Public Land and Democracy in America

Anthropology of Contemporary North America

SERIES EDITORS

James Bielo, Miami University

Carrie Lane, California State University, Fullerton

ADVISORY BOARD

Peter Benson, Washington University in St. Louis

John L. Caughey, University of Maryland

Alyshia Gálvez, Lehman College

Carol Greenhouse, Princeton University

John Hartigan, University of Texas

John Jackson Jr., University of Pennsylvania

Ellen Lewin, University of Iowa

Bonnie McElhinny, University of Toronto

Shalini Shankar, Northwestern University

Carol Stack, University of California, Berkeley

Public Land and Democracy in America

Understanding Conflict over Grand Staircase-Escalante National Monument

Julie Brugger

University of Nebraska Press | Lincoln

© 2025 by the Board of Regents of the University of Nebraska

Acknowledgments for the use of previously published material appear on page xxii, which constitutes an extension of the copyright page.

All rights reserved

The University of Nebraska Press is part of a land-grant institution with campuses and programs on the past, present, and future homelands of the Pawnee, Ponca, Otoe-Missouria, Omaha, Dakota, Lakota, Kaw, Cheyenne, and Arapaho Peoples, as well as those of the relocated Ho-Chunk, Sac and Fox, and Iowa Peoples.

Library of Congress Cataloging-in-Publication Data
Names: Brugger, Julie, author.
Title: Public land and democracy in America: understanding conflict over Grand Staircase-Escalante National Monument / Julie Brugger.
Other titles: Understanding conflict over Grand Staircase-Escalante National Monument
Description: Lincoln: University of Nebraska Press, [2025] | Series: Anthropology of contemporary North America | Includes bibliographical references and index.
Identifiers: LCCN 2024002519
ISBN 9781496233011 (hardback)
ISBN 9781496241054 (paperback)
ISBN 9781496241528 (epub)
ISBN 9781496241535 (pdf)
Subjects: LCSH: Grand Staircase-Escalante National Monument (Utah) | Public lands—Utah—Grand Staircase-Escalante National Monument—Management. | Public lands—United States—Management. | Grazing—Environmental aspects—Utah—Grand Staircase-Escalante National Monument. | Range management—Utah—Grand Staircase-Escalante National Monument. | National monuments—Utah—Management. | Democracy—Utah—Citizen participation. | Democracy—United States—Citizen participation. | BISAC: NATURE / Environmental Conservation & Protection | SOCIAL SCIENCE / Anthropology / Cultural & Social
Classification: LCC HD243.U8 B78 2025 | DDC 333.7409792/5—dc23/eng/20240215
LC record available at https://lccn.loc.gov/2024002519

Typeset in Charter ITC by K. Andresen.

Contents

List of Illustrations	vii
List of Tables	ix
Preface	xi
Acknowledgments	xxi
Abbreviations	xxiii
Introduction	1

PART 1. LANDSCAPE

1. National Landscape	27
2. Regional Landscape	53

PART 2. CONFLICT

3. Conflict over Grazing	85
4. Conflict over Roads	129

PART 3. DEMOCRACY

5. The Locals: Democracy and Community	177
6. The Ranchers: Democracy and Freedom	207
7. The Environmentalists: Democracy and the Environment	249
8. The BLM Employees: Democracy and Bureaucracy	293
Conclusion	333
Notes	361
Bibliography	391
Index	405

Illustrations

1. General location of Grand Staircase-Escalante National Monument — 4
2. The Grand Staircase-Escalante region — 5
3. Federal lands and Indian reservations — 29
4. National conservation lands as of 2017 — 49
5. & 6. Escalante house and old outbuildings — 57
7.–12. Traces of former inhabitants of the Grand Staircase-Escalante region — 60
13. Grazing allotments on GSENM — 91
14. & 15. Cartoons from the *Salt Lake Tribune* — 152
16. Conflicting road signs — 154
17.–20. Sustaining community — 184
21. Brent and Lynette Robinson on their leased property — 225
22. Looking for strays with the Johnsons — 232
23. Delane Griffin at Dance Hall Rock — 236
24. Riparian assessment — 299
25. Ranchers and EIS Team members — 323

Tables

1. Timeline for grazing retirements on GSENM
   up until 2007   99
2. Timeline for roads dispute on GSENM
   up until 2009   136
3. Headlines describing the conflict over roads on
   GSENM before and after August 13, 2003   149

Preface

What does democracy mean to ordinary people in the United States? This question motivated my research on conflict over the management of Grand Staircase-Escalante National Monument (GSENM) in southern Utah, on which this book is based.[1] Because the research was conducted between 1999 and 2008, much of this book serves as an ethnography of recent history in the early twenty-first century, when democracy was on the rise in the world and its final victory over other systems of government was assumed.[2] The understanding of democracy it presents can shed light on how the meaning of democracy in America may be changing today and the role that conflict over the public lands can play in shaping its meaning.

In 1996 President Clinton used the 1906 Antiquities Act to create the 1.9-million-acre GSENM on public land administered by a federal land management agency, the Bureau of Land Management (BLM). Its creation by presidential proclamation provoked widespread opposition in Utah, and during the period of my research, controversial issues concerning the monument continued to arise, often making national news and making its day-to-day management problematic. As public land, GSENM is held in trust by the federal government for all Americans, who, owing to federal environmental legislation, have a voice in its management. Drawing on anthropologist Victor Turner's observation that social conflict brings people's passionately held beliefs and values into prominence, I approached conflict over the management of GSENM using his concept of a "social drama," in which participants mobilized ideas about democracy as they engaged with federal, state, and local governments and each other to have a say in how public land was managed.[3]

I first became interested in what democracy means in 1994, when I was in South Africa during the run-up to the first democratic election ever held in that country, followed by the election on April 27 and the inauguration of Nelson Mandela as the country's first democratically elected president. Although I was not interested in politics in my own country, I was caught up in and irrevocably changed by the emotionally charged atmosphere leading up to and following the election. Preceding it, the national mood was one of tense anticipation and preoccupation with every development. People were hopeful but at the same time worried that the election might be disrupted by violence or boycotted by some faction. On election day, people traveled long distances and waited with great dignity and patience in legendarily long lines to vote. When the election miraculously came off without disruption, a collective sigh of relief could be felt. But it wasn't until May 10, the day Nelson Mandela was inaugurated, with the realization that the years of struggling and believing had finally ended, that overwhelming joy swept the country. As it was transformed into "the new South Africa," I felt transformed by a new awareness that the efforts and conviction of ordinary people really could change their world.

The word "democracy" was on everyone's lips at that time, and the word was radiant, powerful, alive. It was suffused with triumph at the end of the long struggle, and it meant much more to South Africans than the electoral process they had just participated in. It also carried their hopes for the future. The ideals of jobs, peace, and freedom proclaimed by campaign posters could now take tangible shape in their lives. Amid the rejoicing, I paused to consider what democracy would come to mean in this country that had just begun the process of making dreams of democracy into reality. And I wondered why the word "democracy" didn't evoke the same enthusiasm and emotion in the United States, arguably the world's oldest existing democracy. In my experience, Americans seldom used the word, and when they did, it seemed they were more often complaining about how it wasn't working than celebrating it. Nevertheless, the U.S. government had gone to great lengths to defend democracy in, or extend it to, other countries since the mid-twentieth century. So what had democracy come to mean in the United States?

Initially, I planned a comparative study that would seek to compare the meaning of democracy in the two countries. I wanted to site my research in each country in a national park or protected area where collaborative management efforts were underway, assuming that its status as public land in a democratically governed country would bring out participants' ideas about democracy as they created management plans. Attempts to develop more collaborative and democratic approaches to conservation were underway and being celebrated worldwide at the time. Personal reasons also motivated this choice. Because I have come to love wild, rugged, beautiful places through my pursuit of alpine and rock climbing throughout the world, I wanted to be able to conduct my research in such a place, knowing that the landscape would help sustain me during what was likely to be a challenging research process. Choosing a field site based on attachment to the landscape turned out to be a fortunate decision because, from the start, it gave me something in common with the people who lived there.

I chose GSENM as the site for the U.S. side of my project because, despite the conflict its creation had ignited, attempts at collaboration existed. The initial Monument Management Plan had been drawn up by a team that included local residents; tribal representatives; representatives of city, county, and state governments; non-BLM scientists; and monument staff. In 1999, when I first visited GSENM, the beginnings of a collaborative effort among the monument, the state of Utah, Southern Utah University, and local residents existed in the form of the Escalante Center. It aimed to build a cooperatively run nonprofit arts and sciences education and information campus in the community of Escalante adjacent to the monument. For various reasons, some described in this book, these initiatives unraveled or did not result in the desired outcomes. Conflict persisted, and my research focus shifted from collaboration to conflict—a shift that profoundly shaped the understanding of democracy that emerges in this book. When I asked people in the Grand Staircase-Escalante region what they wanted to get from my research, their response was: "Just tell our story. We just want our voices to be heard." That was something I felt I could do.

I returned to South Africa in 2001–2 to scout out a field site there. But I abandoned the South African side of the project when I couldn't come up with a satisfactory answer to the question people inevitably posed to me, in one way or another, at each potential field site I visited. Politicized by their long struggle against apartheid, and having been inundated by researchers since 1994, they wanted to know, "What's in it for us?"

Concern about how the U.S. response to the events of September 11, 2001, was undermining some of the accepted pillars of democracy—free and fair elections, individual rights, and transparency—also suggested to me that the question of what democracy means was more urgent in the United States than in South Africa. Since then, it has become even more urgent.

Finally, the timely appearance of Julia Paley's "Toward an Anthropology of Democracy" in the 2002 *Annual Review of Anthropology* reinforced my decision to make the current status of democracy in America the focus of my research.[4] Paley made a case that anthropologists have a valuable contribution to make to the study of democracy, which had undergone a resurgence among political scientists since the end of the Cold War. She traced the emergence of an "anthropology of democracy" from ethnographic analyses of anthropologists doing fieldwork in countries undergoing regime transitions. For the most part, these anthropologists were not studying democracy specifically, but since democracy was a topic of conversation and debate in day-to-day life, their observations on democracy were often embedded in discussions of other topics.

To further the development of this area of study, Paley encouraged anthropologists to undertake research specifically focused on democracy. She maintained that because of their ethnographic methods and attention to the viewpoints of the nonelite, anthropologists can offer insight into questions about democracy that the statistical methods of political scientists cannot address. She also suggested that an important challenge for the anthropology of democracy was to critically examine democracy in places whose governmental systems had not been undergoing massive change. In particular, she underscored the need for "an interrogation of Western political ideals and institutions . . . given that the United States is regularly taken as the unexamined standard bearer for the rest of the world."[5]

The primary goal of my dissertation was to tell the stories of people in the Grand Staircase-Escalante region by providing a detailed and nuanced account of conflict over GSENM and a better understanding of the experiences and viewpoints of people involved in it. At the same time, I took up Paley's challenges by focusing on ideas about democracy that informed participants' actions as they engage with government and with each other. My hope was that by disclosing the ways that ordinary Americans think about, experience, and practice democracy in their daily lives, my work could contribute to a rethinking and revitalization of democracy in America focused on its inspirational and transformative possibilities, a hope buoyed by the election of Barack Obama as president in 2008. By proposing an agonistic understanding of democracy, I wanted to encourage readers to reevaluate the role of conflict in democracy, to see those on the other side as adversaries rather than enemies, and to appreciate the role that the public lands can play in fostering democracy in America.

Developments since 2009

Much has occurred since 2009, when I completed the dissertation that is the basis for this book, and the word "democracy" has come into widespread circulation again in the United States. I always intended to turn my dissertation into a book, but my academic research jobs got in the way. Meanwhile, the political divide in the United States—between conservatives and liberals, Republicans and Democrats, rural and urban, the working class and the elite—widened and became more antagonistic. Donald Trump exploited that divide and the fears of a shrinking white majority to win the 2016 presidential election. The conclusions about democracy I had come to in 2009 began to seem hopelessly optimistic, even to me.

In 2017 I moved back to Escalante, fulfilling a dream I'd had since 2005 to live there permanently someday. On December 4 of that year President Trump, in response to the urging of anti-monument Utah legislators, used the Antiquities Act to reduce the size of GSENM by 46 percent and open the excluded lands to motorized vehicles, energy and mineral development, and sale or other disposition. The legality of his Proclamation 9682 was immediately challenged by multiple lawsuits, which would take years to settle in court. This action was one of the earliest and most visible in a concerted attack on the public lands during the Trump administration. Political commentators and ordinary people began to characterize many of the Trump administration's actions as threats to democracy. Books for the general public on the declining health of democracy in America began to appear.[6] When Joe Biden won the 2020 presidential election, and against all evidence, Trump continued to claim it had been stolen and galvanized his followers to attack the U.S. Capitol on January 6, 2021, the precariousness of U.S. democracy suddenly became shockingly real.

In Escalante, things had changed too. When I was doing my research, there had been divisions between the "locals," pioneer descendant residents who were primarily conservative and members of the Church of Jesus Christ of Latter-day Saints, and the "move-ins," who were primarily more educated, ex-urban liberals, but in general these groups treated each other with civility. When I moved back, many of my neighbors were flying Trump flags, many locals had dropped the show of civility, and many new move-ins spoke about the locals with contempt.

In light of these developments, I questioned whether my earlier research and the conclusions I had drawn from it were still relevant. You are reading this book because I concluded that they were and could shed light on how democracy in America may be changing. In the intervening years, there has still been little anthropological research on democracy in America, on rural white populations, or on those with ultraconservative, nationalist sentiments, "others" whom most anthropologists consider "the enemy."[7] So I think it is more important than ever to tell their story and try to create understanding that can help bridge the divide that threatens democracy in American today.

Methods

This book is based on ethnographic fieldwork and archival research I carried out in the Grand Staircase-Escalante region between 1999 and 2008: each summer from 1999 to 2003 and 2006 to 2008, and full-time between September 2003 and September 2005 while living in the town of Escalante. My research methodology is based on that used by anthropologist Faye Ginsburg in her study of conflict over the opening of an abortion clinic in Fargo, North Dakota, in the 1980s. The components of Ginsburg's threefold methodology are (1) using historical material to provide a temporal context for the contemporary conflict; (2) following the conflict over time to see how individuals and groups transform the meanings and terms of the debate as they participate in it; and (3) collecting and analyzing life stories from activists to answer questions about the nature of their commitment to the issue.[8] Her work was cited by anthropologist George Marcus as exemplary of a type of multi-sited ethnography called "follow the conflict," which enables anthropologists to understand contested issues in contemporary societies.[9]

For the first component, I drew on library and internet research to understand the ecological, historical, social, economic, and political context for conflict over the management of GSENM. For the second, I followed the conflict over time using multiple ethnographic methods, including participant and direct observation, structured and unstructured interviews, and content analysis of media reports. I attended public meetings and gatherings, including city council and county commission meetings, court hearings, public comment (scoping) meetings held by the federal land management agencies, campaign meetings for local elections, and planning meetings for local events. I participated in community events, some sponsored by the Church of Jesus Christ of Latter-day Saints; in the ordinary activities of daily life; and as a volunteer at the elementary school. Most participant observation of community life took place in the town of Escalante. I also accompanied ranchers, BLM scientists, environmentalists, and others in their everyday work. In relation to GSENM specifically, I attended meetings of the interdisciplinary team working on a monument-wide Rangeland Health Environmental Impact Statement and was a member of the GSENM Monument Advisory Committee for two years, where I represented the social sciences. Altogether, I conducted over one hundred formal and informal interviews with people living and working in the Grand Staircase-Escalante region or involved with GSENM in other ways.[10]

Native American perspectives are conspicuously absent from my research. There are several reasons for this. When I began my research, I consulted with the assistant monument manager for cultural and earth science, Marietta Eaton, an archaeologist who had come to work on

GSENM shortly after its creation and was responsible for consultation with tribes that recognized sites with cultural, historic, or religious significance on GSENM. The Monument Management Plan directed that these sites should be identified, respected, preserved, and managed for continued recognized tradition uses and for public education.[11] Eaton explained that the consultation process had been challenging because there was no precedent, protocol, or mentor to help her figure out what to do. It was proceeding acceptably, if slowly. Not wanting to jeopardize the progress she had made, I felt it was best not to approach the tribes. In addition, there were seven tribal entities with which GSENM consulted: the Hopi, Zuni, Navajo, Ute, Kaibab Paiute, San Juan Paiute, and Paiute tribes of Utah. Had I decided to include Native Americans in my research, the process of getting permission from all seven tribes and the logistics of travel would have added immensely to the time and expense necessary to carry out my research.

For the third component of my research methodology, I carried out more intensive research and developed deeper relationships with key collaborators—collecting life histories, participating in activities, and spending much more time in conversation with them—to gain greater insight into their life experience, their views on GSENM, and what motivated their participation in the conflict over its management. I also asked them specifically what democracy meant to them.

Since I moved back to Escalante, I have followed new developments related to GSENM in the media; attended local events related to the monument; read much new scholarship on public lands issues, rural America, and the current state of democracy in America; and reflected on my more recent experience living in the region. I have used all these to rethink and add to the story and my initial conclusions.

As I considered how to present the results of my research, I read Azar Nafisi's *Reading Lolita in Tehran*. She asserted that a novel is democratic when it "shows the complexity of individuals and creates enough space for all those characters to have a voice," thereby opening readers' eye to their problem and pains and creating empathy. In this passage, Nafisi elaborated on what she meant by the democratic structure of the novel: "In Austen's novels there are spaces for oppositions that do not need to eliminate each other in order to exist. There is also space—not just space but a necessity—for self-reflection and self-criticism. Such reflection is the cause of change. We needed no message, no outright call for plurality, to prove our point. All we needed was to read and appreciate the cacophony of voices to understand its democratic imperative."[12]

As I tell the stories of participants in conflict over GSENM, I aspire to write democratically: presenting the lives, struggles, and values of participants from all sides and groups, letting them speak for themselves as much as possible, and aiming to create space for self-reflection in my readers. My hope is that through this dialogue, readers may come to recognize what they have in common with others they previously felt antagonism toward and perhaps even feel empathy, despite their different experiences and viewpoints, and their antagonism might transform into agonism. Then more Americans would be able work together to maintain and manage our legacy of public lands and our democracy.

Acknowledgments

First, I want to acknowledge the contributions of all who participated in my fieldwork: residents of the Grand Staircase-Escalante region, members of local government, staff of Grand Staircase-Escalante National Monument, and members of the environmental community. I am grateful for their interest in my research; for their time, hospitality, and unfailing courtesy; and for their help in gaining an understanding of what democracy means to ordinary Americans. I especially thank the people of Escalante, who made me feel so at home that I didn't want to leave and aspired to make it my permanent home one day. And a special thanks to Crockett Dumas for allowing me to discover and experience the incredible landscape riding his beautiful Arabian endurance horses.

Mimi Kahn, my advisor when I was a graduate student at the University of Washington and the chair of my dissertation supervisory committee, offered warm support throughout graduate school and read and commented on innumerable revisions of my dissertation. The other members of my dissertation committee—Lucy Jarosz, Danny Hoffman, and Gene Anderson, a late and enthusiastic addition—also gave helpful feedback. Catherine Zeigler, the graduate program assistant in the Anthropology Department, provided unfailingly cheerful and meticulous assistance with all matters administrative.

The writing process that turned my dissertation into this book was a long and lonely endeavor. What motivated me to complete it was the attachment I feel for the landscape of the Grand Staircase-Escalante region, the obligation I took on to tell the stories of local residents, the intellectual curiosity I developed about the meaning of democracy, the excitement I felt when interest in democracy rekindled as it seemed to be going wrong, and just plain stubbornness. Some dear friends were always there for me: Pat, Barbara, and Miriam. As the process neared completion, anonymous readers of the book manuscript for the University of Nebraska Press provided invaluable suggestions for updating the data and conclusions from my original research to make them more relevant to the condition of democracy in America today. The staff at UNP was immensely supportive. And a copyeditor with superpowers, Joyce Bond, eliminated writing evils from the manuscript and made the book much better for it.

Portions of the introduction previously appeared in "'The Other' and 'The Enemy': Reflections on Fieldwork in Utah," *North American Dialogue* 10, no. 1 (2007): 6–10.

Portions of the introduction and chapters 1 and 3 previously appeared in "Re-territorialization and Rule in the United States: Insights from Conflict over the Management of Public Land," in *Negotiating Territoriality: Spatial Dialogues between State and Tradition*, ed. Allan Charles Dawson, Laura Zanotti, and Ismael Vaccaro (New York: Routledge, 2014), 114–28.

Portions of the introduction, chapter 1, and the conclusion previously appeared in "A Genealogy of Grand Staircase-Escalante National Monument: Considering the Future of Federal Public Lands," *Society & Natural Resources* 33, no. 6 (2020): 788–805.

Abbreviations

ATV	all-terrain vehicle
AUM	animal unit month
BLM	Bureau of Land Management
CGC	Canyonlands Grazing Corporation
DOI	Department of the Interior
EA	environmental assessment
EIS	environmental impact statement
FLPMA	Federal Land Policy and Management Act of 1976
FWS	U.S. Fish and Wildlife Service
GCT	Grand Canyon Trust
GSENM	Grand Staircase-Escalante National Monument
MMP	Monument Management Plan
NEPA	National Environmental Policy Act of 1969
NPS	National Park Service
OHV	off-highway vehicle
SUOHP	Southern Utah Oral History Project
SUWA	Southern Utah Wilderness Alliance
TGA	Taylor Grazing Act of 1934
TNC	The Nature Conservancy
USFS	U.S. Forest Service

Public Land and Democracy in America

Introduction

> To believe that a final resolution of conflicts is eventually possible[,] ... far from providing the necessary horizon of the democratic project, is something that puts it at risk.
> —Chantal Mouffe, *The Democratic Paradox*

> A good novel is one that shows the complexity of individuals and creates enough space for all those characters to have a voice; in this way a novel is called democratic—not that it advocates democracy but that by nature it is so.
> —Azar Nafisi, *Reading Lolita in Tehran*

"Left Out of the Loop"

On September 18, 1996, as his campaign for reelection entered its final crucial weeks, President Bill Clinton presented the American people with a monumental surprise. Standing on the south rim of the Grand Canyon in Arizona, he proclaimed 1.7 million acres of public land in southern Utah, a rugged, arid, and sparsely populated region of multi-hued cliffs and labyrinthine canyons, as Grand Staircase-Escalante National Monument (GSENM)—the largest national monument in the United States outside Alaska (see figs. 1 and 2).[1] According to the proclamation, the president created GSENM to protect "the spectacular array of scientific and historic resources" that its "vast and austere landscape embraces."[2] In creating the monument, he was using power granted to the president by the Antiquities Act of 1906 and following a precedent set by earlier presidents to bypass the legislative process required to create national parks and wilderness. The proclamation contained a second surprise: the monument would remain under the management of the Bureau of Land Management (BLM) instead of shifting to the National Park Service, which manages all national monuments created before then, making it the first national monument the BLM would manage and signaling a new role for the agency.

Those invited to the proclamation ceremony included Vice President Al Gore, Interior Secretary Bruce Babbitt, actor and Utah resident Robert Redford, Utah writer Terry Tempest Williams, and representatives from several environmental groups, but not one elected official from Utah. Environmentalists had been working for more than a decade to have even more of Utah's public land designated as wilderness; they applauded the president's action but declared it only a partial victory. However, local residents and Utah elected officials, who had been neither consulted nor informed of the president's intentions beforehand, were outraged.

In the towns adjacent to the new monument, reaction to the proclamation was immediate and explicit. In Kanab, many businesses closed, schoolchildren released dozens of black balloons, and protestors held a Loss of Rights rally where they wore black armbands and carried signs voicing their feelings about the president's action: "Shame on You Clinton" and "Why Clinton, Why? You're Our President." One Kanab resident declared as he emerged from the rally, "The Constitution was not written up for one man to have that much power."[3] Another admitted, "What I'd like to do is declare war on the White House . . . but my church and the laws don't allow me to do that."[4] In Escalante, angry residents burned figures of Clinton and Babbitt in effigy. These emotions, actions, and words revealed Utahns' deeply held beliefs and values about how decisions should be made in a democratic government, which they felt had been violated.

A poll taken by the *Deseret News* of Salt Lake City found that 49 percent of Utahns opposed the monument, and 61 percent said the process used to create it was unfair. Even some environmentalists were displeased about the secretiveness of the process. An attendee at the proclamation ceremony, Bill Hedden of the conservation organization Grand Canyon Trust, told the press, "All kinds of people I work with are angry about the process that didn't happen."[5]

Utah's elected officials expressed their objections in terms of their understanding of the principles of a democratic system of government, pointing out how the president's action had violated them. Republican senator Orrin Hatch fumed, "In all my 20 years in the U.S. Senate, I have never seen a clearer example of the arrogance of federal power." He added, "This declaration has nothing to do with preserving land in southern Utah—which is a goal we all share—and everything to do with scoring political points with a powerful political interest group just 48 days before the presidential election is to take place."[6] Republican senator Bob Bennett called the president's action an "arrogant, outrageous approach to public policy."[7] Senators from other western states joined in their condemnation of the designation, calling it the act of a "tyrant" and a "phenomenal misuse of power."[8] Republican representative Enid Green maintained that what Utahns objected to most about the monument was the "autocratic process" the president had used to sidestep existing legislation, the state's elected representatives, and its people.[9]

Having learned in advance of the president's potential action, Governor Mike Leavitt had met with White House chief of staff Leon Panetta to ask the White House to reconsider it. He told Panetta, "I'm not asking you not to do a monument, because there may be aspects of this that have virtue. I'm asking you not to do it this way." He "made a strong case that there's a win-win opportunity here. That we share their desire to protect this land, but that we also need to be concerned about preserving the assets of the land and being true to the deliberative process of democracy." Democratic representative Bill Orton from Utah reported that he had warned the president that the approach he was taking "would cut out the local people from the decision-making process."[10]

As these statements indicate, many Utahns objected strongly to the creation of GSENM and articulated their objections in terms that expressed opposition not so much to the monument per se as to *the way it was created*. Although they seldom used the word "democracy," their statements reflect underlying normative ideas about how a democratic government should work—people, via their representatives, should have a say in decisions that affect their lives—and practical understanding of how the procedures and institutions of American

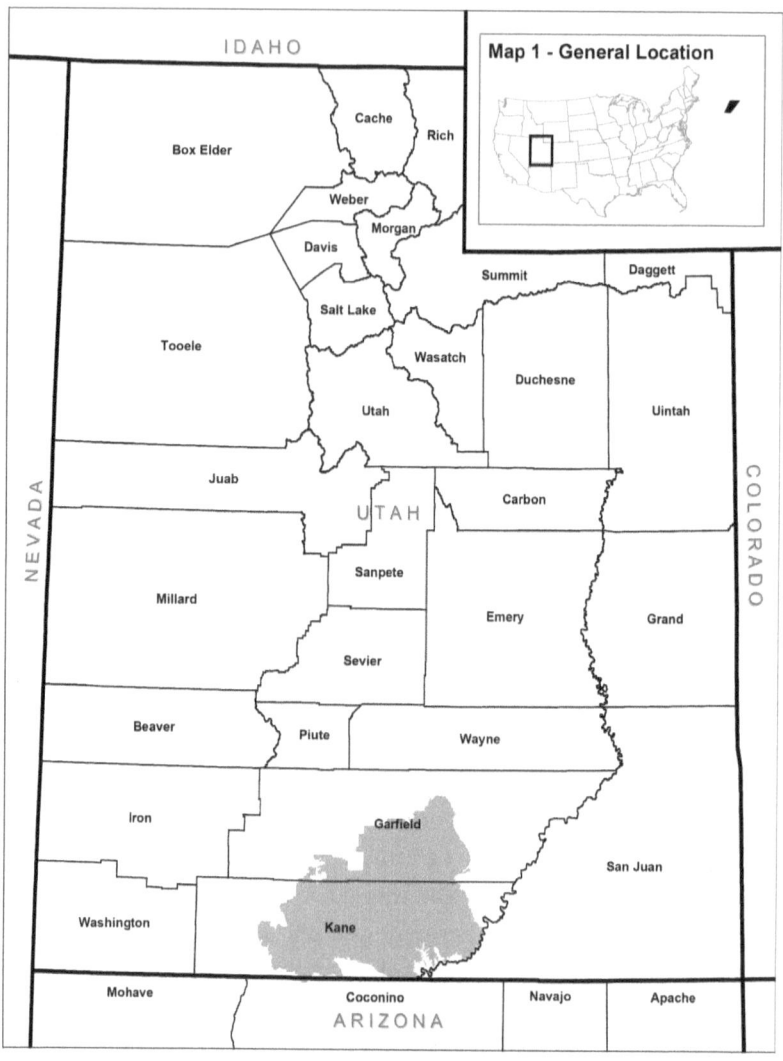

1. General location of Grand Staircase-Escalante National Monument. Source: Bureau of Land Management, *Grand Staircase-Escalante National Monument Draft Monument Management Plan Amendment and Draft Rangeland Health Environmental Impact Statement*, 2008.

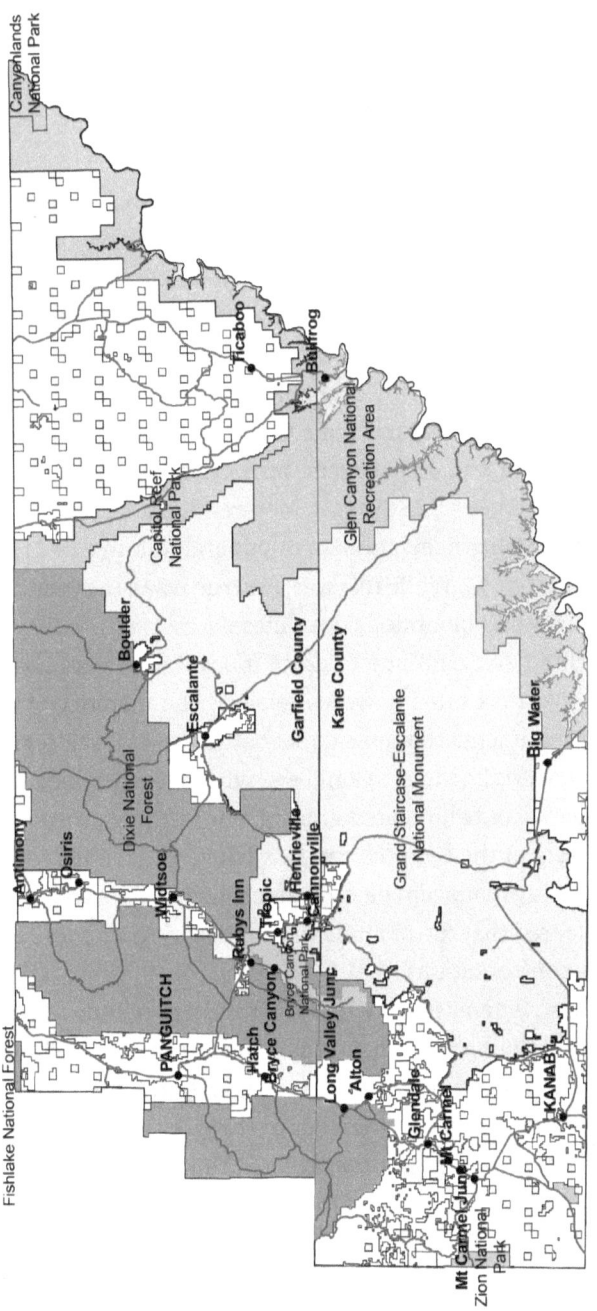

2. The Grand Staircase-Escalante region. Created by the author.

government intended to check the power of the federal government were supposed to work. The violation of what they considered basic democratic principles and procedures aroused strong feelings of outrage and disillusionment. For many, the strength of their feelings then still colors their perceptions of the monument now.

Residents of the Grand Staircase-Escalante region were also concerned about the concrete effects the monument would have on their lives.[11] Their reactions to the creation of the monument were heightened by anxiety about whether the new designation would result in greater restrictions on natural resource use and other traditional activities on the public land included in the monument, threatening local livelihoods and culture. In Garfield and Kane Counties, in which the monument lies, 88.1 percent and 90.5 percent, respectively, of the land was federally owned as of 1999.[12] In the past, most residents of these communities had depended on grazing, timber, or mineral resources on these lands for their livelihoods. While this was less true when the monument was created, many still identified with a lifestyle and culture they associate with ranching and continue to do so today. Local fears about loss of access to livestock grazing were fueled by the memory of two other national monuments that presidents had created in the region, Bryce Canyon and Capitol Reef; Congress subsequently made these into national parks and eliminated grazing. For ranchers, increasing numbers of hikers in the red rock canyons where their cattle grazed were already causing management difficulties, such as gates being left open, and they feared that the monument would bring even more hikers and inevitable confrontations.

Years later, when I spoke with local residents about GSENM, those who had been living in the region at the time remembered clearly how they felt when the monument was created. Carol Sullivan, a resident of Kanab since 1967 and a member of the city council, explained, "It was the way the monument was created that created a lot of feelings within the community, because the citizens of Garfield and Kane Counties and the local officials were totally left out of the loop." She went on to link feelings about the monument with feelings about the local economy:

The bitterness was there, not only because of the way it was done, but also because Kane County was placing a lot of hope on Andalex and jobs for our economy.[13] Because the mill had shut down—they had gone from three shifts to two shifts, to one shift, to no shift.[14] And all those cutbacks we felt in the schools, we felt in the local economy. And so there were people holding on, hoping that they could get a job out there. So you have to kind of put it all in perspective. And this is just after we also had another outfit here that was mining uranium out there on the Arizona Strip . . . and they shut down—Energy Fuels it was called. They got shut down, and that was a hundred employees. And you stop and think about all of the employees in this area, whether you're for or against lumber, whatever it is, the point is, it had a disastrous effect on the local economies. So if you take the background on all of these, and you just build on those, I mean that was just kind of like the last blow. Jobs, economy, tourism, the international dollar—everything was coming at the same time.

For many longtime residents of the Grand Staircase-Escalante region, attitudes toward the monument and feelings about its creation are still intertwined with fears and uncertainty about the future for individuals and their communities. They feel powerless in the face of federal power along with social and economic changes over which they have no control. And they feel bitter about being "left out of the loop" in decision-making concerning both the creation and management of GSENM, in addition to being left out of economic prosperity and perceiving that the federal government is unconcerned about their welfare. These feelings also anticipate, based on past experience, being "left out of the loop" again in future decisions.

Federal officials attempted to reduce some of the ill will toward the federal government the creation of GSENM had generated. They proposed that the management plan for the monument be drawn up by a team that would include local residents, tribal representatives, non-BLM scientists, and representatives of city, county, and state governments, in addition to monument staff. The planning team was also given a say in where monument headquarters would be located. Initially the team chose Escalante, but the town declined, so the headquarters wound up in Kanab. At the request of state and local officials, who were concerned about the effects the monument would have on local economies, Congress appropriated $9.7 million for the construction of visitors' centers and interpretive exhibits in four communities adjacent to the monument. And in light of the prevailing mood in the region, the BLM chose Jerry Meredith, a Utah native and a specialist in public relations, for the monument's first manager.

But despite these measures, resistance to the monument remained strong in the region, making day-to-day management problematic. The resistance took a wide variety of forms, ranging from spur-of-the-moment acts to protracted lawsuits and from individual actions to those at the community, county, or state level. Anonymous individuals vandalized rock art and signage in the monument, floats in Pioneer Day parades displayed anti-monument sentiment, and jokes about the monument were part of the public entertainment at holiday celebrations. Citizen groups such as the Canyon Country Rural Alliance and Canyon Country Ranchers Association formed to consolidate opposition to the monument and prevent loss of access to resources. In October 1996 Garfield and Kane County road crews graded roads within the monument to assert the counties' authority over them. And in 1997, in an attempt to get the proclamation overturned, the Utah Association of Counties and the Utah School and Institutional Trust Lands Administration filed a lawsuit against the federal government, claiming that the president had overstepped his authority in establishing the monument.[15]

This account of the creation of GSENM and reactions to it highlights emotions that were aroused when Utah residents felt that their passionately held beliefs about democracy had been violated by the way the monument was created. These emotions built on long-standing discontent with federal management of the public lands in the rural communities adjacent to the monument and among Utah elected officials. For them, democracy meant they should be included both in decision-making that affected their lives and in national economic prosperity. Although people in the region seldom used the word "democracy," their emotions, words, and actions revealed their beliefs about what democracy means in relation to the federal government and how it is supposed to work. My account of the next event provides insight into what democracy means to people in their everyday lives. It also relates a decisive event in my research that opened my eyes to my own unacknowledged stereotypes of rural Americans and marked a shift in my perceptions of local residents.

"You Don't Have to Agree with Him, but He Has a Right to Speak"

On July 18, 2001, when I arrived for the 7:00 p.m. biweekly Escalante City Council meeting, I was surprised and somewhat apprehensive to see the room packed with attendees. At previous meetings, there had been few people besides the five city council members, the mayor, and the city recorder. This meeting included a public hearing to consider a proposed ordinance for civil emergencies and establishing right to maintain firearms.[16] Residents showed up to hear the views of others and express their own. The ordinance would require "every head of household residing in the Escalante City limits . . . to maintain a firearm." I saw many people I knew, but I took a seat in the back, hoping to remain unobtrusive.

The mayor opened the meeting and began by explaining the rationale for the ordinance. According to him, it was identical to an ordinance originally proposed in Kennesaw County, Georgia, which had been picked up and enacted into law the previous year in Virgin, Utah. It was intended as an extra safeguard to the Second Amendment right to keep and bear arms, which was "slowly being eaten away." He had heard on the news that environmentalists were saying the ordinance was aimed at them, but he insisted this had never crossed his mind when he proposed it. He had heard that senior citizens had been frightened by the ordinance and apologized to them, then assured the audience, "You don't have to have guns if you consciously oppose guns." He concluded by encouraging those who wanted to speak to come up to the microphone in the front and not to "slam each other" but to "let each individual have their chance to talk because the Constitution gives them the right as well as everybody else."

In the summer of 2001 I was still operating under assumptions about the "locals" (which is how I thought of them at the time) based on newspaper reports and accounts of people from outside the region about events surrounding ongoing public meetings on wilderness designations in Utah. In these accounts, the locals were represented as unintelligent, irrational, right-wing, suspicious and intolerant of outsiders, and sometimes violent. These accounts combined with my own unacknowledged stereotypes of rural Americans to create the expectation that local residents would readily support the ordinance. But as each person stepped up to the microphone, most voiced opposition and gave reasons that were varied, well thought out, and well expressed. I began to see local residents in a different light. Although some were people who had moved to Escalante more recently, their statements received approving nods from many longtime residents in the audience.

The meeting proceeded smoothly until Patrick Diehl, a self-described environmentalist, stepped up to the microphone. He was the hero and the victim of local wrath in accounts I had read in newspapers and heard from wilderness advocates. In 1999 he had led the opposition to a new irrigation reservoir for Escalante and crashed an anti-wilderness rally held in town. Having just moved to Escalante the previous year, he had quickly succeeded in stirring up considerable controversy and hard feelings in the town. For his appearance at this city council meeting, he wore a green T-shirt that had an American flag with a white peace symbol in place of the stars. With obvious relish, he began reading a prepared statement that proposed "not only a strengthening amendment to the firearms ordinance we are considering this evening, but three other ordinances that will add significantly to the notoriety of Escalante."

As he read his amendment, which would require heads of households to maintain, in addition to a firearm, "an assault rifle or machine gun, a box of grenades, and a ground-to-air missile programmed to home in on the silhouette, spectrographic image, and infrared signature of a black helicopter," murmurs began to arise from the audience. It became clear that his intent was not to contribute to the discussion but to insult and provoke. As he continued, some in the audience began to shout objections. He read louder to overcome the shouting. Some men in the audience rose to their feet and began to move toward him. Tension in the room rose palpably. The mayor asked Patrick to sit down, but he read louder still, and the agitated audience shouted back even louder, attempting to drown him out.

Just as tension rose to an ominous level, a local rancher stood up and calmly requested that everyone allow Patrick to continue. "You don't have to agree with him," he pointed out, "but he has a right to speak." The audience quieted, and everyone sat back down. Patrick continued with his mock ordinances, and when he finished, the audience responded spontaneously with a round of applause. While they may have been offering it in the same mocking spirit as Patrick's speech, it felt to me as if they were congratulating themselves for the feat they had just accomplished: a feat of democratic discussion.

After Patrick returned to his seat, the rest of the hearing felt anticlimactic. As it drew to a close, the rancher who had asked the audience to let Patrick speak took the floor again. Recognizing that Patrick was a member of the community and likely to continue to voice his opinion in public discussions, he suggested, "When Patrick tries to stir us up, let's just hold our peace and let him go, and we'll all get along." The final speaker thanked everyone for their contributions and added, "I always like listening to everyone, even Patrick." The mayor closed the hearing by informing the audience that in light of the discussion, the council's vote on the ordinance would be postponed.

Most of the audience filed out as the regular city council meeting began. But I sat lost in wonder and admiration. I had acquired a new perspective on the locals, who had just demonstrated what democracy meant to them: the right to free speech, tolerance, and inclusive decision-making. They believed that the opportunity to speak and be heard was so important for getting along that they provided it to someone even when they knew he would use it to taunt them.

This event illustrates the significance that democracy has in people's everyday lives, in their relationships with neighbors and community members, not just in relation to the federal government. While they do not necessarily articulate their actions in terms of democracy, people in democratic societies share norms and expectations that encourage them to deal with differences, disagreements, and conflicts in daily life using democratic principles. This event also suggests that while ordinary people value democracy, their practice of it must be able to embrace paradox. In this case, local residents maintained their commitment to the democratic principle of inclusion at a public hearing despite experiencing exclusion from decision-making in federal land management.

Together, these accounts provide some insight into what democracy means to ordinary people in the Grand Staircase-Escalante region both in relation to government and in everyday life. Next, I consider what it means to the experts: political scientists and political theorists.

Experts' Definitions of Democracy

In his preface to the second edition of *Models of Democracy*, one of the most widely read histories of the idea of democracy, prominent democratic theorist David Held announced that although "we live in the age of democracy," and it has become "the fundamental standard of political legitimacy in the current era," "democracy, as an idea and as a political reality, is fundamentally contested."[17] In an article titled "The Vexed Issue of the Meaning of 'Democracy,'" political scientist Laurence Whitehead concluded that trying to come up with a "minimal" or "realist" definition of democracy for the purposes of evaluation and comparison is a vain effort because such definitions are, paradoxically, both "insufficient" and "too demanding" at the same time. They are insufficient because they exclude the components of democracy that give it its "emotional force" and too demanding because we do not actually expect existing democracies to consistently conform to these minimum standards.[18] So political scientists can't give us a definitive meaning for democracy.

Political scientists faced another paradox at the beginning of the twenty-first century. Democracy had become both "the preeminently acceptable form of governance" in the world and "a universal value."[19] And a long tradition of survey research in the world's oldest and most stable democracies showed that citizens believed overwhelmingly in its desirability.[20] Yet these same countries had low levels of voter turnout and participation in democratic institutions. Eminent democratic theorist Robert Dahl cited this as "overwhelming evidence that citizens do not put much value on actually participating themselves in political life." He proposed a minimal set of political institutions necessary for modern, representative democratic government and a set of rights and opportunities presupposed by these institutions that citizens may choose to exercise. When people say they support democracy, he conjectured, what they have in mind is this minimalist conception and not actually exercising their rights and opportunities to participate in democracy.[21]

More recently, political scientist Yascha Mounk suggested that the problem with trying to define democracy is that most existing definitions conflate three very different things: liberalism, a political philosophy that prioritizes liberty and the protection of individual rights; democracy, a set of electoral institutions that translates the will of the people into public policy; and the historically contingent set of political institutions to which we have become accustomed in North America and western Europe. Mounk used Dahl's procedural minimalist definition to illustrate this problem.[22]

In contrast to the methods of political scientists, I approached the question of what democracy means with the ethnographic methods of anthropology. By analyzing how members of different groups used ideas about democracy as they participated in conflicts over GSENM and by allowing them to explain what democracy meant to them, this book illuminates the ways ordinary Americans imagined and practiced democracy in their daily lives. Several key concepts facilitate this understanding: democratic imaginaries, agonistic democracy, and statemaking and territorialization.

Democratic Imaginaries

To encompass the myriad and contradictory ways ordinary Americans understand democracy, I use the concept of democratic imaginaries. It draws on political philosopher Charles Taylor's concept of the "social imaginary," which he defined as "the ways in which people imagine their social existence."[23] Democratic imaginaries include the ways people imagine and practice democracy—their ideas about how a democratic system of government should work and what would violate its principles, what democratic principles mean in everyday life, and how to get along with others and behave "democratically"; their practical knowledge about how to participate in its official political institutions; and their commitment to these principles—as well as their emotional attachment to these ideas, institutions, and practices. These imaginaries are both idealistic and practical, normative and experience based, and they include the capacity to make sense of new and contradictory experiences and to draw on these in unexpected ways to imagine new possibilities.

In a democratic society, although individuals' imaginaries will be similar in many respects, they will differ based on each person's background and life experiences. They are developed through upbringing, formal education, the media, popular culture, and personal experiences both in their daily lives and in their interactions with government institutions and officials. Much of this becomes internalized and implicit, and people do not necessarily think or talk about their motivations and actions in terms of democracy. Sociologist Ruth Braunstein used the term differently but made the same point: "Democratic imaginaries are rarely made explicit but are embedded and embodied in symbols, discourses, and practices."[24] Therefore, social scientists must use ethnographic methods to illuminate them.

Using the concept of democratic imaginaries allows me to avoid the paradoxes that confronted the political scientists when trying to define democracy or limiting it to the sphere of government. This concept can encompass the astonishing variety of meanings and experiences that people in the Grand Staircase-Escalante region associate with democracy, the value they place in it, and the emotional force it generates.

This variety is exemplified in the responses I received when I asked people what democracy meant to them. Democracy is "one vote, one person"; it is "rule by the majority but with protection of the viewpoints of the minority"; and it is "rule by the people of themselves according to a generally agreed-upon set of rules." Democracy is "something you take for granted, and you don't even think about, when you're born and raised in the United States and you've grown up with it your whole life." And it is "a privilege. It's something that nations, that societies have to make a very conscious effort to develop, to keep, to preserve." It can mean "you need to be involved. You need to be aware of what's going on. And it's much better to be involved in some capacity than to sit back and complain." It can also mean "I can wake up every morning and plan whatever I want to do, and as long as it doesn't have an adverse effect on mankind, or on the earth, I can do it." It can even be simply "living in Escalante" or "a feeling in my heart."

Participants in conflict over GSENM drew on many different understandings of the principles of democratic government to legitimate their point of view and their actions as they interacted with the federal government: respect for individual rights, balance of power, rule of law, deliberative and inclusive decision-making, and expert or science-based decision-making. And they drew on different understandings under different circumstances. At the same time, individuals' understandings of democracy were often contradicted by the circumstances of their daily lives. For example, multigenerational residents often conceived of democracy in terms of their community, but they were concerned that increasing numbers of "move-ins" who did not share their background and values might change the community. Ranchers conceived of democracy as freedom, although they grazed their livestock on the public lands, were dependent on the federal government for that privilege, and were subject to federal grazing regulations.

Agonistic Democracy

Agonistic democracy is a theory of democracy formulated by political theorist Chantal Mouffe. It helped clear up my initial confusion about the ongoing nature of conflict over GSENM and the contradictions between what democracy means to participants in the conflict and the circumstances of their lives. The central proposition of this model, which is captured in the first epigraph to this introduction, is that conflict is integral to the democratic project.[25]

When I began my research in the Grand Staircase-Escalante region, informed by the model of collaborative conservation promoted by social scientists and embraced by federal agencies in the 1990s, I intended to study collaborative management efforts then underway. Collaborative conservation, also referred to as community-based natural resource management, is an approach to management that involves broad participation by regulatory officials and all affected parties (usually called stakeholders), a face-to-face deliberative process, and decision-making by consensus. It is expected to result in decisions and management plans that would satisfy local needs and concerns and at the same conform to state and federal laws. It assumes a discursive or deliberative model of democracy in which citizens are able to find mutually acceptable solutions to public issues through a rational deliberative process. I began my research looking for collaboration, consensus, and conflict resolution, but what I found was ongoing conflict. While the concept of agonistic democracy has most often been applied in a national or international context, it helped me make sense of what I found in the Grand Staircase-Escalante region.

Mouffe began her formulation of agonistic democracy by describing the "democratic paradox." The type of democracy that was established in the West in the last two centuries, and has come to inform modern democratic imaginaries, is the expression of both a conceptual and an actual paradox. Liberal democracy is the expression of a conceptual paradox because it is a contingent historical articulation of two distinct traditions that are irreconcilable in practice. The democratic tradition, which emerged in Greece in the sixth century BC, foregrounds equality and popular sovereignty. The liberal tradition, which emerged in Europe in the seventeenth century, promotes individual liberty, rule of law, and separation of powers. The conceptual paradox is that equality disallows the individual liberty to be unequal, while individual liberty inevitably leads to inequality. Modern liberal democracy is an expression of an actual paradox because existing democracies are characterized by diversity. Their citizens and residents differ in ethnicity, culture, religion, values, age, gender, and socioeconomic status, and diversity is growing as people increasingly move across and within national borders. As a result, the political process of defining the people who are sovereign and possess rights, the will of the people, or the common good always involves forms of exclusion.[26] While the democratic paradox is an abstract concept, my research disclosed some of the ways it is manifested and experienced in people's daily lives in the Grand Staircase-Escalante region.

As a result of conceptual and actual pluralism, no final balance between the democratic and liberal logics is ever possible. Mouffe pointed out that "there can only be temporary, pragmatic, unstable, and precarious negotiations of the tensions between" political forces. Apparent consensus in a modern democratic society—whether achieved by allowing the "highest good" to emerge, as advocated by aggregative models of democracy; by citizens willing the "common good," as advocated by civic republicans; or by rational consensus achieved through public deliberation, as advocated by deliberative democrats—will always mean that one political force has prevailed. According to Mouffe, "What is specific and valuable about modern liberal democracy is that, when properly understood, it creates a space in which this confrontation is kept open, power relations are always being put into question and no victory can be found."[27]

Because politics inevitably entails a dimension of antagonism, the aim of democratic politics should be to transform antagonism, a struggle between enemies, into agonism, a struggle between adversaries. Adversaries are "legitimate enemies," with whom we have some common ground because they share our attachment to the principles of liberal democracy, but with whom we disagree fundamentally about the meaning and implementation of those principles.[28] We oppose their ideas, but we do not question their right to defend them. Participants in conflict over GSENM, and public lands more generally, have additional common ground because they share an attachment to the landscape, whether they perceive it as home, refuge, resource, wilderness, or national landscape. Emotion plays an important role in transforming antagonism to agonism because the recognition of common ground creates empathy and disposes us to give opposing views a more open-minded and compassionate hearing. But even when adversaries reach consensus or compromise, it should be seen as conflictual: temporary agreement in ongoing confrontation. In a modern liberal democracy, a wide variety of practices, institutions, discourses, and forms of life should foster identification with democratic values, generate common affects, and contribute to the development of democratic citizens who can participate in agonistic processes. Federal environmental laws that require public participation in environmental decision-making are an example of such institutions and practices.

Statemaking and Territorialization

The concepts of statemaking and territorialization illuminate the nature of the relationship between the U.S. government and ordinary American citizens, or between what social scientists would call state and society, and highlight the role of democracy in mediating that relationship. They situate conflict over GSENM in a long history of conflict over public lands as the federal government's approach to managing them evolved. They also provide a way of understanding the perspective and rationale of the federal government in these conflicts.

In the Grand Staircase-Escalante region the government plays a more prominent role in the lives of residents than what urban dwellers experience. Because such a large proportion of the counties in which GSENM lies is federally owned, the policies, regulations, and day-to-day activities of the federal agencies that manage these lands—the BLM, U.S. Forest Service, and National Park Service—affect residents' lives directly. The residents interact with employees of these agencies on a regular basis, either as neighbors or as people they are obligated to consult in pursuit of livelihoods that depend on using resources on the surrounding public lands, or both. References to the government, the BLM, or the monument are ubiquitous in daily conversations and usually in an antagonistic sense. In this sparsely populated rural region, county and city government officials are also neighbors. Since these officials are more familiar and accessible than their urban counterparts, local government also plays a more personal and prominent role in residents' lives. Relationships with all levels of government are further intensified for those actively participating in conflicts over GSENM.

At the same time, different levels and branches of government often worked at cross-purposes. For example, interpretations of regulations by the BLM in the executive branch of the federal government can be overturned by decisions of the judicial branch. Plans and actions of local-level BLM officials can be overruled or contradicted by state- or national-level BLM officials, and the local officials may try to find ways around the dictates of their superiors. Regulations and policies are not uniformly enforced because line officers have discretion in enforcing them in their jurisdiction. (Line officers are BLM or Forest Service employees with supervisory and land management responsibilities and decision-making authority over a state or field office or a forest or district, respectively.) In addition, BLM employees may have different motivations and agendas in carrying out their jobs. For example, one local BLM employee was motivated by "dedication to the principles of good land management by the people on the ground, regardless of what the philosophy." Another felt that employees were expected to "get into the groove of just doing what the managers want." One recently hired employee felt that many of the old employees were "just sitting around waiting for retirement." Different levels of government, such as the state of Utah and the counties in which GSENM lies, can pass ordinances and resolutions counter to federal policies and dispute which level of government has jurisdiction. Thus what people thought of as the government did not seem to have a well-defined identity, specific location, or consistent agenda.

Social scientists have grappled with the difficulty of grasping the nature of the state.[29] While they use the term to refer to a centralized political organization that establishes and enforces rules over a population within a territory, there is no agreed-upon definition. Early twentieth-century sociologist Max Weber famously defined the state as "a human community that (successfully) claims the *monopoly of the legitimate use of physical force* within a given territory."[30] However, my observations in the Grand Staircase-Escalante region and the experiences of its residents support more recent conceptions of the state as a process rather than an entity that exists separate from society. The idea of the state is imaginatively constructed as a unified entity from an amalgam of political institutions with conflicting practices, interests, agendas, and disunited powers. Its appearance of comprehensive authority and control comes from the multiplicity of intersecting arenas and strategies in which government is exercised. It serves to legitimate political and economic domination and mask ongoing resistance to it, "which if seen directly and as itself would be illegitimate, an unacceptable domination."[31] This conception better captures the way people actually experience state power and develop ideas about its legitimacy.

Anthropologist Kalyanakrishnan Sivaramakrishnan termed this process "statemaking," which he described as "the ways in which institutions of government and ideas of governance are negotiated in specific contexts by local actors and agents of central design or bearers of official ideologies. Statemaking refers also to the power of the central government to penetrate rural society, exact compliance, and invoke commitment. This power rests on 'a delicate balance between autonomy and control in the relationship between state and society.' Statemaking is fundamentally about defining the forms and legitimations of government and governmentality."[32]

He thus suggested that in statemaking, "the relationship between state and society" is not just one of domination but rather a "delicate balance" in which "local actors" also have power and agency. This also highlights the uncertainty of state power. Monument manager Dave Hunsaker recognized this "delicate balance" in the Grand Staircase-Escalante region when, in the context of the conflict over roads on GSENM, he said, "We have all the power of the federal government behind us. But we don't want to use it." Why not? Because it might upset the "delicate balance." The statemaking concept highlights the state's need to legitimate its actions and directs attentions to "the forms and legitimations of government" that participants in conflict over GSENM have drawn on to support their claims and actions.[33] Since "democracy has become the fundamental standard of political legitimacy in the current era,"[34] local actors drew on their ideas about democracy when they confronted the BLM, while the BLM attempted to legitimate its actions in ways that did not appear to violate democratic principles.

Peter Vandergeest and Nancy Lee Peluso described "territorialization" as a subset of statemaking that refers to the process by which a state attempts to establish and maintain sovereignty to control the territory within its borders, include or exclude people, and control what they do within the territory.[35] Just as statemaking is an ongoing process, the state's control over its territory, borders, and the people within them is never secured once and for all and proceeds differently in different regions of the territory. Nor is territorialization a one-sided process; local actors play a significant role in shaping the specific forms of government that emerge. Because people can have a deep attachment to the place and the way they live, territorialization processes are often strongly resisted and contested. Reterritorialization occurs as conditions or perceptions of territory already under state control change and new ways of governing it must be negotiated.

In the following chapters, I describe three waves of reterritorialization and, drawing on the work of French historian and philosopher Michel Foucault, the rationality of state rule motivating each one:

sovereignty, government, and neoliberal governmentality.[36] The concept of reterritorialization draws on geographer Bruce Braun's insight that when Foucault defined "government" as managing the relation between "men and things," including "the territory with its specific qualities, climate, irrigation, fertility, etc." so that the nation prospers, he assumed that the territory "merely contained a set of pre-given 'things'" and left the question of how the territory and its qualities come to be known largely unexamined.[37] Braun argued that the territory is historically contingent, produced through networks of science, government, and capital. As new ways of seeing it develop, "new" territory emerges, and what it means to govern it is no longer the same. This "open[s] a space—both epistemological and geographical—that could be incorporated into forms of political rationality."[38] So new forms of government arise to govern this new territory.

The first wave of reterritorialization began when Europeans "discovered" North America, bringing diseases that decimated Native populations, and continued as European displacement of remaining Native Americans advanced westward across the continent. Euro-American settlers perceived the territory as vacant because Native Americans did not view or claim the land as property. When the fledgling U.S. government took control of the public domain lands, its goal was to establish sovereignty by filling them with settlers. As these lands came to be seen as possessing resources that were threatened by uncontrolled development, the federal government began to reterritorialize some lands by taking on the role of managing them. These became the public lands. The creation of GSENM is representative of a third wave of reterritorialization of public lands as they came to be seen as "national landscape," more valuable as an amenity than for resource production.

Each wave has been contested by local actors, who shape the forms of management of these lands. Reterritorialization is not a uniform process: it is initiated at different times and proceeds at different speeds in different localities, its progress depends on the degree of resistance it encounters, and it does not eliminate earlier rationalities of state rule, which are retained and intermixed in collective memory and in the laws and state structures that initially enabled and propagated them.

Viewing conflict over GSENM through the lenses of statemaking and reterritorialization brings the state's rationality of rule and forms of legitimating rule into focus, sheds light on internal inconsistencies within the federal government, and provides some understanding of why the federal government does what it does. It also provides a broader context in which to understand residents' resistance to GSENM. Throughout this book, I use these concepts to analyze conflict over GSENM, illuminate what democracy means to participants, and understand how they are practicing democracy as they participate in the conflict and go about their daily lives.

Plan of the Book

This book explores what democracy means to ordinary Americans in three ways. Part 1, "Landscape," describes both the physical and social landscapes in which conflict over GSENM took place and how democratic imaginaries from the local to the national level have shaped and been shaped by these landscapes. The chapters in part 2, "Conflict," follow and analyze specific conflicts over the management of GSENM that arose as local actors contested its reterritorialization as national landscape. This section investigates what democracy means to ordinary Americans in relation to the federal government. It identifies different imaginaries of how a democratic government should operate that participants in the conflicts drew on to inform and legitimate their perspectives and actions. Part 3, "Democracy," analyzes the meaning of democracy to members of different groups of participants in conflict over GSENM.

In part 1, chapter 1 focuses on the national context. This chapter explains what public land is and how the western United States came to have so much of it, describes the development of federal land laws and policies, considers the ideas about democracy informing them, and situates conflict over GSENM in a history of conflict over the public lands in the United States. It shows how the western landscape shaped federal land laws and policies and American democratic imaginaries. Chapter 2 focuses on the regional context. It begins by situating GSENM geographically and describing what makes the Grand Staircase-Escalante region unique, then considers the affective impact of the landscape on democratic imaginaries. Next, it provides a brief history of Mormon settlement of the Great Basin and the Grand Staircase-Escalante region and considers the effect of this experience on Mormon democratic imaginaries. Some knowledge of Mormon history aids in understanding the attitudes of local residents who are members of the Church of Jesus Christ of Latter-day Saints.[39] Finally, it describes the economic and demographic shifts currently affecting the region and residents' everyday lives.

The two chapters in part 2 document and analyze concurrent conflicts over livestock grazing and roads in GSENM between 2000 and 2008 as sites of negotiating the reterritorialization of public land as national landscape. GSENM became the flagship of the BLM's National Landscape Conservation System and the most prominent arena for negotiating the bureau's role as manager of national landscapes. Examining these conflicts in detail goes beyond oversimplified media accounts of ranchers or locals versus BLM or environmentalists to see how "the forms and legitimations of government" are being negotiated and how participants draw on different democratic imaginaries to support their positions. Because one of my goals in this book is to tell the stories of local people in the Grand Staircase-Escalante region, their voices and my explanations of their points of view are given considerable space. This is meant not to convey that they are good, or the BLM and environmentalists are bad, but to provide space for perspectives that have been underrepresented and given insufficient opportunity to be understood.

The four chapters in part 3 explore themes that emerged in the responses of members of four groups in the Grand Staircase-Escalante region—local residents, ranchers, environmentalists, and BLM employees—when asked, "What does democracy mean to you?" The chapters show that their understandings of democracy drew on, but also often conflicted with, the actual circumstances of their lives. I apply political theory to shed light on these democratic paradoxes and show how members of these groups are practicing democracy as they work through them.

The conclusion begins by describing where the conflicts and EIS process stood as of 2006, the tenth anniversary of the creation of GSENM, It then evaluates the understandings of democracy developed in the book by revisiting the three interrelated sets of conclusions about what democracy means to ordinary Americans in relation to landscape, conflict, and democracy and by considering, as Tocqueville did, what each suggests about "what we have to fear or hope" from democracy in America.[40] New text added since I moved to Escalante in 2017 brings the conflict up to date as of the time of this writing. I first tackle the reduction of GSENM and Bears Ears National Monument that same year by President Trump and the onslaught against the public lands during his administration, then describe changes in the region I observed since I moved back and provide an update on GSENM. The book ends with reflections on the value of the understanding of democracy presented here for addressing the deep political divide the United States is facing as of this writing.

# Part 1
Landscape

1 National Landscape

Defining the Terminology of Public Lands

The United States is unique among developed countries in how much of its territory is owned by the federal government.[1] The convoluted story of how this came to be is central to understanding both conflict over Grand Staircase-Escalante National Monument (GSENM) and American democratic imaginaries. The U.S. government owns about 615 million acres (27 percent) of the territory of the United States, and most of it is in the West, where about 46 percent of the land is federally owned (see fig. 3).[2] The terminology referring to this land is somewhat confusing, and some definitions are necessary to clarify the usages in this book. "Public lands" plural and "public land" singular are both used to refer to lands managed by all levels of government, city, county, state, and federal. "Public domain" is the name given officially to U.S. territory acquired through cession by the original thirteen states or from foreign powers or Native peoples. Nearly all U.S. territory outside the original thirteen states was once part of the public domain.

Originally, the federal government aimed to convert all the public domain lands, except for small parcels reserved for specific needs, to private ownership. In the latter half of the nineteenth century, this policy shifted to one of withdrawing more lands from the public domain to be retained and managed in federal ownership. For the purposes of this book, I refer to this land as "federally owned land." Most of this land is held in trust for the American people and managed by the federal land management agencies: the Bureau of Land Management (BLM), National Park Service (NPS), U.S. Fish and Wildlife Service (FWS), and Bureau of Reclamation, all in the Department of the Interior, and the U.S. Forest

Service (USFS) in the Department of Agriculture. I refer to these as "the public lands." They include national parks, national recreation areas, and national monuments managed by the NPS, national forests and wilderness areas managed by the USFS, national wildlife refuges managed by the FWS, and public land managed by the BLM. I use "public land" as opposed to "the public lands" to refer specifically to land managed by the BLM.

The BLM manages more of the federally owned land in the United States by far than the other federal land management agencies: 244.4 million acres for the BLM compared with 192.9 for the USFS, 89.2 million for the FWS, and 79.9 million for the NPS. Among the western states, the highest proportion of federally owned land occurs in Nevada, with 80.1 percent; Utah is second, with 63.1 percent.[3]

Federal ownership of such a vast amount of U.S. territory has had and continues to have significant effects on government and democracy in America. To explain these effects, this chapter tells the story of why there is so much public land in the western United States and of the development of the legal framework governing its management.

From "Vacant" Territory to Resource

The public domain has been crucial to the development of democracy in the United States since 1781, when the Articles of Confederation went into effect, a national government came into existence, and the thirteen original colonies began to cede the "western lands" they claimed to the new federal government.[4] Although Indigenous people inhabited this territory, Euro-American settlers perceived it as vacant because Native Americans did not view or claim the land as property. The first step in reterritorialization for the young government was to secure its territory from claims by foreign powers, which was best accomplished by filling the land with settlers. To facilitate settlement, the Confederation Congress initiated a policy of transferring the public domain lands into private ownership and passed land ordinances in 1784, 1785, and 1787 to promote their orderly inventory, administration, and sale. The management and disposal of the public domain lands remained the chief business of the federal government until after the Civil War.

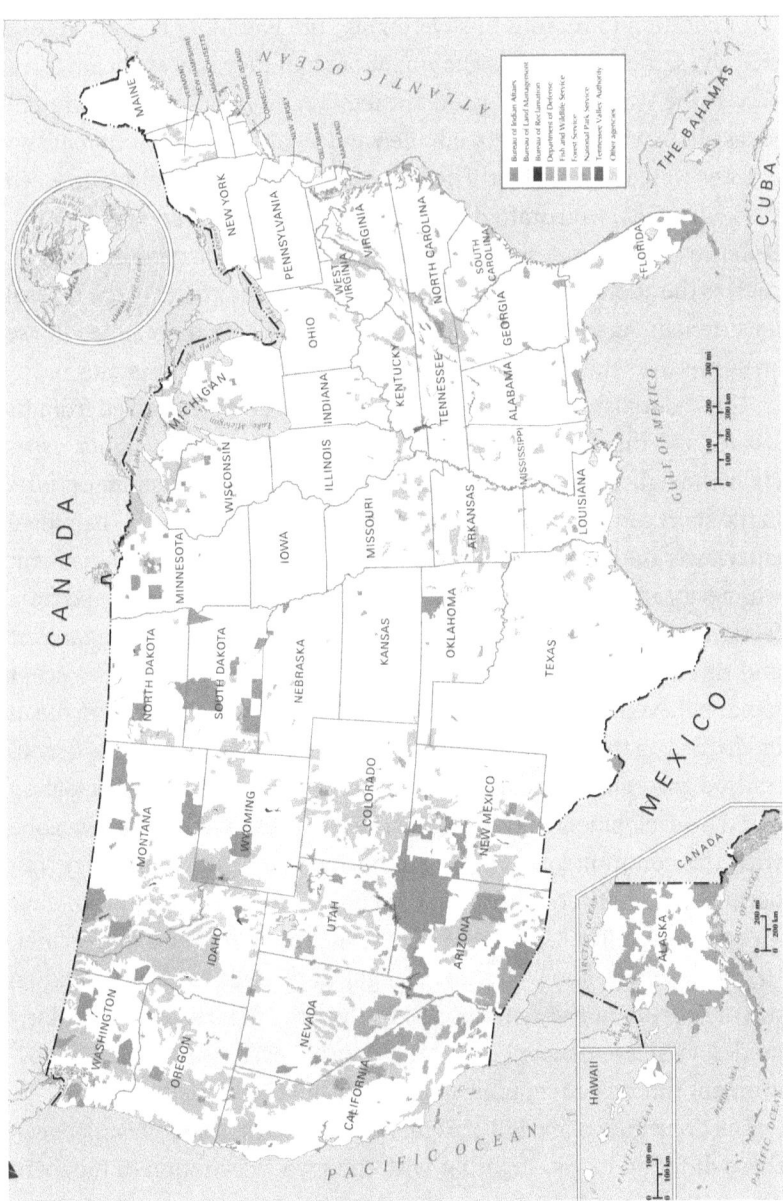

3. Federal lands and Indian reservations. Source: National Atlas of the United States of America, Interior Geological Survey, 2005, accessed June 2, 2006, http://www.nationalatlas.gov/printable/images/pdf/fedlands/fedlands3.pdf (site discontinued).

In addition to reasons of sovereignty, the Founding Fathers agreed that the settlement and development of what they saw as vacant territory of the West would be good for democracy. But they held different ideas about what democracy entailed and what kind of government and citizens would best foster it. This was exemplified by the debate between the Federalists, who drafted the U.S. Constitution in 1787, and the Anti-Federalists, who opposed it as written and insisted on certain changes, such as the addition of the Bill of Rights to limit the power of the federal government. As a result of these differences in beliefs, there were intense struggles over the ratification of the Constitution in many states.

The Federalists believed that the strength of a state derived from its wealth and that democracy should guarantee individual rights, especially the right of property, to promote "individualistic economic efforts in the short run and national wealth and power in the long."[5] Their ideal citizen was the entrepreneur. They believed a strong central government was necessary to protect democracy, both from outside threats and from factions of its own citizens that might unite around a common interest and threaten the rights of others. The Anti-Federalists, on the other hand, believed that the strength of a nation derived from the virtue of its citizens. In their view, democracy was fostered by small-scale, decentralized government and institutions that promoted citizen participation and the development of civic virtue: the identification of one's own good with the common good. They supported the right of property, not because it enhanced wealth, but because it fostered republican civic independence. Their model of the ideal citizen was the small farmer, "the respectable, knowledgeable, frugal, and public-spirited individual who acts deliberatively and cooperatively with other citizens of similarly modest means and independence."[6] They believed a strong central government threatened republican liberties and therefore democracy.

The Constitution and Bill of Rights represented a compromise between these differing views. Together with the 1776 Declaration of Independence, they established the principles of democratic government by which the federal government would operate: popular sovereignty or rule by the people, limited government, republicanism or government through elected representatives, federalism or division of powers between the federal government and states, separation of powers, checks and balances, and individual rights. Equality was limited until the passage of the Thirteenth, Fourteenth, and Fifteenth Amendments. Over time these principles, as well as the tension between Federalist and Anti-Federalist ideas about democracy that they incorporate, have entered deeply into American democratic imaginaries.

The Federalists' ideas about democracy, government, and citizenship led them to conclude that settlement and development of the public domain lands would be good for democracy because it would spread people out over the territory and make it more difficult for factions to form. The Anti-Federalists agreed but for different reasons: expansion of agriculture into this territory would ensure the continued vitality of republican principles. As a result, both Federalist and Anti-Federalist ideas about democracy and government also informed federal land law and policy in contradictory ways since its inception. These ideological differences and the tensions they produce have had a real effect on the western lands.

Early scholars proposed that the western lands had a potent effect on American democratic imaginaries. Perhaps the first to do so was French nobleman Alexis de Tocqueville, who traveled to the United States in 1831 to study prison reform and evaluated the functioning and future of democracy. He reported his observations in three books, including *Democracy in America*, which remains one of the most influential studies of democracy and of American society that has even been written. Tocqueville concluded, "Among the lucky circumstances that favored the establishment and assured the maintenance of a democratic republic in the United States, the most important was the choice of the land itself in which the Americans live. Their fathers gave them a love of equality and liberty, but it was God who, by handing a limitless continent over to them, gave them the means of long remaining equal and free."[7]

For Tocqueville, the existence of so much land ensured prosperity, which was crucial to the stability of a democratic government because if the people became unhappy, they might overthrow the state. At the same time, he anticipated that preoccupation with material comfort could promote excessive individualism and reduce participation in civic life.

American historian Frederick Jackson Turner also considered the relationship between the western lands and democracy. His 1893 essay "The Significance of the Frontier in American History" has been called "the single most influential piece of writing in the history of American history."[8] He surmised that the most important factor that influenced the making of American democracy was "that an area of free land has continually lain on the western border of the settled area of the United States. Whenever social conditions tended to crystallize in the East, whenever capital tended to press upon labor or political restraints to impede the freedom of the mass, there was this gate of escape to the free conditions of the frontier. These free lands promoted individualism, economic equality, freedom to rise, democracy."[9]

For Turner, the experience of frontier conditions promoted a love of individual liberty, antipathy to control, and a "composite nationality for the American people." The existence of free land promoted equality because "everybody could have a farm, almost for taking it."[10] This frontier experience became integral to American democracy, even for those who did not experience it directly.

But Turner also recognized certain dangers inherent in a democracy nurtured by the western lands. Among them were some of the same dangers that Tocqueville had recognized: individualism and a lack of civic spirit. "But the democracy born of free land, strong in selfishness and individualism, intolerant of administrative experience and education, and pressing individual liberty beyond its proper bounds, has its dangers as well as its benefits. Individualism in America has allowed a laxity in regard to governmental affairs which has rendered possible the spoils system and all the manifest evils that follow from a lack of a highly developed civic spirit."[11] Another danger was a tendency toward continuous expansion once the frontier was gone.

It is noteworthy that Tocqueville and Turner, in considering the effects of the western lands on American democratic imaginaries, both warned of the deleterious effects the traits they encouraged could eventually have on democratic government. Western historians have more recently tempered Tocqueville's and Turner's celebration of God-given free land that crucially shaped the character of American democracy with the grim acknowledgment that its existence depended on the extirpation and removal of the Indigenous population.[12] Yet the conclusions they drew so long ago about the relationship between the public domain lands and American democracy still ring true.

For a variety of reasons, the reterritorialization of the public domain lands proceeded quite differently than the Founding Fathers had imagined. First, the rectangular land surveying system set up by the Land Ordinance of 1785, which was intended to provide a simple and failsafe method for describing property and make the territory more legible to the American state, profoundly affected the way settlers interacted with the landscape and with each other.[13] It divided the territory of the United States into townships of thirty-six square miles, further divided into thirty-six sections of 640 acres each, with quarter sections of 160 acres. These were to be disposed of at auction, carving the landscape into a grid and contributing to a settlement pattern of scattered homesteads. While the village arrangement of farms that had developed in New England had promoted interaction among citizens and the development of civic virtue, this pattern promoted isolation and intensified the individualism that Tocqueville had seen developing, which became the celebrated "rugged individualism" of the pioneer. This grid pattern can still be seen on a flight across the country, giving a glimpse into the ways it has shaped Americans' experience of the landscape and of community.

Second, with the Louisiana Purchase in 1803, the Oregon Compromise with England in 1846, and the cession of lands by treaty after the war with Mexico in 1848, the growth of the public domain outstripped the federal government's ability to survey it and regulate its settlement and development in an orderly manner. Federal land laws, rather than setting policy, often attempted to legitimate uses that were already occurring. For example, the Mining Acts of 1866 and 1872 recognized mineral claims on the public domain in accordance with local laws and customs and provided a system for obtaining title to the lands on which these claims were established. Section 8 of the Mining Act of 1866 granted the right-of-way for the construction of highways over public land, recognizing a right-of-way wherever a highway was built. This grant, which became section 2477 of the Revised Statutes (R.S. 2477), came to play a crucial role in the contemporary conflict between Garfield and Kane

Counties and the BLM over who has jurisdiction over R.S. 2477 roads on GSENM (described in chapter 4).

The third and most significant reason reterritorialization did not proceed as imagined was the territory itself. West of the 100th meridian, much of the land was too rugged and the climate too dry for the small-scale farming envisioned by the Founding Fathers. Congress had eased the requirements for purchase of public domain land over the years as U.S. territory expanded rapidly west. The passage of the Homestead Act of 1862 made it possible for settlers to acquire title simply by living on the land, building a home, making improvements, farming the land for five years, and paying a total filing fee of $18. The act embodied the Anti-Federalist ideal of the small farmer in the figure of the homesteader and specified an amount of land eastern legislators believed workable by a single family: 160 acres. When it became apparent that 160 acres could not support a family in the arid West, Congress increased the amount of land that could be acquired in this way in a series of subsequent homesteading acts, but never to more than 640 acres—still not enough for homesteading to be viable in much of the West. The Anti-Federalists' agrarian ideal was still powerful enough that lawmakers considered it undemocratic to allow homesteads of greater size, fearing that such a policy could lead to a feudal system of great landowning barons like those the colonists had left behind in Europe. Although the Mormon pioneers in Utah came closest to reproducing in the West the agrarian landscape the Anti-Federalists had envisioned (see chapter 2), the western landscape made their idea of democracy impossible to realize and profoundly affected American reterritorialization.

Settlement of the land west of the one hundredth meridian proceeded slowly until after the Civil War, when rising beef prices, a supply of free-roaming cattle in the southern states, and an infusion of capital from the eastern United States and Great Britain led to a cattle boom.[14] At first the livestock industry was successful where farming was not. Although it took several hundred acres to support a cow in the arid West, compared with only one or two acres in the East and Midwest, the existence of the vast, unregulated public domain lands made it possible for those who wished to go into the livestock business to acquire a base ranch near water and then run their herds at will on the surrounding public domain land. There was no incentive to acquire the land when it could be used for free, so most of the land west of the 100th meridian remained in the public domain. The image of the cowboy began to take its place in American democratic imaginaries at this time, conveying a very different understanding of democracy and of the ideal citizen than that of the small farmer. But the cattle boom—the heyday of the cowboy—was short-lived. The severe winter of 1886–87 and subsequent drought caused a massive die-off and brought the cattle boom to an end. Stockmen continued to overstock the western rangelands, however, and by the late nineteenth century, these lands were severely damaged.

By the late nineteenth century several factors had converged to bring about a shift in perception of the public domain lands and in the conception of the federal government's role in managing them, along with a corresponding change in the reterritorialization process. First, as in the case of livestock grazing, the unintended consequences of the federal government's policy of encouraging rapid settlement and development of the West were becoming apparent. As a result of concern over deforestation, water, and overgrazing, the public domain lands came to be seen as possessing resources that were threatened by uncontrolled development. Second, by this time no large areas of the West remained unsettled, and the region had achieved a population density of more than two people per square mile. This fact prompted the U.S. Census Bureau to declare the frontier officially closed in 1890 and inspired the famous 1893 Frederick Jackson Turner essay, which considered the effects the closure of the frontier would have on American democracy. These shifts in perception opened an epistemological and geographic space that could be integrated into new forms of political rationality, and a new mode of rule in the form of "government" arose to govern this new territory.[15] The idea of federal management of these resources for the benefit of all citizens began to take hold.

Third, the Progressive movement, which arose during the same period, provided additional impetus and legitimation for federal management. It advocated an expanded role for federal government and citizens to address social, economic, and political reform and to restore democracy, which Progressives believed was eroding as a result of rapid industrialization and the rise of corporate power. Progressive thinking incorporated both Federalist and Anti-Federalist ideas about democracy but developed them further. It advocated using governmental authority to carry out democratic reforms and now relied on technical and scientific expertise and efficiency—"rule of experts"—to legitimate the increase in government power.[16] It also emphasized the civic republican responsibility of citizens in a democracy to use critical and rational judgment to bring about political reform. The conservation movement, which arose during this time, is often considered an aspect of the Progressive movement.[17] It was personified by Theodore Roosevelt, president from 1901 to 1909, who was an ardent conservationist. He extended the powers of the federal government to regulate industry and strengthened the executive branch using presidential initiative and charisma, especially to promote conservation. The shifts in the meaning of democracy in America initiated by the Progressive movement—rule of experts and citizen activism—were taken up by the environmental movement in the 1960s.

These factors drove a second reterritorialization of the public domain lands as resource. The physical territory had largely been settled and secured through the mode of rule of sovereignty. Now the same physical territory was perceived as possessing resources in need of management. The federal government began to take on this role, prefigured in the preamble to the Constitution as one of the purposes of government: to "promote the general welfare." The American state's mode of rule began to shift from sovereignty to "government": how to manage the relationship between "men and things" to ensure the "welfare of the population."[18] The western landscape had significantly affected the outcome of the first reterritorialization, and it would continue to have an impact on subsequent reterritorializations.

To initiate the second reterritorialization, Congress began to provide for the withdrawal of some public domain lands from disposal. In 1872 it created Yellowstone National Park; in 1891 it passed the General Revision Act, which gave the president the power to establish forest reserves; and in 1906 it passed the Antiquities Act, which gave the president the power to establish national monuments. Land withdrawn in these ways became the public lands and soon necessitated the creation of bureaucracies to manage them. Informed by Progressive ideology, their goal was efficient development of the resources on the public lands. Western historian Richard White argued that "the federal government created itself in the West" because federal power increased and took on modern forms through the development of the bureaucracies that managed the public lands and became the federal land management agencies of today.[19] This expansion of federal power was legitimated by the discourses of scientific management and utilitarianism.

Native Americans had contested the reterritorialization of their homeland during the first phase of American reterritorialization; now settlers in the American West contested the reterritorialization of what they saw as theirs. In the 1990s historians began to draw attention to the role of local actors in this reterritorialization process by documenting the ways that changes in federal land management policy were contested. For example, Mark Spence recounted the struggle between Native American users of national park lands and the federal government.[20] Karl Jacoby discussed the strife between subsistence users of the national park lands and the federal government.[21] Karen Merrill described the clash that ensued when the federal government first attempted to regulate livestock grazing on the national forest lands.[22] Contention over this expansion of federal power also took place between different branches of the federal government and between different levels of government. For example, presidents' aggressive use of the General Revision Act created concern among representatives from the western states about the large acreage in forest reserves in their states. In 1907 Congress revoked the president's authority to create new reserves in Colorado, Idaho, Montana, Oregon, Washington, and Wyoming; later, this was extended to Arizona, California, and New Mexico but reinstated in Montana. Local residents, the legislative and judicial branches of the federal government, and state and local governments also contested presidents' expansive use of the 1906 Antiquities Act to create national monuments. A brief description of these struggles will provide additional insight into the conflict over the creation of GSENM.

NATIONAL MONUMENTS

National monuments are different from national parks in that hunting, mining, and other consumptive uses such as grazing are permitted in national monuments but are generally prohibited in national parks.²³ In addition, while Congress must legislate national parks, a process that may take many years, the president can proclaim national monuments with the stroke of a pen. While GSENM was created in what seems to have been an undemocratic manner, it wasn't the first time a president used the Antiquities Act to create a national monument and, in so doing, sparked a national uproar.

The act authorizes the president to proclaim national monuments on federal lands that contain "historic landmarks, historic and prehistoric structures, and other objects of historic or scientific interest," of a size that "in all cases shall be confined to the smallest area compatible with the proper care and management of the objects to be protected."²⁴ The sponsors of the act intended it to protect archaeological sites in the Southwest, such as cliff dwellings and pueblos, and assumed that national monuments would be small in area and geographically limited to the Southwest. However, assertive presidents interpreted it more broadly, and this expansion of executive power was hotly contested.

In 1906 President Theodore Roosevelt used the reference to "objects of scientific interest" to proclaim a natural geological feature, Devils Tower in Wyoming, as the first national monument. In 1908 he used it to proclaim an even larger "object of scientific interest," the 800,000-acre Grand Canyon National Monument. That proclamation was challenged but upheld by the Supreme Court. In 1909, forty-eight hours before he left office, Roosevelt signed a proclamation for Mount Olympus National Monument. Historian Robert Righter suggested that because Mount Olympus was an area of natural beauty rather than historic or scientific, this action "surely stretched the meaning of the Antiquities Act to the limit." As other presidents followed the precedent set by Roosevelt, the Antiquities Act became "a significant executive tool to shape sometimes controversial conservation policies in the United States."²⁵ Since 1906 presidents have proclaimed more than 130 national monuments. Some of the best-known national parks originated as national monuments, among them Grand Canyon, Olympic, Grand Teton, Zion, Bryce Canyon, and Capitol Reef National Parks.

Expansive use of the Antiquities Act first generated a struggle between the president and Congress in 1943, when President Franklin Roosevelt used it to proclaim Jackson Hole National Monument after Congress had declined to authorize an expansion of the adjacent Grand Teton National Park. Congress responded by passing a bill to abolish the monument, but Roosevelt vetoed it. The state of Wyoming joined the struggle by challenging the proclamation in court. Congress did eventually pass legislation that incorporated the monument into Grand Teton National Park, but at the same time, it reduced presidential powers under the Antiquities Act by prohibiting further use of it in Wyoming without congressional approval. Presidents used the act more carefully for decades afterward. But in 1978 President Jimmy Carter antagonized Congress by proclaiming fifteen new national monuments in Alaska after Congress had declined to pass a major Alaska lands bill. Congress responded similarly by reducing the president's power to proclaim national monuments in Alaska. The presidential proclamation authority was not used again until 1996, when President Bill Clinton proclaimed the largest national monument in the contiguous United States: Grand Staircase-Escalante National Monument. Utah's elected officials and local residents reacted to this forceful use of the Antiquities Act just as their counterparts had in the past.

From Desert to Public Land

By the early twentieth century most of the land remaining in the public domain was too dry or too rugged for farming, not considered scenic enough to be a national park, or lacked sufficient trees to be a national forest.[26] It was generally considered desert, good for nothing but livestock grazing or mining, and the rural communities that these activities supported still pursued them relatively unrestricted by federal regulations. In 1929 President Herbert Hoover offered to give the public rangelands back to the states. However, the states declined because the offer did not include mineral rights. Despite evidence that the public rangelands were deteriorating as a result of unregulated grazing, Congress did not take measures to protect them until 1934, when the Great Depression coupled with an extended drought throughout the West provided the necessary impetus for the passage of the Taylor Grazing Act (TGA). The Depression also gave rise to and legitimated an expanded role for the federal government in providing for the welfare of the population, exemplified by Roosevelt's New Deal, which included increased control of the economy and the money supply, support for agriculture and labor, job creation programs, and Social Security.

In keeping with New Deal ideology, one purpose of the TGA was "to stabilize the livestock industry dependent on the public range." The act authorized the secretary of the interior to establish and regulate grazing districts on public domain lands deemed "chiefly valuable for grazing," issue grazing permits for up to ten years, and collect grazing fees. It directed the secretary to cooperate with "local associations of stockmen" in the administration of grazing districts, a feature that the act's sponsor, Representative Edward Taylor from Colorado, referred to as "democracy on the range" or "home rule on the range." The act also gave "preference right" in issuing permits to "those within or near a district who are landowners engaged in the livestock business, bona fide occupants or settlers, or owners of water or water rights." A crucial clause saying "pending its final disposal" indicated that Congress was still trying to decide what to do with the remaining public domain lands and that the arrangements laid out in the TGA might be temporary.[27]

Interior Secretary Harold Ickes established a Grazing Division (which became the Grazing Service in 1939) to guide these procedures and delegated authority to set up an allotment system, decide who would receive permits, and determine initial stocking rates to grazing advisory boards composed of local ranchers. State advisory boards and the National Advisory Board Council took on more general policy issues. But grazing fees were set by Congress, a process that proved to be contentious. The BLM emerged out of one such clash in 1946, as an administrative merger of the Grazing Service and the General Land Office. However, it was given no official power to manage these lands and little funding, so its effectiveness was limited. The BLM did manage to complete range surveys during the late 1950s and early 1960s to determine the capacity of the land for grazing, and following these surveys, decisions on forage were adjudicated and livestock numbers on most allotments were reduced.

As the American economy recovered from the Depression, much of the New Deal legislation came under critique for granting too much power either to the federal government or to special interests. Most assessments of the effects of the TGA conclude that it gave local grazing interests tremendous control over public land administration and imply that these arrangements not only were undemocratic but also contributed to the degradation of public land. Political scientist Grant McConnell used the TGA to illustrate how private interests, in this case the range livestock industry, had largely "captured" American government.[28] However, from the perspective of the community-based, or collaborative, conservation movement, which calls for more participation by local communities in conservation decision-making and practice, the provisions of the TGA seem visionary. Advocates of this approach see it as more just and democratic, and they view it as essential to achieving conservation goals because healthy ecosystems and healthy communities are inextricably linked.

In the 1960s the rise of the environmental movement in the United States led to another shift in perceptions of the public lands and to the passage of legislation that had a profound impact on the operation of the federal land management agencies and laid the groundwork for a third wave of reterritorialization. The 1964 Wilderness Act provided for the creation of the National Wilderness Preservation System to preserve and protect public lands managed by the NPS and USFS as "wilderness areas," places "where the earth and its community of life are untrammeled by man."[29] The 1969 National Environmental Policy Act instructed federal agencies to prepare environmental impact statements (EISs) for all significant federal actions that might affect the environment and required public input as part of this process. For the BLM, this included managing livestock grazing on the public rangelands. However, while this act requires federal agencies to investigate and report environmental impacts, it does not require them to make decisions based on their findings. The 1973 Endangered Species Act added stipulations that federal actions could not contribute to the extinction of native species. With this new legislation, management of the public lands began to come under wider public scrutiny.

It was not until 1976, when Congress passed the Federal Land Policy and Management Act (FLPMA), that the federal government officially recognized that the public rangelands were not just desert, but possessed resources that needed to be managed, and began the second reterritorialization of these lands. FLPMA declared that the remaining public domain lands would be retained in federal ownership, officially ending the policy of disposal; defined these lands as "public lands"; finally gave the BLM authority to manage them; and gave the agency a multiple-use mandate, which required it to find "a combination of balanced and diverse resource uses that takes into account the long-term needs of future generations for renewable and nonrenewable resources."[30] FLPMA also represented the beginnings of a third reterritorialization of public land, which was coming to be seen as wilderness or national landscape, more valuable for amenity consumption—aesthetic appeal, recreation, biological diversity, or nearby real estate development—than for resource production.

The second reterritorialization threatened the long-standing priority of traditional public lands user groups in the West, and they contested it. A loosely organized movement among these groups and state and county governments, deemed the Sagebrush Rebellion, sought greater state and local control or privatization of the public lands. Sagebrush rebels argued that federal ownership and management of the public lands had an adverse effect on local economies and undermined the sovereignty of states. For the most part, they pursued their objectives through government channels: they passed laws in state legislatures claiming the lands, their representatives in Congress introduced legislation to transfer the lands to states, and they used the courts to claim legal rights to the lands. These strategies proved unsuccessful, and the movement was largely defused when Ronald Reagan, who self-identified as a sagebrush rebel, was elected president in 1980. His interior secretary, James Watt, instituted a "good neighbor" policy that provided resource producers with expanded rights. The Sagebrush Rebellion was informed and sometimes funded by organizations that had formed in response to the growing power of the environmental movement. These organizations advocated free enterprise and opposed environmental protections that limited resource development.[31] Environmental historian James Skillen argued that the greater significance of the Sagebrush Rebellion was how this "regional challenge to federal authority in the West aligned with challenges from both business interests and religious conservatives in the New Right and how opposition to federal land authority increasingly became a plank in the conservative platform."[32]

In the late 1980s and 1990s the Wise Use movement, strategically drawing its name from Gifford Pinchot's definition of conservation as "the wise use of the earth and its resources," continued to contest reterritorialization of the public lands as wilderness.[33] Responding to deep downturns in primary production industries since 1980, the growing strength of the environmental movement, and its successes in court, Wise Use consisted of a coalition of industry groups, property rights organizations, and conservative legal foundations supporting commodity development on the public lands. Having learned its strategy from the environmental movement, it supported rural resource users' grassroots efforts to maintain their historically privileged access to the public lands, justified in terms of local rights, custom, and culture versus the national interest and of common sense versus expert knowledge. It labeled the environmental movement as anti–private property and anti-people and promoted the protection of jobs and economic development from federal regulations, as well as multiple use and private property rights. It was joined at the local level with the county supremacy movement, which directly challenged federal ownership and management of the public lands, sometimes resulting in transgression of federal law by county officials and incidents of violence against federal employees. The ideology and rhetoric of these movements later came to inform opposition to GSENM.

From Public Land to National Landscape

FLPMA aimed to systematize and simplify the complex jumble of federal land laws that had developed during the first reterritorialization as Congress tried to encourage settlement and keep pace with western expansion. Three of its provisions are particularly relevant to conflict over GSENM. First, to systematize the management of livestock grazing, FLPMA amended the TGA, eliminated the grazing advisory boards, and set up a system of federal grazing regulations to provide uniform guidance for administration of grazing on public land exclusive of Alaska.[34] Since the 1990s executive branch changes to the grazing regulations have been used to circumvent possible congressional opposition to changes in the management of grazing on public land. For example, during the early part of the Clinton administration, Interior Secretary Bruce Babbitt promoted legislation that would further reduce what many still saw as entrenched privileges held by the range livestock industry. When his efforts failed, he turned to the administrative arena and developed a set of revisions to the federal grazing regulations known as Rangeland Reform '94. The revisions included the removal of the requirement that an applicant must be in the livestock business to obtain a grazing permit, which enabled the Grand Canyon Trust to purchase grazing permits on GSENM (described in chapter 3). Congress also included a provision allowing for conservation use. The Public Lands Council, a trade organization that represents ranchers, challenged the revised regulations in the federal courts. The case, *Public Lands Council v. Babbitt*, made its way to the Supreme Court, which upheld the revised regulations, with the exception of the conservation use provision.[35]

Second, to systematize the management of roads on public land, FLPMA repealed R.S. 2477 and set out new provisions for granting various kinds of rights-of-way in Title V. FLPMA also acknowledged rights-of-way for roads built before 1976 and gave the BLM authority to manage all other roads on lands it administered. However, it did not specify a process for identifying valid R.S. 2477 rights-of-way. As a result, controversy arose over how these rights should be determined. And GSENM became the testing ground for strategies to persuade or force the BLM, the Interior Department, or the federal courts to make a definitive pronouncement on the issue.

Third, FLPMA directed the BLM to inventory the roadless lands it administered for possible inclusion in the National Wilderness Preservation System and to manage those areas it identified as potential wilderness areas (referred to as wilderness study areas) for nonimpairment of their wilderness characteristics until Congress either decided to make them part of the wilderness system or released them for multiple use. Since wilderness designation precludes many of the multiple uses for which public land would otherwise be available, such as logging, mining, other extractive and commodity uses, and motorized recreation, the inventory process was contentious. In particular, the recognition of R.S. 2477 rights-of-way was problematic because it could disqualify areas that were currently considered roadless from inclusion in the National Wilderness Preservation System.[36]

Wilderness became a particularly contentious issue in Utah when conservation groups, dissatisfied with the outcome of the BLM's wilderness inventory in that state, filed a series of appeals.[37] Disappointed with the results of the appeals, they formed the Utah Wilderness Coalition, which began to conduct its own inventory in 1985.[38] In 1989 the results of the coalition's "citizens' proposal" were incorporated into the first version of America's Redrock Wilderness Act, which called for the designation of 5.7 million acres of wilderness in Utah. In 1994 the Utah congressional delegation countered with its own wilderness legislation, which would limit the ability to create more wilderness areas in the state. The Utah Wilderness Coalition fought it. This ongoing legislative battle prompted Interior Secretary Bruce Babbitt in 1996, the same year GSENM was created, to direct the BLM to conduct a new wilderness inventory in the state. In the Grand Staircase-Escalante region, many residents opposed wilderness for the same reasons they opposed GSENM: they believed that it locked up public land, denying them access to resources they had been able to use in the past, and they resented the implication that their use of the land was degrading it. One Escalante resident draped the fence between his property and a public road with signs expressing his anti-wilderness sentiments, including one that read "Let's Make Wilderness Where You Live." The fact that the wilderness reinventory and the creation of GSENM happened about the same time intensified opposition to both.

The creation of GSENM is representative of the third reterritorialization of the public lands as they came to be seen as more valuable for amenity consumption than resource production. This shift is legitimated by a form of rule Foucault refers to as "neoliberal governmentality," which seeks to minimize the role of the state and maximize economic growth by extending market rationality to all domains of life, activities, and subjects.[39] It replaces the welfare of the population with the welfare of the economy as the goal and legitimation of state power. Conflict over GSENM reflects local actors' resistance to this reterritorialization.

When President Clinton created GSENM and made it the first national monument the BLM would manage, he assigned the BLM the difficult and ambiguous role of steering between the management guidance laid out by FLPMA and the responsibilities assigned by his proclamation: to protect the objects of historic and scientific interest the proclamation identified; to respect "valid existing rights" and "existing permits or leases for, or levels of, livestock grazing" within the monument; and to govern "existing grazing uses" by "applicable laws and regulations."[40] When the BLM first came into existence, without official power or funding to manage the public rangelands, its role was also ambiguous, and it could accomplish very little. On the other hand, the executive branch has been able to take advantage of ambiguity in federal laws to expand its power. In this case, supporters of greater protection for public land hoped the BLM would take advantage of this ambiguity to become more oriented toward protection rather than resource use, while opponents of GSENM feared exactly that. To support the agency's new role as manager of a national monument and the reterritorialization of public land as national landscape, Congress granted GSENM generous funding during its early years.[41]

Another reason Utah officials and local residents were angered by the creation of GSENM was that locally based proposals to create a national park or protected area of some kind in the region were already being developed. In 1991 the governor of Utah had endorsed a locally based effort to create a Canyons of the Escalante national heritage and recreation area from public land that is now part of GSENM, but this was stymied by a group of residents who opposed it. In 1996, when GSENM was created, Utah officials were working on two proposals: Republican governor Mike Leavitt's plan for an "eco-region" and Democratic representative Bill Orton's for a national conservation area. Efforts were also ongoing to have much of the area included in the Wilderness Preservation System.

Proposals to protect the region actually dated back to the mid-1930s, when a plan was first proposed for an Escalante National Monument, which took other forms over the years—national park, national recreation area—and eventually grew in size to almost 4.5 million acres. When the governor of Utah was informed of the plans after they were well underway, he and many other Utahns objected strongly. After a long struggle, the proposal was abandoned during World War II.[42] Only a small part of the acreage in the original proposal is included in the present-day GSENM.

In addition to their anger over President Clinton's disregard for ongoing local efforts to create a protected area in the region, residents' opposition to GSENM was fueled by what had happened after two other national monuments were created in the region. In 1923 President Warren G. Harding set aside Bryce Canyon in Garfield County as a national monument. Congress designated it a national park in 1928, and the elimination of livestock grazing became a long-range goal. The process was finally completed in 1964.[43]

In 1937 President Franklin Roosevelt proclaimed Capitol Reef National Monument in neighboring Wayne County, and grazing was soon prohibited on all monument lands. In 1969, in the last hours of his administration, President Lyndon Johnson signed a proclamation that increased the size of the monument by 600 percent, an action that was controversial locally. Some residents remember how the NPS began to acquire private land in and around the town of Fruita, a historic Mormon settlement located inside monument boundaries and the most desirable location for monument headquarters, from "willing sellers" to relieve the agency of "a significant management problem."[44] In 1971 Congress made Capitol Reef a national park, with a plan to end grazing within ten years. The plan also called for razing Fruita's remaining buildings and orchards and returning the landscape to its "natural" condition. Local opposition to this plan eventually influenced the NPS to adopt a new management approach in 1998, which recognized the significance of Mormon settlement and agriculture in the landscape and would preserve the remaining orchards and renovate or restore historic structures. Some of the structures have become residences for park employees. One local resident asked me, "How would you feel if you were kicked out of your house and the park superintendent moved in?"

The phase-out of grazing in Capitol Reef was also contentious and has progressed slowly. It was extended to 1992, and the legislation authorizing the extension also paved the way for the NPS to purchase remaining permits for allotments in the park from ranchers willing to sell. By 1994 only three grazing allotments remained. When increases in the value of permits priced the Park Service out of the market, the conservation organization Grand Canyon Trust stepped in to fill the gap. The trust purchased the permit for the last allotment in the northern range of the park when it came on the market in 1999.

The creation of the park inspired Boulder rancher Dell LeFevre to run for county commissioner in 1976. "They made Capitol Reef Park . . . about the time I was getting out of the service," he recalled in 1998. "I had cattle down in Capitol Reef Park, and these ranchers were just getting pushed around. I did it more for the ranchers than myself back then. I mean, they didn't have a spokesman."[45] The phase-out of grazing in Capitol Reef National Park is not yet complete. And the feeling of injustice is refreshed each time one of the remaining grazing allotments in the park closes.

Although the proclamation creating GSENM stated that it should not be interpreted to affect existing grazing permits or levels on the monument and that grazing uses would continue to be governed by the same laws and regulations as before monument designation, the experience of longtime residents with national monuments in the region has taught them to expect otherwise. They would have been unlikely to look favorably on a proposal for a Grand Staircase-Escalante National Monument, had they been consulted. But the way that GSENM was created ensured their opposition.

The reterritorialization of public land as national landscape proceeded nonetheless. Before he left office, President Clinton created a total of nineteen new national monuments, fourteen of which the BLM would manage. In 2000 Interior Secretary Bruce Babbitt created the National Landscape Conservation System (also referred to as National Conservation Lands) to manage the new national monuments, as well as the national conservation areas, wilderness areas, wilderness study areas, national historic trails, and wild and scenic rivers already under BLM management.[46] To make the system permanent, in 2009 Congress passed the National Landscape Conservation System Act. GSENM became the flagship of the system and the focus of struggles among the federal government, local residents, environmental organizations, and the general public over the meaning of "national landscape" and the understanding of democracy embedded in it. It has continued to attract a high level of scrutiny from officials at the Department of the Interior and conservation groups.

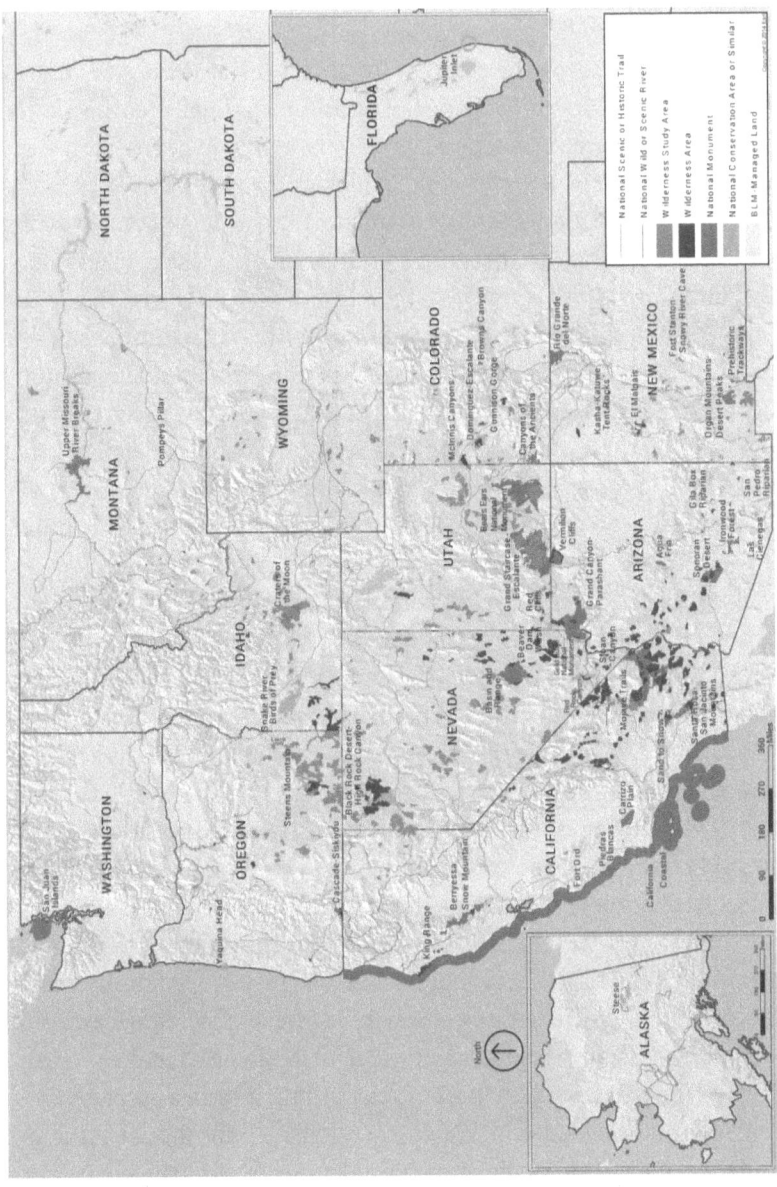

4. National conservation lands as of 2017. Source: Bureau of Land Management, accessed January 31, 2023, https://www.blm.gov/sites/blm.gov/files/documents/files/NLCS_August2017_look%26feel.pdf.

An "October Surprise"

Further complicating the creation story of GSENM is the story of *why* it was created. On April 20, 2004, a decision was finally reached in the lawsuit filed against the federal government in 1997 by the Utah Association of Counties and the Utah School and Institutional Trust Lands Administration in an attempt to overturn the proclamation creating GSENM. The latter group dropped out during the seven years it took for the case to wind its way through the federal courts, and the Mountain States Legal Foundation joined the lawsuit. When the lawsuit was finally decided, the U.S. District Court judge upheld President Clinton's use of the Antiquities Act. In an interview the same day at the Center of the American West, former interior secretary Babbitt explained that since "the last challenge for the Grand Staircase Monument was dismissed by a federal judge in Salt Lake City today," he could "in public for the first time, tell . . . the real story" of how it was created.

According to Babbitt, the idea for an "October surprise"—a last-minute action that might influence the outcome of the election—came from Dick Morris, a "kind of dark, shadowy figure" who worked with the Clinton campaign, "had surely never been near a national park," and had never heard the phrase "national monument." Morris had noticed that environmental issues were beginning to climb back up in the polls and advised the president, who "didn't really hear the music of environmental issues," that the campaign needed "a dramatic environmental initiative." But it couldn't come from Congress because "you can't get anything out of Congress." So the president solicited "some dramatic proposals," and "the Grand Staircase jumped to the top of the list immediately." For political reasons, it had to be "done in secret. Because that was the whole Morris kind of thing. If we're going to make the front page of the national press in a big splash, it's got to be a surprise."

Babbitt acknowledged, "We paid a terrible political price for it and understandably." Although former presidents had "often thrown national monuments over the transom on their way out of office," he continued, "in an era of higher expectation about transparency and process, we paid an awful price." Babbitt concluded, "The political process doesn't always work like you get it in the civics books. It really doesn't."[47]

This interview reveals that Clinton's creation of GSENM reflected a lack of interest in and concern for the people who would be affected, and not even a real concern with protecting the landscape, but simply the desire of the administration to remain in power. Even without hearing this backstory, Utah elected officials and residents of the communities adjacent to the monument keenly felt that disregard.

This brief history of the U.S. public lands, with a focus on those managed by the BLM, shows that the public domain lands were a crucial site for the development of the American state and ideas about government and democracy that legitimated state power. A significant feature of that development not addressed in this chapter was the genocidal campaign against the Indigenous population that made these lands available for settlement. From the inception of the United States, divergent ideas about democracy became associated with the western lands and embedded in federal land law and policy, providing justification for conflicting ideas about how they should be managed. Positioning conflict over GSENM in a series of reterritorializations of these lands draws attention to the ways that people inhabiting the land and, since the passage of the National Environmental Policy Act, the American public more generally have contested reterritorialization and shaped its outcome and the meaning and practice of democracy.

2   Regional Landscape

Grand Staircase-Escalante National Monument (GSENM) is situated in a unique landscape. The physical landscape is spectacular: vast, arid, and sparsely vegetated expanses framed by the sheer cliffs of multihued mesas, punctuated by fantastically shaped spires, dissected by labyrinthine canyons, and strewn with evidence of its former inhabitants. The cultural landscape is shaped by the Mormon pioneers who first settled the region, having moved westward as a group for reasons that differed from those of other settlers of the West. The authoritative history of the American people by Bailyn and colleagues offers the Mormons as "a test case" for dissent in American society.[1] Most of the region's current residents are descendants of these pioneers and are united by religion and a fierce pride in their pioneer heritage.

Situating GSENM

GSENM is in southern Utah in the Intermountain West, the region that lies between the Rocky Mountains to the east and the Sierra Nevada and Cascade Ranges to the west. Geological forces uplifted the whole region and created mountains to the west that block the flow of moisture from the Pacific Ocean, making this high, dry country. Most of the Grand Staircase-Escalante region is either arid or semiarid.[2] Vegetation is sparse except at higher elevations. As a result of its aridity, the Intermountain West is the quintessential Old West of wide-open spaces, glittering blue skies, and small, scattered settlements huddled close to water.

More specifically, GSENM is in the geologically and topographically unique Colorado Plateau region, which includes parts of southern and eastern Utah, northern Arizona, northwest New Mexico, and western Colorado. Its colorful cliffs and towers have been the backdrop for many of the Hollywood westerns that formed an image of the American West throughout the world. Between the 1930s and the 1990s many movies and television shows, including *Gunsmoke* and *The Lone Ranger*, were filmed near the town of Kanab, now the location of monument headquarters.

GSENM takes its name from two of the three topographically distinct areas that it encompasses: from west to east, the Grand Staircase, the Kaiparowits Plateau, and the Escalante Canyons. Maj. John Wesley Powell, who led a series of expeditions beginning in 1869 to explore and map the Colorado River and its tributaries, described the prominent series of cliffs and benches rising northward from the North Rim of the Grand Canyon as the Grand Staircase. Known as the Chocolate, Vermilion, White, Gray, and Pink Cliffs, these were formed by different-colored geological formations. However, longtime residents of the region found the name chosen for the new national monument puzzling. Boulder rancher Dell LeFevre told a *New York Times* reporter, "I don't even know what the Grand Staircase is—nobody around here has ever called this place by that name."[3]

The higher terrain of the Kaiparowits Plateau is extremely rugged and isolated. Its eastern end is known as Fiftymile Mountain, which played a central role in one of the conflicts over livestock grazing on GSENM (described in chapter 3). Formed in the Late Cretaceous geological period, the Kaiparowits Plateau is the site of sometimes smoldering coal deposits, which provided some specific locations with their names (e.g., Smoky Hollow, Burning Hills, and Coal Bed Canyon). Since the 1960s these deposits have been the focus of a series of controversial plans to mine them, the most recent being those of Andalex, which were halted by the creation of the monument. Its creation also stimulated paleontological exploration on the Kaiparowits Plateau, which has proven to be one of the best sites in the world to find fossilized remains of dinosaurs and early mammalian species of the Late Cretaceous. Discoveries of several new dinosaur species and well-preserved details of dinosaur skin, bones, teeth, eggshells, and tracks are advancing understanding of the evolution of dinosaurs and early mammals.

The area most favored by hikers is Escalante Canyons, a set of twisting canyons of Navajo sandstone that form the drainage basin of the

Escalante River. Water from sources high on the Aquarius Plateau to the west runs year-round through many of these canyons, creating inviting green oases and hanging gardens in the midst of a red rock desert.

Because of its rugged and remote character, the Grand Staircase-Escalante region was the last area in the continental United States to be explored and mapped by Euro-Americans. The region remained a blank space on the official military map of Utah until a scientific exploration party headed by Almon H. Thompson, part of Major Powell's expeditions, mapped it between 1871 and 1877. In 1872 Thompson's party named the Escalante River after one of the leaders of the Spanish party that passed through the region in 1776 while scouting a more direct route between missions in Santa Fe and Monterey, California, the first known Euro-Americans to visit this area.[4]

The region remains relatively remote today. The communities adjacent to the monument are still a considerable distance from major freeways, via roads that wind through rugged canyon country or climb over high mountain passes, and from the nearest major airports in Las Vegas and Salt Lake City. Until the Civilian Conservation Corps constructed a road to Boulder in the 1930s, the region was inaccessible from the north. This road, which became State Route 12, commonly known as Highway 12, was not fully paved until 1985. It has been recognized by the U.S. Department of Transportation as a National Scenic Byway and an All-American Road and now brings a steady stream of tourists to the region.

The Monument Management Plan signed in 1999 intended that GSENM should remain an undeveloped "frontier."[5] Visitors will not find the amenities they are accustomed to in national parks. The roads in the monument are unpaved and rough. There are few campgrounds, but primitive camping abounds. The only visitor facilities are in the adjacent towns. The monument has few of the interpretive signs found in abundance in national parks, and hiking routes are marked, if at all, by piles of stones built by thoughtful hikers who came before. Visitors to GSENM are left to discover what the landscape has to offer on their own.

The Grand Staircase-Escalante region encompasses the eastern portions of Garfield and Kane Counties, in which GSENM and the towns of Boulder, Escalante, Henrieville, Cannonville, Tropic, Glendale, Kanab, and Big Water lie. Each of these towns is in a spectacular physical setting framed by massive cliffs in stunning colors. For Kanab, these are the deep-red Vermilion Cliffs; for Glendale, the Gray Cliffs; and for Tropic, the same Pink Cliffs also found in Bryce Canyon National Park. Escalante and Boulder lie among domes of white Navajo sandstone of the Escalante Monocline. Most of the land in the region is federally owned, of which most is public land managed by the Bureau of Land Management (BLM). GSENM is surrounded by national forest, national park, and other BLM-administered lands, as well as three state parks. Garfield and Kane Counties have high proportions of federally owned land, at 88.1 and 90.5 percent, respectively; 18 percent of Garfield County and 49 percent of Kane County lie within the monument boundaries.[6]

With the exception of Kanab, the seat of Kane County, no other town in the region has more than one thousand residents, and most have much fewer. Except for these small and scattered communities, the region is largely unpopulated. In the past, most residents of these communities depended on grazing, timber, or mineral resources on the public lands for their livelihoods, and many still depend on activities such as small-scale ranching and wood gathering on these lands to augment their incomes. Private land surrounding the towns is mainly devoted to irrigated alfalfa fields.

Most Americans would find the communities adjacent to GSENM very different from the urban and suburban environments to which they are accustomed. In 2008 none had shopping malls, big-box stores, movie theaters, or bars. Only Kanab and Escalante had a fast-food restaurant. One couldn't buy a latte in Escalante until 2000. The stores, for the most part, are locally owned and have a limited selection. Residents regularly make trips to larger cities in the area—Cedar City and St. George or, farther still, Las Vegas and Salt Lake City—for more specialized needs. Except for those who live in Kanab, nobody has mail delivery or garbage pickup. The post office is a place to socialize and post notices as well as pick up mail, and the community dumpsters are a place to find useful castoffs as well as deposit garbage. There is little traffic, and people wave to each other when they pass on the roads. It's quiet. Social life centers around the LDS Church and high school athletics.

5. & 6. Escalante house and old outbuildings. Courtesy of the author.

In Escalante, where I lived while conducting my research and live again now, homes are mostly small and unpretentious, but they sit along wide roads, on large lots shaded by great old trees, preserving the feeling of spaciousness of the surrounding landscape within the town limits. Many homes are updates of the brick homes built by early settlers, often in need of repair, and surrounded by outbuildings, unused for years, weathered and tumbling down. Many have large, well-tended gardens and fruit trees. Outside the city limits, as far as the eye can see, are public lands, uninhabited, crisscrossed by fences, and grazed by cattle during certain seasons. Like the Mormon pioneers and the Native Americans before them, people are free to roam and explore.

The Physical Landscape

The physical landscape of the Grand Staircase-Escalante region is austere, stunning, and improbable. A high, arid, sun-scorched region of sparse vegetation, it has wide vistas framed by cliffs and towers in layers of various colors, sculpted by the wind into astounding shapes ranging from graceful to grotesque, dissected by deep, twisting canyons where water seeps and flows year-round, nourishing hanging gardens and carving immense, cathedral-like grottoes, and scented by sagebrush. By day, the bones of the earth lie exposed in the crystalline desert air; by night, the heavens sparkle brilliantly. The stillness and the silence are immense, stopping time, inducing peacefulness. For those willing to venture out into the vastness, there are traces to be discovered everywhere of those who came before: dinosaurs left tracks and fossilized bones; people of the Fremont and Ancestral Puebloan cultures left granaries nestled, steps carved, and figures chipped or painted along the sheer canyon walls;[7] Mormon pioneers left bits of hardware and their names engraved on rocks scattered along old wagon tracks; and cowboys left line shacks and stashes of old tin cans and bottles and brush corrals next to favorite camping sites.

The landscape began to take on its unique physical forms during the Cambrian Period, over 500 million years ago, when the Colorado Plateau region began to form as a distinct piece of the earth's crust.[8] The Colorado Plateau region is geologically unique because it has remained a relatively distinct mass of continental crust, while the landmass that would become North America drifted slowly northward from the equator; was thrust, stretched, folded, and fractured by the movement of the earth's plates; and gradually disengaged from Asia, Africa, and South America about 150 million years ago. Situated on what was then the western edge of the North American landmass, the region was alternately coastline, covered by shallow seas, or a vast Sahara-like desert. Its climate, initially quite warm and varying between tropical-humid and desert-hot, gradually became temperate as it continued to drift northward. The region accumulated vast amounts of sediment, as distinct layers were laid down under different conditions, and gradually sank under its own weight. Heat and pressure hardened the deposits into a mantle of sedimentary rock several miles thick, which served to protect the region from forces that drastically changed nearby regions with thinner crusts. This thick crust forms the magnificent strata exposed today.

The Colorado Plateau region remained intact even when the Ancestral Rockies rose to its east about 300 million years ago, the Sevier orogeny uplifted the region to its west about 100 million years ago, and the Laramide orogeny produced the modern Rockies around 60 million years ago. The forces causing these events were dampened by the thick layer of sedimentary rock, so they are reflected more subtly in the Colorado Plateau region as broad, dome-shaped uplifts, shallow basins, and long folds or reefs. About 10 million years ago, the entire western United States began to rise, initiating the processes that exposed the region's spectacular geology. As the elevation of the region became higher, its climate became wetter. The greater amount of precipitation created a system of meandering streams, increased erosion rates, and removed the most recent deposits. As the uplift continued, the streams cut deeper and deeper, becoming the Colorado River and its many tributaries, and carving the region into its present shape.[9] With an arid climate and little soil, forests, or other vegetation to hide these geological formations, 200 million years of the earth's history are exposed to view on the Colorado Plateau. Today the region has the world's largest concentration of protected landscapes, with over fifty-five national parks, national monuments, and wilderness areas.

The Grand Staircase-Escalante landscape is also exceptional for the wide diversity of native plant species and the high rate of endemic plant

7.–12. Traces on the landscape of former inhabitants of the Grand Staircase-Escalante region: dinosaur tracks; excavation of North Creek Shelter; petroglyphs; granary; pioneer inscription; line shack. Courtesy of the author.

species found there. As a result of its complex geology, the region contains a mosaic of soil types, variations in altitude and annual precipitation (ranging from 6 inches at 4,000 feet near Lake Powell to 25 inches at 9,280 feet at Canaan Peak on the Kaiparowits Plateau), and unique topographic features, such as dunes, potholes, and hanging gardens, creating an abundance of habitats.[10] The predominant vegetation types found in GSENM are sagebrush, pinyon-juniper, and desert shrub. Species distributions have been affected by human activities, fire suppression, the establishment of non-native species, and climate change. Nevertheless, depending on rainfall, in the spring and summer great expanses of forbs, shrubs, and cacti burst into colorful and aromatic bloom, providing one of the most glorious experiences of the region, including white sego lily, sand verbena, cliffrose, and evening primrose; yellow cryptantha, wallflower, prince's plume, and prickly pear; orange globe mallow; red claret cup cactus, scarlet gilia, firecracker penstemon, and paintbrush; lavender fishhook cactus, purple sage, and Palmer's penstemon; and blue lupine, flax, and larkspur.

The diverse habitats in the Grand Staircase-Escalante region also support a rich variety of wildlife, with 83 verified mammal species, 243 bird species, 29 reptile and amphibian species, and 20 fish species.[11] Larger mammal species include mountain lion, black bear, coyote, elk, mule deer, pronghorn antelope, desert bighorn sheep, beaver, cottontail rabbit, and black-tailed jackrabbit. Historically, desert bighorn sheep were the most common large herbivore, but their numbers were decimated when domestic livestock, especially sheep, were introduced in the late nineteenth century. Hunting and trapping have reduced populations of beaver and carnivore species, and management for game hunting has affected those of deer and elk.[12] Several historically more abundant species, including desert bighorn, pronghorn antelope, and otter, have been reintroduced on GSENM since it was created. Today the most common larger species encountered in the region are coyote, mule deer, cottontail rabbit, and black-tailed jackrabbit.

Also as a result of geology and climate, signs of the region's former human inhabitants can be found everywhere in the landscape (see figs. 7–12). Archaeological evidence indicates that the Colorado Plateau's first human inhabitants arrived about twelve thousand years ago, at the end of the last Ice Age.[13] These Paleo-Indians hunted big-game animals, such as mammoth, bison, camel, and horse, and left evidence of their existence in the form of large Clovis and Folsom spear points. In 2004 archaeologist Dr. Joel Janetski and his students from Brigham Young University began excavating a shelter site on private land near Escalante, which yielded the earliest evidence yet of human occupation of the Colorado Plateau.[14] The same site also yielded the earliest evidence of wild potato use in North America, 10,900–10,100 years BP.[15] The next period of cultural history, the Archaic Period, began about nine thousand years ago, when post–Ice Age warming was complete and many of the larger mammals had become extinct. The region's inhabitants adapted to a small-game hunting and gathering way of life.

In the Grand Staircase-Escalante region, an Archaic to Formative transition took place beginning around 3000 BP, when maize was first introduced, complex storage strategies developed, and the population began to increase. By the beginning of the Formative Period, around AD 500, the population had increased substantially and was heavily reliant on agriculture. The people constructed more permanent dwellings and storage facilities and fashioned rock art, pottery, and other, less durable artifacts that the dry desert environment has preserved, such as baskets, clothing, and sandals. Encountering this evidence as one explores the region is an unforgettable experience.

During this time, two different complexes developed in the region: the Fremont in the eastern GSENM and the Ancestral Pueblo in the west. Unique sites that represent contact between the two cultures exist on GSENM, contributing evidence to archaeologists' debate about the relationship between them. Both practiced farming, small-game hunting, and gathering, but the Fremont seem to have been less settled and less socially complex than the Ancestral Pueblo, and the two had their own distinct rock art, pottery, basketry, and sandal styles. Both of these cultures vanished from the region between AD 1300 and 1500, adding an aura of mystery to the artifacts they left behind. The Ancestral Pueblo migrated en masse to the south and southeast, and the Hopi and Puebloan peoples of New Mexico were their descendants. The cause of their decampment has stimulated debate among archaeologists, who offer drought and social strife as interrelated possibilities. Archaeologists also believe that the ancestors of the Ute and Southern Paiute peoples, whom the Euro-Americans encountered when they first explored the region, migrated into the region around this time.

The Spanish expedition that first explored this region, as well as Mormon pioneers who began arriving in southern Utah in the 1850s, encountered Native Americans who belonged to the culture later named the Southern Paiute, a hunting and gathering people who moved around to exploit seasonally available resources. Evidence of the Southern Paiute's habitation is more difficult to find than that of their predecessors, the Fremont and Ancestral Puebloan. However, I learned from a horse-riding companion how to locate old campsites on sandy rises that gave their occupants a view of the surrounding terrain. They can be identified by patches of ash in the sand from campfires, smooth stones called manos and metates that were used to grind corn, chips of stone from making weapons and tools, and shards of pottery.[16]

It is this "spectacular array of scientific and historic resources" that GSENM was created to protect.[17] And this is the landscape that many scientists, federal land managers, environmentalists, and visitors to the region perceive.

Landscape and Affect

But descriptions cannot capture the profound feelings the landscape generates. Anthropologist Kay Milton suggested that landscapes that appeal to us are those that provided the features our distant ancestors needed to survive.[18] Certainly, the region does resemble the East African savanna. Geographer and historian Richard Francaviglia proposed a spiritual connection.[19] Writers of the American West who have attempted to penetrate the aesthetics of western landscapes are more concerned with the effects of the landscape's qualities than of the apparently limitless "free land," as were Tocqueville and Turner. They concur that the experience of distance and space, the result of aridity, evokes strong feelings. Some venture to claim that the specific character of American democracy has been formed by this landscape and these feelings.

For western environmental historian Donald Worster, the landscape evokes a feeling of spaciousness that nourishes the American dream of individual freedom: "Come into the western country, however, and the reactions of travelers were unanimous: here at last was the true promise of American freedom. Here in a landscape generally free of trees, where no forests crowded in and impinged on the view, all physical restraint seemed to be removed." Here one could experience "freedom not available to people living in the East, freedom made possible only by the dry air, the short grass, and the horizon running off into infinity."[20] Worster argued that it is not because westerners view land as property that they are willing to fight over it, but because of the feelings it produces in them:

> The land has entered into western identity in more subtle and complicated ways than as property to be owned and fought over.... Everywhere in the region there is so much space—so much amplitude of rugged rock, soil, climate, and vista—that the landscape, like the gods of old, can leave men and women feeling humbled or diminished, exhilarated or threatened.... Still, for all its difficult traits, the land has entered into people's identities and affections in ways that defy rational analysis or the tests of logic. More than they can quite express or know how to acknowledge, westerners have become attached to this place. They feel a part of it.... You will seldom find this sense of attachment articulated in the halls of politics, for politicians, like businessmen or engineers or accountants, do not commonly deal with such matters. Writers, on the other hand, commonly do.[21]

For Pulitzer Prize–winning author Wallace Stegner, who grew up in Utah and was one of the West's most eloquent spokespeople, the experience of space also contributes to American individualism. "There is the visible, pervasive fact of western space, which acts as a preservative. Space itself, the product of incorrigible aridity and hence more or less permanent, continues to suggest unrestricted freedom, unlimited opportunity for testings and heroisms, a continuing need for self-reliance and physical competence. The untrammeled individualist persists ... partly because runaways from more restricted regions keep reimporting him. The stereotype continues to affect romantic Westerners and non-Westerners in romantic ways, but if I am right, it also affects real Westerners in real ways."[22]

In the Grand Staircase-Escalante region, in addition to the effects of aridity, space, and light, there is something more—something that writers who focus specifically on southern Utah convey. In *Red: Passion and Patience in the Desert*, Utah native and nature writer Terry Tempest Williams described the southern Utah desert as "this spare, raw, broken country, so frightfully true, complex, and elegant in its searing simplicity of form." She continued, "You cannot help but be undone by its sensibility and light, nothing extra. Before the stillness of sandstone cliffs, you stand still, equally bare."[23] For Williams, the landscape connects her to her essential being. She suggested that human beings are drawn to the red rock canyon country because red is the color of blood; after black and white, red is the next color given a name in human languages. In *The Open Space of Democracy*, she also suggested that these open spaces open minds, a necessary prerequisite for democracy.[24] In later chapters of this book, local residents, visitors to the region, and participants in conflict over GSENM also evoke the landscape's affective power and its traces in democratic imaginaries.

The Mormon Experience

For members of the Church of Jesus Christ of Latter-day Saints, perceptions of the landscape are inflected by the Mormon experience of settling the region.[25] Local residents' feelings about the landscape are implicated in their opposition to GSENM.[26] Wallace Stegner, who grew up among Latter-day Saints, touched on these feeling when he compared Mormon history to Jewish history: "It's a history of real persecution and in large part also because the paranoid memory of persecution begets a conviction of continued persecution, with the result that you can't see anything that is critical of the church that isn't a dagger aimed at your heart."[27] Although the federal government is no longer openly critical of the Church, for some Latter-day Saints the government is still associated with that history and those feelings. Understanding the Mormon experience sheds light on local residents' attitudes toward GSENM today.

The Latter-day Saints first arrived in the Salt Lake Valley in what is now Utah on July 24, 1847. Under the leadership of Brigham Young, they had left Nauvoo, Illinois, and headed west for the U.S. border in wagons loaded with what they would need to start a new life. When they crossed into Mexican territory, they began looking for a place to settle where they would be free from the hostility and persecution that had dogged them ever since Joseph Smith founded the religion in Palmyra, New York, in April 1830. Their leaders favored a rugged, mountainous region where they would be isolated from Gentiles and that the latter would find undesirable.[28] Legend has it that when he first saw Utah Valley on July 24, 1847, Young declared, "This is the right place." Today July 24 is Pioneer Day, the most celebrated date in the Church calendar. In southern Utah, it outshines the Fourth of July in importance and patriotic fervor.

Joseph Smith had established the Church during the Second Great Awakening, a time of great religious activity and the founding of many churches, when evangelical Protestantism and denominationalism spread throughout the United States following the abandonment of state-supported churches. This was also a time of democratic awakening, often called the Age of Jackson (for President Andrew Jackson), when equality became a central theme in American democratic imaginaries and political institutions underwent a profound transformation as control was shifted from an older aristocracy of education, position, and wealth to the common man. It was this period that the French nobleman Alexis de Tocqueville described in *Democracy in America*.

The Church of Jesus Christ of Latter-day Saints, like many founded during this time, was conceived as a whole way of life that challenged the ongoing industrialization, urbanization, and secularization of American life. Those attracted to it were people who had not shared in the growing prosperity and social modernization of the early nineteenth century. Bailyn and colleagues described Mormonism as "both a radical protest against the values of an individualistic, competitive, uprooting, and disinheriting world, and a way of achieving solidarity and authority that enabled its members to adjust to that world."[29]

Joseph Smith's new Church immediately encountered hostility in New York. He moved his family and some of his followers to Ohio in 1831 and called on other followers to gather in Missouri. After running into trouble with the law in Ohio, Smith joined the others in Missouri in 1838. There the influx of Latter-day Saints, with their acquisition of large amounts of land purchased with Church funds, communal economy, clannishness, bloc voting, religious doctrines, opposition to slavery, and friendliness with Native Americans, soon generated anti-Mormon sentiment and, beginning in 1833, anti-Mormon violence. Vigilantes terrorized Mormon settlements, trying to force them to leave Jackson County. When the Missouri legislature designated Clay County as a zone of Mormon settlement, most moved there. But violence followed them.

At first Joseph Smith had forbidden the Latter-day Saints to retaliate, but after five years of persecution in Missouri, he reversed his position and urged them to fight back. This caused violence to escalate further, resulting in the Haun's Mill Massacre, where Missouri militia killed eighteen Saints after they had signaled for surrender. To prevent complete annihilation of the Latter-day Saints, Smith gave himself up to the militia. He was tried for treason and sentenced to be executed. The Latter-day Saints were required to surrender their weapons, compensate Missourians for damage to property, and leave Missouri. Smith managed to escape from jail, and in 1839 the Latter-day Saints fled to Illinois.

There they built the city of Nauvoo and soon transformed it into a bustling metropolis. Out of sympathy for the Latter-day Saints' experience in Missouri, the Illinois General Assembly granted Nauvoo an unusual charter, making Joseph Smith the leader of what was effectively a theocracy with its own militia, the Nauvoo Legion. Non-Mormon residents of the county disliked these arrangements, and Smith's new doctrine of plural marriage added to their hostility. When some Latter-day Saints destroyed a press that exposed the polygamy in 1844, the Illinois governor, fearing the outbreak of civil war, called for Smith and those responsible to surrender and face charges in Carthage. A group of anti-Mormon militia attacked the jail where Smith and his brother Hyrum were being held and killed them. When those responsible were tried and found not guilty, violence between Latter-day Saints and Gentiles resumed.

Brigham Young, one of the nineteenth century's great organizers, succeeded Joseph Smith as president and prophet of the Church. He decided that the Latter-day Saints would leave the United States altogether and migrate west to Mexican territory. The exodus began in 1846. The Church actively supported emigration, maintaining a Perpetual

Emigrating Fund to complete the exodus from Illinois and assist newly recruited members in the United States and Europe. By 1860 over forty thousand Euro-Americans had migrated to Utah, virtually all of them Latter-day Saints.

Latter-day Saints brought to Utah democratic imaginaries shaped by the experience of persecution, the hostility of their fellow citizens, the martyrdom of their prophet, the failure of the federal government to protect them, and the grueling emigration from Nauvoo, which recalled the biblical exodus. These experiences welded them into an exceptionally close-knit group, loyal to their leaders and distrustful of the federal government. For them, the Utah landscape was a refuge, which they believed would be "the gathering place in the last days."[30]

However, shortly after the Latter-day Saints arrived in their new Zion, the United States defeated Mexico in a war provoked by the annexation of Texas, and Utah became U.S. territory. A process of reterritorialization of the land acquired through the Treaty of Guadalupe Hidalgo in 1848 and the Gadsden Purchase in 1853, from south of the 42nd parallel to the present northern boundary of Mexico, began. Incorporating the Latter-day Saints posed a particular challenge to the American state. They had already adopted a constitution, elected Brigham Young as governor, and established the provisional state of Deseret, with its own currency and army. In addition, their theocratic institutions, practices such as polygamy based on divine revelation, and communal economy challenged prevailing American concepts of popular sovereignty, secular law and morality, and private property. What Gustive O. Larson called "the 'Americanization' of Utah for statehood" shaped both Mormon and American democratic imaginaries as the two groups negotiated the limits of dissent, the meaning of freedom of religion, and the boundaries between church and state.[31]

Recognizing that statehood would grant them more sovereignty than territorial status, Church leaders immediately applied to be admitted to the United States as the state of Deseret, an area that included most of present-day Utah, Nevada, and Arizona; large portions of present-day Oregon, Wyoming, Colorado, New Mexico, and California; and a small part of present-day Idaho. Congress denied their request and in 1850 created the much smaller Utah Territory. Conflict began when federal officials arrived in Utah Territory to take up their posts, leading eventually to the "Utah War" in 1857–58.

This "war" began when non-Mormon territorial officials appointed by the federal government fled the territory and convinced President James Buchanan that the Mormons were in rebellion against the United States. The president sent a force of 2,500 troops—the largest peacetime army in the nation's history—to escort a new governor and territorial officials to Utah and forcibly establish federal authority. The Utah War never erupted into actual warfare because adverse weather and raiders from the Nauvoo Legion slowed down the advance of the federal troops, allowing criticism of Buchanan's action to gain enough strength that Church leaders were able to negotiate a peaceful settlement.

Reterritorialization of Utah expanded to a new arena in 1862, when Congress passed the Morrill Anti-Bigamy Act outlawing both slavery and bigamy in the territories and disincorporating the Church of Jesus Christ of Latter-day Saints. But the Civil War intervened, and the law was never enforced. Congress renewed the effort when the war ended by proposing a series of bills addressing polygamy, culminating in the 1882 Edmunds Act. That act allowed Mormons to be prosecuted for "unlawful cohabitation," which was easier to prove than bigamy. Federal agents immediately began carrying out a systematic and intensive pursuit and prosecution of Mormon leaders, known by Latter-day Saints as "The Raid." It disrupted family and community life and farm production and caused great hardship for women and children. In 1887 the Edmunds-Tucker Act increased the pressure. In an attempt to destroy the temporal power of the Church, it disincorporated the Church of Jesus Christ of Latter-day Saints and confiscated all Church property in excess of $50,000.

These measures gradually forced Church leaders to back down on their stand for plural marriage, and in 1890 Church president Wilford Woodruff proclaimed its end. Utah had seen its less populated neighbors admitted to statehood, while it had been denied in 1849, 1856, 1862, 1872, 1882, and 1887. Woodruff's Manifesto paved the way for statehood, but not before the Latter-day Saints were required to make further concessions. One of these was disbanding the Latter-day Saints' territory-wide People's Party to eliminate Mormon bloc voting for its candidates. Since the Republican Party had sponsored all the anti-polygamy legislation, Latter-day Saints were unlikely to vote for Republicans. Church leaders had to recruit members to vote Republican to avoid bloc voting for the Democratic Party. Finally, in 1896 Utah was granted statehood.

Reterritorialization continued through the twentieth century as Mormons had to make further accommodations to American secular values and institutions. Throughout, they kept alive the memory of their treatment at the hands of Gentiles and the federal government. The Mormon experience is reflected in Mormon democratic imaginaries today as a deep distrust of the federal government and in their allegiance to the contemporary Republican Party, which advocates "small" government. It is also reflected in the response many Mormon residents of the Grand Staircase-Escalante region gave when asked what democracy means to them: "freedom of religion."

Non-Mormon Americans are less aware of this history, but it has shaped and continues to shape their democratic imaginaries as well. Ongoing reterritorialization is reflected in scrutiny of the Fundamentalist Church of Jesus Christ of Latter-day Saints (FLDS) and other fundamentalist Mormon sects that still practice plural marriage. Examples include the 2007 arrest of FLDS leader Warren Jeffs, who was convicted of accessory to rape, and the 2008 removal of 412 children from an FLDS ranch in Texas into temporary state custody. Finally, the meaning of freedom of religion in the United States today is circumscribed by the fact that many Americans still consider Mormons a "peculiar people," as attested by the 2007 PBS special "The Mormons."[32] In addition, in the 2008 presidential race, while the suitability of Mitt Romney, who is a member of the Church of Jesus Christ of Latter-day Saints and trained in law, was questioned, that of Mike Huckabee, a Baptist pastor with only theological training, was not.

The Mormon Landscape

While the Mormon experience shaped Mormon and American democratic imaginaries, it also shaped the social landscape of the portion of the Intermountain West colonized by Latter-day Saints. Mormon settlement differed from the prevailing mode of land settlement, characterized by unregulated and uncoordinated individualistic efforts to claim and make a living from widely scattered homesteads. In contrast, the Latter-day Saints' method of colonization was Church directed, highly organized, and based on communal effort, egalitarianism, farm villages, and a belief that God had meant the land to be their home.

At the heart of their approach was the Plat of the City of Zion, a plan for the perfect city to be built in preparation for the millennium. Joseph Smith and other Church leaders had devised this plan in 1833 and sent it to their followers in Missouri to guide them in laying out towns there. When the Latter-day Saints arrived in the Salt Lake Valley, they immediately set to work constructing a city according to this plan. The Plat of the City of Zion envisioned a self-sufficient agricultural way of life in which people lived together under similar conditions in towns or villages and farmed outside them. The City of Zion had wide streets running north–south and east–west, marked off into blocks and lots of equal size. Public buildings were in a large block in the center. Home lots were large enough for gardens, fruit trees, chicken coops, and barns in which to keep livestock. Farm lots were outside the town, of equal size and productivity, and farmers traveled to them each day to work. Both home and farm lots were distributed by drawing lots. The inhabitants of the city raised, gathered, or made everything they needed and cooperated in the construction and administration of public works. The city of Escalante provides one of the best remaining examples of what the Mormon village originally looked like.

The Plat of the City of Zion became the basis for settlements Latter-day Saints established throughout the Intermountain West. Using this method of colonization, in ten years they were able to establish ninety-six new settlements that extended in a corridor from Salt Lake City to San Diego. The method proved advantageous for the conditions they encountered in the Great Basin region and allowed them to survive and eventually flourish in an arid, inhospitable region considered uninhabitable by many early explorers. Historian Leonard Arrington called Mormon settlement of the Great Basin the largest and most successful experiment with collective and cooperative living ever carried out in the United States.[33]

Francaviglia devised a way to investigate how Latter-day Saints living in this landscape perceived it in the early twenty-first century using structured interviews and photographs. He concluded that there is a deep attachment to place in the Mormon West.[34] Latter-day Saints are aware that they transformed a difficult environment into a unique physical and social landscape where the Church could flourish. The landscape is not something they consciously perceive; it is incorporated into an entire lifestyle and very much a part of their culture and religion.

The Mormon method of colonization produced a landscape where tracts of private land were smaller than in the rest of the West and where the land between scattered villages remained uninhabited and unclaimed. As a result, in Mormon country, there is a lower proportion of private land and a higher proportion of public land than in other parts of the West, and therefore less potential for the kind and scale of development that has transformed other parts of the West. To non-residents, the landscape appears more like frontier or wilderness than in more populated and developed parts of the West. In addition, since many small Mormon towns, especially those in the Grand Staircase-Escalante region, still look much the same as they did fifty years ago, their appearance and the residents' lifestyle evoke nostalgia for small-town America in many who visit. Finally, the Grand Staircase-Escalante landscape has so many traces of Mormon history that even non-Mormons can get a feeling of the fervor that drove the Mormon pioneers to such great efforts to colonize this rugged and inhospitable landscape and develop respect for what they did.

Regional Settlement

The first Mormon settlers in the Grand Staircase-Escalante region began arriving in 1858 in the vicinity of what is now the town of Kanab in Kane County but did not establish permanent settlements until the 1870s. Irrigated farming was more uncertain than in northern Utah because crops were more frequently lost to drought or flood. Raising livestock—first sheep, then cows—became the main form of livelihood in the region because of the proximity of high plateaus, where livestock could graze in the summers, to lower-elevation desert, where they could graze in the mild winters. The settlers lived in typical Mormon villages, surrounded by small farm plots, and ran their herds on the surrounding public domain lands. As a result, local ranchers own little private land and have depended on permitted use of the public lands to graze their cattle. As they ranged far and wide looking for water and forage for their herds, the early ranchers left many traces on the landscape. They built stock trails, tanks, corrals, line shacks, and cowboy camps and carved their names in the rocks. Their names have been given to features on topographic maps of the areas where they grazed livestock. One can find Johnson, Robinson, and Bunting Canyons; Spencer Flat; and Griffin Springs on maps. And Johnsons, Robinsons, Buntings, Spencers, and Griffins are still ranching on the land. The historical dependence on ranching in the region and the lifestyle it afforded account for the continuing attachment to a lifestyle and culture that local residents associate with ranching, even as economic dependence on ranching diminishes.

Sociologist Lowry Nelson, who conducted surveys in Escalante in 1923 and 1950 as part of his wider study, *The Mormon Village*, provided a glimpse of what life was like and the changes that took place in the region during that period. His findings foreshadowed the experience of today's residents and demonstrated that the social and economic shifts that inform conflict over GSENM have been unfolding for some time. The first change he noted was increased government regulation: the passage of the Taylor Grazing Act in 1934 had brought the public domain under management by the federal government. Second, ranching was declining because of economic shifts. Livestock numbers had decreased precipitously as a result of foreclosure on stockmen's debt during the Great Depression, drought in 1934, and depletion of the range. During the same time, both livestock and landownership became concentrated among fewer families. In 1923 the majority of families had some sheep or cattle from which to derive income, but by 1950 fewer than one-fourth had income from that source. A shift in occupations occurred as the number of farmers decreased by half; the number of laborers, merchants, employees of the Forest Service, and retirees increased; and new occupations of café, motel, and service station operator appeared.

The third change was demographic. As a result of outmigration during World War II, the population of Escalante declined from 1,008 in 1923 to 908 in 1952. There was also a significant shift in age distribution: the percentage of the population in the twenty-five-to-thirty-four age group halved, while that in the sixty-five-and-over group doubled. In addition, many newcomers had arrived. The relief policies of the Depression brought a Civilian Conservation Corps camp to Escalante, populated by outsiders from many parts of the country, and many marriages took place between CCC men and local women.

Fourth, Nelson noted a decline in community. In 1923 he had been impressed with the "we feeling" in Escalante; by 1950 he was equally impressed by its absence. He attributed this to the development of a cleavage between the "haves" and the "have nots." Finally, Nelson reported that residents "had anticipated for several years that tourists would come in large numbers to see the scenic attractions of the area."[35] However, in 1950 these hopes had not been realized, and the motels built to serve the expected tourists were languishing.

The "New West" Landscape

The rate and character of development of the American West changed dramatically after World War II. The defense industry drove the first round of explosive growth; in the 1990s knowledge-based industries accelerated it. Geographers have labeled the landscape the resulting economic and demographic shifts are producing the "New West."[36] Urban populations grew rapidly and real estate prices skyrocketed, driving "equity migration" to cheaper rural areas. The growing workforce flocked to nearby public lands for recreation or escape, and the many national parks, forests, and monuments attracted visitors from all over the country and the world. Soon the tourist industry rivaled all others in growth and income, and the western rangelands were no longer "chiefly valuable for grazing."[37] Private lands were far more valuable for real estate development and public lands for their aesthetic value and for recreation.[38] In 2004 the BLM announced that for the first time in its history, it had collected more from recreation receipts than from grazing fees.[39]

Meanwhile, resource-based rural economies declined as a result of decreasing commodity prices, horizontal integrations in agriculture, and globalization. Reduced trade barriers and inexpensive energy allowed products to enter the market from areas with more productive lands, lower wages, and fewer environmental constraints.[40] By 2000 only about 20 percent of the U.S. population lived in rural areas and less than 3 percent of the U.S. workforce was in primary production, making these groups a political minority. In rural areas, per capita income is much less and the poverty rate much higher than in urban areas.[41] Rural residents who formerly made a good living in resource production jobs have had to cobble together several sources of income to be able to remain in the places they consider home. And families are dispersed when the younger generation is compelled to leave to find work elsewhere.

As jobs in ranching, timber, and mining declined, the main local industries became tourism, recreation, and real estate. The first two typically offer low-paid service employment, while the latter generates tax increases.[42] Many rural residents who have jobs in the tourist industry cannot afford to live where they work. The new industries depend on the existence of landscapes that fit the primarily urban environmental aesthetics of an imagined "pristine" nature. Local livelihoods, in contrast, depend on the existence of working landscapes that local residents experience as home. As the shift in the rural West from a resource-based production economy to an amenity-based consumption economy accelerates, conflict over the management of public lands, which help drive both, has intensified.

Between 1990 and 2005 the combined population of the eight states of the Intermountain West rose three times faster than that of the United States as a whole, and the fastest-growing areas were rural areas.[43] In 2021 states in the Intermountain West continued to be among the fastest-growing.[44] In contrast to longtime residents of these areas, newcomers are primarily urban, college-educated, middle-class professionals. The demographic shift also affects local politics in the rural West as newcomers become economically dominant or the demographic majority. Clashes between newcomers and "the locals" are often characterized as conflicts between cultures or ideologies. However, geographer Peter Walker, who studies the New West, argued that they reflect tensions resulting from "competing capitalisms that commodify nature in incompatible ways" and "an increasingly uneven development and a sharpening of class differences."[45] They also reflect different democratic imaginaries (discussed in chapter 5).

The demographic shift in the New West is also reflected in Utah by a decline in the percentage of the state population that is Mormon.

According to Church records, that percentage has declined each year since 1989. In 2004 it was 62.4 percent; this number reflects Church membership, rather than active participation, which is closer to 41.6 percent. In 2018 a different source reported that these numbers were 62 percent and 40 percent, respectively. Experts attribute this decline to an increase in newcomers from other places and a decline in the fertility rate in Utah.[46]

These economic and demographic shifts took place in Garfield and Kane Counties more slowly than in Utah and the West as a whole but were accelerating. The economic struggles that fueled local residents' fears about the effects the new monument were borne out by economic data for Garfield and Kane Counties in the late twentieth century. Income from mining, timber production, and agriculture (including ranching) had been steadily dropping since 1970, both in total amount and in proportion of total income, while income from nonlabor sources, such as investments and retirement payments, and from jobs in the service and government sectors had been rising. The steep rise in nonlabor income reflects the influx of new residents, retirees, "equity migrants," or those who relocate for quality-of-life reasons. Nonlabor income accounted for 71 percent of net growth in real income in Garfield County between 1970 and 2000, and 32 percent in Kane County.[47] Meanwhile, by 2000 net farm income (which includes ranching) contributed a very small to negative amount to total personal income in both counties.[48] These statistics indicate trends but not the differential effects of these trends on longtime residents of the region. For example, fewer and fewer longtime residents have been able to make a living solely from ranching, the economic activity most closely associated with community identity. In 2004 there were fewer than one hundred ranchers in Garfield and Kane Counties for whom ranching was their primary source of income.[49] Most ranchers in the region are small producers who hold other jobs or derive income from other sources. However, for small producers, their ranching income may make the difference in whether they are able to send their children to college.

While total employment grew 33 percent in Garfield County and 150 percent in Kane County between 1980 and 2000, the average wages per job in inflation-adjusted dollars fell from $19,452 in 1970 to $18,762 in 2000 in Garfield County, and they increased only slightly, from $20,034 in 1970 to $20,134 in 2000, in Kane County. These wage rates were far below the state and national averages of $29,203 and $36,316, respectively. The statistics reflect the fact that jobs lost in resource-based industries often pay better than jobs gained in the services and professional sector, which includes the tourist industry. For example, 40 percent of Garfield County's nonfarm jobs were in the leisure and hospitality sector in 2004. Employment in Garfield County is also extremely seasonal, reflecting the seasonality of the tourist industry. For example, in 2001 the unemployment rate varied from 4.1 percent during the summer to 21 percent during the winter. Overall unemployment in Garfield County was 9.2 percent that year, far above the state and national averages of 4.4 percent and 4.8 percent, respectively. In Kane County, it was 3.5 percent.[50] In both counties, unemployment had decreased from much higher rates in the mid-1990s.[51]

Nonfarm proprietors' income, which had been declining throughout rural Utah, grew significantly in Garfield and Kane Counties between 1996, when the monument was created, and 2000, which might reflect the establishment of more small businesses catering to tourism. However, I observed that most such businesses were owned and operated by people who had moved into the region more recently. This is further evidence of the ways that economic statistics fail to capture the experience of long-time residents.

Demographic statistics showed that the median age in many of these communities was above the national median and well above the median for Utah and that it had been increasing since 1990, as the proportion of residents under twenty decreased and the proportion sixty-five and over increased.[52] In 2004 Utah had the highest birth rate in the nation, with 21.2 live births per 1,000 population, while the U.S. average was 14.0.[53] Therefore, the county figures reflect the fact that a large proportion of Garfield and Kane County youth could not find work that paid well enough to enable them to remain and raise their own families in the region and that few of the newcomers were families with young children. Changing demographics were also accompanied by declines in enrollment and funding for the region's schools.

The communities adjacent to GSENM had not yet experienced as large an influx of newcomers as many others in the New West because they lacked some of the factors that facilitate in-migration and development, such as proximity to a major metropolitan area, a major airport, and medical care facilities.[54] There is also less private land available for development because of the high proportion of federally owned land in Garfield and Kane Counties. By 2008 few "trophy homes" had appeared within or on the outskirts of these communities to proclaim the socioeconomic differences between residents.

A 2017 report focused on GSENM showed that the economies of Garfield and Kane Counties, including population, jobs, real personal income, and real per capita income, continued to grow through 2015.[55] Service industry jobs had increased 42 percent since 2001, while nonservice jobs, which include resource production jobs, had a 3 percent decrease. Nonlabor income, which includes investment and retirement income, grew at a much faster rate than labor earnings and by 2015 made up 44 percent of total personal income. These statistics continued to show that the benefits of economic growth were unevenly distributed and that longtime residents were less likely to share in them.

Longtime residents of the Grand Staircase-Escalante region are experiencing changes in their lives that they are struggling to comprehend and control. In the early twenty-first century, they were concerned about the same kinds of changes that Nelson reported more than fifty years previously: increased government regulation; the decline of ranching; outmigration of their youth; the arrival of newcomers who are not like them; a decline in the pioneer values of hard work, self-reliance, independence, and mutual support on which community identity and solidarity is based; and the failure of the tourist industry to replace the good-paying jobs in resource-based industries that were being lost. For many, the creation of GSENM crystallized fears and uncertainties about personal and community futures, and the monument came to represent something concrete and nearby that they could do something about.

This brief history of the Grand Staircase-Escalante region highlights emotional attachment to the landscape and suggests that the landscape is deeply embedded in American democratic imaginaries. People become attached to the landscape for different reasons. For visitors to GSENM, it is an unforgettable experience of space, light, stunning geological formations, and the feeling of freedom. For Mormon pioneers, it was a refuge. For Latter-day Saints, it still evokes religious freedom and is "the gathering place in the last days." For local residents, it is home, the source of community and livelihood. For environmentalists, it is wilderness or land threatened by resource use. For BLM employees, it represents an opportunity and challenge to balance protection of its "spectacular array of scientific and historic resources" with multiple uses of those resources.[56] These attachments, intertwined with attachment to democracy, have a profound effect on conflict over GSENM and public land more generally.

Part 2
Conflict

3   Conflict over Grazing

The creation of Grand Staircase-Escalante National Monument (GSENM) provoked angry resistance in the Grand Staircase-Escalante region, and conflict continued to erupt on the monument, often making national news. The chapters in this section delve into the details of conflicts that arose in two domains—livestock grazing and roads—to illuminate what democracy means to ordinary Americans in relation to a system of government. Analyses of these conflicts reveal the forms and legitimations of democratic government that local residents, ranchers, environmental groups, the general public, and county, state, and federal government officials drew on and posed against each other as they contested the reterritorialization of GSENM public land as national landscape.

Livestock grazing on GSENM became a domain of conflict, although the proclamation explicitly stated that monument status would not affect existing livestock grazing permits or levels and that grazing uses would continue to be governed by existing laws and regulations. Based on their past experience with national monuments and their mistrust of the federal government, ranchers in the region were not reassured. While they waited for the Bureau of Land Management (BLM) to finalize a grazing plan for GSENM, anxiety about the future of livestock grazing on the monument remained high. The appointment of Kate Cannon as monument manager in 1999 added to their concerns. Cannon came from the National Park Service, which has a preservation mandate rather than the multiple-use mandate of the BLM and had no experience managing livestock grazing.

The Monument Management Plan was signed in November 1999 but deferred decisions about livestock grazing to a grazing management process that was to be completed by July 1, 2003. The process, known as the Grazing Permit Renewal Environmental Impact Statement (EIS) until the title was changed to Monument Management Plan Amendment and Rangeland Health EIS (described in chapter 8), got underway in 1999, when data collection for rangeland health assessments began. A letter announcing the initial scoping period for the EIS sent to the public in September 2000 listed "no grazing" as one of the alternatives to be considered, feeding ranchers' fears that grazing would be eliminated on GSENM. When the conflicts described in this chapter took place, a draft of the EIS had not yet been released, and in fact it had still not been released when I completed my fieldwork in 2008. Without some indication from the BLM of how grazing was to be managed on GSENM, uncertainty and anxiety about the future of livestock grazing on the monument persisted. When I spoke with Cannon in the summer of 2000, she revealed that she planned to manage grazing on GSENM differently than it had been managed in the past: "Grazing is a symbolic issue. It will change in the monument. We're using the same rules" that the BLM uses everywhere to manage grazing. "We're just using them." This statement seemed to corroborate what ranchers had intuited about her intentions.

The federal government's inertia and local anxieties were intangible but significant factors in the conflicts described in this chapter and the next. Another hidden factor was the extent to which, owing to GSENM's high national profile, Department of Interior (DOI) and BLM national-level officials, who are appointed by the presidential administration and respond to presidential politics as well as federal laws and regulations, were directly involved in decision-making. Their participation was largely invisible to residents in the Grand Staircase-Escalante region, leading to local perceptions of hidden agendas and a lack of transparency on the part of the BLM.

Ranching in the Grand Staircase-Escalante region has several unique characteristics that also helped set the stage for the two conflicts over livestock grazing on GSENM described in this chapter. First, it has always been a precarious endeavor. Most of the region is considered desert, with annual precipitation averaging less than ten inches. The complicated topography of the region made it possible for settlers to find forage for livestock by moving their herds to higher-elevation pastures that get more precipitation in the summer and to the drier lowlands in the winter and spring. With the reterritorialization of the public rangelands as resource and the passage of the 1934 Taylor Grazing Act (TGA), livestock grazing on these lands was gradually rationalized by the division of the range into allotments and pastures separated by fences and by the development of a permit and allotment management plan system that specifies when livestock are to be moved and the order of rotation between pastures and allotments. This gives ranchers in the region much less flexibility to adapt to changing conditions than they had in the past.

Second, to qualify for a federal grazing permit, an applicant must own base property in the form of private or leased land or water. The requirements vary by agency and region. In the Grand Staircase-Escalante region, they are minimal because of Mormon settlement patterns. Generally, the base property had to include basic livestock management facilities and the ability to provide some (usually about 50 percent) of the forage needed to sustain the permitted livestock during the offseason. But in the Grand Staircase-Escalante region, this requirement has been reduced or eliminated. According to a rangeland specialist on GSENM, there was no written policy on how many acres were required for base property. BLM field offices in southern Utah each had different requirements, and it was up to the authorized BLM official to decide. As a result, since most ranchers in southern Utah own little or no private rangeland, should they lose access to public land grazing, they would have nowhere else to put their cattle.

Third, before the monument was created, many employees of the BLM resource area offices in the region were local residents who knew the country and the local ranchers well. The staff was familiar with and sympathetic to the difficulties of ranching in the region and attempted to work with ranchers and follow regulations at the same time. These arrangements were consistent with the idea of democracy on the range promoted by the TGA. For those from outside the region, however, this situation appeared to blur the boundary that is supposed to exist between state and society, and the agency came to be seen as ineffective, corrupt, or captured by local interests.[1]

Negative perceptions of public land grazing, which are prevalent among the general public, also played a role in these conflicts.[2]

Opponents of public land grazing claim that livestock grazing damages the land, which will be restored if livestock is removed. However, their arguments are based on questionable assumptions. Undoubtedly, before the federal government began to regulate resources on the public rangelands, competition for the free grazing produced a classic tragedy of the commons and severe degradation of the western rangelands.[3] But in the early twenty-first century, experts disagreed about whether livestock grazing was still damaging these lands. Some said it was; others asserted that the public rangelands had been improving and were in the best ecological condition they had been in for several decades; still others concluded that the lack of data and a uniform methodology made it impossible to determine.[4]

The belief that when a disturbance such as livestock grazing is removed, a plant community will resume its predictable progression toward a single climax community, determined by soil type and climate, is based on an equilibrium model of ecology first proposed by American botanist Frederic Clements in the early twentieth century and institutionalized in range management as the range succession model.[5] This is an outdated understanding of rangeland ecology, however, and has been superseded by a nonequilibrium model of ecology. This model proposes that ecosystems evolve unpredictably in response to random disturbances and may have multiple, relatively stable states that are path dependent. Unpredictability is most pronounced in arid and semi-arid environments like the Intermountain West, where precipitation variability is the main driver of change. Nonequilibrium ecology has given rise to the state and transition model of rangeland ecology, in which disturbance is seen to cause transitions between states that are not easily reversible. Rangelands will not necessarily return to their prior condition if livestock are removed or reduced. Since the 1950s the BLM has significantly decreased the amount of authorized grazing on public land, but improvement in range condition often is extremely slow or fails to occur. Restoration may require active management, such as mechanical or chemical treatment, reseeding, fire, or intensively managed grazing.

These widespread but ill-informed public perceptions weigh heavily in conflicts over grazing on GSENM. They were evident in the highly polarized media reporting of these conflicts. For example, the *Salt Lake Tribune* printed frequent reports that displayed an anti-grazing and anti-local bias by mainly quoting Kate Cannon and environmentalists. Meanwhile, the local paper, the *Garfield County News*, mainly quoted the ranchers and displayed sympathy for their predicament.

Finally, the fact that some ranchers conceive of livestock grazing on public land as a right, even though the TGA explicitly defines it as a privilege, adds to the emotional intensity of conflicts over public land grazing. These ranchers and the county governments that support them feel they are fighting for this right against the federal government or environmental organizations that are trying to deprive them of it.

These factors, coupled with record-breaking drought, set the stage for a confrontation between ranchers and the BLM on GSENM in 2000. It made national news and became the first real test of the BLM's new role as manager of a national monument.

Cattle Impoundment on Fiftymile Mountain

The year 2000 was the third year of a severe drought and one of the driest on record in southern Utah.[6] In June twenty permittees on twenty-one summer allotments in the monument were notified that they would probably have to remove their cattle early that year. All but three permittees, Quinn Griffin and Gene Griffin on the Lake allotment and Mary Bulloch on the Mudholes allotment, had voluntarily removed their livestock by July. BLM range staff inspected the forage on these allotments at the end of July and found it well below the allowable utilization level, and monument manager Kate Cannon gave the permittees until September 1 to remove their livestock or face impoundment. The ranchers did not have another place to take their cattle and would have to sell them at a loss.

When I first met Quinn Griffin in the summer of 2000, before the call to remove the cattle, I was interested in his role as a board member of the Escalante Center. The Escalante Center was a group of people from the local community, Southern Utah University, the Utah governor's office, and the BLM that had formed to promote a vision for a nonprofit arts and sciences education and information campus to be run as a cooperative effort between the local community and the monument. At the time, this seemed to be a promising example of collaborative conservation. Quinn, a fifth-generation resident of Escalante, was on the board because he had been involved in an effort to build a local history museum in Escalante, and his group had decided to join forces with the Escalante Center. He spoke well of Kate Cannon, who was also on the board. He had taken over his father's livestock business because he enjoyed ranching and wanted to raise his kids in the rural environment where he had grown up. But he wasn't making enough money to support his family, so he also juggled various part-time jobs, and his wife worked full-time.

Quinn said that working with the monument was no different from working with the BLM before, except he was "watched more closely." But he admitted he was worried because it was difficult to manage cattle on his allotment, and "they give me no tools and wonder why I can't do it.... I got what I want and I don't mind sharing it, but I don't want them to run me off." He believed that "we need government. Without the federal agencies to control us, we'd be riding the range with guns." But "there needs to be a better partnership between the government and the local people." He recognized that "it's tough because the BLM has to listen to the whole country." However, he believed that "if people could come together, they can work it out."

Quinn disagreed with the BLM's evaluation of his allotment, so he hired a range scientist who had worked in the region for many years to do another evaluation. Local actors in resource conflicts elsewhere have come to employ this strategy to contest reterritorialization as the state increasingly uses scientific and technical knowledge to legitimate and depoliticize its actions.[7] The expert Quinn hired found the utilization on his allotment to be much less than that measured by the BLM's "young scientist with no experience in this area." Nevertheless, the BLM's evaluation prevailed. The fact that experts can disagree is one reason that reliance on the rule of experts to legitimate decision-making on public lands is inadequate.

The Griffins and Mary Bulloch grazed allotments on the remote Fiftymile Mountain, known locally as "the Fifty," which forms the eastern end of the Kaiparowits Plateau and is so named because it is about fifty miles from town. From Escalante, the Griffin allotments are accessed

13. Grazing allotments on GSENM. Source: Bureau of Land Management, Grand Staircase-Escalante National Monument Draft Monument Management Plan Amendment and Draft Rangeland Health Environmental Impact Statement, 2008, map 10.

by rough dirt roads leading to a bench partway up the plateau; these roads become impassable when it rains. From the bench, a steep stock trail, which has claimed the lives of both horses and cattle, winds steeply up through cliff bands to the top of the plateau. The complex and rugged terrain of the Fifty, with its contours obscured by thick stands of pinyon and juniper, makes it difficult to find and gather cattle. In addition to the terrain, permittees contend with unbranded feral cattle that are descendants of animals that escaped roundups in the past.

Citing these difficulties, the permittees appealed to the BLM State Office for more time to remove their cattle. They were given until September 15, but their efforts were hampered by rain that made the roads treacherous and by what they perceived as a lack of flexibility on the part of monument staff. Because both their summer and winter allotments were closed, the gathering process was much more complex than in a normal year when the cattle would head down the mountain to the adjacent winter allotment on their own as the season changed. Now the cattle had to be driven to corrals and held there until they could be trucked off the mountain. Feral cattle cannot be led or herded like those that are regularly handled, and there were few holding corrals to use for gathering because the BLM had not permitted the ranchers to build more.

The BLM State Office reported on September 25 that the ranchers had made "significant progress over the past few weeks" in removing the cattle and that "the majority of the cattle are off the mountain."[8] But when the BLM sent a helicopter to fly over the Fifty in early October, it discovered cattle remaining on the allotments. On the eleventh it notified the permittees that they were in trespass and accruing fines. On the seventeenth monument staff began impounding the cattle. They used helicopters to spot the cattle and a crew of wranglers on horseback to gather them, advantages the ranchers did not have. In addition to the trespass fees, the permittees were held responsible for expenses incurred in this process. Kate Cannon's view was that the ranchers had not made a good effort to remove the cattle: "We had been hopeful that the [ranchers] would have done this themselves. We gave them lots of opportunities to do it. Frankly, we've been very disappointed in their response."[9]

Ranchers and residents of the region saw these measures as extremely harsh and as evidence of a strategy to eliminate grazing on the monument; this galvanized and united them in opposition to the BLM. In the past, the agency had shown more concern for their welfare—the BLM range staff had tried to work with ranchers to solve problems rather than strictly enforce rules—which served to legitimate its authority. A member of the monument range staff who had worked for the BLM in the region for over twenty years explained, "Permittees and local people were more like our partners back when I started. We were trying to help them out, even though we still had to do NEPA [the National Environmental Policy Act]—not be a big brother with our thumb on them." He pointed out that Cannon was not familiar with BLM practices, livestock grazing, or the concerns of local residents. She was choosing to blindly "follow regulations" and agency scientist opinions, he said, instead of consulting with local people. She was thus evoking a democratic imaginary legitimating rule of law or rule of experts, in contrast to local residents' imaginaries of democracy on the range, where local ranchers have some say. Such differences between the attitudes and approaches of BLM officials at the state office, in field offices, on the monument, and between longtime and more recently hired employees illustrate the struggles within the BLM as it tried to take on a new role in the reterritorialization of GSENM as national landscape. In addition, because many of the monument staff who participated in the impoundment were longtime local residents themselves, the BLM's action pitted not only ranchers against the BLM but also neighbor against neighbor.

The BLM staff quietly transported some of the cattle impounded from Mary Bulloch's allotment—rumor had it that they bypassed roadblocks set up by Kane County and a state of Utah brand inspector—to a stockyard in Salina, Utah, where the cattle were scheduled for auction on November 7. When their location was discovered, a group of ranchers from Utah and Nevada, in a show of solidarity, accompanied Mary to Salina to repossess them. The ranchers claimed that the BLM had followed neither its own regulations in impounding the cattle nor Utah state law in transporting them and that it had also broken written agreements with the ranchers. The county sheriff did not intervene while the group loaded the stock into trucks to deliver them to an undisclosed location. The ranchers' actions made national news, which compared them to "a scene out of a Western movie."[10] But local residents saw their actions as justified civil disobedience toward a state that had acted illegally.

The U.S. attorney threatened to prosecute those involved, but because the ranchers had appealed to Utah state law, they were able to shift the focus from their actions to the question of federal versus state jurisdiction. The BLM and the Utah Department of Agriculture and Food met to negotiate a process to be used in future cases of impoundment, and in the end, no charges were filed against the ranchers. Later the same month there was also a tense confrontation between a group of armed Escalante residents and BLM officials guarding impounded cattle at a corral on the Hole-in-the-Rock Road outside Escalante. The cattle were being held there because local auctions and feedlots would no longer accept them. Throughout the impoundment process, those on opposite sides perceived the impounded cattle differently. Cannon saw them as "emaciated . . . nothing but skin and bones," while Quinn Griffin saw them as "fat and healthy."[11] This contrast illustrates that reterritorialization can entail constructing reality to legitimate actions: emaciated cows legitimate the BLM's actions; fat cows call them into question.

Meanwhile, up on the Fifty, the BLM was learning how difficult gathering the remaining cattle was going to be. In January 2001 the monument gave up on more conventional means and hired a Wyoming company to net cattle from the air using helicopters, tranquilize them, and then airlift them off. To justify this extravagant solution, Cannon explained, "Somebody has to go up there and get [the cows]. Since [their owners] themselves are either unwilling or unable to follow through—for whatever reason—we are left with no recourse but to resume our impoundments using the safest and most efficient means available."[12] Assuming that he would be held responsible for cost of this operation, Quinn Griffin found a cheaper solution: he hired his own helicopter and a gunman to shoot the cattle from the air. For a rancher who took pride in his skill raising and handling cattle, it was heartbreaking to destroy them in this way. Despite these extreme efforts to get all the cattle off the Fifty, in July a BLM reconnaissance team discovered that some yet remained.

This added credence to the ranchers' assertions that they had been doing their best to get the cattle off and that the task was made much more difficult by the presence of feral cattle on the Fifty. As Quinn put it, the BLM was beginning to realize "that maybe I was right." Cannon had dismissed the feral cattle as "a wives' tale," although some of the impounded cattle had indeed been unbranded. The BLM was not eager to admit to the presence of feral cattle on public land. Nor was the agency eager to draw Kane County (in which the allotments are located) into the conflict, since according to state law, unbranded cattle are the responsibility of the county in which they are found.

Feral cattle are one of the West's best-kept secrets. Most people are aware that "wild" horses still roam the public lands, but like the cattle, they are feral, not wild. Feral horses and burros on public land are protected by the 1971 Wild Free-Roaming Horses and Burros Act, which recognizes them as "living symbols of the historic and pioneer spirit of the West" and an "integral part of the natural system of the public lands," even though the horse is not native to North America.[13] Since these animals compete with wildlife and domestic livestock for forage, the BLM tries to control the number of horses on public land. But no such recognition has been given to the uncounted feral cattle that roam the public lands; if their existence was acknowledged, it would pose a challenge to both federal land managers and wild horse advocates.

In the end, the ranchers were held financially responsible for the BLM operations. The Griffins faced a combined assessment of $72,000 and Mary Bulloch one of $65,000. With the advent of the George W. Bush administration, GSENM got a new manager. In November 2001 Kate Cannon accepted a position as deputy superintendent of Grand Canyon National Park. *USA Today* reported that she was the victim of a "personnel purge" of BLM land managers whose approach to public land management favored environmental interests too much.[14] *High Country News* was more specific and confirmed a rumor I had heard locally. It reported that several local government officials had flown to Washington DC in the summer of 2001 to complain to high-ranking Interior Department officials about her. A former DOI staff person reported, "She was clearly singled out by disaffected local people, and they definitely had a great deal of influence."[15] Many of the monument staff hired when Cannon was manager also left when she did. Dave Hunsaker, a career BLM employee, took over as acting monument manager and became monument manager in January 2002.

Although the goals of the new administration changed, the BLM had to follow up on actions Cannon had initiated to maintain the effect of authority and legitimacy. Hunsaker pursued negotiations with the Griffins and Mary Bulloch. In July 2003 the BLM reached a settlement with the Griffins, including a large reduction of the fine and a gradual resumption of grazing on the Lake allotment, which had remained closed until then. The Griffins were forced to sell the permit for their winter allotment and part of the permit for the Lake allotment to pay off the debt. They eventually had to sell the remaining permit and give up ranching. In July 2004 the BLM reached an agreement with Mary Bulloch, which included taking possession of all cattle remaining on her allotment and closing it to grazing for several more years. One of the monument range staff pointed out that ironically, "Now the BLM is in trespass."

As owner of the remaining cattle, the BLM could try other options to get them off the Fifty. However, those remaining were the wiliest and most aggressive, which had eluded all efforts to capture them. The BLM first offered the job to a local rancher with the incentive that he could keep whatever cattle he captured. After capturing only a few and losing two horses in the process, he gave up. Finally, the monument received approval to exterminate the cattle. In a final confirmation of the difficulty of removing feral cattle from the Fifty, in December 2005 a helicopter carrying BLM personnel to Fiftymile Mountain to shoot the cattle crashed. No one was seriously injured, and the BLM resolved to continue the effort the following spring. Nevertheless, visitors confirmed that there were feral cattle still roaming and multiplying on the Fifty several years later.

Reterritorialization of Fiftymile Mountain

What is remarkable about this struggle is the great effort and expense the BLM put into removing a relatively small number of cattle from Fiftymile Mountain. Viewed through the lens of reterritorialization of public land as national landscape, however, it illustrates the great effort the

BLM must expend to assert its new role as manager of a national monument. Before the creation of GSENM, the BLM legitimated its management of public land primarily to local residents, in terms of a partnership relationship with them, concern for their welfare in keeping with the purpose of the TGA, and an understanding of democracy on the range to mean that those who use the public rangelands should have a say in their management. As manager of national landscapes, the BLM now had to legitimate its actions at the national scale, in terms that carried weight at that scale: scientific expertise and legal authority, meaning rule of experts and rule of law.

This skirmish in the reterritorialization of public land as national landscape initially called into question whether livestock would have a place on them. But other participants affected its outcome and muddled its ultimate effects. Nonhumans were a significant influence. Drought created the opportunity for the BLM to remove livestock from some allotments temporarily and potentially permanently. But the nature of the terrain and of the feral cattle on Fiftymile Mountain made it impossible for the agency to accomplish this, although it did succeed in putting some ranchers out of business. Ranchers acting as individuals were unable to effectively influence the outcome, and their lives were negatively affected in significant ways. However, when they acted together or appealed to other levels of government to oppose the BLM, as in the recovery of Bulloch's cattle, they were more successful or at least avoided negative consequences.

Perhaps the greatest but unintended effect of the impoundment was to substantiate the belief locally that the BLM intended to eliminate livestock grazing on GSENM and to increase antipathy toward the monument in the region. It also extinguished the democratic possibilities of creating understanding between antagonists, which could have led to solutions acceptable to both parties, and instead turned potential allies into enemies. The BLM pulled out of the Escalante Center, and that effort largely collapsed. Quinn Griffin, who had thought Cannon was "trying to work with locals" and was "the type who will listen to you," admitted that he was "really disappointed" in her. Getting the cows off the Fifty became a "power struggle," and monument management turned into a "dictatorship." What should have happened on the Fifty, Quinn believed, was that "Kate Cannon should have come to Escalante and called all the ranchers together and asked for input. Then she would have gotten their support. . . . She should have shown *leadership* instead of management. She was locked into regulations, not wisdom or common sense." The democratic imaginary informing his vision of how national landscapes ought to be managed is one in which the federal government takes into account the welfare of local residents whose livelihoods, traditions, and recreational activities have been entangled with these lands for generations and gives them a say in how the lands are managed.

Grazing Retirements on GSENM

In contrast to the impoundment on Fiftymile Mountain, in which the BLM used strict interpretation and enforcement of existing regulations to reterritorialize public land as national landscape, the conflict described in this section and the conflict over roads described in the next chapter turn on ambiguity and indeterminacy in the laws governing livestock grazing and rights-of-way on public land, making it possible for actors to interpret them in different ways to promote their vision of national landscapes.[16]

The conflict over grazing retirements began in 2001, when Garfield and Kane Counties initiated a cycle of litigation to stop a conservation organization, the Grand Canyon Trust (GCT), which had purchased permits for grazing allotments on GSENM, from retiring them and ending grazing on the allotments. GCT's market-based approach to reducing the impacts of livestock grazing on public land developed out of an initial successful experiment in 1996. Local residents saw the role that monument staff were playing in facilitating grazing retirements as further evidence that the BLM intended to eliminate grazing on the monument. They also saw GCT's strategy as one that could lead to the elimination of grazing on all public land and therefore as a threat not only to local livelihoods and culture but to the ranching industry throughout the Intermountain West. Table 1 shows a timeline of significant developments in the conflict. A year-by-year description of how it unfolded follows.

TABLE 1. Timeline for grazing retirements on GSENM up until 2007

1996	Grand Staircase-Escalante National Monument (GSENM) is created. Grand Canyon Trust (GCT) begins negotiating with ranchers holding permits along the Escalante River.
1999	Amendment to Escalante Management Framework Plan eliminates grazing along main canyon and many tributaries of the Escalante River.
2000	Bureau of Land Management (BLM) starts sending drought letters to permittees requesting nonuse (2000–2003).
June 2000	GCT begins arrangements to retire Clark Bench allotment permit.
October 2000	Cattle impoundment on Fiftymile Mountains begins.
2001	GCT forms Canyonlands Grazing Corporation (CGC). CGC acquires permits for Last Chance, Willow Gulch, and Big Bowns Bench allotments.
August 2001	Monument staff begins preparing environmental assessments (EAs) for the three allotments.
November 2001	Interior Secretary Gale Norton expresses support for market-based approach in letter to Utah representative Chris Cannon.
December 2001	Assistant Secretary of Policy, Management, and Budget Lynn Scarlett expresses support for "market-based solution" in letter to GCT. GCT sends conditional offers to relinquish permits to BLM.
January 2002	BLM requests, and GCT sends, unconditional offers of relinquishment. Trevor Stewart applies for Clark Bench permit. Subsequently, five other local ranchers apply for the permits held by CGC.
February 2002	Final EAs released.
April 2002	Kane and Garfield Counties protest findings of the EAs to director of BLM. GCT withdraws all offers to relinquish permits.
October 2002	First memo released from Interior Department chief solicitor William Myers on grazing retirements. (Second memo released a few months later.)
2003	Bill Hedden becomes executive director of GCT.

January 2003	BLM denies the counties' protests. BLM state director Sally Wisely decides to defer action with respect to grazing reallocation on the allotments until completion of ongoing monument-wide Rangeland Health Environmental Impact Statement (EIS).
February 2003	CGC officially acquires Clark Bench permit.
September 2003	BLM denies local ranchers' applications for permits held by CGC.
October 2003	Ranchers' appeal denial. CGC leases Brent Robinson's cattle to graze the Clark Bench allotment.
November 2003	State of Utah Permanent Community Impact Board Fund grants Garfield and Kane Counties funds for the appeal.
July 2004	GCT announces plans to buy Kane and Two-Mile Ranches.
January 2005	The counties sue BLM for failure to follow regulations in the 1999 grazing retirements.
March 2005	Utah State Legislature passes H.B. 264, State Land Use Management Plans Amendments.
May 2005	Interior Department Office of Hearings and Appeals hears appeal of denial of applications for permits held by CGC in Kanab May 9–11.
September 2005	Office of Hearings and Appeals continues to hear appeal on September 8–9. GCT acquires Kane and Two-Mile Ranches.
January 2006	Judge James Heffernan denies appeal.
March 2006	Kane and Garfield Counties appeal Judge Heffernan's decision to Interior Board of Land Appeals and sue BLM in U.S. District Court, claiming economic harm.
April 2006	GCT files injunction to keep state funds from being used in the lawsuit is granted.
September 2006	Interior Board of Land Appeals denies ranchers' appeal. U.S. district judge rules the counties lack standing to continue their lawsuit against BLM.
2007	BLM releases official policy on relinquishment.

Source: Created by the author.

1996-99

According to the GCT's website when I conducted my research in the early 2000s, the trust was formed in 1985 with the mission "to protect and restore the Colorado Plateau," and its approach was to "work for common sense, balanced solutions to significant problems affecting the region's natural resources."[17] Up until 1996, however, GCT's conservation projects did not include any related to livestock grazing.

That year, the superintendent of Glen Canyon National Recreation Area approached Bill Hedden, the Utah representative of GCT, about buying a grazing permit from a rancher with an allotment on BLM-managed land bordering Canyonlands National Park. The rancher was anxious to sell, but no ranchers were interested in buying the permit. The presence of livestock had led to conflicts with park visitors, and the superintendent felt that the best way to avoid further conflict was to remove the livestock. He proposed that GCT offer to compensate the rancher for relinquishing the permit to the BLM if the agency concluded, through the appropriate NEPA process, that the allotment should be permanently closed to grazing and the permit retired. This seemed like a solution that would benefit all parties involved, and the process was successfully carried out. However, the solution the parties came up with explored options not addressed by existing laws and regulations governing grazing on the public lands. It bore a resemblance to some of the Rangeland Reform '94 revisions to the federal grazing regulations (described in chapter 1), which were currently under appeal in the federal courts. In addition, relinquishment and retirement were neither defined nor anticipated by federal grazing regulations.

When GSENM was created the same year, Boulder rancher Arthur Lyman, whose great-grandfather had helped found the town, foresaw that the new designation would bring more conflict with hikers and tighter regulation of his operation, making ranching in the region even more difficult. He reluctantly decided to move his operation somewhere else. Having learned of GCT's recent purchase of a grazing permit in the region, he and several other ranchers holding permits for allotments in the Escalante Canyons approached Bill Hedden with an offer to sell their permits.

Working with five ranching families and the BLM, GCT put together an agreement involving the purchase and trade of grazing permits that resulted in the removal of grazing from most of the canyons in the Escalante River drainage. In 1999 the BLM incorporated these changes into an amendment to the Escalante Management Framework Plan, the plan guiding livestock grazing on the monument. These retirements furthered the trust's goal of reducing the impact of grazing on public land by curtailing grazing in some of what it considered the more ecologically sensitive areas in the monument.[18] Bill Hedden called the agreement "a nice example of environmentalists and the community working together," adding, "It has been rare to see that in southern Utah."[19]

Ranchers benefited because they were compensated for permits that would have been difficult to sell or traded their permits for allotments that would be more productive and easier to manage. However, they could hardly be considered willing sellers in a free market. Arthur Lyman described his decision this way: "I'm not happy to be leaving Boulder. I would have liked to stay, but I just couldn't do it. I've seen the writing on the wall, and I want to try somewhere else."[20] Dell LeFevre, another Boulder rancher, said at the time, "I worked with Grand Canyon Trust and I got as good [a deal] as I could have ever got."[21] He later explained, "I was afraid the BLM would add so many restrictions that I wouldn't be able to use the land anyway, and I'd be out the $100,000 I spent for the permits. The BLM just shuts you down."[22]

As a result of successes arising from these unexpected opportunities, GCT began to develop an actual Grazing Retirement Program. The GCT's "market-based" approach involved negotiating with willing ranchers to create agreements in which either the trust compensated the rancher for relinquishing a grazing permit to the BLM or the trust's nonprofit corporation, Canyonlands Grazing Corporation (CGC), purchased the permit and offered to relinquish it to the BLM. The agency would then undertake the NEPA process required to determine whether the allotment should be permanently closed to livestock grazing. GCT's website in 2004 described its approach as less oppositional than that of environmental groups seeking to eliminate livestock grazing on public lands, which had largely been unsuccessful, and in fact supportive of livestock grazing. It pointed out that GCT had "never filed an appeal, protest, or lawsuit on any grazing issue anywhere. In fact, ranchers in the region have been nearly free of environmentalist interference because the conservation community has been giving this market-based approach a chance, to learn if it can work." It also stated, "Our payments [have] allowed all the ranchers involved to pay off debt and stay in business."[23]

"Relinquish" ostensibly meant giving a permit back to the BLM, which could then grant it to another qualified applicant. But the expectation underlying GCT's offer to relinquish was that the BLM's environmental assessment of the allotment would recommend that it be permanently closed to grazing. In practice, this process took some time and might not result in the expected recommendation. According to GCT, the Grazing Retirement Program evolved as these shortcomings became apparent. However, as discussed in the section on the events of 2005, Kane and Garfield Counties offered a different interpretation of why the program changed.

GCT formed the Canyonlands Grazing Corporation in 2001 as a tax-exempt corporate subsidiary so it would qualify to hold federal grazing permits. This addressed several shortcomings in the program. First, the ranchers could now be compensated immediately instead of holding the permits and assuming the risk until the retirement process was complete. Second, CGC was "more nimble in the market," able to take advantage of opportunities to buy permits when they came up and was shielded from tax liability. Third, as a permit holder, CGC had more standing in the planning process. Finally, CGC made what Bill Hedden called "Plan B" possible: in case the BLM decided not to close the allotment, CGC could "buy cows and graze it at an appropriate level, take non-use as allowed under law, or transfer the permit to someone else."[24]

The Grazing Retirement Program relied on the idea of a free market and a creative and expansive interpretation of the federal laws and regulations governing grazing to realize GCT's vision of national landscapes that were more valuable for aesthetic, recreational, and ecological reasons than for livestock grazing. But it produced an unintended effect:

less than five years after the cattle had been removed from the Escalante River canyon, the banks had become choked with thorny, invasive Russian olive, which the cattle had helped keep down, making it more difficult for recreationists to hike or boat the canyon. And the program was soon challenged.

2000–2001

The grazing retirements along the Escalante River had attracted little attention when they occurred. However, GCT's next purchases of grazing permits in GSENM, which took place while Kate Cannon was monument manager, proved extremely controversial. These began in June 2000, when extreme drought gripped southern Utah, with the acquisition of the permit for the 55,000-acre Clark Bench allotment in the southern part of the monument from Brent Robinson. Robinson explained that he had been trying to sell the permit for some time, but interested buyers were discouraged after consulting with the BLM because the agency expressed uncertainty over how the allotment would be managed in the future. Discouraging potential buyers of grazing permits could be seen as a tactic in the reterritorialization of GSENM as national landscape without livestock grazing.

In 2001 CGC purchased permits for the 12,000-acre Willow Gulch allotment, the Drip Tank pasture of the Headwaters allotment, the 43,000-acre Moody allotment, and the 256,985-acre Last Chance allotment, the largest in the monument. With these purchases, CGC became the largest permit holder on GSENM in terms of acreage. GCT negotiated a deal with Dell LeFevre to exchange a permit to graze the developed area of Last Chance for his permit for the 18,245-acre Big Bowns Bench allotment, the last allotment along the Escalante River still open to grazing. These transactions took place during what meteorologists were calling the worst drought in southern Utah in five hundred years, which threatened ranchers' entire livestock operations. It is questionable whether the ranchers could be considered willing sellers and whether the market could be considered free at a time when those in the livestock business were in desperate straits.

When GCT offered to relinquish the permits to the BLM, members of the monument staff, specifically those who had been hired since

Cannon became monument manager, began preparing EAs to consider a plan amendment to retire grazing simultaneously on the Clark Bench, Willow Gulch, the undeveloped part of Last Chance, and Big Bowns Bench allotments. In a comment that revealed her vision of national landscapes, Cannon told a *Salt Lake Tribune* reporter that she found GCT's approach "a real useful tool to us," adding, "I'd like to turn it into an even more useful tool."[25] During the public comment period for the draft EAs, Kane County submitted forty pages of comments, which had been drawn up by a newcomer to Kanab, Mark Habbeshaw.

Habbeshaw can be seen as representative of the economic and demographic changes that have been taking place in the New West. He chose Kanab as "the perfect place to retire" in 1997, after a thirty-year law enforcement career with the Clark County Sheriff's Department and the Las Vegas Metropolitan Police Department. He grew up in Las Vegas and described himself as a "city boy" who had "always been interested in public lands" and liked to spend time outdoors, hiking, mountain biking, snowshoeing, and horseback riding. He moved to Mount Charleston outside Las Vegas and got to know the mountain so well that the Forest Service asked him to be a wilderness ranger when he retired. The job gave him "insight into public land management and how land management agencies operate," but it was not as much of "a wilderness experience" as he had expected. He spent too much time in the campgrounds and the front county, so he left after one year. After moving to Kanab, as a "community service responsibility," he volunteered for the Kane County Resource Committee, which gives advice to the Kane County Commission on public lands issues. A thorough researcher, he educated himself further to gain an understanding of federal land law and grazing regulations, range management, and the local environment. It became "a kind of a passion" for him.

His study of the EAs led him to conclude that they were flawed in serious ways, displayed an anti-grazing and anti-rural bias, and revealed that the BLM was colluding with GCT to facilitate grazing retirements. He said he was shocked because his career in law enforcement had given him a great respect for the law: "The law is our friend. Where we have had success in protecting our rights is by using the law. When we get into trouble is when agencies deviate from the law. A federal agency needs to have authority for everything they do; they need to be able to show where it derives from." In his democratic imaginary, rule of law applied to the federal government as well as citizens.

Since GCT had invested a great deal of money in the permits it had purchased, Bill Hedden wrote to Utah representative Chris Cannon seeking reassurance that the procedure the trust was following to retire the permits was correct. Both Interior Secretary Gale Norton and Assistant Secretary of Policy, Management, and Budget Lynn Scarlett responded to his inquiry, expressed support for GCT's "market-based solution" to resolving resource conflicts, and reassured him that GCT was following the appropriate process. The Interior Department supported GCT's approach not because it shared GCT's vision of national landscapes, but because it supported the idea that the market should decide how national landscapes should be managed, which was consistent with the philosophy and policy of the George W. Bush administration.

GCT's Grazing Retirement Program illustrates the effects of neoliberal rationality, which has infiltrated and become hegemonic in political-economic thinking and practices since the 1980s and informed the reterritorialization of public land as national landscape. It exemplifies a neoliberal approach to conservation, in which a nongovernmental organization uses the market to gain access to conservation decision-making that is officially the responsibility of a government agency. Geographer David Harvey defined neoliberalism as "a theory of political economic practices that proposes that human well-being can best be advanced by liberating individual entrepreneurial freedoms and skills within an institutional framework characterized by strong private property rights, free markets, and free trade."[26] According to this theory, the market is better than government institutions at making decisions that will improve the welfare of the population and preserve individual freedom and is therefore a more legitimate form of governance.

Neoliberalization is a process characterized by deregulation, privatization, and withdrawal of the state from many areas of providing for social welfare. At the same time, the state must create and preserve the institutional framework that supports private property rights, free markets, and free trade and "liberates" individuals to be entrepreneurs. This process entails much "creative destruction": "of prior institutional frameworks and powers, . . . divisions of labor, social relations, welfare provisions, technological mixes, ways of life and thought, reproductive activities, attachments to the land, and habits of the heart," to "bring all human actions into the domain of the market."[27] So while GCT perceived its Grazing Retirement Program as an approach to reducing the impacts of livestock grazing on public land that was less oppositional than the approaches of other environmental groups and that gave ranchers greater choice, and high-ranking officials in the Interior Department saw it as a market-based approach to resolving resource conflicts, many residents of the Grand Staircase-Escalante region perceived it as an attempt to destroy their way of life. By contesting GCT's Grazing Retirement Program, they were also contesting the legitimacy of the market as a form of rule in a democratic society. Participants in this conflict drew on neoliberal rationality in various ways, sometimes advocating it when they saw the market as preferable to federal government control, sometimes resisting it when they called on the federal government to control the excesses of the market.

2002

When the final EAs were released in February 2002, they had been revised based on Kane County's comments, but they still recommended that the allotments be closed to livestock grazing. Ranchers agreed that Big Bowns Bench should be closed because water was a problem on that allotment, and it had not been grazed for years. But the other closures did not make sense to local residents, in particular, the closure of the Clark Bench allotment, which a BLM rangeland specialist had described as a "showcase allotment" and "the best native grassland on the monument." The closures strengthened their conviction that the BLM intended to eliminate grazing from the monument. With Habbeshaw in the lead, the Canyon Country Ranchers Association, a group of about eighty ranchers from southern Utah and northern Arizona, announced it would challenge the BLM in court if the agency decided to carry out the recommendations. Because the first set of grazing retirements on GSENM went "under the radar," they aimed to "stop the process" this time. Habbeshaw explained why: "It's a very dangerous precedent. If they can eliminate grazing in these areas, then it sets a precedent for further restricting and eliminating grazing in other parts of the monument and even outside the monument."[28] The group believed, "The BLM is clearly biased to achieve the trust's purposes. . . . This has been publicized as a 'market-approach' to stabilize the livestock industry. It's just the opposite of that."[29]

At the urging of some local residents, Habbeshaw ran for Kane County commissioner in 2002, a decision that came to have significant effects on the reterritorialization process in the Grand Staircase-Escalante region. Because of his experience in law enforcement and as a wilderness ranger on the public lands, as county commissioner he was initially interested in making sure the BLM was following authorized procedures in the grazing retirements and other actions on the monument. But his approach to the job reflected a shift in his democratic imaginary, as he soon came to see himself as a spokesperson for people in the county whose voices were not being heard. The experience he had gained on the Kane County Resource Committee helped Habbeshaw realize that a need existed for someone to speak for the "people who weren't having their interests represented." A member of the Church of Jesus Christ, he learned that southern Utah members were not comfortable with conflict and would go to great lengths to avoid it, while he was a person who liked to get the issues out on the table. This shift reflected a republican democratic imaginary in which elected officials should represent the voice of the people. In addition, Habbeshaw saw his political office as an extension of his career helping people in law enforcement and a way of being able to pay back the community for living there. This reflects a civic republican democratic imaginary in which citizens have responsibilities as well as rights.

Kane and Garfield Counties developed a variety of strategies to contest the vision of national landscapes without livestock grazing that GCT and the BLM seemed to be promoting. They protested the findings of the EAs to the director of the BLM, and they encouraged local ranchers to apply for, or file over, the permits held by CGC. Three local ranchers, including Dell LeFevre, filed for the permits. While it may have appeared at first that Dell was betraying his benefactor, he later testified that he had discussed the reasons for his action ahead of time with Bill Hedden, and Hedden had agreed with his reasoning. Now, unsure what the outcome of the ranchers' actions might be, GCT withdrew its offer to relinquish the permits.

While the BLM in Washington DC was considering the counties' protest, the Interior Department's chief solicitor, William Myers, issued two memos that clarified some of the ambiguity in the legal framework governing grazing on public land and invalidated the interpretation assumed by GCT's Grazing Retirement Program. The memos indicated that the BLM could retire grazing permits, but "a decision to foreclose livestock grazing is not permanent. It is subject to reconsideration, modification and reversal in subsequent land use plan decisions. Only Congress can permanently exclude lands from grazing use."[30] The memos contradicted the assurances Interior Department officials had given Hedden and seemed to constitute a setback for GCT. This is another example of what sociologist Philip Abrams called "the actual disunity of political power" of the state, revealing "the conflicting practices, interests, and agendas of political institutions that the idea of the state conceals," even within the Washington DC headquarters of the DOI.[31]

During this period, a series of unrelated legal actions against public land grazing that took place close to home helped reinforce the belief locally that GCT's Grazing Retirement Program was part of a conspiracy among environmental organizations to eliminate grazing on all public lands. In the fall of 2001 a group of environmental organizations appealed more than 180 grazing permit renewals in northern Utah. In April 2002 the National Public Lands Grazing Campaign announced a proposal to enact federal legislation creating a grazing buyout fund coupled with permanent retirement of allotments purchased with these public moneys. And in the summer of 2003 a coalition of environmental organizations appealed a group of permit renewals that had been approved by the Kanab Field Office of the BLM. Meanwhile, according to Hedden, other environmental organizations were holding off on becoming involved in grazing issues on GSENM while they waited to see whether GCT's approach worked.

Throughout this series of legal actions, the BLM continually tried to counter local perceptions that it was trying to eliminate grazing on the monument. Dave Wolf, assistant manager for planning on the monument, asserted, "There will always be grazing in the Monument. That doesn't mean it will continue in every area, in every way, and at the same levels it has always occurred. There are times when adjustments are made. There are no conspiracies or secret deals, but there will be changes in the future."[32] Monument manager Dave Hunsaker reiterated that the BLM was following public process and that grazing would always be "an integral part" of monument management.[33] However, in the absence of any concrete action by the BLM or any results from the Rangeland Health EIS process to indicate otherwise, local residents were not convinced.

Meanwhile, the drought continued. The BLM sent letters to all permittees on the monument requesting them to graze reduced numbers of cattle or take nonuse. While ranchers had to reduce their herds or ship them to places where they could lease grazing, the drought worked to GCT's advantage because it did not have to stock its allotments.

2003–4

In January 2003 the BLM denied the counties' protests of the recommended decisions in the EAs. However, BLM state director Sally Wisely decided to defer action on the recommendations until completion of the ongoing Rangeland Health EIS. This seemed like a reasonable solution since the EIS was required by the Monument Management Plan to be finished on July 1 of that year. But the Draft EIS was not released by that date, and it still had not been released when the events in this account took place, leaving the fate of these allotments up in the air and local residents concerned about the future of grazing on GSENM.

Hedden, who became director of GCT in 2003, interpreted the Wisely decision as an about-face on the part of the Interior Department:

> Working with the federal agencies and ranchers to actually get the agency to evaluate realistically whether grazing was in the best interest of the American public on a particular piece of land, under the Bush administration they decided they won't do that. So that particular approach doesn't have much of a future until we have different leadership in the Department of the Interior. Gale Norton says, we

like using the market and we want decisions to be made at the local level. So we used the market, the range scientists at Grand Staircase do three extensive EAs, . . . and Washington, at the highest level, intervened to subvert those environmental assessments.

The decision demonstrated, to his disappointment, the conflicting practices, interests, and agendas concealed by the idea of the state. In this case, the agenda of "Washington, at the highest level" trumped the DOI's commitment to market-based and collaborative approaches to resource conflicts and its assurance to Hedden in 2001 that GCT was following the appropriate process.

Hedden was not the only one who believed that the decisions made by monument and state BLM managers in the grazing retirement process on GSENM were being handed down from higher up. Habbeshaw, who continued to lead the opposition to grazing retirements on GSENM after becoming a Kane County commissioner, expressed similar beliefs about the recommendations in the EAs. He had hoped that management of the monument would change with the advent of the Bush administration and was puzzled and disappointment when high-level administration appointees in the Interior Department seemed to be supporting GCT's Grazing Retirement Program. The conflicting agendas of the state sent conflicting messages to both GCT and the counties.

In February the monument staff denied the local ranchers' applications for the permits held by CGC. Now the state of Utah was drawn into the conflict, further complicating the dynamics. The ranchers appealed the denial, backed by funding for legal expenses granted to the counties by the Utah Permanent Community Impact Board Fund. The counties had applied for funding for "lawsuits against the federal government regarding grazing" in GSENM. Their application was initially turned down, but the fund agreed their cause was worthy and encouraged them to apply for a grant for "alternate eligible projects of roughly the same dollar value." The board director explained later that the procedure was "straightforward," saying, "We try to maintain a lot of flexibility to help an applicant get to the resources they need."[34] However, an editorial in the *Salt Lake Tribune*, with the title "Poisoning the Well," condemned the state's grant as "improper use of public money, undermining the free market, and abuse of precious natural resources."[35] This statement reflects contradictory positions: the neoliberal position that the state should not interfere with the market and the progressive position that the state should protect natural resources. Ironically, the Permanent Community Impact Board Fund is a state agency whose purpose is to help mitigate the effects of the market on rural communities.

The ranchers' appeal was to be heard by the Interior Department Office of Hearings and Appeals, with CGC participating as an intervenor. GCT, which had refrained from using the courts to pursue its vision for grazing in national landscapes, now had to defend its actions in court. In addition, while ranchers' expenses were to be paid by the state of Utah, GCT, which had already spent more than $600,000 for the permits in question, had to foot its own bill for legal expenses. The date of the hearing was pushed back several times, prolonging local uncertainty about the future of grazing on the monument; it did not take place until May 2005.

Hedden admitted that he had not anticipated the high level of local opposition to GCT's Grazing Retirement Program and was dismayed by it. In 2004 GCT's website maintained that the socioeconomic effects of the proposed retirements would be "minimal" because "ranching is so unprofitable."[36] Hedden saw the program as a way to provide individual ranchers with more options and expected local residents to see it that way too. But local government officials and many local residents were more concerned about the welfare of local culture and of public lands ranching in general than they were about the welfare of individual ranchers. State representative Mike Noel explained, "It doesn't matter if the ranchers want to do it. . . . They're selling their heritage for a mess of pottage."[37] Garfield County commissioner Maloy Dodds noted, "We have a lot of people's living made on public lands. We want those lands made available to viable ranchers. If the Grand Canyon Trust is a viable rancher, good. But we don't think they are."[38]

The discrepancy between the views of GCT and the counties brings out another underlying assumption of neoliberal market logic: benefits to individuals aggregate and will benefit the whole. Opponents of neoliberalism argue that this is not the case: the market distributes benefits unequally, and the state needs to step in to ameliorate this tendency. In this case, the counties were insisting that GCT's logic did not take into account ranching culture, which includes local knowledge, relationships, and attachments to the landscape. Local people value ranching culture, but the market does not. Ranchers acknowledge the value of ranching culture when they say that they are in ranching for the lifestyle and not the money. If the free market eliminated public lands grazing, it would deprive them of their freedom to pursue and enjoy the ranching lifestyle.

GCT and the counties also disagreed about the economic significance of ranching in the Grand Staircase-Escalante region and the effects of the proposed grazing retirements on the local economy, and they turned to different experts to provide authoritative economic evidence they could use in the appeal. Although the judge in the appeal declined to use the resulting reports, their contradictory findings illustrate the problematic role of expert knowledge in legitimizing public lands management decisions.

Kane County commissioned John Groesbeck, a professor in the School of Business at Southern Utah University, who produced two reports demonstrating that the reductions would have a significant negative effect on personal income, jobs, and tax revenue in the two counties.[39] GCT commissioned Thomas Michael Power, a professor of economics at the University of Montana, who used different assumptions and methodology and found the impacts of the proposed grazing retirements to be minor. Power's report was suffused with the discourse of neoliberalism. For example, he critiqued the input-output model Groesbeck used for his calculations because it ignored "the genius of a market economy," which "harnesses both freedom and responsibility," ensuring that "individuals are free to pursue what they perceive as their own interests, harvesting the benefits of their actions, but also accepting the costs." His report constructed ranchers as "economic actors" whose only concern was their bottom line and who were "free" to "adapt [their] behavior to minimize the costs and maximize the opportunities."[40] This was is not, however, an accurate representation of real ranchers, who were significantly affected by changing BLM livestock management policies and more motivated by lifestyle than economic opportunities.

Meanwhile, like many permittees on the monument, CGC had been taking nonuse during the drought years of 2000–2002. However, when limited grazing was permitted in 2003, the trust had to put plan B into effect. CGC leased cattle from Brent Robinson to graze the Clark Bench allotment and purchased trespass cattle still on the Last Chance allotment to graze it. Robinson managed the cattle on Clark Bench, and LeFevre ran GCT's cattle with his own herd on Last Chance. Hedden came to know Robinson as a "good rancher" and a "straight shooter," and he developed a "trustful" relationship and "a great personal fondness" for LeFevre, "one of the few full-time ranchers out there on the land with his animals." As a result of working closely with these ranchers, he came to see them as "exemplary livestock operators," regarding their operations as "sustainable" with an "appropriate level of grazing," and learned that there are "benefits to very carefully managed operations."[41] His perception of ranching had changed, causing him to rethink GCT's approach to reducing the impacts of livestock grazing on public land.

At the same time, both LeFevre and Robinson felt they had benefited from working with GCT. According to Robinson, "The trust can run half the amount of cattle that we ought to have out there, so the range will always look pristine and good. And I don't . . . have to stock it up to where it's bulging to make a payment. My cattle are fat; I don't worry about them; and the range looks good."

The experience of these three men, whose points of view all were changed by these relationships, illustrates the transformative potential of conflict in agonistic democracy: the transformation of antagonism into agonism. Working together provided an opportunity for these men to recognize that they shared a passion for the landscape and a respect for a job well done. Instead of perceiving ranchers or environmentalists as the enemy, these men came to see that they could agree on some things. In this case. drought conditions made working together necessary. Chantal Mouffe asserts that the aim of democratic politics should be to provide a wide variety of opportunities for citizens to engage with difference in order to encourage this kind of transformation.[42] Generalizing from this example, I argue that public land promotes American democracy because it provides such an opportunity. People who are passionately attached to the land, even if for different reasons, are motivated to engage with each other in struggles over its management.

Initially, GCT's effort to reterritorialize public land as national landscape without livestock grazing was supported by the federal government. Then, after a change in presidential administration and after GCT's approach aroused opposition both locally and by the state of Utah, the federal government's position changed, and its role in the process became more equivocal. The tactics employed by the DOI and BLM—long delays in the time it takes to complete official processes, such as EAs and grazing permit applications, and to resolve responses to protests and appeals, as well as mixed signals about the BLM's intentions—allowed the federal government to avoid direct confrontation and maintain the status quo.

2005

In January 2005 Kane and Garfield Counties sought to break this stalemate and stepped up their crusade against grazing retirements by contesting those that GCT had helped arrange along the Escalante River in 1996. They filed a lawsuit in the U.S. District Court of Utah charging that the BLM had failed to follow regulations when it eliminated grazing on those allotments in 1999. In March the state of Utah offered the counties further support in their opposition to GCT's Grazing Retirement Program when the state legislature passed H.B. 264, State Land Use Management Plans Amendments. The bill said, "The state opposes the relinquishment or retirement of grazing animal unit months (AUMs) in favor of conservation, wildlife, and other uses."

The hearing with the Interior Department Office of Hearings and Appeals for the ranchers' appeal of the denial of their applications for the Clark Bench, Last Chance, and Big Bowns Bench permits finally got underway on May 9, 2005, in the Kane County Courthouse in Kanab with Judge James Heffernan presiding. The BLM was the respondent in the appeal, and CGC and Kane and Garfield Counties were intervenors. Most participants in the hearing referred to the counties as the appellants and to GCT and the BLM as respondents—evidence that they conceived the hearing as a contest that pitted the counties' vision of national landscape against GCT's, rather than just local ranchers against the BLM.

The appeal was based on two specific procedural questions: whether CGC was qualified to hold a grazing permit and whether the permits in question were available to other applicants. However, in his opening remarks, the BLM solicitor recognized that the counties intended to broaden the scope of the hearing and "to put on trial the whole issue of retirements." In doing so, they would draw not only on legal frameworks and factual evidence but also on arguments about legal, institutional, and individual intent. Their approach to the issue highlights another aspect of statemaking: the question of transparency and hidden agendas behind what takes place.

The BLM began by using the legal framework governing public land grazing, expert witnesses, and documentary evidence to argue that (1) CGC did qualify to hold grazing permits; (2) the permits had not actually been relinquished during the retirement process, so they had not become available to other applicants; and (3) there was insufficient forage on the allotments in question to support additional permittees. Demonstrating these arguments would preclude the ranchers from filing over the permits held by CGC. However, Judge Heffernan explained that he would allow the counties to pursue other lines of argument so that they would feel their case had been heard. At the conclusion of the hearing, he acknowledged he had "been pretty liberal with letting them make their case."

To broaden the hearing from a focus on the ranchers' file overs to one on the whole retirement process, the counties contended that (1) the process was "inconsistent with law," and the BLM had worked with GCT in "unauthorized" ways to facilitate it; (2) the EAs were "outside driven" and a "top-down action" by high-level Interior Department officials, and their findings were "based on market opportunity, not on a scientific basis"; (3) GCT should not be considered a bona fide applicant because it was not in the livestock business and did not have an "intent to graze"; and (4) the change in GCT's approach, from grazing retirements to "carefully managed" grazing, was due to "local actions" that challenged the process and did not demonstrate a genuine "intent to graze."

The counties turned to the original intent of the TGA, one of the purposes of which was "to stabilize the livestock industry dependent on the public range," and to the objectives of the federal grazing regulations, one of which was "to provide for the sustainability of the western livestock industry and communities that are dependent on productive, healthy public rangelands," to make their first and third arguments, contending that the BLM had an obligation to support the livestock industry and the communities dependent on it. But instead, it appeared to be supporting GCT's Grazing Retirement Program, which, as Commissioner Habbeshaw testified, "undercuts the foundation of the agriculture and ranching that has sustained our communities." In this argument, what legitimates the actions of a democratic government is their contribution to the welfare of its citizens, which is very different from the neoliberal proposition that the role of the state in providing for social welfare should be minimal and that the market should determine the fate of the livestock industry and communities traditionally tied to it.

The counties also argued that the intent of the TGA was for permit holders to be in the livestock business. The idea behind democracy on the range was that local people making a living from the livestock business, who knew the landscape through their daily interactions with it, whose livelihoods depended on it, and who therefore had the knowledge and motivation to manage it in a sustainable way, should have a say in how it was managed. Grazing retirements threatened to cut local people and concerns out of this process because only as permittees did they have the standing to participate. The counties were trying to cut GCT out of the process by questioning its standing. They argued that it was not really in the livestock business because it had been forced to graze and did not really have an "intent to graze." Instead, its 2004 website revealed that GCT's intention was "to eliminate grazing use on allotments under its control." What the counties did not acknowledge was that since the passage of the TGA, as more people had come to see public land as national landscape that is valuable for the aesthetic and recreational experiences it provides and the ecological diversity it supports, local people were no longer the sole users and best experts they used to be. In this context, democracy on the range should involve more user groups and more experts, and GCT would be a legitimate participant.

The counties' argument also depended on the assumption that ranchers are a community with a common interest. However, the testimony of six ranchers who filed over CGC's permits suggests that the ranchers may not have seen themselves that way and may have thought very differently from one another. When the ranchers were asked why they had filed for the permits, they gave diverse reasons. For example, one rancher stated, "My feeling was that once you put a crack in the dam, it's all going to come down, and so I didn't want to see that go." He filed to "stop the process" and "preserve public land ranching." Another rancher explained that the permit would benefit his existing operation: "If you weren't going to use [the AUMs], we could." LeFevre's reason was that he "didn't want anyone else out there." He continued, "If you want problems, get someone in an allotment with you. There are too many weekend cowboys and too many people with money." Ranchers also gave different reasons for participating in the appeal and selling their permits to GCT. While the ranchers may have constituted more of a community in the past, the fences the BLM put up to divide allotments had also divided ranchers from each other and freed them to be individual entrepreneurs. But despite their differences, on their day in court, the feeling of solidarity among them and other ranchers in the courtroom was palpable.

Another key part of the counties' first and second arguments was that the findings in the EAs were determined not by science, but by the hidden agendas of monument manager Kate Cannon, who wanted to eliminate grazing on GSENM, and of high-ranking Interior Department officials, who wanted to promote market-based solutions to natural resource conflicts. While the EA process might have appeared to be consistent with NEPA, the counties argued that the BLM's intentions were inconsistent with it and with the intent of the TGA and FLPMA. To make these arguments, the counties called a series of witnesses, who confirmed under oath local rumors I had heard. For example, to reveal the monument manager's real intentions, the counties called a BLM employee who testified that while waiting outside her office, he had overheard a conversation between her and another staff member about "how they would go about getting rid of grazing on the monument." He added, "They went through a number of approaches, and I was quite disturbed by it." The counties' fourth argument also relied on being able to discern the hidden motives behind GCT's change in approach from grazing retirements to "carefully managed" grazing. Commissioner Habbeshaw testified that the counties had hoped that the new monument manager, Dave Hunsaker, would be more sympathetic to grazing, but Hunsaker had advised them that the EAs were "outside driven" and "a top-down action." The counties' second argument also assumed that the BLM made decisions based on science. However, science is only one tool the BLM used to make multiple-use decisions. In an era of neoliberalization, the BLM might have considered economics to be a better tool: "the combination that will best meet the present and future needs of the American people" would be that which would produce the highest return. Following neoliberal ideology, Interior Department officials allied themselves with GCT in this reterritorialization process, not because they were against grazing, but because amenity use of GSENM was expected to produce a higher return than grazing use. The reterritorialization of GSENM as national landscape without livestock grazing thus emerged from a contingent combination of circumstances: drought; the generosity of donors convinced by the prevailing, but outdated, environmentalist argument that removing livestock grazing would improve the condition of public land, which made it possible for GCT to purchase grazing permits on GSENM; ranchers who wanted to sell grazing permits at a time when no one in the livestock business was able to buy; and the alignment of the objectives of GCT's Grazing Retirement Program with monument manager Kate Cannon's preservationist ideology and with the market-based ideology prevailing at high levels of the Interior Department. But when high-ranking Interior Department officials become aware of the counties' opposition to GCT's Grazing Retirement Program, their support for it faded; they did not want to antagonize rural Utahns, some of the staunchest supporters of the Republican Party and the George W. Bush administration.

After three days of testimony, the hearing was continued until September 8. Up until then, the participants in the hearing had been civil, and emotion, though sometimes evident, was controlled. But when the hearing reconvened with Hedden in the witness stand, the new counsel for the appellants was very confrontational, and I was extremely impressed by Hedden's ability to remain calm.

He testified that he *was* in the livestock business, but not to make money. He pointed out that ranchers also "will tell you they're not it in for the money." He had "a different bottom line: the health of the public lands." Instead of an economic interest, "our interest was in facilitating a review by the BLM of whether grazing should be reduced or eliminated in certain areas. And we did that by alleviating the financial pressure that will normally prevent a rancher from, or make a rancher oppose that kind of review. And so by compensating or offering to compensate those ranchers while BLM did an environmental review, we were . . . facilitating a look by . . . the management agency of whether grazing on . . . those areas was at appropriate levels."[43]

When Hedden was asked about the evolution of the Grazing Retirement Program, he explained it in detail to show that its strategy had changed not simply in response to the counties' "relentless litigation" but as "part of the learning process" and because "we have begun to realize our potential as permittees to achieve our goals." He stated that he was not anti-grazing, but believed that grazing was an appropriate use on the vast majority of public lands. "That said," however, "there are particular places where there are exceptional ecological values where we think . . . that it would be better if the cows could be removed."[44]

To confirm GCT's "intent to graze," Hedden also described the most recent development in the evolution of the trust's approach to reducing the impacts of livestock grazing on the Colorado Plateau. In partnership with the Conservation Fund, GCT had just purchased the Kane and Two-Mile Ranches—1,000 acres of private land and grazing permits for 830,000 acres of public lands managed by the BLM and Forest Service—which border GSENM and Grand Canyon National Park and encompass most of the Vermilion Cliffs National Monument.[45] When the proposed purchase was first announced, he had explained, "Our interest is in restoring habitat and trying to do grazing in the most sustainable way possible that is focused on the health of the habitat."[46] He testified that the partners had already hired a ranch manager, were putting together a science advisory team, and would soon buy cattle.

The media's announcement of GCT's new approach to reducing the impacts of livestock grazing on the Colorado Plateau underlined the fact that it was still market-based. The *Salt Lake Tribune* called GCT's purchase of the Kane and Two-Mile Ranches "possibly the biggest splash for free-market environmentalism, a put-your-money-where-your-mouth-is approach that is gaining converts in an arena that is otherwise marked by polarization, litigation, and gridlock." When the partners created the North Rim Ranch Limited Liability Company to own and operate the ranches, it became the largest ranching operation in the region. The words of Michael Ford of the Conservation Fund exemplify the neoliberal approach to conservation: "We believe you can do more for conservation with money than without money. We believe we have helped create a brand of conservation that engages all Americans. And you do that by involving the private sector—foundations, major corporations, etc.—as partners. There are other models that work, but we like this model and so do our partners." On the other hand, Commissioner Habbeshaw worried that "the little rancher cannot compete with environmental funding. If this keeps up, everybody's going to get bought out and all of our public lands will be run by conservation groups. Where do our ranching families fit into this picture?"[47]

Hedden's testimony lasted for two days. Afterward, a few witnesses were called back to clarify their testimony, and the hearing then concluded.

2006

In January 2006 the Interior Department announced the decision in the case. The appeal was denied because Judge Heffernan found that the BLM had established the procedural basis on which the ranchers' applications could be denied and that GCT had never actually relinquished the permits. Based on the letter of the current grazing regulations, rather than the intent of the TGA, he found that CGC did qualify to hold a grazing permit. This finding was based on a key administrative revision to the federal grazing regulations, one of a number that occurred as public land came to be seen as national landscape. The revision reduced the qualifications for applicants for grazing permits to two: an applicant must own or control water or base property and must have either citizenship or authorization to conduct business in the state where grazing is sought. Finally, the judge found the counties' argument that BLM actions were based on hidden political agendas and "pre-ordained outcomes" frivolous because "appellants are attempting to litigate pre-decisional proposals that have never been implemented into final, effective decisions by BLM."[48] However, the counties' perception that the BLM had violated the democratic principle of transparency played a role in the reterritorialization process because it further diminished the agency's legitimacy in their eyes.

Its victory in the appeal was a hollow one for GCT, which had expected local support for the Grazing Retirement Program. As Hedden testified during the hearing, "We believe we will be most successful when we have buy-in from the local community. Obviously, we failed this time." The counties, on the other hand, felt they had succeeded in what they set out to do. Commissioner Habbeshaw stated that if the trust had not been challenged, it would have returned "to its program of permanently eliminating livestock grazing on its allotments. . . . Our legal challenge forced the trust to reinvent itself. . . . Counties and ranchers have, at least superficially, converted the trust from an organization dedicated to eliminating public lands grazing to an organization required to make grazing use of its allotments."[49] According to Garfield County commissioner Clare Ramsay, "Although the judge ruled against us in the grazing lawsuit, we feel we achieved a victory by stopping the Grand Canyon Trust from buying permits and permanently retiring them, thereby eliminating grazing on public lands. Also the trust has been forced to become a legitimate cattle company."[50] At this point, GCT was more than just "a legitimate cattle company": it had transformed from an organization committed to grazing retirements in "places where there are exceptional ecological values" into both the largest permit holder on GSENM in terms of acreage and the manager of the largest ranching operation in the region.

The counties continued their strenuous opposition to the reterritorialization of public land as national landscape without livestock grazing by appealing Judge Heffernan's decision to the Interior Board of Land Appeals in March. Together with the ranchers, they also filed a lawsuit against the BLM in U.S. District Court, claiming economic harm. In response, GCT filed an injunction to make sure that state money would not be used to fund the ranchers' legal expenses in this lawsuit. In April 2007 a federal judge granted the injunction. Legal decisions continued to go against the counties. In September the Interior Board of Land Appeals denied their appeal, and U.S. District Court judge Tena Campbell ruled they had failed to prove economic harm and lacked standing to continue their lawsuit against the BLM. However, the ranchers were allowed to continue theirs.

The counties' new legal actions stimulated a debate in the *Salt Lake Tribune* about the nature of the free market. When a columnist opined that the counties' latest efforts demonstrated that they "had a problem with the free-enterprise system," a second columnist responded that this was a "warped view of free enterprise" because it "allows tax-sheltered, anti-grazing environmental groups, using tax deductible donations from across America to compete in Kane County against hardworking, tax-paying ranchers contributing to local schools, law enforcement and roads while creating jobs and new wealth."[51] Commissioner Habbeshaw also responded, asserting that the counties could "cope with free enterprise," but first they were "creating a level playing field" by "assuring compliance regarding the permitted use of public lands grazing allotments under the requirements of the TGA."[52] In his view, government intervention was needed to keep markets free by leveling the playing field between "little ranchers" and conservation groups with "environmental funding."[53] Both responses relied on the democratic principle of equality for their force.

The struggle over grazing retirements on GSENM alerted the BLM to the need to develop an official policy on relinquishment. The Rangeland Health Plan Amendment and EIS for GSENM, which was supposed to resolve the fate of the Clark Bench, Last Chance, and Big Bowns Bench allotments, was delayed further while the BLM in Washington DC formulated this policy. It was released on February 20, 2007, as Instruction Memorandum No. 2007-067, Relinquishment of Grazing Preference on BLM Administered Lands, complete with a relinquishment flow diagram.⁵⁴ This rationalized relinquishment and attempted to forestall other innovative interpretations of grazing regulations. Subsequently, work on the EIS resumed. Meanwhile, range restoration projects in two areas in the southern part of the monument, which began in the fall of 2006, gave local ranchers some hope that the BLM still intended to support livestock grazing on the monument.

Reterritorialization and Grazing Retirement

The conflict over grazing retirements on GSENM appeared to have had little material effect on the reterritorialization of public land as national landscape other than to produce an official policy on grazing retirement. Livestock continued to graze for now. As of 2008 CGC was still the permittee for the Clark Bench, Last Chance, and Big Bowns Bench allotments; livestock still grazed on Clark Bench and Last Chance; but GCT had not purchased any more grazing permits on the monument. Its Grazing Retirement Program had evolved into the Kane and Two-Mile Ranches Program, and it was focusing there. Ranchers Robinson and LeFevre, who had sold their permits to GCT, as well as the ranchers who had filed over, were still in business.

How livestock grazing would be managed in the future on GSENM was still up in the air until the Draft Rangeland Health EIS was finally released. Neither GCT nor the counties got exactly what they wanted; instead, the federal government steered a course between their contrasting visions of national landscapes without and with livestock grazing and of rule of the market and democracy on the range, effectively maintaining the status quo.

Local opposition to grazing retirements on GSENM had a significant effect on this outcome. The ranchers' and counties' legal actions and the lack of "buy-in from the local community" contributed to the change in GCT's approach and its transition into the livestock business. The legal actions also made DOI officials aware that while rural Utahns might be staunch supporters of free enterprise, in the case of grazing permits this meant "a free market to buy and sell. But if you buy it, you use it."⁵⁵ These actions prompted the DOI's investigation into the legal subtleties of retirements, which informed the BLM's decision to put off the question of retirement of the contested permits by leaving it to the Rangeland

Health EIS. Because ranchers were mobilized and represented by the counties and unified by a shared attachment to the lifestyle the landscape affords, they were able to exercise more influence in this reterritorialization process than in the conflict over impoundments on Fiftymile Mountain. Commissioner Habbeshaw's role in the process demonstrated the impact that an informed and committed individual can have.

While the purpose of GCT's Grazing Retirement Program was to reduce the impacts of livestock grazing on public land, it is not clear what effect the 1999 retirements or the subsequent purchases of permits by GCT had on the physical landscape. Following the conflict over the impoundments on Fiftymile Mountain, the BLM more intensely monitored the Lake and Mudholes allotments. But as of 2012, neither the BLM nor GCT had conducted any monitoring in the closed allotments in the Escalante River drainage to evaluate their condition, nor had they systematically studied the effects of the changed grazing regime on the landscape since CGC became permittee on the Clark Bench and Last Chance allotments. This raises the question of why, when so much effort was spent to determine whether a conservation organization could hold a grazing permit on public land, so little attention was paid to the effects of that decision on the physical landscape.

Perennial underfunding and understaffing are the usual answers given to the question of why there is not better monitoring of public land grazing allotments. However, GSENM was still operating with a generous budget when these conflicts over grazing took place, so funding could have been made available if rangeland health were a priority. Another possible explanation takes into consideration GSENM's high national profile. To be considered a legitimate manager of national landscapes in national eyes, the BLM must take actions on GSENM that indicate something other than business as usual to the public. Under these circumstances, the performance of an action may matter more than its outcome.

Local opposition to the grazing retirements can be seen as opposition to the creative destruction of local livelihoods and culture based on resource production by a neoliberal reterritorialization process seeking to produce national landscapes more attractive to amenity consumption.

The opposition prefigured debates about the moral limits of neoliberal rationality as it began to pervade more and more aspects of public and private life. In *What Money Can't Buy*, political scientist Michael Sandel questioned whether everything should be for sale. The counties proposed that the market should not be able to determine the value of the traditional ranching lifestyle, nor should the highest bidder be able to determine how public lands are used.

According to neoliberal rationality, the role of the state is to facilitate the market. Initially, the Interior Department supported a vision of national landscapes governed by the market. The counties counterposed one of democracy on the range, in which ranchers should have some say in how livestock grazing is managed on public land and the federal government had a responsibility to ensure the welfare of the livestock industry. This vision resonated with a strengthening conservative agenda that advocated local control or privatization of the public lands. Caught in the contradiction between these two agendas, in the face of opposition from conservative allies in rural Utah, the Interior Department backpedaled.

Viewed through the lens of agonistic democracy, the conflict provided opportunities for antagonists to engage and perhaps transform their antagonism into agonism. For example, the DOI hearing provided an opportunity for ranchers who testified to temporarily overcome individual differences, participate in a common action, express their views in public, and experience a feeling of solidarity with each other. At the same time, members of the public attending the hearing were able to hear ranchers express their feelings in their own words and might empathize with their attachment to their way of life. The conflict also led to longer-lasting transformation in some participants. Working with local ranchers transformed Bill Hedden's vision of permanently retiring grazing into one of carefully managing grazing on national landscapes. Mark Habbeshaw's experience participating in public processes required by NEPA contributed to his transformation into a local government official. GCT transformed into a "legitimate cattle company." And the Interior Department's wholehearted embrace of market-based solutions to resolving resource conflicts transformed into more cautious support. The transformations in individuals and groups that took place may, in the long run, be more significant than any concrete outcome of the conflict.

Finally, the conflict offered a glimpse of the kind of subject that neoliberalism calls into being, as opposed to the democratic citizen of agonistic democracy. Eric Freyfogle, a professor of natural resource law, argued that market-based approaches to conservation are problematic because of the "powerful messages" they convey "about the natural world, how people ought to live in that world, and how people ought to relate to each other."[56] These messages call into being a self-centered individual subject, the consumer, who relates competitively to others as producers or consumers and for whom nature is a collection of resources that are available to buy and sell, valued in purely human-centered terms. Local residents were contesting these messages with a democratic imaginary that calls into being citizens who look beyond individual interests toward communal goods, relate cooperatively with others, and participate in governing national landscapes they view as home. From the perspective of agonistic democracy, this conflict, and conflicts over the management of public land more generally, promote democracy because attachments to the landscape motivate people to participate and have the potential to transform antagonism into agonism.

Both conflicts described in this chapter erupted when one side tried to change the status quo. In the first conflict, it was the BLM; in the second, it was GCT. Both threatened livestock grazing on GSENM and already precarious ranching livelihoods. Both pitted the perception of public land as national landscape against the perception of public land as resource and the national interest in maintaining healthy public rangelands against the local interest in maintaining a traditional lifestyle, historically supported by BLM policy. In both cases, little change occurred. Change upsets the "delicate balance between autonomy and control in the relationship between state and society" and threatens state power.[57] Thus change generated from within state structures can be incremental at best. While change may be incremental, the detailed analyses in this chapter show that the negotiation of institutions of government and ideas of governance, reflected in changing alliances, arguments, positions, and strategies among local and state actors, is intense, ongoing, and animated by ideas about democracy.

But what if antagonists in these conflicts had sat down together to work on the issue of livestock grazing on GSENM? What if the amount of energy and money spent on removing cattle from Fiftymile Mountain and on litigation over grazing retirements had instead been spent to understand and improve the impacts of livestock grazing on GSENM so that all could benefit?[58]

4   Conflict over Roads

What is a road? In southern Utah, where most roads on public land are unpaved, the answer to this question is not always obvious. These roads, which have surfaces of gravel, sand, clay, or slickrock, are constantly being modified by the same forces of nature that sculpted the landscapes they traverse. They may have originated as wildlife trails or as footpaths worn by the feet of Native Americans, subsequently deepened by the hooves of the horses of Spanish explorers and itinerant trappers and traders. They may have been wagon or stock roads constructed by Mormon pioneers, connecting communities or low- and high-elevation pastures or providing access to water. They may have been engineered and constructed through and across deep canyons by the Civilian Conservation Corps during the Great Depression to connect remote towns accessible only by horse or wagon. Or they may have been created with a bulldozer blade by mining companies exploring for valuable minerals on the public lands or by ranchers creating better access to stock tanks and salt licks. They may have names that recall historic events or figures or refer to geographic features, like Hole-in-the-Rock, Bowington, and Smoky Mountain, or they may have no name at all. Their names may appear on maps or may be known only to local residents.

    Some roads that once may have provided a crucial passageway for residents have since faded to no more than a vague track, passable only to hikers and horseback riders. Others may dip in and out of washes and be erased after each heavy rainstorm. Still others may have fallen into disuse when the economic activities they supported became unprofitable. Roads on public land may acquire new uses and value for recreation, especially with the advent of all-terrain vehicles (ATVs), also referred to as off-highway vehicles (OHVs).

Roads are playing a major role in the reterritorialization of public land as national landscape. Questions such as whether a road exists; whether it has been constructed; whether it could be considered a highway; and whether those that are no longer used, are becoming impassable, or have vanished into the landscape could still be considered roads illustrate that this reterritorialization involves a struggle not just over how to govern national landscapes but also over how to *see* them. It requires materializing or dematerializing roads. My description of events in the first few sections begins in 1996, when Grand Staircase-Escalante National Monument (GSENM) was created, and ends in 2009, when I completed my dissertation. The section "Events since 2009" brings the discussion up to the date of this writing.

Background to the Conflict

People living in the Grand Staircase-Escalante region had used these backcountry roads all their lives and took for granted their ability to do so until the passage of the Federal Land Policy and Management Act (FLPMA) in 1976.[1] For them, the county governments, the Bureau of Land Management (BLM), and wilderness advocates, because FLPMA made jurisdiction over these roads unclear, there was now more significance to the question "What is a road?" Counties claim jurisdiction under the 1866 Mining Act, which granted "the right-of-way for the construction of highways over public lands, not reserved for public uses." This grant became section 2477 of the Revised Statutes (R.S. 2477), the law that gave its name to the contemporary conflict over roads. FLPMA repealed R.S. 2477, setting out new provisions for granting rights-of-way in Title V, acknowledging rights-of-way for roads built before 1976, and giving the BLM authority to manage all other roads on lands it administered, but it did not specify how these rights-of-way could be claimed. FLPMA also required the BLM to inventory the roadless lands it administered for potential inclusion in the National Wilderness Preservation System, raising the possibility that some public land could be reterritorialized as wilderness. This possibility could be eliminated, however, by the existence of heretofore unrecognized R.S. 2477 roads.

R.S. 2477 highways played a significant role in the development of the West, as many state and county highways originated under this grant.² But most of these rights-of-way were never recorded. After the passage of FLPMA, county governments began to assert their claims in southern Utah and throughout the West. Kane and Garfield Counties contend that these roads are part of their transportation infrastructure and support resource-based economic activities, such as ranching, as well as tourism and four-wheel and ATV recreation, and they benefit from money received from the federal government to maintain them.

Environmental groups oppose counties' claims to R.S. 2477 roads on public land administered by the BLM for several reasons. First, they argue that the roads have a negative physical impact on the landscape, causing erosion; threatening ecological systems, wildlife and wildlife habitat, and water quality; and leading to losses of archaeological sites. The roads also affect visitors' experience of the landscape, having a visual impact and allowing for uses that produce air and noise pollution. In addition, the roads open adjacent public lands to destructive off-road vehicle use. Second, they point out that these roads would cause a management nightmare for the federal land management agencies. But most important, they note that the roads could disqualify public lands from wilderness designation. These arguments rely on several underlying assumptions. First, they assume that many of the roads that counties would claim are not highways or even roads, "but instead are remote jeep trails, dry desert streambeds, even cow paths" that "do little, if anything, to meet reasonable transportation needs." In addition, they assume that the counties plan to develop these non-existent roads and that vehicle use would increase even on undisputed existing roads.³ Underlying this assumption is another about the counties' desire for economic development on public land. Finally, there is a more problematic assumption about the character of both the county officials and those who would be using these roads. The latter are seen to be likely to indulge in reckless behavior and illegal activities such as engaging in destructive ATV use, looting archaeological sites, and poaching, while the former are seen to condone such activities. I consider the implications of this representation of rural Americans in the section "August 2003."

Since the early 1970s longtime residents of the Grand Staircase-Escalante region have been experiencing opposition to the use and development of resources on the public lands that have traditionally supported their livelihoods. As these lands come to be valued more for amenity consumption than resource production, environmental groups have fought the development of coal mines on the Kaiparowits Plateau, the construction of a dam near Escalante, a proposed Trans-Escalante Highway that would have traversed the most rugged part of the region, the construction of Highway 12 between Boulder and Escalante, and road construction and timber sales in the Dixie National Forest, among other issues in the region. Local residents see environmental groups' oppositional stance on R.S. 2477 rights-of-way as one in a long series of environmentalist actions that threaten their livelihoods, culture, and sense of place. These accumulated experiences engender feelings that are reinforced in each new confrontation with environmental groups in the region. They help explain the intensity of local reactions and why the question of what was a road was so fraught.

The R.S. 2477 issue potentially affects private and state lands, in addition to public land. The public domain lands to which R.S. 2477 applies may have become private between 1866 and 1976 through homesteading or mining law provisions or may have been granted to states or other parties. Depending on how the gap in understanding R.S. 2477 rights-of-way is resolved, it could allow counties to claim access to roads that once existed on land that is now private or that federal land management agencies have already closed. For example, a couple who had bought a ranch in Kane County in the 1970s returned from a trip in 1997 to find that the lock on a gate and several No Trespassing signs had been removed from their property. They learned that the county attorney had taken these actions, without notification or explanation, because Kane County was claiming an R.S. 2477 road through their property. For more than two years, they tried to negotiate with county officials. Finally, after the county ran a road grader through their property in 1999, they filed a lawsuit and won.[4]

Beginning in 1979 the federal government issued regulations to implement the provisions of FLPMA and resolve its ambiguity about roads. Initially, the regulations provided an opportunity for state and county governments to file maps with the BLM showing the location of roads constructed under the authority of R.S. 2477 that they claimed as valid existing rights. The federal government would then establish an administrative process for validating these claims. But little progress was made because attempts were subject to the changing policies of successive presidential administrations and whichever party controlled Congress. For example, during the Carter administration, the Attorney General's Office issued a letter concluding that "in order for a valid right-of-way to come into existence, there must have been the actual building of a highway." The Reagan administration adopted a different interpretation in the Hodel Policy, which provided that "road maintenance over several years" and "the passage of vehicles by users over time may equal actual construction."[5] During the Clinton administration, the Interior Department proposed new regulations that would have established such a process, but the rules were never finalized because Republicans took over Congress later that year and imposed a temporary moratorium on further R.S. 2477 regulations, making it permanent in 1996. The moratorium meant that progress on the R.S. 2477 roads issue could be made only through Congress or the federal courts. Prevented from creating new regulations, Interior Secretary Bruce Babbitt issued a departmental policy statement that revoked the Hodel Policy and declared that state law should be used to decide R.S. 2477, to the extent it is consistent with federal law.

The Grand Staircase-Escalante region became a focus for the R.S. 2477 road issue as early as the 1980s. Responding to the opportunity to file maps, Garfield and Kane Counties, following the lead of San Juan County in southeast Utah, produced maps for the BLM of what they considered their R.S. 2477 roads. Environmental groups participating in the Utah Wilderness Coalition's citizen wilderness reinventory in the 1980s took photographs of roads on county maps and used them to challenge the roads' existence and discredit the counties' claims. In response, because only roadless areas were to be considered for inclusion in the National Wilderness Preservation System, the counties used GPS devices to map county roads in areas the coalition claimed should be classified as wilderness and published photographs of them. The tactic of using photographs and maps of specific roads to discredit the other side continued to be employed throughout the conflict over R.S. 2477 roads in Utah.

Lacking an administrative process for resolving R.S. 2477 disputes, they often wound up in the federal courts, whose findings filled in some of the gaps left by FLPMA. Two prominent cases involving R.S. 2477 rights-of-way originated in Garfield County. In the mid-1980s the county's plan to improve and pave the Burr Trail, which traverses what is now the northeastern part of GSENM, became contentious locally when some residents who had recently moved to Boulder, the Burr Trail's western terminus, organized to oppose the county's plan. Their organization later became the wilderness advocacy group Southern Utah Wilderness Alliance (SUWA), a key actor in the roads dispute on GSENM. While the county's right-of-way was not in question, the opponents sued to challenge whether FLPMA gave the county the right to widen and pave the road. The case established that state law should control the scope of the right-of-way, and the county was able to proceed with its plan. In early 1996 the federal government sued Garfield County after road crews performed what they called routine maintenance at the entrance to Capitol Reef National Park without obtaining a permit from the National Park Service. The county lost that case, which established that even when a county has an R.S. 2477 right-of-way, it does not have unfettered ability to control what happens within the right-of-way. Thus when GSENM was created, it was still unclear how local governments could establish a valid R.S. 2477 right-of-way. As long as this was the case, the roads remained under the de facto control of the federal government.

Since the creation of GSENM, the struggle to resolve the R.S. 2477 roads issue has largely played out on GSENM because the Monument Management Plan, approved in 1999, proposed to limit access to or close many primitive roads, implying that the BLM would ignore county rights-of-way as it reterritorialized GSENM as national landscape. Kane and Garfield Counties were determined to claim their rights-of-way and prevent that from happening. Until 2017 the conflict over who controls backcountry roads in GSENM was the longest-running, most divisive and acrimonious conflict locally and statewide, and the most publicized issue on GSENM since the monument was created. What is at stake is not just how public land will be managed but who owns it. The question of who controls roads on GSENM is a question of sovereignty—who controls the territory—as well as government, meaning how the territory is managed. The contrasting agendas of different administrations and opposing rulings of federal court judges appointed by the various administrations continued to complicate the road conflict on GSENM described in this chapter.

"Road Wars" on GSENM

Table 2 is a timeline of events in the conflict over roads from 1996 to 2009.[6] A year-by-year description of how it unfolded follows. This detailed analysis is meant to illuminate the intricate and drawn-out process by which the participants—Kane and Garfield Counties, the state of Utah, the BLM, all branches of the federal government, local residents, environmental groups, the media, and the general public—negotiated the answer to "What is a road?" This struggle had implications for public land throughout the West. The analysis shows how participants adjusted prior understandings; altered their strategies and tactics, alliances, and oppositions; and drew on different forms of legitimation and understandings of democracy in response to new circumstances. In particular, it focuses on the efforts of local actors to have rights-of-way recognized de jure by FLPMA also recognized de facto by the federal government. Their efforts were overwhelmingly characterized by the media and environmental groups in derogatory ways that dismissed the significance and logic of their participation in an agonistic process that contested the reterritorialization of public land as national landscape.

TABLE 2. Timeline for roads dispute on GSENM up until 2009

1996	Grand Staircase-Escalante National Monument (GSENM) created.
September 1996	Garfield and Kane Counties grade R.S. 2477 claimed roads in GSENM, wilderness study areas, and lands being considered for wilderness study areas.
October 1996	SUWA files suit against the counties and against BLM for failing to protect these areas. Federal government files trespass actions against the counties.
1997	Congress imposes moratorium on Interior Department R.S. 2477 regulations.
November 1998	Draft Monument Management Plan (MMP) released.
December 1998	Kane County and BLM reach tentative agreement on roads in GSENM (which later breaks down).
February 2000	MMP goes into effect.
March 2000	Governor Mike Leavitt announces massive lawsuit to determine R.S. 2477 road ownership (which was never filed).
December 2000	Monument manager Kate Cannon and Kane County Commission reach agreement on numbering system for roads within GSENM.
2001	U.S. District Court judge Tena Campbell rules against R.S. 2477 highway claims asserted by Garfield and Kane Counties in 1996 case. Counties appeal.
January 2003	Interior Department publishes final regulations on "disclaimers of interest."
April 2003	Memorandum of Understanding between the State of Utah and the Department of the Interior on State and County Road Acknowledgment signed.
August 2003	Kane County officials remove BLM signs from roads in GSENM.
November 2003	Kane County officials receive grand jury subpoenas.
February 2004	Judge Campbell reaffirms 2001 ruling; counties appeal again. General Accounting Office finds Utah memorandum of understanding (MOU) illegal.

February 2005	Kane County begins installing signs on class D county roads.
March 2005	Utah State Legislature passes H.B. 264 to clarify state's position on public land issues.
April 2005	BLM Utah state director gives Kane County two weeks to remove signs or face legal action.
June 2005	Deadline passes without removal of signs. Case referred to U.S. attorney for Utah.
September 2005	Tenth Circuit Court of Appeals reverses Judge Campbell's 2004 decision. Kane County passes an ordinance opening all roads in the county to ATVs unless closed by it.
October 2005	Environmental groups file suit against Kane County for enacting road ordinance. Kane and Garfield Counties file suit against Interior Department challenging transportation and water planning in MMP.
March 2006	Outgoing secretary of the interior Gale Norton signs new guidelines for resolving R.S. 2477 rights-of-way.
December 2006	Kane County rescinds ATV ordinance.
June 2007	Kame and Garfield Counties' 2005 lawsuit dismissed as premature because the counties first had to prove ownership of each road.
September 2007	BLM issues preliminary decision in its first nonbinding determination under the Norton policy for Bald Knoll Road in Kane County.
May 2008	Judge Campbell rules against Kane County in lawsuit filed in October 2005, finding that the county had violated the Constitution's Supremacy Clause.
April 2009	Tenth Circuit Court of Appeals upholds 2007 dismissal of Kane and Garfield Counties' lawsuit.
May 2009	Protest ride in Paria Canyon.

Source: Created by the author.

1996

In October 1996, in a decisive action that could be interpreted as protest against the creation of GSENM the previous month, Garfield and Kane Counties sent out road crews with bulldozers to grade R.S. 2477 claimed roads within the new monument, including roads in existing and proposed wilderness study areas.[7] SUWA, which by that time had developed into a large organization with substantial funding and pursued wilderness advocacy primarily through litigation, immediately sued the counties for illegal actions and the BLM for failing to protect the areas. Later that month the federal government sued the counties for trespass. The resulting court cases dragged on for ten years and turned out to be crucial in the ongoing R.S. 2477 debate. Then Garfield County commissioner Louise Liston explained the county's actions this way: "We've been debating and fighting over [this issue] for a long time, and maybe the courts will have to decide. We've been harassed, threatened, and intimidated by federal officials for working on those roads. Maybe it's time to find out who they really belong to."[8]

The counties accomplished two things with this action. First, they asserted local government power in response to what they perceived as a misuse of federal executive power when the monument was created. And second, they took an action that intentionally provoked a federal court case in expectation that it would result in a judicial decision resolving the ambiguous status of R.S. 2477 roads in their favor. This strategy of deploying different levels and branches of government against each other to try to achieve a goal draws on several principles of democratic government established in the Constitution: limited government, separation of powers, checks and balances, and federalism. It was a strategy that was used repeatedly by various participants in the conflict over roads.

In response to the counties' actions, U.S. Attorney Scott Matheson asserted, "There is a right way and a wrong way for the counties to assert their road claims. The course they have followed is the wrong way because it violates our fundamental commitment to the rule of law. We obviously feel the need to assert the claims of the federal government in the face of their outright defiance. The counties should pursue their road claims within our legal framework, not bulldoze first and litigate later."[9]

In fact, there was no "right way" and "wrong way," and no "legal framework" existed for the counties to "pursue their road claims," which was the point they were trying to make. The U.S. attorney drew on a democratic imaginary of the rule of law in which local governments must respect public land laws made by the federal government. Drawing attention to the counties' unruliness deflected attention from the fact that the federal government had failed to provide a clear rule. Spokespeople for environmental groups described the counties as "spoiled, rotten children desecrating our national monument" and declared their alarm at "this rash of lawless behavior."[10] By characterizing the counties' actions as unruly or childish, these comments dismissed their arguments and excluded them from the arena of rational debate central to a deliberative understanding of democracy. Opponents of the counties' position used this tactic throughout the conflict over roads.

This initial provocation set up a dynamic among the executive and judicial branches of the federal government, Garfield and Kane Counties, and environmental organizations, principally SUWA, that shifted throughout the timeline of events as new developments occurred and new participants entered the conflict.

1998–99

The process of developing a Monument Management Plan (MMP) for GSENM, including a Transportation Plan, set the stage for the next developments in the unfolding roads conflict. The 1969 National Environmental Policy Act required public input into the federal land use planning processes—a requirement that reflects a democratic imaginary that decision-making should include the input of all affected and interested parties. Therefore, when the monument released a draft MMP in November 1998, it held a series of open houses to gather public comment on the draft. Locally, the open houses were poorly attended. Garfield County commissioner Maloy Dodds explained why: "The attitude here is we have been beat down [by the federal government] so many times, what's the use of getting involved." Kane County commissioner Norm Carroll offered a similar rationale: "People here still don't agree with the way it all happened, and some of them still feel very strongly about that. But they feel the management plan is a done deal, and any input at this point isn't going to do a lot of good."[11] These comments confirm what an Escalante resident told me about why local people didn't go to the federal agencies' public comment meetings anymore: "We've been whipped every time. For us, the battle goes back before the monument, before the reservoir. You get tired of losing all the time."

These comments identify another area of accumulated experience in the region and the feelings associated with it that affect longtime residents' perceptions of GSENM: that it was futile to participate in public input processes and expect their voices to be heard. They believed that the agencies had already made their decisions and the meetings were just a formality required by law, rather than a real opportunity for participation. Residents who had moved into the region more recently did not share this experience and were more likely to attend the meetings.

In addition to the public meetings, the BLM solicited written comments on the draft MMP. One local citizen who submitted comments was Mark Habbeshaw. His experience with the MMP preceded his experience commenting on the environmental assessments described in the previous chapter. To pursue his love of the outdoors, as he got older, Habbeshaw had taken up off-road motorcycling. He joined the local jeep club when he moved to Kanab and volunteered to investigate the roads issue for the newly formed Kanab branch of People for the USA, an organization formed in 1988 to further the goals of the Wise Use movement. He started with one of the roads he had ridden many times that was slated for closure and tried to understand the rationale for its closure. He spoke with several key people, documented their conversation, and included this information in his comments. When the final MMP was released, the road remained open. Looking back, he identified this as the pivotal experience that propelled him into local politics. It gave him confidence in the process, showed him that "if you validly participate, you can make a difference," and inspired him to volunteer for the Kane County Resource Committee. His experience validated an imaginary of participatory democracy. As he had in the conflict over grazing retirements on GSENM, Habbeshaw went on to become a leading figure in the dispute over roads on the monument.

While the process of preparing an MMP was underway, monument manager Jerry Meredith was holding discussions with the Garfield and Kane County Commissions about which roads on the new monument they would maintain. Counties take responsibility for maintaining the roads in their transportation systems and receive money from the federal government to do so. By maintaining the roads, they feel they are both maintaining their claims to them and providing jobs for local residents. Meredith hoped to forestall problems with the counties if the MMP recommended closing some the roads.[12]

In December 1998 Meredith reached a tentative agreement with Kane County, in which Garfield County did not participate. He was pleased that the county seemed to be working with the monument: "Everybody is really trying. Both sides would like to find an agreement that doesn't mean years in court and millions of dollars in attorney fees." Kane County commissioner Joe Judd, who had been fiercely opposed to GSENM when it was created, confirmed that county officials were trying to work in partnership with the monument to resolve conflicts in an amicable way. SUWA also altered its attitude toward Kane County, acknowledging, "Kane County deserves a lot of credit."[13] The groups who had opposed each other over the road-grading incident seemed to be working together toward a consensus. However, the theory of agonistic democracy maintains that in modern pluralistic democracies, consensus can be achieved only by excluding or overpowering some viewpoints. In this case, a group of Kane County citizens, who had not been part of the discussions between the county commissioners and the monument manager, voiced strong opposition to the agreement because it would require that the county give up R.S. 2477 rights-of-way on the monument. As a result, the agreement eventually fell through.

2000

In February 2000 the final MMP went into effect. The Transportation Plan divided the monument into four zones—Frontcountry, Passage, Outback, and Primitive—that would be managed differently to allow or exclude specific activities. It prohibited all off-road vehicle use, including bicycling, and limited street-legal vehicles, ATVs, and bicycles to roads posted as open to them, none of which would be in the Primitive Zone.[14] By the time the MMP went into effect, Kate Cannon was monument manager. She also tried to negotiate a road agreement with Kane and Garfield Counties. She was able to reach an agreement with the Kane County Commission by conceding that the county would not have to give up its R.S. 2477 rights-of-way. Garfield County again declined to participate in any agreement. When I first met Cannon in August 2000, she had just finalized the agreement with Kane County and was ecstatic. She admitted that the roads issue was being closely monitored in Washington DC and that her negotiating guidelines came "from above," although she had "some wiggle room." Before making an agreement, she would call to check whether it was acceptable.

In March the state of Utah joined the R.S. 2477 debate, altering its dynamics. Utah governor Mike Leavitt, frustrated by the piecemeal creation of R.S. 2477 policy from individual federal-county court cases or agreements, proposed a more comprehensive approach to the issue: a massive lawsuit against the federal government involving the thousands of R.S. 2477 roads claims made by Utah counties. He invoked the welfare of Utah's rural population to legitimate the state's intervention: "We have to resolve this.... The issue is too fundamental to the future of rural Utah to leave it alone."[15]

When the state of Utah entered the debate, possibilities for alliances and oppositions increased, and strategies for negotiating power shifted. The same group of Kane County citizens who had opposed their commissioners' first roads agreement with the monument also opposed the new agreement with Cannon. But this time they opposed the agreement because they feared it would undermine the state's proposed lawsuit. They brought the second agreement before a Utah district court, which put it on hold. The state's proposed lawsuit never materialized, however. Anticipating that the George W. Bush administration, which had just taken office, would be more sympathetic to its goals, the state changed its strategy and began negotiating with the Department of Interior (DOI).

In December the Kane County Commission approved the road-numbering system for GSENM proposed by Cannon. Minutes from the commission meeting indicate that three types of signs were approved: those for numbering roads, indicating points of interest, and warning drivers to stay on the road. However, when the signs were installed, some also displayed restrictions prohibiting motorcycles and ATVs. The commissioners expressed their disapproval of the restrictions to Cannon, who said they were a "mistake" and would be removed.[16]

It is not clear whether the restrictive road signs were really a mistake or an attempt to make the Transportation Plan in the MMP an accomplished fact without officially recognizing Kane County's rights-of-way. The state operates in many zones of indeterminacy where things happen or do not happen for unknown reasons, and it is often difficult to distinguish the personal motivations of bureaucrats from official rationales. In this case, this seemingly small "mistake" violated the democratic principle of transparency in government and had a disproportionately large effect on how events in the dispute over roads on GSENM played out.

2001–3

In June 2001 U.S. District Court judge Tena Campbell, who was appointed during the Clinton administration, ruled against the counties in the lawsuit SUWA brought against them for grading roads in GSENM in 1996. The counties claimed they were maintaining existing rights-of-way. Her decision hinged on the interpretation of the word "highway" in the original 1866 Mining Act. She ruled that to be valid claims, roads must lead to specific destinations and show evidence of purposeful, mechanical construction, offering a new answer to the question "What is a road?" A spokesperson for SUWA concluded, "This ruling will finally bring some reason to the debate," once again casting the counties as "unreasonable."[17] The counties appealed the ruling.

In light of this decision, the new Bush administration, which supported more local control of public land, turned to the administrative arena to facilitate federal recognition of R.S. 2477 rights-of-way. In January 2003 the BLM finalized revised regulations on a "disclaimer of interest," mentioned in FLPMA. This procedure eliminates the necessity for legislation or court action to decide whether the federal government has an ownership or lesser interest in a disputed piece of property and effectively allows the BLM to relinquish the right-of-way for a road to a county. Environmentalists anticipated the new rule would result in thousands of proposals, saying, "We're going to have to fight them route by route."[18]

In April 2003 the state of Utah's negotiations with the DOI resulted in the Memorandum of Understanding between the State of Utah and the Department of the Interior on State and County Road Acknowledgment, which established an acknowledgment process for determining R.S. 2477 rights-of-way in Utah using the new disclaimer rule. The state agreed not to use this new rule in national parks, wildlife refuges, wilderness areas, and wilderness study areas. Governor Leavitt and Interior Secretary Gale Norton extolled the cooperation between the federal government and the state of Utah as a breakthrough in the R.S. 2477 saga. "For more than 25 years, road-ownership disputes have strained relationships between Western states and the federal government," said Norton. "It's time to find solutions and we're doing that in Utah with this agreement."[19] Garfield County commissioner Maloy Dodds was less enthusiastic about R.S. 2477 agreements that did not include the counties' input. SUWA saw the disclaimer rule and the memorandum of understanding (MOU) as being the result of "secret, closed-door negotiations" and "part of an overall strategy to attack wilderness lands in Utah and to make sure any lands designated for wilderness are held to the barest minimum."[20] Changing tactics, environmental groups invoked the Republican Congress's 1996 moratorium on new R.S. 2477 regulations, which had formerly been used against them, to oppose the disclaimer rule and the MOU, arguing that they violated the moratorium.

The disclaimer rule and the MOU could be seen as reflecting a civic republican democratic imaginary of smaller, decentralized government where decisions that affect local residents should be made by local governments. More realistically, the agreement represents an attempt to exclude dissenting voices from the R.S. 2477 debate. For once, the counties and environmentalists shared the same concern over being left out of the negotiations between the state of Utah and the Interior

Department, and both felt mistrustful of the process. Their feelings reflect a democratic imaginary in which decision-making should be inclusive and transparent.

Habbeshaw took on his duties as county commissioner in early 2003. Soon after taking office, he wrote to monument manager Dave Hunsaker and requested that the restrictive roads signs placed when Cannon was monument manager, which were still in place, be removed. Both Commissioner Habbeshaw's words and actions indicated that in his view, democracy works through the rule of law, and when the government fails to obey its own laws, it is up to citizens to force compliance. Nevertheless, one of his first actions in office, which was intended to further discussion of the roads issue on GSENM, was condemned by many as illegal.

AUGUST 2003

On August 13, 2003, the issue of R.S. 2477 roads, which remained unresolved despite the continuing negotiation among environmental groups, different levels and branches of government, and local actors to clarify it, suddenly took on a new urgency. That day Commissioner Habbeshaw and Kane County sheriff Lamont Smith drove through the portion of GSENM lying in Kane County and removed thirty-one road signs with restrictions on motorcycle and ATV use that had been placed by the BLM when Kate Cannon was the monument manager. They deposited the signs at monument headquarters in Kanab, along with a letter citing a state law that allows removal of unauthorized signs on state and county rights-of-way and requesting that the monument manager remove remaining signs on county roads.

Habbeshaw explained later that when no progress in negotiations with Dave Hunsaker had been made by August, he decided that "a definite action that would create change" was needed. "Had we not removed the signs there would be no impetus to consider this. We had to force the issue somehow."[21] Sheriff Smith evoked the experience and feelings of many longtime residents: "As usual, we have been totally ignored. We felt this was the only way to let them know we are serious."[22] Monument manager Dave Hunsaker claimed that the officials' action "completely took us by surprise. At no time was there an indication that we were at an impasse."[23] Invoking a zone of indeterminacy in the state created by the discontinuity of government service and bureaucracy's insistence on authorized procedure and documentation, he denied knowledge of the disputed signs: "I have heard various stories. But I have nothing in writing."[24] Habbeshaw understood that the signs signified more than restrictions the county had not agreed to: "A federal road number connotes federal ownership."[25]

The county officials' objectives were the same as those of the counties that had graded roads in the monument in 1996: to assert county authority over the roads and to provoke the federal government into taking some action that would bring the issue to court. These actions shared the same democratic impulse as that of the ranchers who recovered cattle impounded from the monument in 2000 as well as the Declaration of Independence: to assert the sovereignty of the people in the face of a sovereign whose action, or inaction, they feel has rendered that authority illegitimate. Democratic theorist Iris Marion Young pointed out, "Disorderly, disruptive, annoying or distracting means of communication are often necessary or effective elements in . . . efforts to engage others in debate over issues and outcomes."[26]

In this case, inaction was to the BLM's advantage: as long as the issue of R.S. 2477 rights-of-way was left unresolved, the BLM had de facto control over the roads while the counties continued to maintain them. Since the BLM did not officially recognize any Kane County roads in GSENM, and since removing federal signs from federal lands was a crime, the BLM could have charged the local officials with a crime. But then the officials would have the opportunity to argue in court that their actions were lawful because the roads belonged to the county. Habbeshaw insisted that he was only trying to keep the federal government from asserting a power it did not legitimately possess: "I'm not a criminal. I'm protecting the rights of the county with as much good faith as I can do it."[27] He was confident that the county had the law on its side: "County officials have acted responsibly and believe their actions will not only receive public support but, more importantly, will prevail in judicial review, whether in state or federal court."[28]

The county officials' definitive action succeeded in rousing all the participants in the R.S. 2477 dispute and made state and national news, thereby mobilizing even more participants. A BLM law enforcement official said the agency was "looking into" the incident.[29] State officials reacted with dismay. Referring to the recently signed MOU, an aide to Governor Leavitt stated, "It's very unfortunate. We have a cooperative process going on here to identify roads. I just think it's not good timing to be doing things outside that effort."[30] The *Salt Lake Tribune* published letters to the editor that either vehemently supported or condemned the officials' actions. The Garfield County commissioners expressed their support for the action. SUWA used the incident as an opportunity to claim common ground with Kane County residents, whom they perceived to be typical conservatives: anti-environmental, anti-tax, and pro-property rights. The organization sent a letter to Kane and Garfield County residents warning them that their private property rights were threatened by their commissioners' interpretation of R.S. 2477 and that their tax dollars were being wasted in legal battles to claim R.S. 2477 rights-of-way.[31]

The incident sent the town of Kanab into an uproar. Some residents praised the county officials for protecting local rights and challenging federal "tyranny"; others condemned them for exacerbating local divisions and tarnishing Kanab's image. The Kanab City Council split evenly in its appraisal of the incident. People from all over the country sent letters to the editor to the local newspaper, the *Southern Utah News*, supporting one side or the other. The words of a Montana resident illustrate the predominant perception of the events by someone outside of southern Utah: "In planning future vacation travel, my wife and I came across your website, but after reading about the actions of the Kane County Commissioners we consider travel to your area right up there with war-torn third world countries in Africa."[32] Some friends who met over coffee to discuss how they could support the monument formed a group called Friends of the Monument. It eventually developed into Grand Staircase Escalante Partners, whose mission was "to assist Grand Staircase-Escalante National Monument in its mission by raising public awareness, support and funding."[33]

On August 25 the Kane County commissioners, joined by the Garfield County commissioners, the mayor of Kanab, and the local state representative and state senator, sent a letter to BLM state director Sally Wisely expressing dissatisfaction not just with the way the roads issue was being handled but with the way the monument was being managed in general. The letter criticized the environmentalist leanings of the monument staff and suggested that the staff should be downsized and the monument manager reduced in grade.[34] The *Southern Utah News* published the letter, stirring up the controversy even more. In September Utah senator Orrin Hatch sent a letter to the DOI's Office of Inspector General asking for an investigation of monument management practices. The investigators interviewed twenty-one current and former monument employees, including Kate Cannon, and concluded that while most believed that Cannon had "a strong anti-grazing management philosophy," confirming longtime residents' beliefs about her, there was no evidence that she or Dave Hunsaker had broken the law.[35]

The county officials had explained their actions in terms reflecting the idea that in a democracy, local voices should be heard and their concerns should be addressed by the federal government. Whether or not their actions would be successful in provoking a response from the federal government, they had succeeded in broadening awareness of the R.S. 2477 issue, heightening its emotional impact, and drawing more people into the conflict in some way. Many residents experienced these events negatively, as something that was "tearing the community of Kanab apart"; in contrast, Commissioner Habbeshaw felt, "We should embrace honest debate," reflecting an imaginary of deliberative or agonistic democracy.

The *Salt Lake Tribune* had been attentively reporting events on GSENM ever since the uproar over its creation. With the latest developments in the conflict over roads, its coverage became more sensational and more openly biased. Table 3 gives examples of headlines describing the conflict before and after August 13, 2003. After this date headlines introducing developments in the roads conflict labeled it as a "road war," "revolt," "feud," or "fray," in which the counties were on the wrong side. County officials were represented as "road warriors" and their actions as "road rage," "vandalism," and "the tactics of a scofflaw."[36]

TABLE 3. Headlines describing the conflict over roads on GSENM before and after August 13, 2003

Year	Headline
1996	"Feds Sue to Halt Road Work in Wild Utah Areas" (October 19)
1998	"Monument Roads Issue Resolved" (December 11)
2000	"Leavitt Takes On Dirt-Road Ownership" (March 17) "Kane Considers Roads Deal with Feds" (August 16) "Burr Case Crucial to Road War" (October 30)
2001	"Conservationists Smell Victory in Road Ruling" (June 28)
2003	"Deal Struck on Control of Roads on Public Land" (April 10)
2003	"Removal of Signs Reignites Road War" (August 20) "AG Didn't OK Kane Revolt" (August 26)
2005	"County Is Again Raising Kane over Roads" (February 16) "Kane County Ups Ante in Road Feud with Feds" (March 19) "Monument Fray Heats Up" (April 27) "Rural Road-Sign Rage Erupting Again" (July 16) "Feud over Monument Signs Just Keeps Heating Up" (November 15) "Rebellion in Kane County" (November 21) "In Utah, Trying to Undo a Federal Claim Bit by Bit" (*New York Times*, November 24)
2006	"Garfield May Join Kane County Road War" (January 11)
2009	"Road Warriors to Roar vs. BLM Ban" (May 7)

Note: All were printed in the *Salt Lake Tribune* except for the one designated otherwise.

Source: Created by the author.

The *Tribune* published an interview with a former BLM employee who referred to the county officials and signatories of the letter of August 24 as "the village idiot choir" and "local criminals" who were "taking the law into their own hands and proclaiming their own glory."[37] The paper repeatedly referred to the 1866 Mining Act as "a Civil War–era law," implying that it was outdated and those who used it to legitimate their claims were therefore backward, ignorant, and behind the times. It also published cartoons that depicted county officials with small heads and large bellies encouraging unrestricted off-road vehicle use on public land (see figs. 14 and 15). The *Tribune* continued to use this type of rhetoric and representation in reporting subsequent developments in the conflict. SUWA reported on the events in its quarterly member newsletter in an article titled "Kane Kounty Kapers": "It had all the makings of a Wild West showdown: a sheriff, a county official, a pair of vigilantes, a federal government office, a dispute over who owns property, and dramatic scenery as a backdrop. But in this case, there was a peculiar twist to the facts—the sheriff and county official were the vigilantes."[38] This portrayal was consistent with the way the organization typically represented residents of rural Utah in its newsletter. This biased media coverage may have contributed to the polarization of the issue as well as the anger of local actors portrayed in this way.

The representation of rural residents as backward, irrational, lawless, and disorderly reinforces an image of the federal government as enlightened, rational, lawful, and orderly and validates the claim that public land should be under the control of federal and not local government. This technique of representation creates a dichotomy between reason and emotion and therefore "between a rational elite and social categories that are ruled by their passions" and are thus unfit to govern.[39] Demonizing the other is also a typical strategy in resource conflicts where the state or an environmental organization is trying to gain control over resources to "protect" them from local inhabitants who use them and could be considered to have a prior right.[40]

In their 2002 study, geographers Lucy Jarosz and Victoria Lawson offered further insight into why rural people in the United States might be represented in this way. They examined "redneck" discourse as it is applied to poor, white, rural people in the contemporary United States, arguing that in the current context of rapid economic restructuring in the United States and, in particular, of rural restructuring in the American West, this discourse served to obscure these materialist processes, the increasingly uneven development between rural and urban areas, and the sharpening of class differences that was resulting. "Redneck" discourse represents rural poverty as a lifestyle choice or a cultural trait, reinforcing a neoliberal ideology that emphasizes personal freedom and responsibility. Individuals are seen to be free to choose not only products but also lifestyles and cultures; therefore, personal failure is a result of personal failings. Jarosz and Larson added that "redneck" discourse also served to defuse middle-class anxiety about upward mobility and disguise white racism as redneck racism.[41] This discourse and the ignorance of rural life and contempt for rural Americans it reflects have real effects, contributing to rural anger, the feeling that the federal government serves only urban and elite interests, and the election of Donald Trump.[42]

In September 2003 monument manager Dave Hunsaker turned the road sign removal incident over to BLM law enforcement officials. In November the two county officials received subpoenas to appear before a federal grand jury. When I interviewed Commissioner Habbeshaw in December, he admitted he was worried but willing to accept the consequences of his actions. "We're not looking for fights," he told me. "All we're looking for is recognition of local needs and then we'll bend over backward to make it work." However, in what appeared to be a continuation of the federal government's strategy of keeping the R.S. 2477 road issue out of the courts, it did not proceed with a case against the two officials.

2004

In February 2004 Judge Campbell reaffirmed her 2001 ruling in the 1996 case against Garfield and Kane Counties. The counties again appealed the decision, and the case went to the Tenth Circuit Court of Appeals. That same month the General Accounting Office (renamed the Government Accountability Office later in 2004) found that while the BLM's disclaimer regulations did not violate the moratorium on federal regulations that the 1996 Republican Congress had passed, the state of Utah–Interior

14. & 15. Cartoons from the *Salt Lake Tribune*, August 27, 2003, A12, and September 10, 2003, A8.

Department MOU did and was therefore illegal. This rendered the state of Utah's current strategy of partnering with the federal government to resolve the R.S. 2477 roads issue untenable. When progress on resolving the R.S. 2477 issue seemed to have stalled again, Kane County tried a new tactic to prod the federal government into taking action.

2005

In early 2005 Kane County began installing its own signs on all class D roads on BLM-administered land within the county, including GSENM.[43] County crews first began installing signs on land, including wilderness study areas, administered by the Kanab Field Office, then on roads in GSENM. The signs used a road-numbering system devised by the county that differed from the one the BLM was using on the monument. In some cases, the county placed signs allowing ATV access close to existing BLM signs prohibiting it (see fig. 16). Commissioner Habbeshaw explained why the county had adopted the new tactic: "We decided we needed to start managing our roads instead of being afraid to act like they are our roads."[44] He emphasized, "We are trying to work with the BLM, and I think that's been demonstrated in a number of instances. At the same time, we can't let them dictate over our property rights."[45] This last statement reveals one reason rural Utah counties so doggedly pursued the R.S. 2477 issue: they considered rights-of-way property rights, and thus they were defending their private property from confiscation by the federal government. However, because there is a not a single right of ownership but rather a bundle of legal rights associated with property ownership, the county soon learned that rights-of-way and the right to manage the roads the way it wanted to were two different issues.[46]

In addition to keeping primitive roads open to provide access to public land for local residents, southern Utah counties wanted to keep them open to ATVs both to support a form of recreation enjoyed by many county residents and to encourage off-road tourism as a source of income. To mitigate local opposition when GSENM was created, its supporters had assured local residents that they would benefit from the increased tourism the monument would bring. However, the kind of tourism monument supporters had in mind was class-based: hikers, backpackers,

16. Conflicting road signs from BLM (foreground) and Kane County (background). Courtesy of the author.

and genteel automotive tourists who stop at visitors' centers and overlooks, stay in motels or campgrounds, and eat in local restaurants. From their perspective, ATVs represented a threat to monument lands, not a tourism opportunity, and ATV users were seen as the same kind of "rednecks" as local residents.

At first the BLM responded to Kane County's new tactic by representing it as a refusal to participate in an ongoing federal planning process. An official in the Utah BLM office told a reporter, "It's disappointing. We've had a standing request, expressing our desire to help them with a map identifying trails. For them to act unilaterally seems more confrontational than collaborative."[47] From Habbeshaw's perspective, however, it was "clear that BLM planning will attempt to close and restrict county roads while failing to properly recognize existing county rights on those same roads."[48] The *Salt Lake Tribune* continued to portray the county's signing project as a "road war."

With the state of Utah–Interior Department MOU invalidated, the state needed a new strategy. In March it solidified an alliance with rural Utah counties by passing H.B. 264, State Land Use Management Plans Amendments. The bill was intended to unify and clarify the state's position on several public land issues. Regarding roads, the bill stated that "transportation and access provisions for all other existing routes, roads, and trails across federal, state, and school trust lands within the state should be determined and identified, and agreements should be executed and implemented, as necessary to fully authorize and determine responsibility for maintenance of all routes, roads, and trails." To implement the new law, the state developed the Public Roads over Public Lands Project (which gave rise to the Public Lands Policy Coordination Office), a joint effort between the Governor's Office and the Attorney General's Office to assert state and local ownership over "established public roads" on federal lands.[49] The project's first effort included filing lawsuits against the federal government over roads in Emery and Box Elder Counties.

The next development in the road sign dispute was a letter to Kane County in April from BLM state director Sally Wisely that gave the county two weeks to take down the signs it had posted or face legal action. In addition to representing the signs as unauthorized, the letter characterized them as a public safety issue: "These signs have been placed without proper authorization and most are in conflict with current management plans and direction. I am very concerned that such actions, which result in conflicting management directives, may likely present serious safety issues to members of the public, possibly subject them to legal exposure, and cause resource damage."[50] With sovereignty over roads on public land in question, the letter portrayed the BLM as more fit to "govern" roads because it was more concerned with "the welfare of the population" than was Kane County. The letter called on county officials, as fellow "public servants" concerned with the public welfare, to work with the BLM to resolve the roads issue without endangering their constituents and without litigation.

The May deadline came and went, with Kane County resolutely refusing to remove the signs. Commissioner Habbeshaw affirmed that the county was preparing to meet the BLM in court. Meanwhile, some of the county signs disappeared, and others had the ATV-permitted symbols covered with ATV-prohibited symbols. Eventually, the county removed some of the signs itself. In June the state of Utah began to take on the role of mediator. At the request of Utah lieutenant governor Gary Herbert, Kane and Garfield County commissioners began meeting with BLM officials and the state attorney general's staff over the issue. Herbert explained why the state got involved: "Our hope is to lower the rhetoric and get something done, as opposed to all this saber rattling. This meeting was a start in that direction." After the meeting, Sally Wisely commented, "I don't know if at this point anything has really changed, but we did have a good dialog, and I hope that can continue." And although Habbeshaw still insisted that Kane County wanted its day in court, he acknowledged that "there was some movement toward common ground."[51] Later that month the DOI formally asked the U.S. Attorney's Office to take action against the county. Recognizing the "delicate balance between autonomy and control in the relationship between state and society," a former U.S. attorney for Utah expressed the opinion that the U.S. Attorney's Office was unlikely to take any immediate action because "any court action really intensifies feelings down there."[52]

In view of these developments, a group of Kane County citizens who did not agree with their commission's actions sent a letter to Interior

Secretary Gale Norton, asking her to take action in the dispute. Appealing to her known support of free-market solutions to public land conflicts, the letter asserted, "The economy of Kane County is largely dependent upon the scenic beauty of the nearby public lands, and we want to protect the goose that lays the golden egg for our economy."[53] Senator Dick Durbin of Illinois also urged the DOI to take action against Kane County, which he claimed was openly defying federal authority. To strengthen his request, he reminded the Interior Department that he could block the pending appointment of Lynn Scarlett as deputy secretary if necessary.

Fuel was added to the fire in July, when speakers at the Farm Bureau's annual conference compared Kane County's actions to a "fight against tyranny," "the shot heard 'round the world," "a man standing against a line of tanks," and "Tiananmen Square."[54] These comments received a jeering comeback in a *Salt Lake Tribune* editorial titled "Incendiary Inanities."[55] While the speakers' comments were hyperbolic, they celebrated the democratic impulse in the face of illegitimate authority.

On September 8, almost ten years after Garfield and Kane Counties had graded roads in GSENM in 1996, the Tenth Circuit Court of Appeals issued its final decision in the resulting lawsuit. In a complete about-face, it overturned the District Court's decision, which had been favorable to SUWA; rejected the argument that mechanical construction was necessary to establish an R.S. 2477 right-of-way; and held that a valid right-of-way could be created by use alone. It also ruled that the BLM did not have primary jurisdiction over R.S. 2477 disputes, although the bureau could make nonbinding determinations for land use planning purposes. It emphasized that courts should use state law to determine what actions were required for acceptance of an R.S. 2477 right-of-way, to the extent that state law did not conflict with federal law or policy. In Utah, this meant a road must have been in continuous use for ten years before 1976 to be a valid R.S. 2477 right-of-way.

This reversal strengthened Kane County's position and rewarded its persistence in appealing decisions unfavorable to it (with the help of funding from the state of Utah). Judges appointed by Democratic versus Republican administrations are likely to have different biases. By continuing to appeal, plaintiffs may eventually get a judge favorable to their position. Commissioner Habbeshaw found it "particularly supportive of the validity of our claims." The Utah assistant attorney general shared the county's approval of the decision: "We think this is a big step forward in fixing what the rules are."[56] The Interior Department admitted that the decision would compel it to reassess its policies on roads and to delay taking action against Kane County for its road signing. The Kane County Commission felt sufficiently confident to pass an ordinance later in September that opened all class D roads in Kane County to ATVs unless explicitly closed by the county.

SUWA was least satisfied with the decision. At first a spokesperson called it "a mixed bag," saying, "There's still a lot of confusion."[57] But soon environmental groups decided to take a definitive action of their own to bring clarity to the R.S. 2477 roads issue and end what they saw as the federal government's stalling tactics. In October, together with Earthjustice and the Wilderness Society, SUWA filed a suit against Kane County challenging its new road ordinance, which opened roads to ATVs that the BLM had closed to them. A spokesperson for the Wilderness Society explained, "The stakes are unbelievably high for public lands West-wide, not just in Utah. And what we have is an Interior Department that's essentially motionless."[58] Habbeshaw approved of the lawsuit: "All in all, I think this puts us on the proper course. Once they're judicially recognized, they're our rights-of-way forever. If a court tells us it's not our road, then we know and we can have certainty about it and we can move forward."[59]

Since 1996 environmental groups and southern Utah counties had been trying to get the judicial branch of the federal government to resolve the R.S. 2477 road issue in the face of Congress's inaction and the congressional moratorium on executive branch rulemaking. But the federal courts, too, seemed reluctant to resolve the issue once and for all. What might explain the federal government's inertia in the face of so much public pressure to resolve the issue? Habbeshaw believed that the federal government was avoiding having to recognize that the counties' claims were valid. The fact that the federal government did not pursue a case in the sign removal incident and again did nothing when Kane County failed to remove the signs it had placed reinforced his belief that the federal government was avoiding a confrontation that might decide the issue. A decision would be a lose-lose proposition: if the issue were decided in the counties' favor, the federal government would lose sovereignty over roads; if the decision went in the federal government's favor, it would have to start maintaining the roads.

In November Kane and Garfield Counties followed up on what they perceived to be the advantage they had gained in the Tenth Circuit decision. Adopting the tactic most often used by SUWA, the counties filed a lawsuit against the DOI, contesting the validity of the transportation planning in the MMP just before the statute of limitations for challenging it expired. In response, SUWA again appealed to local residents' assumed conservative sentiments with an advertisement in the *Southern Utah News* titled "Latest Lawsuit Is Un-American." The advertisement asserted that the lawsuit "contradicts the fundamental wisdom of our country's founding fathers," who intended that "the federal lands be managed for the good of all," implying that the counties were trying to promote the interests of a few over the those of all county residents and the national interest.[60]

A group of Kane County residents agreed and continued to make it known that their commissioners' stance on roads did not represent the views of everyone in the county. In a guest editorial in the *Southern Utah News*, a spokesperson for the group said, "There are a lot of locals—even some who ride [ATVs]—who are not pleased with the county's road [position]. They're holding their cards close to their chests because they don't want to be bullied." The group also circulated a petition in Kanab expressing their views. Habbeshaw contested the implication of these statements, insisting, "The Commission is open and listens to everyone." He also objected to the petition the group had circulated: "We've been seeking a judicial solution for years because that's the proper solution, not a petition initiated by a small segment of county residents."[61] In this exchange, participants evinced a democratic imaginary in which the right to free speech allows a variety of ways to express their opinions. The exchange also illustrates the actual paradox of modern liberal democracy resulting from the diversity of views among citizens. On the one hand, Habbeshaw believed he had been elected by, and was representing the views and interests of, "people who weren't having their interests represented." On the other hand, because of the demographic shifts taking place in the rural West, many Kane County residents who had moved in more recently did not share the views of longtime residents and felt that their county government did not represent them.

Throughout the summer and fall Kane County, BLM, and DOI officials continued to meet to try to work out an agreement on the road signs the county had placed. In December the *Salt Lake Tribune* reported that they were close to agreement. Participants offered encouraging comments, but no details, about the meetings. A SUWA representative again objected to the lack of transparency in the process, questioning, "Why is it that the Department of Interior and Kane County are comfortable only operating behind closed doors?"[62] But before an agreement could be reached, new developments intervened.

2006–7

In March 2006, before resigning her post, Interior Secretary Gale Norton signed new department guidelines for resolving R.S. 2477 road claims to replace the 1997 Babbitt policy. These guidelines largely reflected the Tenth Circuit decision and laid out a process the BLM could use to make administrative decisions on roads claimed by counties or states. The process would acknowledge that the BLM believed a right-of-way existed but did not "impose binding rights or obligations."[63] These nonbinding determinations would grant a virtual right-of-way: the counties would have the same road management decision-making power they would have with an actual right-of-way. The state of Utah hailed the new policy as a victory for states' rights and local control. But SUWA and the *Salt Lake Tribune* opposed it because they believed it defined a highway more broadly than the court ruling, did not exempt national parks and wilderness, and did not involve a public process.

In August a federal judge dismissed the lawsuit that SUWA and other environmental groups had filed against the BLM in connection with the counties' 1996 grading of roads in the monument. In the wake of the Tenth Circuit decision, the BLM had declined to contest the counties' action. But a spokesperson for SUWA insisted, "It's not over as long as the state and the counties fail to recognize what this is about. This isn't about roads. It's about who will control the future of our public lands, whether there will be any wilderness left to protect when the fallout clears."[64]

Two months later the legislative branch got involved in trying to resolve the R.S. 2477 roads issue. Republican representative Steve Pearce from New Mexico introduced H.R. 6298, a bill intended to start a discussion of what needed to be done to resolve the protracted R.S. 2477 roads dispute. It proposed a process for state and local governments to claim rights-of-way that bypassed the federal land management agencies, relaxed the standards for road claims the courts had established, but did not exempt national parks or defense installations from such claims. Although he expected the bill to be controversial, Commissioner Habbeshaw was pleased to see Congress finally taking a role in the R.S. 2477 roads debate. But a spokesperson for the Wilderness Society called the bill "the mother of all public land giveaways," saying, "This is such a threat to parks and wilderness that the public should be very concerned about this legislation."[65] The bill went nowhere.

Habbeshaw was reelected for a second term as county commissioner in November. Later that month Kane County was among the first Utah counties to submit requests to the BLM for nonbinding determinations of road claims under the new Norton policy. In December the Kane County Commission rescinded the ATV ordinance it had passed and announced its intent to remove ATV-permitted decals from county road signs. The decisions were based on advice received from the legal counsel representing Kane County in the lawsuit challenging the ordinance. Habbeshaw explained, "It's essentially too big a bite of the apple to defend our property rights and the management of OHVs at the same time. We're trying to secure our rights-of-way under R.S. 2477, and that is being overshadowed by the issue of OHV damage on federal lands, whether it's a real problem or not."[66] He indicated that his understanding of the county's rights-of-way had shifted, and so had his stance on managing the roads: "It is not a right, it is permitted use. We are rescinding it [the ordinance] to fix it with the state and federal government. The County does not have carte-blanche authority over the roads. The state and federal government are involved. This action will result in long range protection of our rights and roads."[67]

In June 2007 a Democratic member of Congress, Representative Mark Udall of Colorado, proposed an amendment to the budget bill that would stop a "public land giveaway" by preventing the BLM from spending money to make nonbinding determinations under the Norton policy. He withdrew the amendment when the DOI agreed to more congressional oversight of administrative decisions on R.S. 2477 claims. At the end of the month another judicial milestone in the R.S. 2477 roads debate occurred. A federal judge dismissed the lawsuit that Kane and Garfield Counties had filed in November 2005 to challenge the GSENM MMP. He ruled that the lawsuit was premature because the counties first had to prove ownership for each road under a legally required "quiet title" action.[68] Habbeshaw recognized the implications: to litigate every road claim "would be overwhelmingly expensive to everybody, to us, to the federal court."[69] The counties once again appealed the decision.

The BLM took the initiative in September 2007 by employing a tactic that avoided the need for litigation over every road. It issued a preliminary decision in its first nonbinding determination under the Norton policy for the Bald Knoll Road in Kane County. The county had submitted a request for a nonbinding determination in November 2006 in order to proceed with improvements needed to make the road safe for trucks that would be hauling rock from a proposed shale-collecting operation. The county saw this request as a good test case for the Norton policy because the road did not go through GSENM or a wilderness study area. In response, SUWA and the Wilderness Society sent letters to Interior Secretary Dirk Kempthorne and the new director of the Utah BLM, Selma Sierra, insisting that the agency postpone its final decision on the Bald Knoll Road until Kane County removed the road signs remaining from 2003. Habbeshaw explained that the county had left the signs because it believed the June decision that counties must make R.S. 2477 claims road by road would be overturned in its appeal. If a federal court issued an injunction demanding the signs be removed, the county would consider the roads to be federal roads and comply, but it would also stop maintaining the roads.

In December 2007 the state of Utah dropped a lawsuit it had filed against the federal government in 2005 over six roads in Box Elder

County. It looked as though the action might signal greater cooperation between the state and the federal government on the R.S. 2477 roads issue. An assistant attorney general for the state explained, "We have simply decided to concentrate our resources on more important matters that can't be resolved through cooperation with the BLM."[70]

2008–9

It became apparent what the "more important matters" were in January 2008. The state of Utah used a two-year-old state law that had been sponsored by Representative Mike Noel, a Republican from Kanab, to begin a process of claiming roads on public land. The law allows counties to record roads on their master land documents, and if a road is not challenged in state court within sixty days, the county assumes ownership of the right-of-way. The State Public Lands Policy Coordination Office began the process of road reviews by sending a list of sixty roads to Box Elder County for recording. "We're recording [our] belief we have a property interest," the coordinator said. "We're putting the BLM and the rest of the world on notice."[71] The review process included examination of historical aerial photographs, topographic maps, road maps, maintenance records, site visits, and interviews with hundreds of witnesses. "People are going to be furious," a SUWA spokesperson predicted. "What's driving this is wilderness."[72] Utah governor Jon Huntsman and the counties explained that this process would avoid the expense of proving each road claim in court. Since 2001 the state had spent $9.6 million on legal and other fees for road claims, including assistance provided to counties for their legal actions.

In May 2008 Judge Campbell ruled, in SUWA's October 2005 lawsuit against Kane County, that the county had violated the Constitution's Supremacy Clause, both when it opened roads that the monument had closed and when it passed an ordinance in September 2005 opening roads in Kane County to ATVs. She also ordered Kane County to remove its signs. SUWA called the ruling a "legal victory" and said it "confirms a basic point of law that continues to escape the county. Federal law trumps state and county law on federal public lands."[73] Representative Noel decried the ruling: "It took away the things the 10th Circuit gave us. There will be an appeal on this. It's very, very important."[74] In June both the U.S. District Court and the Tenth Circuit Court of Appeals denied Kane County's request to allow the signs to remain while it appealed the judge's order to remove them.

Kane County removed the signs, but as Habbeshaw had warned, the county also stopped maintaining roads it had agreed with the BLM in 1972 and 1977 to maintain, contending that whether the county possessed the authority to "drop a blade on the ground" was no longer clear.[75] When I returned to Escalante for a visit in September 2008, the eastern end of the Hole-in-the-Rock Road, which lies in Kane County and is one of the most popular recreation routes in the monument, was barely navigable by two-wheel-drive vehicles. The Cottonwood Road and the Skutumpah Road, which traverse the monument north to south, were no longer passable with two-wheel drive. Ranchers were worried that roads that accessed their allotments in Kane County might become completely impassable without being maintained.

In January 2009 the Kane County commissioners met with BLM officials to try to work out a maintenance agreement, but the meeting ended in a deadlock. After the meeting, Commissioner Dan Hulet expressed his feelings about the issue: "My frustration is with Washington itself. Congress passed [R.S. 2477 in 1976] and it allows recognition of rights-of-way. Just because a federal department, not responsible to anyone, doesn't recognize those rights is not appropriate. It makes me angry. It makes me mad as hell as an American."[76] He was angry because he felt that by obstructing recognition of rights-of-way granted by Congress, the BLM was violating principles of democratic government laid out in the Constitution: separation of powers and rule of law. Kane County saw its fight over R.S. 2477 roads as a fight for its rights against the overreach of the federal government.

Representative Noel continued pushing a bill through the Utah State Legislature that would help Utah counties pay for court costs as they pursued R.S. 2477 road claims by diverting some of their share of road maintenance funds from the state gas tax. Meanwhile, some Kane County taxpayers were getting impatient with their County Commission's continued expenditure of tax money, estimated to be around $1 million, for R.S. 2477 roads litigation that had yet to produce a single road claim.

On April 13, 2009, a Tenth Circuit Court of Appeals judge upheld the lower court's decision of June 2007 in the counties' lawsuit against the MMP, which had ruled that road claims had to be adjudicated road by road. In early May Kanab residents organized a protest ride of OHVs up the Paria River in GSENM. The MMP had prohibited motorized access to the river, which had been used as a road since the time of the Mormon pioneers. Because of the controversy over roads locally, the monument had only asked for "voluntary compliance." But after the April 13 ruling, the BLM notified county officials that enforcement would begin soon. The group organized the protest to let the BLM know that local residents had a stake in who controls the roads on GSENM. Another group of local residents planned a peaceful "picnic with a purpose" along the banks of the river "to show the world that local people care about protecting our land from illegal and irresponsible use."[77] At the ride on May 9, the organizer asserted, "People are the government. . . . We're standing up for our rights to access." The protest ride temporarily reinvigorated the roads controversy locally. Evidence from the ride was turned over to the U.S. Attorney's Office, but no action was taken.

Reterritorialization and Rights-of-Way on Public Land

The conflict over roads on GSENM represents another front for negotiating the reterritorialization of public land as it becomes more valuable for amenity consumption than resource production. FLPMA called into question accustomed management of roads on public land and raised the possibility that public land could be designated wilderness, suggesting that local actors would have less access to it and less say in its management than they had in the past. FLPMA initiated, and the GSENM MMP Transportation Plan reinforced, a reterritorialization of public land as wilderness or national landscape with less motorized access. But FLPMA's ambiguity opened a political space, and a democratic system of government provided the institutional space, for local actors to contest that reterritorialization.

The efforts of Kane and Garfield Counties drew the BLM, all branches of the federal government, the state of Utah, environmental groups, local residents, the media, and the general public into the conflict over roads on GSENM. The protracted nature of the conflict, the proliferation of participants, and the amount of time, money, and human resources invested in it are evidence that something highly valued by each group was at risk. The emotions aroused locally by the creation of GSENM also fueled the conflict. Longtime residents perceived their home and way of life threatened because they would no longer be able to access places they used to go and pursue accustomed activities. Some newer residents wanted the impacts of traditional uses of public land reduced to increase its ecological health and aesthetic appeal. Counties felt that their property rights, local autonomy, and traditional resource-dependent economies were threatened. They stood to lose their standing and say in how public land was managed and control over their future. Each group defended its own understanding of how a democratic government should work. The state of Utah staunchly supported local control over public land and did not want federal control to increase. Environmental organizations wanted to reduce human impact on public land and promote its protection as wilderness. The general public felt it had ownership in public land. Different presidential administrations were committed to different agendas: Democrats to conservation, Republicans to more local control over public lands. The American state sought to maintain legitimacy to "exact compliance" and "invoke commitment" from rural actors at a distance from state power, who had the potential to disrupt it.[78] At the same time, it was reluctant to give up sovereignty over roads.

In 2009, after thirteen years of definitive actions, court decisions and appeals, negotiations, administrative rulings, shifting strategies and alliances, and name calling, the question of who owned the roads on GSENM, and how they would be managed, was still not resolved. There had been incremental change, but roads were being managed much the same as they had been before the creation of GSENM. The federal courts had filled in the gap in FLPMA, ruling that the BLM did not have the power to make right-of-way decisions. Counties could claim ownership of roads on public land, but only by proving it for each road in federal court using applicable state law. However, management of their rights-of-way would still be subject to BLM oversight. This resolution of FLPMA's ambiguity left rights-of-way effectively in the hands of the federal government because counties could not afford to litigate every road. To make it easier for counites to continue to manage roads as they had in the past without obtaining an actual right-of-way, the Bush administration stepped in with the Norton policy. But the counties seemed to want actual rights-of-way.

The conflict over roads also had little effect on most people's daily lives in the region. Events that occurred locally stirred up emotions and caused people to talk about them, but then they returned to their daily routines. Little physical change to the landscape had occurred on GSENM. Since 1996 Kane and Garfield Counties had maintained only authorized roads, and while Kane County refrained from maintaining roads on GSENM, these were being rapidly reclaimed by natural forces. Further road development was put on hold while the lawsuits wound their way through the courts. Signs were placed and removed by the BLM, Kane County, and unknown persons. The road development and off-road vehicle use that environmental groups feared if counties were granted rights-of-way had not yet occurred on GSENM. Why had so little change resulted from so much effort?

Viewing this conflict through the lens of agonistic democracy, I argue that the major accomplishment in the roads dispute was not something tangible. It was the ongoing participation of a wide variety of groups who valued public land in different ways in an agonistic confrontation whose provisional outcomes they accepted because they perceived its procedures to be democratic. The detailed analysis of the conflict in this chapter makes it possible to see the variety of ways participants used the principles and institutions afforded by a democratic system of government. The fact that they participated indicates that democracy meant to them the ability to participate in political decision-making and the institutional arrangements that promote it. Because negotiation was protracted, each group had an opportunity to have its voice heard in a variety of venues: in court, on the ground, in meetings, in the media. And each group tried different strategies and alliances to advance its point of view. As the groups participated, they drew opportunistically on different democratic imaginaries as circumstances changed to legitimate their positions and actions or discredit those of antagonists. For example, the U.S. attorney drew on a democratic imaginary of rule of law to condemn the counties' 1996 unauthorized grazing of roads, while

Kane County also drew on rule of law to condemn the BLM's placement of road signs that it had not agreed on.

Participants drew on a democratic imaginary of inclusive decision-making when they took action to undermine a decision in which they felt left out, such as when the counties and environmental groups objected to the MOU between the state of Utah and the DOI. Even when the actions of Kane County commissioner Mark Habbeshaw appeared to be illegal, he drew on ideas about democracy to justify them. Because the process was seen as democratic, the American state could maintain legitimacy even as the forms and legitimation of the government of public land and the balance of power in public land decision-making tipped away from traditional resource users.

But because the dispute over roads was largely conducted in the courts and in meetings between high-level state and DOI officials, antagonists had little opportunity to engage face-to-face and perhaps to discover common ground and develop understanding of and empathy for the other's point of view. What if, instead of expending so much effort and resources on conflict, representatives from SUWA and the counties had sat down together in a collaborative effort to identify and discuss which roads should remain open and why?

Events since 2009

By the time I moved to Escalante in 2017, it appeared that substantial progress was finally being made toward resolving the R.S. 2477 roads issue in Utah. In August 2010, in a quiet title suit filed by Kane County in the U.S. District Court, the federal government acknowledged the county's ownership and jurisdiction of a portion of the Skutumpah Road. This is believed to have been the first Utah R.S. 2477 road with title confirmed in court. After celebrating this victory, the county immediately began signing and maintaining the road, which was in serious disrepair.[79] In March 2013 U.S. District Court judge Clark Waddoups, appointed by President George W. Bush, determined that twelve of fifteen more roads Kane County had claimed, four of which run through GSENM, were roads and that the county had jurisdiction to manage them.[80] However, in 2014 parts of that decision were overruled by the Tenth Circuit Court of Appeals.[81]

In 2012 the Utah Attorney General's Office had begun filing a series of lawsuits seeking quiet title to more than twelve thousand roads on public land in Utah, based on the results of the road review begun in 2008.[82] On July 31, 2015, on its own initiative, the U.S. District Court established a "bellwether" process to more efficiently process those right-of-way claims. The parties agreed to, and the court approved, the inclusion in the process of fifteen rights-of-way in Kane County that "exemplif[ied] remaining legal issues regarding the determination of R.S. 2477 rights-of-way."[83] Most are in GSENM. Decisions on these roads would provide guidance for future decisions that could be made outside of courts. A spokesperson for SUWA, which was granted intervenor status on the side of the federal government, expressed skepticism about the process: "These are, for the most part, roads to nowhere. They start nowhere; they end nowhere. They were used for ranching. That's what the primary use really was, for cutting posts, for rockhounding, for sightseeing, for hunting. The statute [R.S. 2477] was meant to encourage the settlement of the West. To try and shoehorn in this modern-day recreation use or permitted use in ranching to fit that statute is very inapt."[84]

These fifteen rights-of-way were tried in the U.S. District Court in February 2020 with Judge Waddoups presiding. In light of the reluctance on the part of the federal government to make definitive decisions on R.S. 2477 rights-of way, it is not surprising that by February 2024 no decision had yet been made in the bellwether process. The judge's decision will be accompanied by guidance on how to begin resolving R.S. 2477 right-of-way claims throughout the state. When all legal issues have been resolved, the court will appoint special masters to ensure speedy resolution of all claims throughout the state.

Conflict over Public Land and Democracy

The conflicts analyzed in this section pitted local actors against the BLM, the federal government, and environmental groups. Local actors often conceived of these conflicts as a fight for their rights or freedom against a dominating or tyrannical government, a potent symbol in U.S. history and American identity, which they felt gave them the moral high ground. These conflicts can also be framed as the efforts of a minority, whose traditional way of life depends on the land, to defend themselves against what Tocqueville termed "the tyranny of the majority," in this case the American public who owns the land and has different ideas about how it should be managed.[85] For the most part, local actors were portrayed derisively as rednecks, idiots, criminals, childish, and other pejoratives that dismissed the need to consider their motives and arguments.

This and the previous chapter have framed these conflicts as resistance to reterritorialization of public land, in which the legitimation of government is shifting from welfare of the population to neoliberal rationality and the form of government is shifting from democracy on the range to rule of the market, and have situated them in a history of resistance to reterritorialization. From this perspective, the logic of local actors' actions can be grasped, and their predicament may even elicit some sympathy. Their efforts prefigured current debates about the moral limits of neoliberal rationality as it has pervaded more and more aspects of public and private life.[86] They succeeded in influencing the reterritorialization of public land as national landscape: livestock will still graze on national landscapes, and counties will control some rights-of-way, although which ones is yet to be determined.

The conflicts illustrate that ability to participate is enhanced when participants are organized. Ranchers who organized could stand up against actions of the BLM they disagreed with. Environmental groups, particularly GCT and SUWA, were effective in representing preservationist views of national landscapes. But at the same time, the conflicts demonstrate the far-reaching effects that the actions of individuals and groups can have on reterritorialization processes. Kate Cannon's autocratic actions as monument manager, although they may have been dictated by her superiors and intended to resolve grazing and road issues, instead intensified conflict. Commissioner Habbeshaw's leadership in both the grazing retirement and roads issues largely catalyzed the counties' efforts to oppose them. Without the counties' and SUWA's efforts in the roads dispute, the Justice Department would have continued to drag its feet.

From the perspective of the American state, the slow progression of these conflicts through the courts and other channels is beneficial: it allows strong emotions to die down, and it achieves new forms and legitimations of government slowly enough to maintain the delicate balance between local autonomy and state control. The lack of progress in addressing both livestock grazing and roads on GSENM can also be attributed to the fact that the political sympathies of high-level officials in the Interior Department, who are presidential appointees, change with administrations, and the BLM's priorities and management philosophy change with them. The BLM's lack of autonomy and a clear vision for public land makes long-range planning difficult and jeopardizes the future of this land, even if retained in federal ownership.[87]

Analysis of these conflicts also illuminates what democracy means to participants in relation to government. For example, ranchers perceived the strict enforcement of rule of law in the cattle impoundment on Fiftymile Mountain as dictatorship, not democracy in which the BLM and ranchers worked together to address problems. In the conflicts over grazing retirements and roads, by using the legal framework governing public land, participants evinced an understanding of democracy as the ability to participate in decision-making, as well as acceptance of the procedures and institutions for participation and the results, because they perceived these things to be based on democratic principles, such as equality, freedom of expression, and rule of law. Much of their participation took the form of an agonistic confrontation via the judicial system, in which they drew on different understandings of democracy to justify their positions and actions: "democracy on the range," the idea that local actors should have a say in public land decision-making that affects their livelihoods and culture; rule of law, applied to the federal government as well as citizens; defense of individual rights; rule of the market, which preserves individual freedom; equality, as in a level playing field; and inclusive and transparent decision-making. From the perspective of agonistic democracy, these conflicts provided an opportunity for the creation of democratic citizens who engaged in disputes with adversaries according to procedures accepted by both.

Participants in the conflicts were able to contest the reterritorialization of public land as national landscape because the territory is public land. In the United States, public participation in management of public land is guaranteed by law, and a system of procedures and institutions is in place to facilitate this. If the land was private or belonged to the state, they would not have had this opportunity.[88] Public land is valuable to the American people not only for the resources, biodiversity, recreation, spiritual renewal, and scientific research it can provide, but also because it strengthens American democracy. It provides opportunities for ordinary Americans to participate in decision-making about its management and in agonistic confrontations with others who have different ideas about how it should be managed. And they are motivated to participate because they are attached to this land for all the various reasons mentioned in these two chapters.

But public land and democracy are threatened by a conservative movement that promotes local control and privatization of public lands. It grew in strength after the passage of FLPMA and was advanced by the Reagan administration and the Wise Use movement. The movement dovetails with the basic premise of neoliberal ideology—that the market should decide the best use of these lands—and the process of neoliberalization, characterized by deregulation, privatization, and withdrawal of the state from many areas of providing for social welfare. This process is represented by a variety of seemingly unrelated and uncoordinated actions and programs, which do not necessarily have the explicit goal of privatization. For example, in the 1980s the Reagan administration proposed to sell off 35 million acres of federally owned land to, according to Interior Secretary James Watt, "make it more beneficial to the individual taxpayer."[89] This proposal was dropped when it generated widespread bipartisan opposition among the American public. This conservative movement can be seen as a new attempt to reterritorialize the public lands as private land, which the American public has strongly resisted.

Subsequently, the move toward privatization became more indirect. In the 1990s the Republican Congress slashed the budgets of federal land management agencies, allegedly in the interest of "streamlining" government. The agencies began encouraging public-private partnerships and volunteerism to perform much of the work they used to do, such as maintaining trails, overseeing campgrounds, and building wildlife management structures. In 1996 a rider for the Recreational Fee Demonstration Program, tacked on to an unrelated piece of legislation, allowed the agencies to collect, and retain in the budget for the area where they were collected, fees to recover costs from operating and maintaining recreation areas and sites. To show their opposition to this program, many recreationists refused to pay the fee, and citizen groups such as Wild Wilderness and the Western Slope No-Fee Coalition arose to oppose it.

The George W. Bush administration continued the privatization process by outsourcing thousands of jobs in the federal agencies; aggressively promoting oil, gas, and mineral development on public land; and passing the Federal Lands Recreation Enhancement Act, tacked on to an appropriations bill, making failure to pay a recreation fee a criminal offense punishable by up to a $5,000 fine, six months in jail, or both. Funding for GSENM and the NLCS was drastically reduced during this administration. Bush's fiscal year 2008 budget proposed the lowest level of funding ever, not enough to hire on-the-ground staff to protect these areas or fund scientific research needed to make better management decisions. While the conservative offensive against public lands receded during the Obama administration, it returned with increased ferocity when Donald Trump took office.

Part 3
Democracy

5 The Locals

DEMOCRACY AND COMMUNITY

The four chapters in part 3 consider the meaning of democracy to people in the Grand Staircase-Escalante region in the early twenty-first century. They are based on the responses of interviewees when asked, "What does democracy mean to you?" Each chapter focuses on the meaning of democracy to a particular group involved in conflict over Grand Staircase-Escalante National Monument (GSENM): local residents, ranchers, environmentalists, and Bureau of Land Management (BLM) employees. In each of these groups, a specific theme was prominent. For local residents, it was democracy as community; for ranchers, it was democracy as freedom; for environmentalists, it was how to protect the environment in a democracy; and for BLM employees, it was the tension between democracy and bureaucracy. Each chapter also illuminates a paradox that arose between the group's understanding of democracy and the actual circumstances of their lives and explores how they struggled to resolve that paradox. This chapter considers what democracy meant to residents of the communities adjacent to GSENM.

Who Are the Locals?

I am using the term "locals" differently than it is usually used in discussions of politics in the rural American West, where it bears connotations of priority, culture, and class and often appears in opposition to another group: newcomers, environmentalists, or the government. There were differences and divisions among residents of the Grand Staircase-Escalante region, and they often spoke in "us and them" ways. But the way they used these terms indicated that community dynamics were much more complex than simple dichotomies indicate. People who had lived in the region for a long time sometimes referred to those who had moved in more recently as "newcomers" or "move-ins," and the latter sometimes referred to the former as "locals." But the locals may have been newcomers themselves in the past, and move-ins might regard themselves as locals simply by virtue of living there and refer to those who have moved in even more recently as the newcomers.

Everyone agreed that descendants of the Mormon pioneers who settled the region were locals. But those who moved away and lived elsewhere for most of their lives were not always considered locals if they moved back. Interpreting community dynamics in terms of a dichotomy between Mormons and non-Mormons was also an oversimplification. For people who were not members of the Church of Jesus Christ of Latter-day Saints, the "locals" or "them" could mean both people who were and were not LDS. And people who were LDS might refer to other members of the Church who had moved in from somewhere else as "newcomers" or "them" and to people who had lived in the region for a long time but were not LDS as "locals." "Them" could also refer to people who were of a different political persuasion than the speaker.

Local residents provided several alternate understandings of who the locals were. For a woman who retired to Escalante in 1996, the "three-year rule" determined who was a local: "Their attitude changes after three years, when they decide you're going to stay." According to her definition, she was a local. Yet she still thought in terms of "us and them," and the people she socialized with were others who had moved in more recently. A young man in his thirties, a descendant of the Mormon pioneers who founded Escalante, explained who the locals were for him: "I don't count local people as members of the Mormon Church, whose families have been here forever, and that vote Republican. . . . There are a lot of people who move into here regardless of their background, who fit right in, and they become what I call local people. I think it's a state of mind and not an issue of your background."

Finally, both longtime residents and those who had more recently moved into the region made a distinction between community members and the extremely vocal and oppositional residents whose activities and words provided fodder for the media. These media reports had colored my own impressions of the locals. A woman who was a descendant of the Mormon pioneers who had founded Escalante emphasized that "the loudmouths don't represent the community. The media go to the local café where the backbiters hang out, and some of the people they interview, I think, 'Oh no!'" At public meetings, they "stand up and rail." This woman felt that the hostility of "the loudmouths" made it "a big problem trying to get the community to work together." Another woman, who had moved to Escalante in the 1980s, explained that people who are more representative of the community "aren't vocal. They live their lives the way they've always done. They've gone through a lot of bumps, and the monument is just one of them." A woman who had moved to Kanab in 2001 felt that "your typical townsfolk, your typical rancher, they're more moderate. But their voice is not heard. Because the people who get involved are more radical."

I came to agree with the "state of mind" theory. Being a local comes down to mutual recognition of having something in common, feeling like one belongs. Where I have ethnographic insight into someone's state of mind, I use this criterion; otherwise, I default to the "three-year rule." This methodology enables me to avoid simple dichotomies; to recognize that communities are not static, but always changing; and to suggest possibilities beyond what political philosopher Charles Taylor described as "'us and them' ways of talking, thinking, doing politics."[1] I also distinguish residents as "pioneer descendants" or "longtime residents" by the more objective criteria of descent and length of residency. Regardless of their length of residency, residents of the communities adjacent to GSENM came to be involved in conflicts over its management, whether they took an active role or not, because the monument was such a prominent topic in everyday conversation.

Feelings of Belonging and Community Identity

I was surprised by how much I enjoyed living in the small town of Escalante while I was doing fieldwork. I had anticipated feeling lonely and bored, but instead, I experienced a feeling of belonging and a lively community life. I will never forget the first morning I woke up in the place I had rented, watching the sun rise over the far desert horizon from the front porch. As the seasons changed, I could mark the sun's slow march southward and back north again along the crest of the sandstone monocline in the far distance. In the vast, quiet landscape, I felt a sense of cosmic belonging. Moreover, residents included me in their practice of greeting each other and stopping to talk on the street, in the grocery store and post office, and even when driving by. People were genuinely friendly and interested in what I was doing. I felt looked after and much less alone than when living as a single woman in Seattle.

In addition, participating in community life was more accessible in this small community than in the large city I came from. The Mormon church sponsored events that everyone was welcome to attend, and I found them to be occasions for socializing rather than proselytizing. Community celebrations were held for many of the major holidays: the Escalante Heritage Festival on Memorial Day weekend; Pioneer Day festivities on July 24, which included a parade, rodeo, and fireworks; a Veterans Day program at the high school; and for Christmas, a play by the elementary school and a concert at the Mormon church. At first I looked on these activities as part of my research, but as time went on, I realized that people appreciated my participation, and I began to feel like part of the community. The nearby communities also held unique events, like Cannonville's Old Time Fiddlers and Bear Festival, Tropic's Ebenezer Bryce Festival, Kanab's Western Legends Roundup, and Panguitch's Quilt Walk, which were intended to celebrate community identity as well as attract tourists. I also found many meetings to attend—city council, county commission, irrigation company, scoping meetings held by the federal land management agencies, community improvement groups—and volunteer activities to participate in. GSENM held many events in the local communities, such as regular Walks and Talks and Brown Bags; a Science Forum, where the public could learn about scientific, historic, and cultural resources on the monument; and celebrations for the opening of visitors' centers and the monument's tenth anniversary. Meetings of local government were sparsely attended, and those sponsored by the federal land management agencies were attended mainly by more recent arrivals.

Many residents of the region, both longtime and more recent arrivals, expressed to me their appreciation of this feeling of belonging. And while not everyone felt that way, they did agree that their communities had a unique identity. This feeling may be a feature of all small towns to some extent, but in the Grand Staircase-Escalante region, I attribute it to three main factors: the landscape, the pioneer experience, and the influence of the Church of Jesus Christ of Latter-day Saints. The historically shared occupation and lifestyle of ranching on the landscape, the pioneer experience, and the influence of the LDS Church, enhanced by the small size and relative isolation of the communities, have all contributed to strong community identities in the Grand Staircase-Escalante region. However, I would argue that it is not these objective factors per se but rather the subjective attachment to the values that they fostered—self-reliance, hard work, and mutual support—that determines who the locals are, who feel like they belong, and who are seen to fit in.

THE LANDSCAPE

As their comments throughout this book indicate, an appreciation of the landscape was shared across whatever divisions and differences exist among residents of these communities, as well as with the environmentalists who wanted to protect it. Most people who had moved into the region more recently said they came because of the landscape, and many pioneer descendants said they stayed, even though it was a struggle to make a living, because of it. But they did not necessarily experience the landscape in the same way. Those who grew up in the region knew it as home and a source of livelihood, as well as the gathering place in the last days, but they did not necessarily see the topography as unique. A Tropic resident said that when he was growing up in Long Valley, people thought the landscape was "common." A rancher in his eighties who grew up herding sheep in Bryce Canyon said that when he was young, he thought "everyone had a Bryce Canyon where they lived." Sometimes it took being away for lifelong residents to realize the uniqueness of the surroundings they grew up in and to understand why other people see it as special and in need of protection. Many who had moved there more recently saw the landscape more as a setting, which they described, photographed, went hiking in, and wanted to preserve. Some immersed themselves in it more deeply, spending as much time as they could outside. Some experienced its immensity as a feeling of peacefulness and contentment. Across these differences in how they perceived the landscape, residents were often unaware of the attachment to it that they shared.

THE PIONEER EXPERIENCE

Most residents of the communities in the Grand Staircase-Escalante region are descendants of the Mormon pioneers who originally settled the region and established the towns beginning in the 1870s. New residents soon come to recognize the surnames that dominate in the region, such as Alvey, Griffin, Lyman, Roundy, Spencer, and Woolsey, as those of the original pioneers. Residents' pioneer ancestry was a source of great pride and identity. They described themselves by generation (such as fourth or fifth generation) and still placed a high value on the qualities that had enabled the Mormon pioneers to succeed in the demanding environment of Utah: hard work, self-sufficiency, simple living, and communal effort. Everyone had to participate for the community to survive. The importance of communal, not just individual, effort distinguished the Mormon pioneers from those who settled other parts of the American West. I would argue that the desire for a united community is still an ideal for their descendants in these small rural communities and acts as a counterweight to Mormon clannishness. However, both demographics and values in these communities are changing as the older generation passes away, their offspring leave for better job opportunities elsewhere, and new people move in.

Mormon pioneer values were even more important in southern Utah, where the landscape is more rugged, the climate more arid, and the communities more isolated than in northern Utah, where the Mormons first settled. Cooperation in the construction of irrigation systems was crucial to farming, and livestock belonging to different owners grazed together. But crops were still often lost to drought or flood. Raising livestock—first sheep, then cattle—became the mainstay of the region because it was less uncertain than farming and because of the proximity of high-elevation summer and lower-elevation winter pasturage.

Ranching contributes much less to the local economy today, but many residents still identify with a lifestyle and culture they associate with ranching. A Glendale pioneer descendant's description of his "simple community" reflected the effects of pioneer values. It was "pretty much self-reliant, we don't rely on much from the outside world.... Just kind of make do." He believed that most people lived there "not because they ever intend to get rich, but because they enjoy living with friends and neighbors and just making do.... There's a lot of pride in the community. People like the community the way it is." The communities still have a pioneer look and feel that people who have moved in more recently are attracted to, and many respect the pioneer values.

Members of the oldest generations, those in their seventies, eighties, and nineties, grew up when these towns were still very isolated and self-sufficiency was necessary. I spent many hours enjoying their stories of life in those days, which they told to preserve the history of the region and pass on the values of their generation to younger ones.[2] But that generation was dwindling fast. A man who moved to Boulder in 1977 had observed their passing: "When I first moved to Boulder, there were sixty old-timers, and there were only a couple kids; mostly old-timers, with their kids having moved away. Today there are probably only ten people that have been in Boulder longer than me. Because they all left and died mainly. All the old-timers died."

As the old-timers pass on, memories of the pioneer experience that gave rise to the values that pioneer descendants hold in such high esteem pass on with them. When the next generation, in their fifties and sixties at the time of my research, grew up, life in the region had changed significantly, so their experience was different. They were trying to hold on to and pass on the pioneer values of their forebears, but they recognized that these would diminish further in the younger generations.

THE CHURCH OF JESUS CHRIST OF LATTER-DAY SAINTS

While my research did not specifically focus on the role of the Mormon Church in conflicts over GSENM, it is impossible to ignore its role in community life. What I learned about it was mostly from the women I met when we worked out together at the high school gym on weekday mornings. Before 7:00 a.m. it was ladies only, and many of the regulars,

17.–20. Sustaining community: July 24 parade in Escalante, 2004; July 24 dedication of Veterans Memorial, 2005; LDS church and old tithing house in Escalante; Easter picnic at Devil's Garden, 2005. Courtesy of the author.

who got there at 5:00 every morning before heading off to a full day of jobs and caring for families, occupied important positions in the local church: the president and vice president of the Relief Society, a first counselor, the wife of a bishop. Discussion of church matters often accompanied pulldowns on the lat machine and sessions on the elliptical trainer.

Pioneer descendants are members of the LDS Church by virtue of their descent, but not all members actively participate in church activities.[3] For active members, community life centers around church activities. Besides services, Sunday School, and Primary for children between three and eleven on Sundays, there are Priesthood Quorums for boys and men of various levels of Priesthood and auxiliary organizations, such as the Relief Society for women eighteen and older and Mutual for teenagers, that meet on weekday evenings other than Monday, which is Family Home Evening. Church members may also be "called" to perform other church-related duties or community service, such as organizing meals served at funerals, leading a Boy Scout troop, or serving as the city judge. They also contribute to distribution centers that sell goods at cost or give them away to members and nonmembers in need, a practice that enabled Mormons to be among the first to arrive with goods to help victims of Hurricane Katrina. Mormons also place a strong emphasis on family, and their families often have more children than the national average.[4] Huge family reunions are annual events for pioneer descendant families in the region. All these activities contribute to the solidarity of the Mormon community but also leave little free time for socializing with those who are not active Church members.

Mormon solidarity can make non-Mormon residents feel unwelcome. But the way the Mormon community in Escalante responded to tragedy while I was living there illustrates that its support is not offered only to members of the Church. When the partner of a woman who was not LDS committed suicide, the Mormon community offered her support, organized a service at the Mormon church, where members spoke highly of the deceased man, and held a luncheon afterward.

The Mormon community is not homogeneous, however. One fifth-generation man perceived a difference between the older generations—"people who haven't been away"—and his generation, which "has been away": the former "don't want to see anything change. They don't realize it's been changing all the time." There are also differences between Mormons who are pioneer descendants and those who have moved into the region more recently. For example, Mormons in Escalante had developed a local tradition of celebrating March 17, which commemorates the Relief Society, with a big dinner and entertainment for the whole community. But according to another fifth-generation resident, "new people, Mormons from other places, are changing it back to just something for the Relief Society." In addition, some members are more active than others, and members of the Church do not necessarily all share the same values. Carol Sullivan, a longtime resident of Kanab, a member of the LDS Church and the city council, and childless, made national news for her opposition to a city council resolution proclaiming support for the "natural family."[5] Finally, being LDS does not guarantee unqualified acceptance by the Mormon community, as an LDS man who moved to Boulder in 1970 was dismayed to learn when he "tried to get involved and smooth things over" at a meeting on an environmental issue: "You weren't allowed to have a different opinion."

Challenges to Community Identity

The existence of strong community identity in the region helps explain the strength of emotion when that identity and community viability are perceived to be threatened. Residents experienced three sources of challenge to personal and community identities in the region: the monument, changes in the local economy, and changing demographics.

THE MONUMENT

Concern about how GSENM would affect community identity was a central feature in my conversations with residents about the monument. While the creation of GSENM reflected processes that had been underway for some time—changing perceptions of public land and changing economics and demographics in the American West—many longtime residents of the region tended to lump their experience of these processes together with the bitterness and powerlessness they felt when the monument was created and saw the monument as the main challenge to their community identity.

For example, a retired pioneer descendant in Escalante felt that "since the monument, there has been more animosity—neighbor against neighbor. Everyone used to love one another." His wife interjected, "It wasn't really like that." "But it was more harmonious than now," he responded. According to another older pioneer descendant woman in Escalante, "We were a really a nice community—of course, there are always some problems—until the monument came along." Longtime residents' feelings of powerlessness in the face of the president's action and of bitterness that the federal government was unconcerned with their welfare were compounded by the historical memory of the Mormons' treatment at the hands of the federal government and more recent memories of being left out of the loop in the creation of other national monuments in the region. All this resonated with their feelings in the face of other changes in their lives and communities that were beyond their control.

Not all longtime residents felt this way. Some decided to learn to live with the monument and make the best of it—to "take lemons and make lemonade," as Carol Sullivan put it. A group in Escalante formed the Escalante Center, a nonprofit arts and sciences education and information campus that would provide educational opportunities to residents and visitors and be built and run in partnership with the monument. The idea foundered in part because of objections by the "loudmouths." When a couple who retired to Kanab in 1996 helped start Friends of the Monument, they learned, "There's a sizable group that's just thrilled about the monument and how it preserves this beautiful land." But some longtime residents were "a little afraid to speak out if they were in favor of the monument and saw that it had benefits to the community. And so, once people stepped forward and were brave enough to say, 'This is what we are doing. We are supporting the science and this spectacular treasure,' it gave a lot of people the courage to step forward and say, 'Hey, I'm supporting this.'"

Some residents' fears about stricter regulation of resources or losing access to them were confirmed. Although local government representatives helped draw up the Monument Management Plan and a public comment period on a draft plan was required, many residents felt that their views had been ignored. The final plan restricted fuelwood harvesting on the monument to a limited area and prohibited wood gathering elsewhere. Residents who depended on wood harvested from nearby public land to heat their homes in winter or to use for fence posts now had to travel farther to get it. Escalante residents could no longer dig gravel from a nearby wash or clay from pits used since pioneer days for their small construction projects. Little things like that make a big difference to people already struggling economically. Outfitters and guides were also "getting hammered" by strict enforcement on the monument, as an Escalante pioneer descendant man put it. New restrictions on group size and new fees affected traditional recreational activities for Mormon families, such as Eastering, when extended families gather for picnics at favorite spots at Easter (see fig. 20); Boy Scout outings; and family outings to Calf Creek. As a result, "locals don't use public land anymore," said another Escalante pioneer descendant man who worked for the BLM.

While many local residents' fears about the effects of the monument on their communities had been confirmed, they did not believe that promised benefits from tourism had materialized. A front country visitor study by the Institute for Outdoor Recreation and Tourism at Utah State University, undertaken in 2004, estimated that more than $20.6 million had been spent in Garfield and Kane Counties by visitors to the monument, an income that supported 430 full-time equivalent jobs with almost $10 million in employment value added on.[6] Nevertheless, the comments of a Kane County commissioner from Glendale are typical of longtime residents' perceptions: "[In] arguments for the national monument, . . . the ones that shouted the loudest were, 'Oh, you'll do so much more on tourism. It'll just be great. It'll be a lure for people. People will just come.' Well, statistics have shown us that that hasn't happened. . . . We always try to increase ways of getting people to come, but we also argue that your economic activity is really in the production of natural resources and other things. . . . We need to have good stable jobs, . . . enough to support families and schools."

Many longtime residents pointed out that an economy based on tourism would not support the kind of community they want it to be. They worried that increased tourism could turn their communities into "another Moab"; that the monument would attract people with money to move into the region, changing the character of their communities;

and that an increase in monument employees would have an effect on their communities.

CHANGING LOCAL ECONOMY

As traditional occupations in ranching, farming, timber production, and mining became less viable, longtime residents looked for other ways to make a living. But there were not many in the region, and few offered wages that could support a family. Most of the businesses that catered to tourism were owned by people who had moved to the region more recently. Jobs in tourism, which many residents referred to as "cleaning toilets," brought neither the income nor the dignity and satisfaction of traditional occupations in resource production. Jobs with the federal government were more reliable and paid well, but they didn't really produce anything. Most young people left after high school to find work. Those who remained often held multiple jobs and still struggled to make ends meet, but they stayed, or came back, because of their attachment to the community and to the landscape.

For example, an Escalante woman whose great-grandfather was the first person to bring cattle to the valley explained that her family had sold their grazing permits and were trying to diversify. "It's a sacrifice to stay here," she said. But they stayed "for the quality of life, to raise children who could learn the work ethic and moral values and share family ties, because of the land and the type of beauty—the red rocks, the mountains, and the desert—and the traditional heritage that roots you to a place."

A fifth-generation Escalante man who grew up elsewhere and moved back to Escalante to raise his children had to do "all kinds of work to stay." He took over his father's ranching operation but had to hold several other jobs to support his family of six children. He worked at the local hamburger stand and the sawmill in Escalante but hadn't been able to find a full-time job since the sawmill closed.[7] For a short time he received an income as director of the Escalante Center. His wife was working at the telephone company and taking college classes to get a teaching certificate. He and his wife were trying to earn additional income as real estate agents. He feared that economic change might force him to leave the community. He wanted the farms to stay, with "the green fields and red and white rock," but he also wanted to see better-paying jobs.

As a result of economic change, work had taken on a different meaning for longtime residents. Once it meant physical labor in the surrounding landscape, producing something tangible and being able to support a family. It required knowledge of the environment and skills that were a source of pride and satisfaction. It also involved a certain amount of adventure and freedom. Once a source of personal identity and self-esteem, work was now, for many, just "something you do to stay." The changing nature of work, the experience that what one knew how to do was no longer valued, and the discontinuity of work experience between the older and younger generations were challenging pioneer values and both personal and community identities in the Grand Staircase-Escalante region.

CHANGING DEMOGRAPHICS

Community identities were also being challenged by increasing numbers of new people moving into the region. Many longtime residents associated the influx of new residents with the monument. But demographic changes that had been taking place throughout the West for some time were beginning to affect the Grand Staircase-Escalante region as well. The people moving in were different from longtime residents in a variety of ways. Many came from urban areas and had no experience of how people lived and interacted in a small, rural community. Many had attained a higher level of education, held white-collar jobs, and had a more affluent lifestyle. Many were not members of the LDS Church. These new residents saw and experienced the landscape differently. They posed another challenge to community identities in the region, and longtime residents considered their impact with some anxiety. They wanted to see "growth that's good for the community," but at the same time, they wanted to "preserve the lifestyle."

Most of the people I spoke with who had moved into the Grand Staircase-Escalante region before the 1980s either married someone living there or came for a job in the resource production economy or to teach in the schools. A few were drawn by the landscape and took whatever work they could find when they moved there. As a result, this group was more likely to share a rural background, work experience, or membership in the Mormon Church with pioneer descendant residents. For example, a man who had lived in Boulder since 1977 said he came "for the beauty of the canyons," although his first job was mining uranium. Later he worked for a contractor building roads for the Forest Service. In the 1990s he and his wife started a horse guiding business in the Escalante Canyons. Their best friends were the old-timers. His wife traced her affinity with the old-timers to the "Protestant work ethic" of her Yankee upbringing: "Out here it's the Mormon work ethic, you know, the Beehive State. If you work hard and you're honest and do what you say you're gonna do, you're okay." A pioneer descendant Boulder rancher explained why he eventually came to accept the couple, despite their environmentalist leanings: "They fit in my class now: they're working people. I can forgive anybody anything if they're hard workers." This was the only time I heard someone use the word "class," although the values I characterize as pioneer values are similar to what other writers have characterized as working-class values.[8]

People who moved to the region in the 1980s or later identified the landscape as their primary reason for doing so. In the 1980s and 1990s their means of supporting themselves reflected the shift from resource-based production to amenity-based consumption: they ran businesses catering to tourism or worked via the internet. In their work and daily lives, they had less need and opportunity to interact with pioneer descendant residents. As a result, their feelings of belonging to the local communities were usually more tenuous. The 1990s also brought more retirees to the region. With free time on their hands, many of them decided to get involved in their communities for the first time.

For example, a man who moved to Escalante in 1991 from a city in California to work for a wilderness outfitter said he didn't "get involved" in that city because "it's a full-time thing. It takes more commitment." A woman who moved to Escalante from California in 1986 volunteered to be on the committee making recommendations to the Utah Department of Transportation for improving Highway 12; she said it was the first time she had "gotten involved in a town." The couple who retired to Kanab in 1996 said of helping start Friends of the Monument, "We've never been involved in anything like this." But the efforts of new people to get involved were not always appreciated by longtime residents. A man who retired to Escalante in 1996 and got involved in city government learned that "people in power in small towns can stonewall your ideas." A BLM employee who came to Kanab in 2001 found it "frustrating," saying, "There are people here that are way, way, way different from me, and they have the power."

The number of people moving into the region increased since the monument was created. Those who had opened businesses catering to the tourist industry saw the monument as a major draw for business. One of the owners of the Hell's Backbone Grill, Boulder's largest employer as of this writing, came from Flagstaff, Arizona, to open the upscale organic restaurant in 2000. She explained, "For us, if the monument didn't exist, we couldn't do what we're doing. We need a certain kind of people who come to Boulder for the style of food we're doing."[9] In 2003 a man from Kansas City retired to Escalante and bought the Escalante Outfitters, an outfitting shop, restaurant, and motel, along with several residential properties he intended to rent out as holiday houses. People from elsewhere had also begun purchasing residential property in Escalante for vacation homes, including a woman from Washington who worked for Microsoft, a doctor from Las Vegas, and another doctor from Salt Lake City. As a result of the influx of outsiders, a young pioneer descendant in Escalante predicted a bleak future for his community.

> Whether we like it or not, I expect that in the long run, Escalante will be more of a summer vacation, retirement kind of town. And it's really hard to make something like that work. When you start to stratify the society, when you have local people here that are trying to get by earning low wages on one hand, and then you've got people who have a half a million house that they come to a few weeks out of the year, and they want to be just involved enough to make a mess, it makes it hard for the community.

While it appeared that the monument was there to stay and that nothing could be done about demographic changes taking place in their communities, longtime residents still hoped to maintain their cherished community identity. They struggled to encompass more recent arrivals, while the newcomers struggled to understand how to belong to a small rural community for perhaps the first time in their lives.

Community Dynamics

Together with shifting local economies, the influx of newcomers into these communities with strong identities based on shared history, culture, and religion generated complex community dynamics. Residents often characterized their communities in terms of divisions but perceived the divisions differently. The very articulate pioneer descendant man who offered the "state of mind" theory characterized people moving into the region as being of two distinct types:

> There are those that come here expecting to change the community, and before long they leave very frustrated because we're all stubborn, hardheaded people that just can't see the light. And those people don't really contribute anything positive here, and frankly, I don't feel a bit bad to see them go. But we've had a lot of people, too, who've moved here who . . . keep their mouths shut until they understand a little bit about the town, and then they make a positive impact on it. And it's not an issue that they belong to a particular religion, or they vote a particular way, or they drive a certain color vehicle. Some people just come in receptive to the fact that the town's not going to change for them. They're here hopefully because they like the community. . . . I've noticed a lot more of the people who come here because they just love the area, but one of the first things they want to do is to start making changes. I have very little patience for hearing, "In Los Angeles, we . . ." or, "In Portland, we . . ."

An older pioneer descendant Escalante man thought that new people moving in could help bring needed change to the community: "It's going to take some outside people to bring something in this valley. If you don't shut us out, we'll help you go for it." But, he added, they could be successful only by "taking their time and getting to know us and our ways and then suggesting some changes."

People who had moved here from elsewhere often described the communities as split or layered, but these terms could also indicate different kinds of divisions. For example, Carol Sullivan saw Kanab as split between people who were open to change and those who were resistant to change. "We've had a lot of new people that have moved in that are a little bit more supportive of some of the changes since they've moved in. And we have . . . the locals that have been here for several generations and are a little bit more diehard. And some, even if they're not the locals, that are more resistant to change. But I see a growing tolerance in the community for new thoughts and new innovations." However, some of the "new people that have moved in" are also opposed to change: "Any time you have growth happen, when somebody comes in, they bought the place as it is now, and they don't want to see a lot of dramatic change." She admitted that she felt that way about change herself.

A woman who retired with her husband to Kanab in 1996 from Salt Lake City described the community as "layered," with the layers being several different groups:

> You've got basically your core community, which is people who have generations. They've been here since the Mormon pioneers settled Kanab, so they have families that have deep, deep roots in southern Utah and religious roots as well. And then I think there's a growing community—we call it the alternative community—all of us who think differently. And there's a liberal group. Somebody was telling me when we first moved here, the percent of non-Mormons to Mormons was about 40 percent to 60 percent. So the dynamics are changing. We've both been involved with community stuff. It's allowed me to become acquainted with more of the core community, and they're just as nice as they can be.

However, she added, their friends were people who, like themselves, had moved to Kanab from somewhere else: people who had left "the comfort of a city, the conveniences of a city, and move[d] to a little place in the middle of nowhere, . . . people who are kind of willing to push the envelope a little bit, . . . people living their lives, choosing their lives, really creating their lives the way they want, owning their lives."

Some of those who had moved in from elsewhere, especially those who shared a rural background or work experience, felt more in common with the pioneer descendants than with more recent arrivals. For example, the Yankee woman from Boulder felt that "people don't have as much community" as when she moved there in the 1980s. "And they don't have the same kind of rural value of doing what you say, understanding the power of your words. Now you get together for dinner and chat. I'd rather do something, be engaged. To a large extent, they could be anywhere, any pretty place."

However, the way residents of the region experience community is not based solely on their background. Sometimes more recent arrivals still felt like part of the community even if they didn't share a background with longtime residents. One woman in her forties moved to Escalante in 1999 because it was more affordable than the California community she came from and was able to keep her job there and work remotely. She called the community a "cultural democracy," a place where "people culturally learn to take care of each other," and described an experience similar to mine:

> Coming here was another way of me seeking a spot where I could really put down roots and be some place. And I didn't really have a sense of what that would be like. When I got here, I did in a sense originally come here because it's pretty countryside, but when I saw this town, the town intrigues me as much or more—I mean it's part of the landscape, so you can't separate it. That has been a really important thing to me. But what I have found really most profound about being here is, I really like the culture. Even though there are some idiosyncrasies about it that could potentially get on my nerves, I like living in an LDS community. I like having that sense of some community that ties things together. Because that's not easy to come by. More and more in this culture, it's a very difficult thing to find. So it's neat being in a place that it feels like an extended family. People really do look out for each other here.

Geographer Peter Walker, who has studied environmental conflict in the rural American West, critiqued "New West" literature that characterizes conflicts between the locals and those who have moved into their communities more recently as "clashes of cultures or ideologies." Instead, he asserted that the political dynamics of these conflicts reflect a clash between three different expressions of modern capitalism—the older resource-based economy, a development industry, and the newer rural-residential, amenity-based economy—each having a distinctive relationship with nature and set of ideologies. He argued that "the desire among 'locals' to take back their communities reflects not just personal experiences but also experiences that are manifestations of regional processes." Therefore, a focus on cultures or ideologies "misses the point that these conflicts reflect underlying tensions between competing capitalisms that commodify nature in incompatible ways" and "an increasingly uneven development and a sharpening of class differences."[10]

However, explanations in terms of differences in culture or class can't fully account for the ways that residents experienced and described community in the Grand Staircase-Escalante region. And they don't explain why some people who move into the region come to feel like they belong in their communities but some do not, or why some come to be seen by the locals as locals but some do not. Neither the New West literature nor Walker's explanation considers that people who have or develop a commitment to their community may be willing to accommodate different cultures, ideologies, or classes and to gain new shared understandings to maintain it, as some of the people who shared their thoughts with me have been willing to do.

For further insight into community dynamics, I turned to *Habits of the Heart*, a much-cited qualitative study of individualism and community in American society. Sociologist Robert Bellah and his coauthors found that the people in their study understood community and politics in fundamentally different ways. One group thought of community as if it were an extension of the notion of family. This could be called a community of belonging. This type of community has formed over time. It has a history and is defined in part by its past and its memory of its past. Its members share similar experiences and values, so it is easy for them to come to agreement and get along. Bellah and colleagues called the corresponding understanding of politics the "politics of community." "Getting involved" expressed "a genuine concern for one's local community, a concern expressed in working for its betterment and caring for those in need within it."[11]

What holds this kind of community together and motivates its ethic of care is a feeling of belonging akin to belonging to a family. The problem with this understanding of community is that it is static: it cannot easily accommodate economic, social, or cultural change, or people who are different. Longtime residents of the Grand Staircase-Escalante region seemed to share this understanding of community and politics. One does not have to be a pioneer descendant to become part of such a community, but it takes time for more recent arrivals to come to understand it and feel like they belong. These newcomers were accepted by longtime residents because they "keep their mouths shut until they understand a little bit about the town, and then they make a positive impact on it." This understanding of community and politics has much in common with the deliberative model of democracy: for people to be able to deliberate together, they must also share some degree of understanding, commitment, and trust.

Another group in this study conceived of community as an assortment of self-interested individuals and groups who "join together to maximize individual good."[12] This could be called a community of association. What holds this type of community together is rational interest. Corresponding to this understanding of community is an understanding of politics as "the politics of interest": "the pursuit of differing interests according to agreed-upon, neutral rules." While political scientists sometimes celebrate this as pluralism, ordinary Americans often view it suspiciously: "One enters the politics of interest for reasons of utility, to get what one or one's group needs or wants, rather than because of spontaneous involvement with others to whom one feels akin."[13] This understanding of community and politics has much in common with the aggregative model of democracy in which decisions are made by autonomous individuals, each person expresses their preference, preferences are aggregated, and the one with the greatest support would become the decision of the community.

The problem with this understanding of community is that a group that finds itself in the minority does not have much incentive to abide by decisions they disagree with and continue to consider themselves part of the community. Bellah and colleagues pointed out that while many urban Americans are nostalgic for the small town and the image of its face-to-face politics, their idea of politics and community is interest based. People who moved into the Grand Staircase-Escalante region and got involved in their community for the first time before "taking their time and getting to know" the locals and their ways were practicing the politics of interest. Lacking understanding of the community, they could promote only their own personal vision of its future. As a result, they posed a challenge to community identities and the politics of community, and longtime residents might feel inclined to exclude them.

A third group in the study understood community as a "lifestyle enclave": "formed by people who share some feature of private life," such as "shared patterns of appearance, consumption, and leisure activities, which often serve to differentiate them sharply from those with other lifestyles," and who are "not interdependent, do not act together politically, and do not share a history." What holds a lifestyle enclave together is similar habits. Bellah and colleagues did not consider a lifestyle enclave a community. While a community "attempts to be an inclusive whole, celebrating the interdependence of public and private life and of the different callings of all," a lifestyle enclave involves "only a segment of each individual," that concerned with private life, and only a segment of society, "those with a common lifestyle."[14] Those who moved into the Grand Staircase-Escalante region and found friends like themselves seem to fall into this group. They excluded themselves from the community, did not feel like they belonged, and saw it as split. New residents like this pose a challenge to the politics of community, which aims to include everyone despite their differences.

Bellah and colleagues began to develop a fourth understanding of community "in a strong sense," as "a group of people who are socially interdependent, who participate together in discussion and decision-making, and who share certain practices that both define the community and are nurtured by it." What holds community in this sense together is moral or ethical commitment. It is based neither on the metaphor of kinship nor on common interests but rather on a conception of "a common good or a public interest that recognizes economic, social, and cultural differences between people but sees them all as parts of a single society on which they depend."[15] Those in the communities adjacent to GSENM who are willing to accommodate differences and develop new shared understandings to maintain a commitment to their community seem to understand community in this way. This understanding of community and politics has much in common with the agonistic model of democracy.

Two further examples illustrate how different understandings of community and politics affected interactions between longtime residents and those who have moved to the region more recently. The first year I lived in Escalante, several newer residents had volunteered to be on the Planning and Zoning Committee. The committee thought it would be a good idea to put out a survey to learn what kind of development residents wanted to see in Escalante. According to the mayor:

> The survey was a spectacular flop, I'm happy to say. Because I thought they had poor questions, some of them were leading, and a lot of them just weren't pertinent. The majority of the community just ignored it. They saw it as an attempt by some of these people who want Escalante to be a certain way—more of a retirement vacation town, a little-bitty Moab, and people don't want that here. I hate to make it sound like I'm picking on people who move into the community, because by and large most of them fit right in and they become the town. It's just these, one little group of what I would call exclusionists. People here in Escalante hear things like that, roll their eyes, and go back to their lives. If you want to know what people think, ask them, rather than telling people, "Oh come fill out a little survey." All you really need to do is go to the grocery store or to . . . , and hear what people really think about the community.

The group the mayor referred to as "exclusionists" thought of community as a community of interest, as evinced by their use of a survey. In their view, a survey would objectively and efficiently solicit the preferences of community members, conceived of as autonomous, self-interested individuals, which the Planning and Zoning Committee could aggregate and base its decisions on. The mayor recognized this approach as "the politics of interest" and felt that the "exclusionists" were trying to promote their own vision of development with a biased survey. People who belonged to the community practiced the politics of community: they talked things over at the grocery store, the post office, the café, city council meetings, and basketball games, so they had a good idea of "what people think."

A pioneer descendant Boulder rancher described another example of the politics of interest on Boulder's Planning and Zoning Committee. He said they wanted to pass zoning ordinances that would preserve Boulder's rural character by restricting the way large agricultural landowners could subdivide and sell their property. The ordinances would not affect any of the committee members, since none of them owned more than three acres. According to him, their intention expressed the idea that "we came and got what we want, and now we're going to tell you what we want you to do."[16]

Based on this discussion of the meaning of community, I would argue that the salient difference between the locals and newcomers in rural western communities is not so much culture, ideology, or class, but different understandings of community and politics. These differences became especially problematic when newcomers wanted to get involved in local politics. Longtime residents want to preserve community identities and conceive of democracy as the politics of community. They are being challenged by newcomers with a different understanding of community and politics at the same time that they are being challenged by the monument and the changing local economy.

The Meaning of Democracy

When I asked local residents what democracy meant to them, community figured prominently in their responses. For example, for a woman whose family had moved to Boulder in 1970, democracy was feeling that she had a say in her community: "Just the fact that I know in this small town that I do have a voice in government, that I can be personally involved in it, that it does make a difference in how the community is run and the values that are brought out in my community, and that I personally can make a difference in the community." In contrast, residents felt they didn't have a voice in national government when the monument was created.

For Carol Sullivan, democracy was about "caring for your community": "I've always had the sense that being part of a community means that you need to be involved, that sense of commitment to your community means you care. And if you care, in some capacity you're doing something for your community. Because democracy isn't just taking; it's also giving." In contrast, local residents felt the federal government didn't care about them when the president created the monument without consulting them.

For a man who had lived in Escalante in the 1980s and returned after retiring, democracy was simply "living in Escalante."

> You want to know why? Well, you have probably the closest thing to basic democracy, the very basis of it right here, which is freedom to choose and work together. And that's because of the lack of population here. This is the least populated area in the United States, so it's not as complicated. People can get along better. People are more individually self-reliant. However, at the same time, with the Mormon pioneer culture that developed here, if you need help, all you have to do is holler or ask. . . . They'll get you by with things.

The response of a Kanab woman who worked in county government and was married to a pioneer descendant extended the idea of community to a national scale. She began by pointing out, "First of all, we don't live in a democracy; we live in a republic. A democracy is a majority rule. You vote, the majority rules. A republic protects the rights of the weakest of citizens. And the closer we stay to a republic and protect the rights of the innocent and the weaker, the more we substantiate the community as a whole." She believed that "the government that governs best is the closest to the people," and to illustrate how the federal government should work, she drew on examples from her community: "You can call your county commissioners and your city council and every single elected official that works in local government. You go to church with them. You meet them in the grocery store. You go to the movies. You see them everywhere. You have that contact. And if they are not doing what they're supposed to be doing, the pressure to behave yourself is tremendous." She thought that was one of the main reasons

> the cities and the rural areas have different perspectives on things. And why the rural people feel like they have more ownership of their government and more ownership of the direction of the land, and

more ownership of whether the land should be used in what manner or the other, because they're closer to it. And why sometimes people who are born and raised in the city don't have that same perspective, they don't see it. Because we are a small community and people care. And we fight for that freedom. We don't want to see the rural ambience ruined. And it can only be maintained when we have the ability to maintain these kinds of resource jobs. Jobs that are these lifestyle jobs. You do away with the cows, you do away with the western ambience.

Her words echoed the civic republicanism of the Anti-Federalists. For her, democracy rested on the strength of rural communities, and the ethics of care that bound rural communities provided a model for the national community.

An important aspect of caring for the national community, and therefore of democracy, was coming to its defense in times of war. Longtime residents of the region have a high proportion of veterans; military service is highly respected, and veterans are honored by community celebrations on Veterans Day and Memorial Day. While I was living in Escalante, a campaign to raise funds for a memorial to local veterans came to fruition. I attended the groundbreaking ceremony on Memorial Day 2004 and the highly attended dedication of the memorial the following July 24 (see fig. 18). Its theme was "Freedom Isn't Free." I heard many residents express pride in the memorial and how they had overcome disagreements to come together to make it happen.

Democracy and Community

A theoretical consideration of the relationship between democracy and community reveals a paradox of democracy that longtime residents experienced in relation to change in their communities. Since many residents of the communities adjacent to GSENM understand democracy in terms of community, and the legitimacy of democracy as rule of the people is based on inclusion of all the people, this means that for democracy and community to be congruent, the community should include all the people. But as more and more people with different backgrounds and values move into these communities, the dilemma for longtime residents is how to maintain community identity and democratic legitimacy at the same time. The paradox for more recent arrivals is that in attempting to belong and contribute to the community, they may push out the voices of those with less social and financial capital.

In his essay "No Community, No Democracy," political philosopher Charles Taylor asserted that a strong form of community is necessary for democracy, but at the same time, it creates a dilemma for democracy. He began by arguing that a modern democratic state demands a people with a high degree of mutual understanding, trust, and commitment, which he referred to as a "strong collective identity."[17] What he had in mind sounds like the community of belonging. Taylor was specifically discussing community at the national scale, and he referred to a strong collective identity at the national scale as "political identity." However, his argument, and the paradoxical relationship between democracy and community he identified, applies to communities of all scales and is relevant to the experience of longtime residents of the Grand Staircase-Escalante region.

Taylor went on to point out that while the existence of a strong collective identity makes democracy possible, it also "provides a strong temptation to exclude those who can't or won't fit into the identity which the majority feels comfortable with or believes alone can hold them together."[18] However, exclusion not only is morally objectionable to the community but also goes against the democratic principle of inclusion of *all* the people, on which the legitimacy of democracy as rule of the people is based. As diversity becomes a more significant feature of communities at all scales, a tension arises between democratic inclusion and a strong collective identity because "the exact content of the mutual understanding, the bases of the mutual trust, and the shape of the mutual commitment, all have to be redefined, reinvented. This is not easy, and there is an understandable temptation to fall back on the old ways and deny the problem; either by straight exclusion from citizenship or by the perpetuation of 'us and them' ways of talking, thinking, doing politics."[19] Some residents of the communities adjacent to GSENM observed this happening in their communities.

According to Taylor, this "dynamic of exclusion" is built into democracy and cannot be resolved either by appeals to an original agreement, contract, or constitution or by appeals to a preexisting unity of culture, history, or language. Both deny the fact that personal and community identities shift over time through economic, social, and cultural change, which can bring the established identity "out of touch with the people who are supposed to live with it."[20] Taylor referred to this as "inner exclusion"; it poses the same dilemma for community and democratic legitimacy as the overt kind of exclusion.

Taylor added that liberalism's appeal to individual rights and official procedures based on rule of law cannot overcome this "standing dilemma of democracy." For one reason, "the condition of a viable political identity is that people must actually be able to relate to it."[21] But many people would not forsake a historical collective identity for that of an autonomous and isolated liberal subject. In addition, liberalism's supposedly neutral procedures usually turn out to be based on non-neutral assumptions. And finally, reliance on official procedures does not give people the opportunity to consider other points of view, the first step toward redefining or reinventing the bases of mutual understanding, trust, and commitment.

Residents of the Grand Staircase-Escalante region were experiencing this paradox of democracy in multiple ways. First, longtime residents experienced a kind of reverse "inner exclusion" as national identity shifted but historical community identities did not. As rural residents, they are a political minority in a U.S. population that in 2009 was less than 20 percent rural and by 2022 had declined to 17 percent rural.[22] Mainstream American values have diverged from their pioneer values. Since per capita income and average earnings per job were well below the national average in Garfield and Kane Counties, residents of the Grand Staircase-Escalante region struggled to be included in national prosperity. And more Americans are coming to perceive the landscape surrounding them differently than they do and clamor for different management. They were excluded from decision-making when the monument was created and continue to feel excluded from decisions that affect their lives.

Not only was their strong community identity out of touch with the national identity in many ways, but it also was being challenged by increasing numbers of new people moving into the region. As a result, longtime residents were tempted to exclude new residents or to include only those who shared their conceptions of community and politics. While some new residents' attempts to get involved in their communities were rebuffed and they felt excluded, others who proceeded more cautiously felt like they belonged. In the story in the introduction about the public hearing for a gun ordinance in Escalante, local residents attempted to include a new resident who didn't fit into the identity the majority felt comfortable with, didn't try to understand it, and in fact denigrated it. Local officials opposed changes in the management of GSENM they perceived to threaten traditional livelihoods and culture. These are some examples of the ways that residents of the Grand Staircase-Escalante region were trying to negotiate the democratic paradox they experienced as they clung to historical community identities while their communities and the nation changed around them.

For Taylor, the key to facing the dilemma of democratic exclusion creatively is the idea of sharing identity space. What he meant by this is that "political identities have to be worked out, negotiated, creatively compromised between peoples who want to or have to live together under the same political roof."[23] By engaging in this effort, they begin to form what Bellah and colleagues called community "in a strong sense": one based on ethical commitment to being a community that recognizes interdependence and the contributions that difference can make. Taylor also said that these identities "are never meant to last forever, but have to be discovered/invented anew by succeeding generations."[24] This resonates with Chantal Mouffe's assertion that solutions to conflict will always be "temporary respites in an ongoing confrontation."[25]

Taylor and Mouffe have provided a broader understanding of political life that can be applied to how residents of the Grand Staircase-Escalante region were practicing democracy as they struggled to get along with each other. Residents shared an attachment to the landscape, to their communities, and to democracy, although they understood each in different ways. These emotional attachments could potentially provide the motivation for them to "work out, negotiate, and creatively compromise" changing community identities, as well as common ground from which to begin.[26]

6   The Ranchers

DEMOCRACY AND FREEDOM

This chapter considers the meaning of democracy to ranchers in the Grand Staircase-Escalante region in the early twenty-first century. It presents the stories and perspectives of five ranching families who had grazing permits for allotments in Grand Staircase-Escalante National Monument (GSENM) to provide a better understanding of their way of life and values, as well as the challenges to both that GSENM represented. Two of the families lived in Boulder and one in Escalante and ranched in the northern part of the region, and two lived in Kanab and ranched in its southern part. All except the Cochrans were pioneer descendants, but they differed in many ways. Their ranching operations varied in size and were in different ecological settings. They had gotten into ranching in different ways, used different strategies to remain in ranching, and had different perspectives on working with the Bureau of Land Management (BLM) and how things had changed since the monument was created. But despite these differences, they also had much in common with each other, with other ranchers in the region, and with public land ranchers in general. Several were involved in the conflicts over grazing described in chapter 3, and these stories provide more insight into their experiences.

Their stories highlight the noneconomic values they derived from ranching, in terms of their experience of freedom, enjoyment of their work, family and community life, and ability to make a contribution to American democracy. The stories also aid in understanding how larger socioeconomic processes—the transforming economy of the rural West from resource production to amenity consumption, altering perceptions of public land from "chiefly valuable for grazing" to national landscape, and the changing role of the BLM—played out both materially and emotionally in ranchers' lives and informed their preoccupation with the monument.[1] Ranchers had to work harder, negotiate shifting BLM grazing management policies, navigate increased uncertainty about the future, and devise new strategies to stay in ranching, while they also faced negative perceptions of public land ranching. Finally, the stories bring out a democratic paradox that ranchers in the Grand Staircase-Escalante region, who understood democracy in terms of freedom, experienced as they saw their daily lives and futures circumscribed more tightly by BLM management of grazing on the monument.

Dell LeFevre

When I began my fieldwork at GSENM and asked people I met for the names of ranchers I should talk to, the first name mentioned was always Dell LeFevre. That was not just because Dell ran the largest locally owned cattle operation ("outfit") on the monument, but because he was larger than life himself. He was elected to the Garfield County Commission in 2000, so he was also a central figure in local politics.

Dell was in his sixties when I first met him, but he didn't look it. He was big and brawny, his hair and mustache were still blond, and his eyes were blue and shrewd. He spoke with what I came to recognize as the distinctive southern Utah accent. In the years I knew him, he didn't change much. He came across as the quintessential cowboy, knew it, and used it to his advantage. Media reporters covering issues on GSENM always went to him for the rancher's perspective. They came away with quotes that got right to the heart of the issue and, at the same time, convinced readers and listeners they were hearing from a real cowboy. He has been featured in articles in the *New York Times*, the *Denver Post*, and *High Country News*, where he represented himself as "a bitter old cowboy."[2] But that was just for the media. Despite the difficulties of the ranching life and its increasing tenuousness, he loved it.

Dell was one of the few full-time ranchers in the region. He ran a cow-calf operation out of Salt Gulch outside Boulder, which means that his herd consisted of "momma cows" that he hoped would have a calf each year that could be sold as yearlings. He usually ran about 1,000 cows, but he was down to about 600 to 650 during the drought that lasted from 1999 to 2005. He held permits for hundreds of thousands of acres of grazing allotments on the Dixie National Forest for summer and fall grazing and on GSENM for winter and spring grazing, and he owned about 1,000 acres of private ground, where he raised hay for feed when it was needed. His ranching operation was larger by far than any other in the region except Steve Sorensen's, whom local ranchers described as a millionaire from California whose ranch, run by hired help, provided a tax write-off. Dell saw him as a competitor and someone who drove up the price of grazing permits. Full-time ranchers in the region typically ran 300 head at most, and part-time ranchers only a few. Most owned only a small amount of land and did all the ranching work with the help of their families.

Dell described himself as fifth generation. He was born in 1940 in Boulder and grew up on a small farm his father owned in Salt Gulch. Although his father "always wanted a big ranch" and "had a lot of opportunities," he never acquired one because, according to Dell, he was scared: "They went broke during the Depression," and "my dad never would go in debt." So Dell didn't inherit a ranch, but he did inherit his father's dream. His dad had sheep, but Dell wanted to be a cowboy: "I didn't know how I was going to buy a ranch, but that was my dream."[3] He got to work early making his dream come true:

> When I was about twelve years old I started coming here working for the Lymans [Ivan Lyman's ranch] because they had a lot of cattle.... I hung around these guys that knew cattle, and I started getting cows. When I started working for [the] Lymans they'd give me dogie calves, and I put quite a little herd together.... [But] I didn't want to work for someone else. I knew I had to own my own ranch. When I was about 13 or 14, I decided the only way I could get a ranch was, I was going to be a bull rider, so I started riding bulls.[4]

Dell found a ranch he wanted to buy in the early 1960s, but no one would sign for him to get a loan except his mother, and "back then it had to be a man." But before he could buy a ranch, he got drafted. While in the army, he acquired "bad lungs" and a "bad shoulder" that still give him trouble. When Dell got out of the army, he worked for the Lymans and rodeoed some more. Eventually he realized he didn't have what it took to make enough money bull riding, so he went to Casper, Wyoming, to work on the oil rigs, taking his new wife, Gladys, one of Ivan Lyman's daughters, with him. He worked there for nine years, starting as a roughneck, working his way up, and eventually buying into the drilling company. He thought of buying a ranch in Wyoming, but "coming from here, I guess it's always been Boulder."[5]

As soon as he had saved enough money, he came home and bought half of the Lyman ranch in 1965 and the other half in 1973. "It has been a struggle ever since, but I just kept buying. Every time I got a chance, I think because my dad wouldn't, I would. I bought out like thirteen or fourteen ranches over in Escalante, and we just kept going, and we're still broke. . . . It's going to be tight, but I figured out, if you're going to make it, you've got to get big enough to survive it."[6] By the time I met him, his operation had grown so large, and he had become so busy with his duties as county commissioner, that he hired a local as foreman.

To expand and improve his livestock operation, Dell participated in several transactions with the Grand Canyon Trust (described in chapter 3). In 1996 he decided to sell his permits in the Escalante River canyons because working those allotments became increasingly difficult as the canyons became more and more popular with hikers. Hikers who were opposed to livestock grazing in the canyons were sometimes antagonistic toward local ranchers. His allotment was "one of the most hiked spots and one of the most fenced spots" on the river. "People keep going through and leaving the gates open. Then my cows get into areas they're not supposed to be, and that means trouble for me. So I decided it was time to get out."[7] Dell recounted an unpleasant incident that ensued when thirty-four of his cows died from eating copperweed (*Oxytenia acerosa*). While he was still going through the process of getting permission from the BLM to take a bulldozer in to remove the carcasses, a group of hikers came upon them and tried to burn them: "They cut down a lot of cottonwoods, but only did half the job. I had to finish. I just about felt like quitting. People wrote a lot of letters about what a bad rancher I was."

According to Dell, his strategy for staying in ranching was to be "aggressive." He kept buying ranches; he got into politics, where he learned about programs that were available to help ranchers; he used the contacts he made there; and he was always thinking up ways to improve his operation. He knew cows, saying he had "a doctorate in the beef business," and his calves were "reputation calves."[8] He still pushed, getting up at daylight and going until dark. There are no typical days for ranchers: something always needs to be done, and something unexpected often comes up that puts off getting it done. If it's not problems with the sprinklers or a hurt calf, it might be cows that have to be brought back from someplace they're not supposed to be, a broken fence that has to be mended, or ranch equipment that has broken down and has to be fixed.

Dell decided to run for county commissioner in 1976 to be a spokesman for ranchers, including himself, who were "getting kicked off some ranges" when Capitol Reef National Monument became a national park.[9] He explained how getting into politics had helped his ranching business:

> This is a political arena we're in. I get along with BLM. I get along with the Forest Service and I get along with the Park Service. I've learned that you don't throw stones at somebody and call them names and expect to work with them. You go in and you set down, like we're talking here. A lot of these old-time ranchers wouldn't do that. They just would not. I could side-effect early in life that these guys was losing out because they just bulled their neck and then they'd take a big cut [in permitted cattle] and hate everybody instead of trying to work [with the agencies].[10]

He was a commissioner from 1977 to 1987 and ran again in 2000, feeling that this time would be his "final payback." "I've had it good. I've done what I wanted to do." And he wanted to make it possible for others to keep ranching: "I like cowboys. They're different. They're a breed all their own. And that's why I'm fighting so hard." To do that, "we gotta figure out how to get along."

While Dell made an effort to get along with the federal agencies on a professional level, on a personal level it wasn't so easy. For example, when a *New York Times* reporter asked him why he sold his permits along the Escalante River to GCT in 1996, he explained, "I was afraid the BLM would add so many restrictions that I wouldn't be able to use the land anyway, and I'd be out the $100,000 I spent for the permits."[11] And when I asked him why he was interested in trading his remaining permit along the river to GCT for one on the Last Chance allotment, he responded, "You couldn't run in the rivers anymore and I had to go somewhere. I always liked it out there, way out, and I didn't think BLM could find me out there." The deals he made with GCT were one of the strategies he used to keep ranching. They benefited his ranching operation financially, increased his animal unit months (AUMs), and gave him easier allotments to work. Dell was also frustrated with the BLM because few of the range improvement projects he proposed ever got done, telling me, "You can go back thirty years and none of it's ever been done. You can study it and study it and study it and no money ever seems to come. The only reason there's been anything done on my allotments is because I've been beating these guys' doors." Other ranchers expressed similar frustration about the BLM's inertia on range improvements.

However, Dell recognized that neither the BLM nor the monument was the real problem facing ranchers in the region: "The economics is what's killing us in the cow business." He explained to me that he was going to get the same price for cattle in 2000 that he did in 1973. But in 1973 a gallon of gas was 39 cents and a new pickup was $3,000. Cattle prices were 25 cents a pound less that year than the year before, so he was going to lose $100 a calf. And on top of that, "this free-trade"—imported cattle—"is just killing us."

With all these difficulties, what did he get out of ranching? Among other things: "I'm alone. You think a lot. You're just riding along. It's therapy is what it is. It's made me what I am. Everybody has to have an escape of some kind. I guess maybe that's it, but if you escape and do something at the same time, if you can do your work, I don't care if checking fences, riding through your cows or doctoring calves, or what you're doing, I enjoy being alone."[12] Ranching is "a lasting love affair with me."

Dell didn't much like the changes he saw in Boulder, changes that reflected the shifting economics and demographics in the rural West:

> That's what bothers me today, the make-up of Boulder is changing, and every one of these old boys we put in the grave, like we did Kirk [Lyman] the other day, it just breaks my heart because there's another piece of history gone. There's not another of that type. We're not raising that type anymore.... The people come into Boulder, they're good people, but they're not of that pioneer stock people, and they don't know what tough times is. These old-timers, they may have talked about each other, but if somebody broke his leg or got sick, they done his work. They just teamed together. It was nothing.... I don't like the change that's coming. Little ranchettes down the road here, and motels, and Garfield County, and the State of Utah, all we can talk about is tourism. That's a damn poor industry. Tourism don't do nothing. There's not a tax base in tourism. One good oil field out here produces more taxes than all the tourists in Garfield County, but the schools is going down. Everything is going down because you can't pay people $5 an hour and expect them to live....
>
> It's not neighbors now, but years ago it was neighbors. You was neighbors and you was friends, and you accepted each other. If you had faults, you accepted them. If another guy had a fault, you accepted it. To me now, you could be a neighbor, and not be in agriculture. Back then it was a bond. They was all struggling to make it. It was kind of a bond. Now . . . I have neighbors would just as soon my cows went off the hill. I have neighbors who walk right past me in church and won't say a word. . . . They're not bad people, it's a different culture, different customs.[13]

He told a reporter in 2002, "You can't blame the monument for everything. I'd like to, but you can't. I see my world going away."[14]

All these things about Dell I learned bit by bit. After our first interview, I asked if I could see what a typical day of work was like on his ranch. I didn't realize at the time what a big favor I was asking. He asked me if I could ride. Yes, I was one of those horse crazy girls when I was a kid and had a horse of my own in high school. So he suggested I come along while he set out salt for the cows on one of his summer allotments on Boulder Mountain the following week.

It was almost 10:00 in the morning in late July in the hot, dry summer of 2000, but it was still cool in the shade of the aspens at 7,000 feet, where I waited to meet Dell. He was almost two hours late. Still unaware of the unpredictability of ranch work, I was wondering whether I should give up waiting. Finally, a big, white American pickup truck pulling a stock trailer came up the hill and parked across the road from the trailhead. As I walked toward it, a large figure emerged from the driver's side and a small, slight figure from the other. Dell introduced me to his daughter Ariul, who had dark, liquid eyes, long black hair, and South Asian features. He seemed as shy of her as she was of him. As we unloaded the horses, Dell explained that they were late because his brand-new pickup had gotten a flat tire. "This outfit cost more than my first ranch," he informed me, saying it was one of only two new pickups he had ever owned in his life.

Dell and his wife, Gladys, had started adopting children after they had been married for fourteen years and still had none of their own. They adopted a total of fourteen, including eight girls from India, two boys from Bolivia, and a girl from Colombia. Ariul, sixteen, was the oldest girl. According to Dell, the boys were shaping up to be good cowboys, and the girls could all ride. Local residents joked that thanks to Dell and Gladys, Boulder (population 180 in the 2000 census) was the most ethnically diverse town in Utah.

Dell loaded the salt blocks, weighing fifty pounds each, onto the packhorse and carefully adjusted the packsaddle. We tightened the cinches on the other horses' saddles, mounted, and rode off with Dell leading the packhorse. We soon left the trail, and Dell led the way at a fast trot through groves of aspen and spruce, taking a route that seemed perfectly obvious to him but was indiscernible to me. As we wove and ducked our way through the trees, I was thankful that I could still ride a horse even though I hadn't ridden since I was in high school. Dell didn't slow down or look back to see how Ariul and I were doing. In the rancher's code, this does not indicate disregard for our welfare but rather respect for our independence. When the trees opened, Dell rode alongside me and pointed things out, while Ariul silently brought up the rear.

We passed groups of cows in the forest, and Dell showed me the ones that didn't belong to him; they belonged to the permittee on the adjacent allotment who didn't repair his fences. But he said it wouldn't do any good to tell the man, because all he did was drink whiskey, or to tell the Forest Service, because it seemed to be doing nothing these days. We passed herds of elk and deer. Dell commented that the elk ate his salt and competed with his cows for grazing, but it didn't do any good to complain about that either. Permits for hunting deer and elk are a major source of income for the Utah Division of Wildlife Resources. Pointing out clumps of lupine we passed, Dell explained that the Forest Service was concerned about the amount of forage on his allotment on account of the drought, but he could tell his cows had enough to eat because they weren't eating the lupine yet.

Each time we came to a salting site, Dell would dismount slowly, unload a block of salt from the packhorse, and place it next to the block that was nearly used up. Putting out salt for the cows is not just a way to supply them with minerals; it is also a way to distribute them. Ranchers use the siting of salt licks—and more importantly, water sources—to control where cattle gather and graze and how they affect the landscape. After rebalancing the load on the packhorse, Dell would lead his horse over to a stump or rock to remount. He had sustained multiple injuries while riding bulls and serving in the army, so the procedure involved painfully hoisting himself up instead of neatly throwing a leg over. He laughed at himself, the old cowboy who could hardly get on his horse.

On the way back, we rode more slowly and Dell seemed pensive. He talked about how hard it was to make a living ranching. He could switch to tourism and get rich, but he liked people on his terms, not theirs. He regretted that his kids wouldn't be able to ranch, which he attributed to the economics, having to deal with the government, and the fact that no one wanted to work that hard anymore. He could sell all his land and then his kids wouldn't have to work, but then what would they do? Why does he stay? "Because it's home, I guess, and because of this old mountain."

Dell asked me whether I would like his life. That was when I realized that I felt an affinity with the ranchers because of the many years I had spent climbing in mountain ranges throughout the world, and I began to see them in a different light. What I loved about mountain climbing was being outside all day, in remote, rugged, beautiful places where there were no people. Free of society's rules and trappings, you survive and succeed by learning to understand and work with the mountain environment and the bare essentials. You come to feel at home there. I concluded that I would like his life because it involved many of the same things. In addition, because Dell stayed in the same place, he knew the shape and smell and feel of this particular landscape, the habits of what lives on it, and the changes from season to season and year to year. This experience of freedom and belonging in nature is one that many who work in resource production industries express.[15] It helps explain their attachment to occupations that otherwise seem too physically demanding, dangerous, and financially uncertain. As we rode fittingly into the sunset, I could imagine this as my life, and I began to feel more at home in the Escalante country. Dell most likely was thinking about all he had to do the next day.

At many of the meetings and local events I attended in my role as researcher, I spoke with Dell, who was there in his role as county commissioner. He would always tell me he was still trying to figure out which side I was on. He had "spies all over the place," he said, so he knew I also went to BLM meetings and talked with environmentalists. I kept telling him I wasn't on any side: as an anthropologist, I was trying to understand all sides. But I don't think I ever convinced him. When it came to other things about me, however, his insight was uncanny. Dell helped shatter preconceptions I had brought with me to my research and made me realize that while anthropologists are in the field trying to figure people out, those people are also trying to figure us out, and they might be better at it than we are. I continued to be impressed by the penetrating observations he made, always delivered in a deceptively disarming southern Utah drawl.

Dell's "plain cowboy down" understanding of democracy sounded very much like the ranching life he lived. "Democracy is freedom," he explained to me. "It means that I can *go* where I want, *do* what I want, *become* what I want. I can get on my horse, I can ride on the Boulder Mountain, without being told where and how and what to do. I can make up my own mind and thoughts. I can sit on a point and look for thirty days walking in some direction. I've been in every one of those canyons because I've been free." Freedom also meant being responsible for one's own destiny and being self-sufficient. "Freedom is being born poor, making something of yourself, or being born rich and winding up as a junkie. I mean, think about it. I was born in a log cabin basically. We didn't have electricity until I was twelve years old. We didn't get indoor plumbing until I was about thirteen, fourteen years old. But we were happy. We were poor, we had to work, and my folks taught me to have a goal and go for it."

But democracy to Dell did not mean just personal freedom. "Democracy is a big word, but you have to have it to have a free society. Freedom is helping other people that are not free. We in America, as a government, it's a long way from perfect, but it's the best government in the world. I've traveled to enough countries to know what freedom really is. And I think we are so blessed to live [in this country], especially in this part of America. Freedom is learning to live with others without a conflict, respecting others' views."

Dell's understanding of freedom included two different aspects, which political theorist Isaiah Berlin referred to as "positive" and "negative" liberty. Positive liberty is "the freedom which consists in being one's own master," while negative liberty is "the freedom which consists in not being prevented from choosing as I do by other men."[16] Positive liberty is often conceived as freedom *to* and negative liberty as freedom *from*. Dell felt he was free *to* become what he wanted and make up his own mind and thoughts and *from* someone else telling him "where and how and what to do." While Dell lumped these together, Berlin saw positive and negative liberty as distinct ends of free individuals, conceptually different even if related in practice.

However, while Dell felt free because no one told him "where and how and what to do" when he rode on Boulder Mountain, as a public lands rancher his ranching operation was both enabled and constrained by the federal government. Because he equated democracy with individual freedom, he struggled to get along with the BLM. Dell's experience reflected a democratic paradox, which Berlin captured by suggesting a third aspect of liberty that comes into play when we consider people in the collective. Then positive liberty becomes the collective right to self-government—that is, democracy. But there is no corresponding collective negative liberty: no freedom *from* rules collectively agreed on. So while liberal democracy may guarantee individual rights, it cannot be equated with individual liberty because negative liberty is limited by those rules. Dell recognized that democracy, or collective freedom, meant "learning to live with others," and because he grazed on public lands, he was not free from federal land laws and policies to graze however he wanted. At the same time, environmentalists who oppose public land grazing are not free to eliminate it, because ranchers are also protected by federal laws and policies. Members of a democratic society experience this democratic paradox—the tension between democracy and negative liberty—both in the political arena and in their daily lives. Dell and other ranchers in the Grand Staircase-Escalante region may experience this democratic paradox more acutely than most because they value individual liberty so highly yet are confronted daily with restrictions on their freedom to pursue their livelihood.

Brent Robinson

Brent Robinson lived with his wife, Lynette, and their family on their ranch in the southern part of the monument, along the Skutumpah Road about fifty miles from Kanab. Because of the historical Mormon settlement patterns and livestock herding practices in the region, it was unusual for ranchers in southern Utah to live on an isolated ranch far out of town. Brent was a pioneer descendant like Dell, but the way he got into ranching and his approach to it were quite different.

At forty-two, Brent Robinson was tall and slender, with dark hair, a mustache, and blue eyes, as good-looking as any movie star cowboy. He was a quieter man than Dell but projected a strong presence nevertheless. He spoke slowly and thoughtfully. When I arrived at the Skutumpah Ranch, there was a For Sale sign out where his property meets the road. The three hundred acres of private ground belonged to his father and, before that, his father's father. Using this as their base ranch, Brent and his father had been running up to 280 head of cattle on several BLM allotments. Brent's great-grandfather, whose family came from Cedar City, bought all the land in the valley, over one thousand acres, in 1917. The house we were sitting in was the original ranch headquarters, which

Brent had rebuilt. When Brent's great-grandfather died, each of his sons got a third of the land. Brent's grandfather kept his third and continued ranching, but his brothers sold theirs.

Brent grew up in Kanab, where his father worked, but he spent a lot of time on the ranch. He decided he wanted to be a rancher, so he got his college degree in animal science and found a job on a cattle ranch in Colorado. He never dreamed he would come back. But when his grandfather died and his father and uncle inherited the ranch, he bought his uncle out. Later, when Brent's father decided to sell his share "for pennies on the dollar," Brent saw a "business opportunity" and offered to come back and help his father fix up the ranch so they could sell it together for a better price. "That was eighteen years ago," Brent told me. "It's just taken a lot longer. But we've enjoyed every day of it. We've loved the lifestyle. The lifestyle is why we're in it. And this has been just perfect."

Brent lacked access to high-elevation country for summer grazing, so his ranching operation worked differently than Dell's. He tried to balance out his winter and summer grazing by selling the permits for some of the allotments his grandfather used and buying permits for or leasing others. During 2002 and 2003, when the drought was at its worst, he pared down his herd, leased pasture in New Mexico, and moved his whole operation there. After he brought his herd back, he kept it down to 100 to 150 head and operated his allotments at about one-third of what the BLM defined as their carrying capacity.

While Dell was a shrewd businessman, Brent spoke about ranching in business terms more than Dell did. He explained that he had bought the West Clark Bench permit in the early 1990s with the intention of selling the permit as soon as he was able to improve the Ford Well allotment, adjacent to the ranch, to increase its value. When, according to his business plan, it was time to sell, potential buyers backed off after they discussed the transaction with the BLM. West Clark Bench was considered a "showcase allotment," but Buckskin Gulch and Coyote Butte, which border it, had recently become popular hiking objectives. Brent surmised that the BLM conveyed uncertainty about how the allotment would be managed in the future to discourage interested parties from buying it. He had not previously heard of the Grand Canyon Trust

(GCT), but he sold the permit to Bill Hedden, the trust's executive director, because no one else would buy it.

When the drought improved and he could bring his herd back, it coincided with the timing of the challenge to GCT's Grazing Retirement Program. Brent proposed leasing his cattle to the trust's Canyonlands Grazing Corporation to graze the allotment, an arrangement that would benefit them both. As the permit holder, he "had the capital exposure and risk, but they [BLM] could tell me how to manage [the allotment]." Leasing to GCT, he no longer worried about making payments on the loan for the permit and had "as much certainty from year to year as . . . with BLM. Every time I turned around it seemed like they were trying to get me off."[17]

Brent's ranching business had always been a family operation: his wife was a "top hand," and his five children started helping out as soon as they were old enough. But he always had to find additional sources of income. Now that his kids were older, they were running the ranching business while he devoted more time to his other work. The previous summer he had paid his oldest daughter, who was fifteen, to run the whole cattle operation: "move 'em, haul 'em, do everything." The day I was at the ranch, another daughter, eleven, stayed home from school to help gather cows for the spring roundup.

Brent explained that his "intention was always to sell" the ranch. He had lived in a lot of places and did not have the same attachment to the Skutumpah Ranch as Dell did to Boulder Mountain:

> You can get that same feeling for home wherever. I'm not allowing myself to become too sentimentally attached because it's always been, this is a business venture. We're gonna sell it. That's good and that's bad. It's really neat to be putting labor into something you know you might just die on the place, and I haven't been able to put that kind of pride into it here. But I don't want my kids to end up with it or they'll go broke. I believe I do my kids a better service by reinvesting the money somewhere else.

Brent felt that it had become more difficult to ranch since the monument was created. He pointed toward a ridge north of the ranch. "You see this land that's just starting to green up? That was all sagebrush." He described how he and his father had worked with the BLM and "Fish and Game" to burn and reseed the ridge to increase forage in the fall of 1996, the year the monument was created. They put up some cash and did all the labor. But from 1996 to 2005 the BLM had not increased his AUMs to take advantage of the increased forage, nor would they let him build fences. "So we're in limbo. It's little subtle things. They don't want us out there salting the cattle, only certain times of the year. We can't cut cedar posts. We've got to go through all this red tape if we want to clean a reservoir. . . . So it's a lot of small little things." These "small little things" added up to a lot of uncertainty:

> For me and for other people coming in and wanting to get into business, one of the things that the monument has done is knock any certainty at all that we used to have in public grazing—you can't count on it. When uncertainty looms in any business, then the overall morale goes down, you don't seem to be a big thinker anymore, and to be more specific, with the uncertainty, then it's hard to justify doing a whole lot of improvements if you don't know if you're going to be there for the next ten years to be able to pay those improvements back off. Working with the monument, their regulations are pretty tight and stringent, so it might take them five years to give you the go[-ahead] to do some burning or some land reclamation or put a new fence in or a new water source, and in today's business age you've got be able to operate a lot quicker than that. . . . In any small business you've got to be able to somewhat predict the future so you can get the capital to operate on, and have a business plan, and not have this big variable out there, this wild card that can come and dictate whether you're going to make it or not from year to year.

Brent pointed out that in addition to the need for flexibility to ranch sustainably in arid environments, ranchers need flexibility to be successful in the current business environment.

The lack of flexibility to run their ranching operations in the way they thought was best was compounded by a disregard for ranchers' experiential knowledge of the landscape. Brent explained:

We don't claim ownership on any of this land, even our own private land. It's something you don't gloat over: it's more of an opportunity you have to care for the land. It's more of a traditional value that's within yourself. So then all of a sudden when you have somebody begin to dictate that you can't cut a cedar post, you can't take care of the range through burning it or erosion control, you can't go clean a spring out for wildlife or for livestock, then they begin to encroach on this traditional lifestyle. And so it's really bothered my dad. I'm a little younger and open-minded maybe, but it still eats at me. I have a problem when egg-headed type people from the East or whatever . . . begin to try to come and micromanage my operation here or try to come and micromanage the range when they're making their assessment and judging it from the seat of a pickup, and mine is from 360 days looking at it. And I've got a gut feeling that I think probably would rival and be more accurate than their educated hypothesis.

These experiences detract from the feeling of freedom and self-reliance ranchers derive from ranching. Their willingness to clash with the BLM over how to manage their allotments is limited by the amount of risk they perceive they are running: "These crusty old guys, they have nothing to lose. Everything is paid for. But take a young guy like me with a lot of debt. . . . I don't really feel like I can stand up to these guys, but I have a code of ethics and I try to work with 'em."

Brent predicted that ranching would decline in the region, not just because of economics but also because ranchers' kids see the effects of this struggle on their fathers:

I personally think that a lot of the leadership in the monument, they're realizing they can only push the older generation ranchers so far. But what it does is, mentally, these old guys are unhappy, and so their offspring or their kids are reading into it and can see, "Man, this is tough, Dad's struggling. We don't want to do this." And so I think their timeline will outlive our ambition and desire to ranch. You roll one generation away, and that generation won't fight quite as hard. . . . And I really believe, whether that be a conscious thing that they've discussed, I can just see that happening with really anything that's ag [agriculture] related in the United States.

He pointed out that when he was young, almost everyone in school in Kanab could be tied in with agriculture one generation back. But now only a few of the kids can do that, "so they don't even have the appreciation, the sensitivity, nothing, to this way of life."

Brent had originally intended, after selling the Skutumpah Ranch, to buy a ranch in a place where the price of land reflected its value for ranching. In the Grand Staircase-Escalante region, the value is "recreation and scenery. The value in the land makes it almost impossible to expand and turn it into a good outfit. Whereas you can take the money here and buy more productive land in Nebraska, wherever." But his plans changed. His other businesses were doing well enough that he didn't want to leave, his kids were doing well in school, and he had learned from his business arrangements with GCT. He had leased some land at the mouth of Johnson Canyon, much closer to Kanab and its schools (see fig. 21), and when the ranch sold, his family would relocate there and keep ranching, not "big time into the cattle, but just have 100 head or 150 head to take care of college and missions and marriages."

Brent expressed much the same understanding as Dell's of democracy as individual freedom, encompassing positive and negative liberty. Both recognized that democracy also entails limits on individual freedom. For Brent:

> Democracy is to be able to independently do what I want to do, how I want to do it. Nobody's going to tell me what to do as long as I don't encroach or devalue or demean anybody else. It's that freedom that you have to be able to treat people—not to bring religion into it, but to treat them like the golden rule or Christ-like, but nobody's got their thumb on you. It's really hard for me to come up with a Webster's definition. It's more of a feeling in my heart. For me, I can wake up every morning and plan whatever I want to do, and as long as it doesn't have an adverse effect on mankind, or on the earth, I can do it. And for me, that means a lot. There are some people that would rather go to work from eight to five and have someone pretty well tell them what to do. There's those people who work for the BLM, and I can't imagine what would motivate them to get out of bed in the morning to go have somebody tell them what they're gonna do. But

that's it there: just that freedom that we all can grasp hold [of]. But it comes with respect for other people. You've gotta have respect for people and for the land and for other people's values.

Brent saw individual freedom as what made America great, and he feared that these qualities were being lost as government came to regulate people's lives more and more:

And actually, I think we're still doing good as a nation. . . . And yet I look at the way that the government is getting involved in subsidies in agriculture and welfare and discipline in the school systems, and we could go on and on and on with their regulations. And then the financial aspect. And what I see is we're breeding a generation that is becoming completely dependent upon government, or on third world countries to feed us, and it's just not healthy. If you study the history of eastern Europe, Russia and all that, that was a great nation until communism come in, and they took the poor old peasants and farmers off the land and turned them into big government plantations, and it took their pride away. It took their incentive to be creative and work hard and put pride into what they did. And then what you do is you breed a weak bunch of people that can't act for themselves. Sorry, I see us heading in that direction.

Paradoxically, ranching gave Brent the freedom he prized while it also made him more dependent on the federal government and brought him more directly under its control. He was aware of the contradictions in his convictions: "But really, I'm not living this free life." Although he had used people who work for the BLM as an example of not being free, he admitted that he saw similar behavior in himself. For example, he hired himself and his heavy equipment out to the federal agencies for fighting fires, and he could see all kinds of inefficiencies in how they did things. But he told himself, "They're not hiring me to think, they're hiring me for my dozer or my water tender, so keep your mouth shut; the paycheck will come in."

Brent explained his approach to negotiating the paradox between personal freedom and the compromises required of a public land rancher:

21. Brent and Lynette Robinson on their leased property, March 2005. Courtesy of the author.

You can't be an extreme. And that's when I'm trying to teach my kids that you've got to get right in the mainstream, try to keep ethics, keep your moral values and your beliefs intact, because that's what makes the moral fiber of this nation strong. But you still gotta get out there and compete and play by those rules. And it's hard to quantify where your comfort zone is and what's right. I just consider myself really blessed to live like we do. I have lots of people come and say, "I'd give everything to live like this." And I say, "Well, that's about what you gotta do."

"Everything" included Brent's cherished personal convictions about democracy as freedom.

Que and Karla Johnson

Que Johnson was a gentle giant of a man, quiet and soft-spoken, with blue eyes and, at fifty-three when I met him in 2005, thinning brown hair. I was on the GSENM Monument Advisory Committee with Que, where he was the representative for the ranching community. He seldom offered comments during meetings, but when he did, he had a way of distilling an analysis of the topic under discussion into a few simple words that got right to the issue.

Que and his father, Calvin, eighty-two, were full-time ranchers who, like Brent Robinson, also ranched out of Kanab in the southern part of the monument. They had a permit to run about 350 to 400 head on the Mollie's Nipple allotment. While Calvin was obviously the physical mold that Que sprang from, he had the opposite temperament. Irascible and domineering, Calvin had managed to intimidate the whole BLM range staff, none of whom wanted to stand up to him or disagree with him. Calvin owned 1,160 acres of private land within the allotment, including the lush Nipple Pasture, as well as land closer to Kanab where Que grew hay.

Because of its proximity to Kanab, the Mollie's Nipple allotment has been historically overgrazed. The BLM conducted extensive range improvements in the region during the 1960s and 1970s to increase forage production for livestock, which included planting a non-native species, crested wheatgrass (*Agropyron cristatum*), that is more productive than native species. However, much of that grass on the Mollie's Nipple allotment died out in the drought that had been going on since 1999. Rangeland health assessments carried out between 1999 and 2002 to provide data for the monument-wide Rangeland Health Environmental Impact Statement (EIS) found that Mollie's Nipple was one of the allotments in the worst condition. The EIS Team was considering redoing the seedings; if they did, a large area of the allotment would be closed to grazing for two years, and the Johnsons would have to cut back on AUMs. But things were looking up in 2005. Precipitation had been three times the average during the winter of 2004–5, and Que said it was the best winter he'd seen in his life.

Que was fifth generation, descended from Joel Hill Johnson, who first settled in the eponymous Johnson Canyon, east of Kanab. The fourth child and third boy of six children, he grew up working on his father's ranch, but he didn't know whether he would be able to count on ranching in the future. In 1976 he left for Salt Lake City to learn a trade. There he met his wife, Karla, the daughter of a dairy farmer from northern Utah. In 1981, since Calvin was getting older, Que and Karla returned to Kanab to help him out.

Their ranching income was not enough to support the family, so Karla crocheted and baked for people to make extra money. Once their three boys were in school, she found a full-time job as the county clerk for Kane County. "Good thing I've got my wife," Que quipped. "She's the one that brings in the income. And the one that's got the insurance." "It's what you call a partnership," Karla added. "He works, I earn." Their three boys all worked on the ranch growing up, but they also got paying jobs during high school. Their middle son was about to graduate from Northwestern University with a degree in economics, and their youngest had graduated from high school the previous year. The Johnsons and the Robinsons are typical of public land ranching families, most of whom have members with other jobs to help support their ranches and provide health insurance.[18]

Karla conveyed what she valued about ranching by recalling what her youngest son had just said to her as they were talking about what he wanted to do with his life. She advised him that he needed to think about what kind of work would allow him to be the kind of father he wanted to be. "Then I'll have to be a rancher," he responded. "Because my dad always had time for me and always needed me, and I always knew where he was." Karla pointed out that ranching allowed her kids to feel "not just wanted, but needed."

But despite the benefits of ranching for raising children, Que and Karla also mentioned its many hardships. Que spoke about the hidden expenses of public land ranching and why ranchers aren't really subsidized by low grazing fees, as most anti–public land grazing rhetoric claims:

> This is just an arid country. On our range, we run cattle over 100,000 something acres, and it comes to be almost 250 acres per cow. It takes a lot of country to raise a pound of beef. If we could lease enough

private ground, we'd rather run on private ground. But it's just not here. On private ground, you have the best feed, the best water. Out on the BLM ground, it's mostly sagebrush. They're trailing three to five miles to water every day. Then there's a lot of expenses: pumping water, keeping water lines going, fuel costs, and the time and the help you have to have to maintain it. On private ground, the calves get fatter and you get a five- to six-hundred-pound calf versus a three- to four-hundred-pound calf. A lot of years we buy more hay than we put up. There's so much work that needs to be done that we're always just behind.

Karla noted that to have their vaunted "freedom," ranchers had to "work twenty-four seven." And because of the constant workload, ranchers didn't have time to organize, attend meetings, or speak up for themselves, which was why people didn't hear their side of the story.

Que's assessment of the changes since the monument was created was conditionally positive. When the monument was designated, "We figured doomsday had hit." But "most of the changes, surprisingly, have been good changes. And I keep saying that the monument's still new and it's still trying to get established and get their policies and things in place. But I keep hoping that this isn't the calm before the storm." From his and his dad's perspective, the monument has been better to work with than the BLM was in the past: "The people we work with have got some agricultural background, and they've got what we call good sense. They're more reasonable and more flexible and have more range understanding." Karla added, "We have the perspective of looking down the road for our boys and their children and their children. So to keep the range in good condition is vital to that traditional way of life. And they appear to be supportive of wise use of the range."

However, Que identified the same problem that Dell and Brent had: little seems to get done in the way of needed range improvements, even though the ranchers supply much of the work and expense and the BLM only has to give approval. He explained:

> They keep talking about things they're going to do, and they've got things on the table. And we just met with them today. And they've

got some seeding programs and some water development programs and programs that we had in the works for years. And if they could get those things going, it'd really be beneficial to the range and the cattle. The thing that disappointed me is we talked about things that would be good for the range, wildlife, everything. After the meeting, the only thing they can do right now is fence off the Jenny Clay Hole. All these good ideas, but that's the only thing that can be done.

Que also identified the constant change of personnel as another difficulty of working with the BLM and a negative aspect of public land ranching. Like Brent, he contrasted the rancher's long-term knowledge with that of the BLM range staff. "You just get them used to how we do things, they come in, and they don't know what cows eat." He also observed that range science can be used in different ways:

We have experienced that range technicians that are pro-grazing will use the science that they have and will find conditions good. Range technicians that we feel are anti-grazing, they'll take the same science and use it against us. So we question a lot of their science because it depends on the person that is using that science.... We feel as ranchers that we've seen the experiences going back, we've seen what happens to overgrazing, we've seen what happens to undergrazing, and we think that we have pretty good knowledge of the range ourselves.

The government employees, they get an education, they get a job in the government, and they work their twenty or thirty years and retire, and their time on that range is gone. They transfer around to different localities, three to five years is the top they'll ever be there, and so we question their motives.... Where we as the ranchers, we go back five, six generations, and we want that to continue.... It's not a job; it's a lifestyle that we enjoy, and we want it to continue. And our interest in the range is very much there. We want healthy ranges so we get healthy cattle.

Que's and Karla's comments about working with the BLM elaborated on topics the other ranchers mentioned and revealed that the difficulties public land ranchers experienced were not simply due to their resistance to limitations on their freedom but were also caused by the bureaucratic institutional arrangements of the agency. Ranchers were willing to work within BLM guidelines, and they used them to plan their operations, as Brent pointed out. But the guidelines were always changing, such as when BLM staff changed or when staff with different attitudes toward grazing used science differently. In addition, the BLM often did not uphold its side of agreements, such as when projects that ranchers were counting on never materialized or when the agency failed to increase AUMs after ranchers had invested in projects that increased forage on their allotments. This created uncertainty for ranchers and the feeling that the BLM didn't really care about the range. They also saw it as unfair. Ranchers were penalized if they didn't adhere to the regulations, their permits, and allotment management plans, but the BLM could disregard agreements with ranchers at will.[19] Ranchers experienced a paradox between democracy and *freedom to* because they were blamed for the perceived poor condition of the public rangelands but powerless to improve on the poor job of managing them that they saw the BLM doing.

Like Dell and Brent, Que was also concerned about the future of ranching. It seemed to him that BLM studies, like the EIS currently being done on the monument, always resulted in a decrease of AUMs. BLM statistics corroborate this observation. But Que hoped that the BLM would "continue to be good to work with, and doing things to enhance the range, and there won't be cutbacks. Hopefully, there'll be good programs put in place that can increase AUMs."

Que also felt that environmental groups' strategy of opposing natural resource production on public lands was a threat to the future of public land ranching. He suggested an alternate approach, based on a critique of consumption:

> To me these environmental groups are always fighting the wrong end of the stick. Politically, they come to where the resources are and say, "Hey, we need to shut this down. We need to drain Lake Powell. We need to stop the cutting of the forest." The people in the cities, they think, "Hey, yeah, we don't want things to be destroyed." So the people

vote for that. In my mind, to send a man to the moon, whenever you turn on your computer, your radio, your TV, your air-conditioning, your heat—it all takes natural resources. And so, if they want that Lake Powell, if they want the dam to go, why don't they go down to Vegas and say, "Hey, shut your casinos down." Go to California and say, "Hey, you guys can't run your lights at night. You've got to shut these buildings down." But do you think that'd go over politically? No way.... They attack the dam, they attack the timber, but they don't attack the people where it's going. So that's always been a dilemma in my mind. How come they fight the wrong end of the stick? Fight where it's going, not where it's coming from.

Karla thought that a large part of the reason for opposition to public land grazing was that most people in the United States didn't understand what public land ranchers do. "So many people have no idea because we're so far removed from agriculture. There's even a difference between people in agriculture in the East and West. Once people in the East understand that out here it's 100,000 acres and 300 cows, instead of 600 cows and 600 acres, they are amazed and impressed." Que added, "I've never seen anyone against cattle ranching that's familiar with it. After they see what we're trying to do, their whole perspective changes. I'll bet in the BLM, those who are against grazing are the ones who have no experience with agriculture."

Karla's understanding of democracy was also informed by an awareness of the difference in perspectives between people from rural and urban backgrounds. In rural areas, the government was closer to the people and people were closer to the public lands. As a result, they felt they had more "ownership of their government" and of how public land should be used. This made them feel freer, but they recognized that, paradoxically, this freedom required responsibility "for their actions" and "for the land." On the other hand, "we have a huge group in the U.S. that's not responsible for the outcome," although they want to have a say in how public land is managed.

I had an opportunity to learn more about what public land ranchers do, and to hear the Johnsons' perspective on how their allotment should

22. Looking for strays with the Johnsons, June 2005. Courtesy of the author.

be managed, when Que invited me to their spring gathering at the Rock House, an old line shack they had fixed up for these occasions. Que gave me a job inoculating calves, then I rode out looking for strays missed in the initial gathering with Calvin, Que's youngest son, a cousin, and a friend of the Johnsons' from Arizona who had been coming to help for twenty years (see fig. 22).

Calvin knew I was a member of the Grazing Subcommittee of the Monument Advisory Committee with Que, so he rode alongside me to point out things he thought I should see: "crested wheat" (*Agropyron cristatum*), which was coming up although the monument staff said the seedings had died, and "grama" (*Bouteloua gracilis*), a grass they hadn't seen for years that was coming up because of the rain. Calvin didn't think the BLM needed to reseed; he thought the grass would come back on its own. In one place, he pointed out some serious gullying and explained that for years he had been trying to get the BLM to build earthworks to stop the erosion. I got a much different perspective on the condition of the allotment and ways to improve it from Calvin than I had sitting in on the meetings of the EIS Team, who attributed the allotment's problems to the Johnsons' management. I had never understood the reasoning behind this conclusion, since the allotment had been historically overgrazed, there was a drought, and it is the BLM that sets, and should enforce, the guidelines for management. However, to figure out what was really happening on the landscape would require research, resources, and time that neither Calvin and Que nor the BLM had.

A long day in the corral and in the saddle ended with everyone hanging out on the porch of the Rock House eating bologna sandwiches and watermelon as the sun was sinking and a breeze frisked in the cottonwoods. A feeling of contentment stole over me after having worked outside all day in this beautiful vast, empty country. Calvin invited me to come back any time, and I felt as if I'd passed some kind of test.

Delane and Quinn Griffin

Delane Griffin (see fig. 23) and his son, Quinn, lived in Escalante and ranched on Fiftymile Mountain, at the southeastern end of the Kaiparowits Plateau. The Fifty is buttressed on three sides by steep cliffs that make access difficult: those on the north are called the Straight Cliffs; those on the east and south drop away to Lake Powell. Locally, it has acquired a lore and mystique because of its extreme remoteness in an already remote region and the difficulties it posed to ranchers who grazed their livestock in the verdant, spring-watered meadows on top, a rare treasure in the arid environment. The controversial events that occurred there in the fall of 2000 (described in chapter 3) seemed to add to the reputation of the Fifty.

The ancestral Griffins ran sheep all over the southern part of the Aquarius Plateau, north of Escalante. The many landscape features that bear the family name attest to the extent of their former grazing grounds: Griffin Top, Griffin Spring, Griffin Ranch. Delane was born in Escalante in 1923 and "raised at the sheep herd" until he was a teenager. However, when World War II broke out, all the young men were drafted, leaving no one to herd the sheep, so they were sold. Delane first went up on the Fifty in 1942, when he was hired to help the ranchers on its lower end bring their cattle down to sell. He came to know the Fifty well over the years by working for different ranchers who ran sheep or cattle up there, but he didn't own his own outfit.

After he got out of the service, Delane went to Provo to find work, but he came back to Escalante during layoffs to try to find a job closer to home. He eventually landed a job with a BLM survey crew that lasted sixteen years. It took him to Nevada and northern Utah, but he returned frequently to Escalante. One of those times, around 1968, Gail Bailey, who had a summer grazing permit for the Lake allotment on the Fifty, was looking to sell it. He asked Delane, who had worked for him, and Delane's two brothers, Cecil and Gene, if they wanted to buy him out. So the brothers borrowed the money and bought the permit in 1969. To acquire the winter grazing for their ranching operation, they did some permit trading and ended up with the adjoining Soda Springs allotment on the Escalante Desert below for their winter grazing. Moving between the two required negotiating a short, but steep and treacherous stock trail that threads its way through the Straight Cliffs.

Now part owner of his own outfit, Delane and his family moved back to Escalante to become full-time ranchers. Delane, Gene, and Quinn, after he moved back, did most of the cowboying. It is a long way from Escalante to their allotments, on rough roads that are impassable when it rains hard or snows, so they had to stay out there for days or weeks, like cowboys did when Delane was young, to do the cattle work. On the Soda allotment, they stayed in an old line shack they had fixed up and called the Soda Cabin; it was burned down on April 18, 1996, one of several targets of unidentified arsonists. On the Lake allotment, they camped, then decided to build a cabin up there. They began cutting and dragging the poles in the summer of 1975, and in the fall they started laying them up. It was hard work, according to Delane, "riding for cattle in the daytime, laying up the logs at night." The cabin became a gathering place for members of the extended Griffin family, and the many experiences they shared on the Fifty made it a prominent landmark in the Griffin family's emotional landscape.

Delane kept a loose-leaf binder where he recorded the history of ranching on Fiftymile Mountain and stories of his own adventures, many in cowboy poetry, illustrated with humorous drawings and photographs from family get-togethers. He and his wife, Leah, were my next-door neighbors in Escalante, and I loved to visit and listen to Delane tell the stories and recite the poetry himself. I recognized that they were some of the best memories of his life. Many of the stories were about trying to capture the feral cattle that lived on the Fifty and consumed the forage that the BLM had allocated to his cattle. Delane's book began with this introduction: "When the Griffin boys purchased the cattle setup of the Fifty Mile Mountain, little did they know the experiences that awaited them that could come from chasing and capturing wild cattle."

He surmised that the wild cattle on the Fifty were descendants of the first cattle brought up there in the 1890s by a family named the Doughertys and left behind when the ranch failed. Their numbers were probably augmented by domestic cattle missed during fall gatherings because there were so many places for them to hide in the intricate system of canyons and gullies and in the dense thickets of pinyon and juniper. The wild cattle were sometimes called "long-ears" because they had never had their ears notched to indicate ownership. There was enough water year-round on the Fifty from springs and snowfall for them to survive. They became wilder, wilier, and harder to catch with each successive generation. Even if they could be caught, they couldn't be tied, herded, or led, making it difficult to get them off the Fifty. Sometimes they had to be shot.

One of Delane's favorite stories was about an old spotted bull, which they had been after for a long time but always managed to elude them. Delane described what happened when they finally roped him:

> We worked with him for about three days, but he wouldn't give up; he wouldn't lead. And we turned him loose with an old cow, and he'd still break away and we'd have to chase him. One time he hit us in the back—me and my horse—so hard he knocked my hat and glasses off. We'd just done everything, and we just couldn't. . . . Anyway, the last time we caught him, he ran so hard, after three days he fell down and died, his legs up in the air, and just quivered. We pushed him and

23. Delane Griffin at Dance Hall Rock during a Hole-in-the-Rock Expedition re-enactment, 2005. Courtesy of the author.

pushed him to try to get him up, but he was gone. As we were leaving, one of the dogs went up and sniffed in his ear. All of a sudden, he jumped up and stared at us with eyes as big as saucers, like he'd never seen us before. He didn't know whether to fight or run. Then he ran off. We decided that he had fought so hard and so well that we'd give him his freedom.

Delane's understanding of democracy was remarkably similar to Dell's and Brent's: "You're free to live like you want and let everyone else have the same privilege. As long as I don't interfere with somebody else's way of life, I have the right to do what I want, and he has the right to do what he wants."

In 2000 Quinn and Gene were running the Griffin Cattle Company. It was more a labor of love than a source of income. Quinn, who was born in Provo in 1950, had moved back to Escalante in 1968 after high school. After he married, he moved to Salt Lake to work but returned again to Escalante to raise his kids. He wanted them to learn to ranch. Quinn's ranching income was not enough to support his family, as it had been for Delane, so Quinn had to find other work and ranch part-time.

Quinn had been captivated by the Fifty, just as his dad had. He liked ranching to be "a little rough and tough," the way it was up there, liked "to take down his rope and use it," and liked solitude. He would be "bored in a pasture." He also described himself as an up-to-date cowboy who "packs a cell phone and a PalmPilot," which made him "unusual around here." Quinn took after his dad as a composer of cowboy poetry. His ode to the Fifty, which simply and eloquently captures the rancher's experience of place, freedom, and belonging, is the first poem in Delane's book:

> You're sitting on your horse looking off a high, flat mesa,
> and the desert stretches out below you for miles around.
> The cold desert wind is ever present,
> causing you to hunch up and pull your coat up around your neck.
> It's Christmas Eve 1969.
> Father and son are out on the Escalante Desert looking for long-eared yearlings

that have eluded the late fall riders.
To the west, the vertical cliffs of the Fifty Mile Mountain rise up out
   of the ground
to brood over their kingdom of sand dunes, ledges, and stretching
   pinnacles.
A man feels quite small in the shadows of the awesome
   surroundings.
No wonder that the Indian worshipped the sun with its power over
   life and death,
and the earth with her towering whispering pines and whirling
   sand funnels of the devil.
No one can fully know the magnitude of nature until they are at
   the mercy of it.
The power of the wind sweeping the desert clean,
the huge threatening clouds with their bellies full of snow and rain,
ready to wash the futile attempts of man's roads clear to the
   Colorado River.
Sitting astride your horse,
listening to his rhythmic breathing,
watching his ears search for the sounds of the desert,
you feel apart from the modern age of technology.
You feel alone.
Alone as those who once roamed unrestricted upon this land
and felt that only God shared their ownership of it.

Quinn agreed that it was difficult to manage cattle on the Fifty, but he was confident he could do it if the BLM would give him the tools he needed, especially permission to build more corrals for temporarily holding cattle during gathering. So he was frustrated in the late summer of 2000, when it seemed to him that the BLM was making it difficult for him to do what he needed to do to get his cows off the Fifty after the agency had closed his allotment early due to drought. He experienced the paradox between democracy and individual freedom as he tried to comply with the BLM's rules in the best way he knew how, while the agency made it nearly impossible to do that. His frustration turned to anger when the BLM began taking what most local people considered an extreme measure, impounding his cattle and eventually airlifting them off the mountain. As he struggled to reconcile his convictions with his experience, he was attempting to work through this democratic paradox.

When I talked with Quinn again in the summer of 2001, he was remarkably philosophical about his situation. The experience had been devastating for him as a rancher whose feelings of independence and self-esteem were tied to his skill in handling cattle. He was faced with large fees for the BLM's impoundment costs, he had to resort to hiring a helicopter to find and shoot the remaining cattle to avoid incurring further trespass fines, he was involved in litigation to appeal the trespass, and the BLM had revoked his winter grazing privileges on the Soda allotment. His private ground was only ten acres, so he had had nowhere to take his remaining cattle and had to sell them in the winter when prices were low. The Lake allotment was still closed.

He was disappointed with Kate Cannon, whom he had thought of as a friend, and the BLM had dropped out of the Escalante Center. He had tried to work with the BLM, but the agency had come down on him hard. He had dealt with his anger by writing in his journal, writing letters, thinking, walking, and praying. In particular, it had been hard on his family. "It was the only topic we talked about for a while. At one point I sat my family down and said, we've still got the greatest government in the world. A small town like this struggles when something big blows up. Everyone went to church together—those who work for the BLM and had to do the impounding, and those on the other side." He had considered getting out of ranching, but his family wanted him to stay. He was considering some options: sell his Soda permit to another rancher or sell his permit on the Fifty to the Grand Canyon Trust and lease some of it back for hobby ranching or raising horses.

By the summer of 2002 Quinn was upbeat. He described several accomplishments of the Escalante Center during the past year and plans for future projects. Both the new monument manager, Dave Hunsaker, and the BLM state director, Sally Wisely, had contacted him to ask whether he would meet with them to try to sort out the Fiftymile issue. He had already had several lengthy meetings with Dave. Meanwhile, the BLM had still not been able to remove all the cattle from the Fifty and was beginning to realize "that you just can't find the cows up there and that maybe I was right." BLM staff had just finished a rangeland health assessment of the Lake allotment for the monument-wide Rangeland Health EIS and found it in "the best condition they had even seen," in his eyes, proof that its condition in 2000 was due to drought, not poor management. People all over the West had been contacting him for advice and inviting him to come and speak. And he was still considering his options with his grazing permits.

As a result of the controversy surrounding the impoundment, the BLM continued to monitor conditions on the Fifty. The agency flew Delane up in a helicopter to help because he still knew the country better than anyone else. He told a story that vividly illustrated the difference between the experiential knowledge of ranchers and the science-based knowledge of BLM experts. He was with a group doing a riparian assessment of a wash when they came to a place where a fence was suspended high in the air across the wash. The group took this as evidence of rapid downcutting of the wash bed and started discussing possible causes. As they were concluding that it was erosion from overgrazing, Delane explained that he knew what had caused it because he had built the fence. To keep cattle from getting under the fence, he had attached large rocks to the bottom to pull it down. The fence was up in the air because the rocks had come loose.

By the summer of 2003 the Griffins had reached an agreement with the BLM about the Fiftymile impoundment. The fine was less harsh than what they had originally faced, but they would still have to sell permits to pay the debt. They eventually sold part of the Soda Springs permit to Steve Sorensen, and the BLM incorporated the rest of it into the Lake allotment. They also sold part of the Lake allotment to a rancher from Beaver, Utah, and were partnering with him to work the allotment. Quinn really regretted having to do that: "We have had the Fifty Mile permit for thirty-three or thirty-four years. It has become an emotional thing in our family." Delane and Leah had been counting on the ranching operation to help with their retirement. Leah asked, "How would you feel if someone came along and took away your retirement?" In 2006 Quinn finally sold the remainder of the Fiftymile permit to his partner.

After hearing all the stories about the Fifty, I wanted to see it myself, preferably on horseback with Delane or Quinn. But the opportunity never presented itself, so I went on foot with friends. We had taken notes while Delane gave instructions on how to find some of the landmarks in his stories, drawing on his remarkable memory of the Fifty's complex topography. We spent four days exploring the Fifty and searching out the places he had told us about: springs, aspen groves, strange rock formations, Native American ruins, and rock art. But even with a topographic map and Delane's directions, it was easy to get lost on the flat plateau top, with its features obscured by trees. We saw no other people, just a couple of horses and a few cows in the meadows near the cabin, and many heaps of bleached white bones, reminders of the drama that had taken place there in 2000. The aura of the Fifty is unique in the Grand Staircase-Escalante region, giving one a feeling of being on an island suspended in the sky, alone and outside of time even more than when down in the desert. I could understand why ranchers accepted its challenges and the BLM's limitations to have this experience.

Sioux and Bob Cochran

Sioux and Bob Cochran ran the Boulder Mountain Ranch, a ranch lodging, trail ride, and cattle business, out of Salt Gulch, outside Boulder. They were neighbors of Dell LeFevre and his father, Mac. In 2004 I found their place by the multicolored surfboard hanging next to the front gate. It was a keepsake from the time they spent in Northern California surfing and running a trail-riding business before they moved to Boulder in 1989. They are the only ranchers in this chapter who were not pioneer descendants and who ran a "dude ranch." Their foray into ranching can be seen as facilitated, rather than threatened, by the shift to an amenity-based consumption economy in the region.

Bob was the strong, silent type. Tall and in his fifties, he still had the look of a blond surfer dude, a look that also could easily pass for that of an experienced, weather-beaten cowboy. Sioux, in her forties, was a petite bundle of energy. Bob was originally from northern Utah, and Sioux was from Wisconsin. Bob had an uncle in the ranching business whom he had visited in the summers as a kid, but before buying a ranch in Boulder, the Cochrans had no actual experience in the cattle business.

They had first come to Boulder for Bob's brother's wedding; while there, his other brother suggested they look for a ranch in the vicinity, which he would help them buy. Their business in Northern California wasn't doing very well, so they decided to make the move. Boulder was already being "discovered" by amenity seekers and developers, and the couple bought the 160-acre Boulder Mountain Ranch from an investor from Hawaii. He had built a big log lodge on the property, one of the first "trophy homes" in the Boulder area, which they used as a guest lodge. In 2004 they had just finished building a much more modest home for themselves and their three sons, sixteen, fourteen, and twelve.

Sioux recalled what it was like being newcomers in the community and new to ranching at the same time. When they first arrived, they "took some flak from the locals, of course. Everyone gets territorial, and they thought we didn't know a thing. Which, they were partly true, but . . . Our interest was really kind of a trial and error, and I think we did quite well." She felt the fact that Bob's family was Mormon had helped them be accepted by the Mormon community, and the fact that they bought cows helped them be accepted by the ranching community. They also made an effort to get to know people: "We went to the Fourth of July thing; we rode in the parade. People would always say, 'Oh, it's so good to see you joining in.' We went to the school functions; we went to the church functions. We did everything that was offered because we wanted to socialize." But in the end, Sioux felt they were accepted for this reason: "We do our own thing. We don't need them to survive. We know they're here, we're here for each other, but we don't depend on each other." In other words, they subscribed to the same values that longtime residents of the region did: hard work and self-reliance.

Sioux and Bob started out in Boulder in the trail-riding business, without any intention of getting into cattle. But back then there wasn't much tourism in Boulder, and Highway 12 through Boulder was not paved until 1986. According to Sioux, "You needed to be real diverse in your ways of making money." They came up with the idea that instead of just doing the usual type of trail rides, they would do cattle drives. At first they paid another rancher to let their guests move his cows. In 1992, when he had to sell some of his permit, they bought part of it: 80 head. Bob wanted to buy the whole permit, which was for 260 head, but Sioux was appalled by the cost of the part they did buy—$52,000 for 80 head—and wanted to hold back. Since then, cattle drives for the guests had become a popular feature of their business. And cattle ranching, for its own sake, had become more popular with them.

Sioux and Bob had permits that allowed them to graze for nine months, half the time on BLM land and half the time on Forest Service land. That left three months when they had to "bring them home" and feed them. They raised hay, but not enough to feed that many cows plus the horses. So they also bought hay. Sioux believed they had been able to make it because they carried less debt than many people in the cattle business. The potential for development had since driven the value of ranch property far beyond the return it could provide from ranching, so anyone who bought a ranch would now incur a debt that ranching would not be able to pay off. Sioux explained, "The first thing I heard about the struggle with the cattle is that you're not gonna make it with cattle. And then one guy said, you can make it with cattle, if you don't have debt. And that key word there, that debt, is everything. . . . I mean this is really a beautiful ranch and it wasn't handed to us, so we still have debt. You know people have told us that, our debt, people would be envious of our debt." Bob added, "The advantage to public lands ranching is it allows people like us to stay in ranching. When people say you can't make it, that's a narrow view of ranching. Eighty percent of small businesses don't make it: it's the small-business person, not the small rancher. We've succeeded because we have a small investment." But they still worked hard to keep the ranch. Their motto summed it up: "Cowboys do it all."

According to Sioux, Bob was the one with the "stronger dream about the cattle. It's not my dream, but I can enjoy it. My dream is the horses, and he loves horses too." And her boys, whom she had feared were beginning to take for granted the things they did outside all the time and would want to move to the city when they grew up, had "come back to the idea of ranching." Another thing she liked about ranching was that her boys all had chores they had to do. "And I think that builds character and gives them a sense of well-being."

Like the other ranchers, Sioux and Bob expressed ambivalent feelings about the monument, even though it had probably helped their trail-riding business. Their opinion of the GSENM range staff differed from that of the more experienced ranchers. Since they were new to ranching, they deferred to the range staff's knowledge. Sioux said they got along well with their "range guy." "We like him. And we agree with what he generally has to say. I think they know, and other ranchers would probably disagree with me, but I think they know, because they've studied intensely plant life and soil conservation and all kinds of things, they know better than we know what's best for our range." She saw the monument as "a good thing. It's protected the land."

But, she continued, "the only issue I worry about is that they want to get the grazing off." She believed that was because of "radical environmentalists," who were

> so uptight about something they really don't know anything about. And because there's a lot of them and they have nothing to do. I don't understand why they pick on grazing when they could be picking on healthy water sources in the city or sewage problems, or . . . There are so many other issues that they could use their energy towards a good thing, but they come and pick on us. And I keep thinking, and I've said this forever, that they're envious of our lifestyle. That we have a stress-free life, and we can be out in the country and following a cow and just enjoying our day on a horse—I just can't help but think that they wish that they could do that.

Aware of the negative perceptions of public land ranching, she worried that because it was a monument, it would attract more visitors, who would convey their negative perceptions to the BLM:

> When the hikers see the cows, they don't know about how the range looked to begin with. And the range may look really hammered to them, because it's a desert—it's not like a Colorado mountain—and they come out here and they don't know what it's supposed to look like, but they think that it's hammered. So they go back to the office and say, "Oh, these cows." Or they write these things at the trailheads, and they [the BLM] take that to heart.
>
> The funny thing is, we hear about this and how hammered our range was, and this and this and this, and then they actually had some

people come out and assess the range, someone special. They sent some people from Colorado, and they came out and assessed all the ranges, and our range came in at the top.

In addition, because Sioux and Bob take trail rides down the Escalante River, they have experienced the changes that have taken place since GSENM was created and the cows were removed. Sioux described the canyon as a "nightmare" now: "The trails have grown up because the cattle kept things chopped down and eaten." Bob added, "The tamarisk wasn't near as bad—none to speak of. You look in there now, and the Russian olive has taken over and the tamarisk."[20] Sioux continued, "When Dell had his cows in there, we'd go down and just cruise the river. We took trail rides down there and it was just great, and the banks weren't that steep, I guess because the cows kept pushing the banks down so that there was a trail into the river. Now they're like, you're jumping off the bank. You have to find a place to get in." Their observations contradicted the assumption of anti–public land grazing rhetoric that removing cows from riparian areas was always beneficial: the cows may have played a part in keeping invasive species in check and maintaining the trails that recreationists used.

Sioux told a story that helped explain why they liked ranching. Every time her neighbor Dell LeFevre saw her, he would ask, "Do you like it here?"

> And I would say, "I love it here." And finally, one time I said, "Why do you always ask me that? Why would I be here if I didn't like it?" And he said, "Because I've seen so many people come and go." And since then Bob and I have seen people come and go: trophy house people or people from the East. People who come here and think they can make it, and not necessarily only them. I've seen young people who think they can live on the land, almost communal-type people. A lot of alternative lifestylers, which I think we fall into that category. But I think it takes a certain type of person, and Bob and I are that type of person. We like to live "out." We like the privacy.

But when I interviewed them, Sioux and Bob themselves were thinking of leaving. They had realized how much they enjoyed ranching and living in a ranching community, believed they could make it in the ranching business, and had been looking at buying a ranch in a region of New Mexico that was still "really ranching strong" They were disappointed with the way the community of Boulder had changed:

> It used to be a ranching community, and now the air of the community is more, and I don't mean anything offensive by this, but the yuppieism of [it]. . . . And the people again, they move here because they love the view. They're getting a visual thing. And they're also getting community. When they move in, they like the people. But then they complain a lot. About the cows and the this and the that.
>
> When we moved here, there was probably 80 percent Mormon and 20 percent alternative lifestylers, for lack of a better word. And now a lot of the old-timers are gone as well, and the children of the settlers that were here left, just like children leave everywhere. And some of them try to come back, but if they don't have something to come back to, like ranching, there's nothing for them here.

They also wanted to get out of the tourist business and pay off their debt. Their idea was to sell half their property—the lower eighty acres with the trophy home—and keep the rest. Then they could buy a ranch in New Mexico, where land values and permits were less expensive, and they would be out of debt.

"We'd like to keep some of our cows because we have a young herd, and we have a good herd," Sioux said. She pointed out another "thing about ranching": in addition to attachment to the landscape, ranchers become attached to their livestock. "It's like a physical thing. You get attached to your animals and you want the best for them. And that's where I think these, and for lack of a better word, I'll say environmentalists, I don't really like to use that term, but . . . The outsiders, maybe the outside people, they don't see it as an attachment to something you care about." Sioux and Bob could address the tension between positive and negative liberty, represented by increased scrutiny of their ranching operation by leaving, because they were not as attached to Boulder Mountain as Dell and other ranchers with a long family history in the region were.

In the fall of 2006 Sioux and Bob were still in Boulder. Their place hadn't sold and their business was going well; they were paying off their debt faster than they had expected. Sioux was as upbeat as ever. Perhaps her closing remarks at the end of the interview we did two years earlier can explain her always ebullient spirits: "If you remember what you really liked when you were about nine, ten, eleven years old—that's what will make you the happiest in your life. I was always in love with horses. I was horse crazy as a kid, and here I am living my dream." But not long afterward, they moved to a ranch near Reserve, New Mexico.

Democracy and Freedom on Public Land

These ranchers' stories illustrate the economic, social, political, and personal struggles that ranchers in the Grand Staircase-Escalante region face and reveal the powerful motivation behind their desire to continue ranching in the face of these difficulties. Studies have shown that many ranchers stay in business because the lifestyle is more important to them than profit.[21] These stories provide more insight into what they value about the ranching lifestyle: the feelings of freedom, self-reliance, and belonging in nature; the opportunity to pass these values and experiences on to their children; being part of a community that shares these values; and contributing to what they believe makes America great. The nature of their work allows them to experience a feeling of freedom in their daily lives to a much greater degree than most Americans, and they come to associate democracy with that feeling.

But public land ranchers' ability to live the ranching life that provides this experience paradoxically makes them more dependent on the federal government and brings them more directly under its control than most Americans. As a result, they experience a democratic paradox resulting from the tension between democracy and individual freedom to a greater degree than most Americans. These ranchers are practicing democracy as they struggle to reconcile the positive freedom of the ranching lifestyle with what most Americans would consider a high level of interference in their daily lives from the federal government. Their freedom is actually restricted in many more ways than just by the BLM; these include the economics of ranching, the structure of the beef industry, and the American public's negative perceptions of public land ranching. In the Grand Staircase-Escalante region, GSENM became the focus of ranchers' frustrations and the site where they have been trying to work out this paradox, because it has a concrete and immediate presence in their lives, and it seems like something they have the ability to address.

This chapter and the previous one have conveyed the experiences of people who, in the face of the reterritorialization of public land as national landscape, feared the loss of a way of life they cherished. They also raise questions about the nature of democratic government and what should be its responsibility to citizens who suffer as a result of policy changes in the interest of the majority or of economic efficiency. In the case of federal land management, when policy changes, what claims should rural residents living near public lands have to a way of life that depends on using them and that policy has supported historically? In his book on public lands versus private interests in the Grand Canyon, journalist Stephen Nash suggested that the situation of public lands ranchers is similar to that of steel workers who lost their jobs when steel plants shut down for economic reasons: they are both unfortunate casualties of economic change.[22] The steel corporations had no obligation to help their ex-workers; why should the federal government help ranchers? But would a democratic government that treats its citizens in the same way as a corporation whose only incentive is profit treats its workers be seen as legitimate?

Historian Leisl Carr Childers, in her book on histories of the impacts of multiple use on public land ranchers and rural residents who live adjacent to public land in the Great Basin, pointed out that while most Americans have benefited from the shift in public land management to prioritize other uses over grazing, such as outdoor recreation and environment protection, these benefits have occurred at the expense of certain groups.[23] Public land ranchers and rural residents have borne the brunt of the costs and at the same time have been vilified or ignored. Carr Childers argued that because they have managed to navigate "the conflicts that created and were created by multiple use," their persistence in living in a place most Americans would find too difficult "should encourage us to think differently about our public lands and to include them in our thought processes." She concluded, "If we fail to recognize our collective responsibility, we will callously continue to casually sacrifice the region's population and its environment for the greater good of the nation."[24]

7 The Environmentalists

DEMOCRACY AND THE ENVIRONMENT

This chapter presents the stories and perspectives of five environmentalists who worked in the Grand Staircase-Escalante region during the time I did my research (1999–2008) and of the organizations with which they were associated. Grand Staircase-Escalante National Monument (GSENM) attracted the attention of environmental groups because many interpreted its creation as evidence of the federal government's support for their goals and its intention to redirect the Bureau of Land Management (BLM) toward them and as an opportunity to pursue them there. I am using the term "environmentalist" hesitantly because the term can carry negative or positive connotations depending on who uses it. For many local residents, it was an epithet. Moreover, some of the people in this chapter might not identify themselves as environmentalists. The accounts that follow describe some of the events that helped create a negative stereotype of environmentalists among some residents of the Grand Staircase-Escalante region and show that the narrators' and local residents' perceptions of these events often differ. They also illustrate a range of approaches to protecting the environment and different ways of being an environmentalist. These stories reflect diverse backgrounds and personalities, various ways environmentalism has shaped conflict over GSENM, and the unique ways these individuals experienced and attempted to work out the tension between environmentalism and democracy.

This tension has been explored by environmental or green political theory, which is political theory that explicitly reflects on the social and political dimensions of environmental issues, as well as on the environmental implications of political discourses and practices. Since the environment did not exist as a concept in policy or policy-making in any country until the 1960s, environmental political theory is a recent development.[1] One of the first problems it took up was the relationship between environmentalism and democracy. According to green political theorist Andrew Dobson, political theorist Robert Goodin initiated the debate with a provocative query: Is it possible to protect the environment while safeguarding democratic values and practices?[2] This question suggests that environmentalism might pose a problem for democracy because environmentalists are likely to prioritize achieving certain outcomes over democratic means of achieving them. For example, if environmentalists argue that environmental problems are dire, urgent, or a matter of survival—claims that contribute to their political persuasiveness—then it becomes easy to justify any means, even authoritarian ones, to solve them. If they argue that we must protect nature against human destruction because it has intrinsic value, then the intrinsic value of nature can trump the contingent value of democracy.

At the same time, democracy poses a problem for environmentalism because its procedures are slow and cumbersome and may not result in majority support for addressing what are seen as urgent environmental problems. Andrew Dobson stated the problem this way: "Democratic and green thinking seem opposed in that the former is concerned with means and the latter with ends."[3] The opposition between democracy and environmentalism has also been conceived of in terms of anthropocentrism versus biocentrism. Democracy as it is presently understood is anthropocentric, placing human interests foremost, while environmentalism prioritizes the well-being of the environment.[4] To resolve the apparent opposition between environmentalism and democracy, green political theorists began to theorize what an "environmental democracy" or a "green state" should look like.[5] The stories that follow show that this opposition creates a real tension for environmentalists who value democracy as well.

Grant Johnson and SUWA

In the Grand Staircase-Escalante region, the best known, and by some the most reviled, environmental organization is the Southern Utah Wilderness Alliance (SUWA). The fact that SUWA originated in the region in the 1980s and has been involved in conflicts over roads and wilderness in the region since then partly explains its notoriety. Grant Johnson's stories provide further insight into some local residents' antipathy toward the organization.

Grant is one of the original founders of SUWA and still lives near Boulder. At the time of my research, he ran a horse-packing and guide service with his wife, Sue Fearon.[6] Grant, Sue, and their daughter lived on 40 acres along Deer Creek, about half a mile upstream on a very rough road from where the Burr Trail crosses the creek. This former cattle trail connects Boulder with the Notom-Bullfrog Road 36.5 miles to the east, and its name became firmly associated in local memory with confrontation between SUWA and local residents. While Grant was building a unique home for them, a sandstone dome hollowed out using the blasting skills he had developed as a miner, the whole family was living in the same small trailer Grant had lived in since he first moved to the property. They raised horses for packing and riding, grew hay to feed the horses, and took temporary jobs in the area when available. Their current lifestyle seemed closer to the way the original Mormon pioneers lived than that of most residents of the region today.

Grant Johnson did not fit the usual mold for an environmentalist. He first came to Utah from Wisconsin in 1973, after he dropped out of high school. He moved to eastern Garfield County in 1975 and Deer Creek in 1977, and he has lived there ever since, except when he went to Evergreen College in Washington State, a couple of quarters at a time. Initially, he made his living by mining for uranium. "I only came here," he said, "for the beauty of the canyons. And I didn't care what I did; I wanted to work here. And mining was the job that was going on. Mining was really fun and interesting. And it was always out in the wilderness. I don't want to live in a town."

When he first moved to Boulder, much of the road connecting Escalante and Boulder (now Highway 12) was still a one-lane dirt road.

He first got into trouble in 1979, when work to widen and pave that road was underway:

> My first big trouble was, I saw a bulldozer up on the cliff up above Calf Creek, and I couldn't believe they were going to put that road through the canyon wall. . . . I called the Sierra Club—Jim Catlin, who worked for them, is who I called—and he said, "That's in a wilderness study area—they can't do that." The next day it was shut down. The *Salt Lake Tribune* called me up and interviewed me, and the next day the paper said that I shut them down. So Escalante, of course, wanted to kill me.

In 1980 the uranium market crashed, and Grant had to find other work. However, he felt this was fortunate because mining companies "were about to open a whole lot of new mines in the Circle Cliffs" (an area now in GSENM), and he had seen what "they did to the surface." Being involved in mining also motivated him to become an environmental activist: "After seeing that, that's when I really jumped on the wilderness bandwagon, seeing that they could just bulldoze roads everywhere they wanted to, and nothing would stop them." From his experience in mining, he became aware that it was not necessarily natural resource extraction in general that was the problem, but *how* people went about it.

Having realized how roadbuilding affected the landscape, Grant helped initiate an effort in 1982 to oppose a proposal by the federal government to build a "highly engineered" road to replace the Burr Trail, which traverses the remote and austere landscape bounded by the Circle Cliffs, then descends precipitously down the Waterpocket Fold in Capitol Reef National Park. Feeling that he "knew the land, and could be a spokesperson," Grant joined Gordon Anderson, a friend of Sierra Club luminary David Brower, and Lucy Wallingford, an environmental activist from Moab, in forming the Save the Burr Trail Committee. In the long run, their efforts resulted in "a compromise, a partial victory," Grant said. "Even though they sprayed some oil on it, we ended up with a little county road. But we got press. And I got heat." And the heat grew as he continued to work on environmental issues.

Grant explained that local animosity toward environmentalists was encouraged by energy corporations that had come in the early to mid-1980s with plans for mining development. "The big corporations would come in and promise everybody that they were going to get rich because they were going to have a coal mine and a power plant. And everybody would get all whipped up. And then the coal mine or power plant would be found to not be a feasible operation. And then the companies would say it's because of the environmentalists, and they would have all of this anti-environmentalist sentiment whipped up for something that didn't happen and wasn't going to happen."[7]

In 1983 Grant started SUWA with Clive Kincaid and Robert Weed, wilderness activists who had moved to Boulder in the early 1980s. People who knew the two remarked on their abrasive personalities and confrontational style. Clive bought land near Grant's place on Deer Creek, and Robert along the Escalante River, where Highway 12 crosses it. Their new organization got to work opposing the paving of the Burr Trail, inventorying Utah's BLM wilderness lands, fighting the exclusion of Antone Ridge from the Box-Death Hollow Wilderness, and appealing the sale of the last virgin stand of ponderosa on Boulder Mountain. Many local residents interpreted these efforts as a campaign against the resource production jobs that had traditionally supported the local economy. Some began to express their displeasure. According to Grant, "One day Robert Weed had some boards with nails buried in his driveway. And then someone salted his well. And apparently people were shooting from the Highway 12 overlook that looks down on his house. That's when we got hung in effigy, the three of us." Grant emphasized that the people who did these things were not from Boulder. Others implied the perpetrators were among the group of "loudmouths" that Escalante residents disassociated themselves from (described in chapter 5). However, those responsible were never identified. Partly because of this harassment, Kincaid and Weed eventually moved away.

Grant recounted one of his experiences with harassment that occurred about 1985:

Garfield County was pushing to pave the Burr Trail really heavily. And it was in court. A judge had said not to begin construction, so the construction company said they wouldn't begin construction until they got permission. So the county commissioners called their buddies and got a bunch of bulldozers from local firms, and they brought equipment here and started bulldozing the right-of-way. And it was illegal. So the next morning, instead of it being the issue that they went in and bulldozed illegally, they came up with this issue that someone had vandalized four of the bulldozers. And all the news stations came down, and there's the story: someone had monkey-wrenched them. There was no mention that they were there illegally. The police couldn't find any evidence, so they came here and made up a bunch of evidence and threw me in jail for half-a-million-dollar bail. . . . They charged me with every crime they could come up with, and all these crimes had a minimum mandatory of five years in prison, all these drugs that I didn't have. When it came to a preliminary hearing, everything got thrown out because there was no evidence. . . . Then when we met bail, the sheriff said he couldn't protect me and wanted it to be on condition that I didn't go home. The judge . . . advised me that my life was in danger, and they couldn't protect me. We weren't leaving. A friend from Boulder came down one time and said, "You guys need to leave. People are talking about shooting you and you lives are in danger." And we said, "Go ahead. They can go for it. This is our home. We're not moving." Nowadays, there's all these environmentalists around, and they have no idea what it was like then. It was so hostile.

Sue met Grant in the 1980s, while she was working for the National Park Service in Zion National Park. She recalled that a job offer in Bryce Canyon National Park was retracted after this incident and attributed it to the machinations of the county commissioners.

These events in the 1980s, SUWA's continued work on wilderness in the region, and environmentalists' opposition to other potential development in the region described in this chapter help explain attitudes toward environmentalists in the Grand Staircase-Escalante region and how SUWA came to be perceived by some as the archenemy. Grant refused to leave Boulder, but SUWA did. In 1986 the board voted to move the office to Springdale, outside Zion National Park, and later the organization moved to Salt Lake City. SUWA's focus became working to have more wilderness designated in Utah. In 1989 the organization helped put together the first version of America's Redrock Wilderness Act, which called for the designation of 5.7 million acres of wilderness in Utah. In the 1990s SUWA fought the Andalex mine on the Kaiparowits Plateau in what later became GSENM.[8]

After Grant got out of mining, he worked as a grade setter, the person who interprets stakes set by survey crews, for a contractor building roads for the U.S. Forest Service. He admitted that he sometimes moved stakes to save trees, in a way that would not affect the road. However, the work he did led to a falling out with his environmentalist associates:

> Robert Weed and I, we butted heads. I had a really hard time with Weed because he would say, "What are you doing building roads? You ought to do something good, like work for the Park Service," because that's what he did. And I'd say, "You think that's good, working for the Park Service? Look what they're doing. They're developers. That's just a whole different angle." These same people that blame me for working on a road down here, if they went to China and saw the Yangtze Dam and how terrible that is and what it's doing, and they look at those peasants carrying those buckets of dirt to that dam, I'll bet they don't blame them. Well, we're here trying to survive. I've never lived anywhere but southern Utah as far as an adult making money. So I'm not going to go anywhere else to make money. The government decides to pave Boulder Mountain Road and build it, so that's where the money is around here. So I go up just like one of those peasants in China working on the Yangtze Dam, that's what I gotta do to support my family. That disconnect—that's the hardest time I have with environmentalists. I throw my chain saw in the back; they flip their heat on. We all contribute. Let's look at our own hypocrisy.

By staying and trying to make a living in Boulder, Grant experienced the paradox between environmental ends and democratic means as conflict with his associates, who perceived the work he did as "helping to destroy this country" and not "good, like work for the Park Service." They put the environmental end of protecting wilderness ahead of rural people's need to make a living. Grant asked how working for the Park Service can be good, when it promotes development in national parks. He pointed out that their attitude was hypocritical, since they would not hold a worker in a developing country responsible for the environmental degradation caused by natural resource development there, and because their own consumption contributed to environmental problems. By comparing himself to "one of those peasants in China," Grant also drew attention to class differences that inform environmentalism, between people who do manual work like he does and his associates. It was because of these differences over work, Grant said, that he was kicked off the board of directors of SUWA. He described this paradox in terms of a schism in the environmental movement:

> Environmentalists are urban people, and they have no idea what it takes to live down here. . . . They come from a polluted valley up there, that is completely ruined, and then come down here and say that this country shouldn't be ruined. . . . They're pointing their fingers at the cattlemen. Yeah, sure, cattle destroyed this country at the turn of the century, and it's never recovered, never will really in our lifetime, although there has been a lot of recoveries. But, for example, I was heading out one day on the horses for a week or so. And I hit the Gulch from Sand Hollow. And I looked up from the mouth of Sand Hollow, and there's these bright-colored tents, right in the flood zone, right in the trail. And you can imagine what the people are going through, ecstatic, they're there. And I headed downstream and went around a corner, and there's a herd of cows there, and there's a kid with no shirt on and this long willow. He was kind of herding the cows, and they're just walking along slowly. And then I saw Ivan Lyman, this classic old cowboy. He'd spent all his life in these canyons, and he and I talk a little bit. And then I went on and realized, these people here, these cattlemen . . . they were just so much a part of the land. And then here's these people coming in that probably just hated cows. Although I hate cows too. And they just had no idea of the realities of this country. That's a big thing for me—I see that all the time. I see the

environmentalists, instead of going after—I shouldn't say instead, they're going after the big corporations, too—but they also go after the little guys.

Grant pointed out the urban background of most environmentalists, their class status, and their lack of knowledge of the landscape and contrasted the way that urban people experience the landscape—as spectacle, something unique and precious to be preserved—with the way that rural residents experience it: as home. By contrasting the cattlemen who are "part of the land" with the people in "bright-colored tents," he also expressed what environmental historian William Cronon saw as "the trouble with wilderness": "it embodies a dualistic vision in which the human is entirely outside the natural."[9] And finally, he implied that instead of focusing on wilderness and going after "the little guys," environmentalists should be "going after the big corporations."

Grant's differences with SUWA over the work he did, and with urban environmentalists, are reflected in critiques of the American environmental movement. For example, western historian Richard White—in a 1996 essay titled "Are You an Environmentalist or Do You Work for a Living?"—argued that environmentalists' position toward work was problematic because they associated productive work in nature with environmental degradation and, with the possible exception of more "primitive" forms of such work, "most typically the farming of peasants" (Grant's example), ignored the ways this work was a means of knowing nature.[10] As a result, nature became an arena solely for play and leisure, and the world was divided into separate domains of work and play, humans and nature. White saw wilderness and old-growth forests as a victory for biodiversity but also as a victory for leisure and a defeat for work. He feared that if we did not come to terms with work, we would "turn public lands into a public playground." He asserted that "environmentalists so often seem self-righteous, privileged, and arrogant because they so readily consent to identifying nature with play and making it by definition a place where leisured humans only come to visit and not to work, stay, or live."[11]

White did not mention class in his essay, but Cronon did. He asked, "Why, for instance, is the 'wilderness experience' so often conceived as a form of recreation best enjoyed by those whose class privileges give them the time and resources to leave their jobs behind and 'get away from it all'?"[12] White claimed that this position antagonized people who worked in resource production and made it difficult for environmentalists to address the ways that *all* work, not just the work of miners, loggers, farmers, and ranchers, intersected with nature. It was also antidemocratic because it was based on an implicit hierarchy of work and workers. White's and Cronon's analyses help explain the antagonism of some residents of the Grand Staircase-Escalate region toward environmentalists. While environmentalism is not synonymous with wilderness advocacy, in the experience of local residents it was.

Environmental historian Ramachandra Guha presented a "third world critique" of the focus on wilderness preservation in American environmentalism, in which he argued that this focus avoided facing the real roots of global environmental problems: overconsumption by the industrialized world and third world urban elites, and militarization. In his view, "a truly radical ecology in the American context ought to work toward a synthesis of the appropriate technology, alternate lifestyle, and peace movements."[13]

White argued that to grapple with the current complex environmental problems, environmentalists needed to reexamine the connections between work and nature. Grant tried to negotiate the paradox he experienced in being an environmentalist who worked for a living by using the knowledge he gained through productive work in nature to find less destructive ways of carrying out that work—for example, ways to build roads that took the landscape and trees into account. He eventually found a way to live and work in the redrock country he loved that did not involve extraction of resources and a way to be an environmentalist that did not involve representing the landscape as wilderness. He learned everything he could about the social history of the landscape, such as the location of Indian ruins and rock art and old mines, cattle trails, and camps, by exploring it on solo horse-packing trips, talking to the "old-timers," and reading everything he could get his hands on about the geology, archaeology, and history of the region, including thirty volumes of Glen Canyon archaeological history. He probably knew more about the Escalante canyon country than anyone, with the possible exception of Bill Wolverton (discussed later in this chapter).

Grant's dream had been to be a guide and run trips in the Escalante Canyons since he majored in outdoor education in college, and in 1991 he and Sue started Escalante Canyon Outfitters. They used horses to pack their guests in to base camps along the Escalante River, from which the visitors could explore on foot and benefit from Grant's vast store of knowledge and experience to learn more about the landscape. In addition, Grant and Sue chose a nonmaterialistic lifestyle that made them "radical environmentalists" in Guha's sense.

The paradox between environmentalism and democracy that Grant experienced was also evident in his understanding of democracy. At first he described democracy as "one vote, one person." But when it came to democracy in relation to public lands, he admitted:

> That's tricky because . . . you have an issue of outsiders from New York, outsiders from elsewhere, saying, "That's our public lands. We want it run the way we want it run." The majority, not just the locals here. That's a really tough one because, . . . say the people in Escalante, they grow up and that's all they know. They don't realize that you can live in LA or somewhere where there is no open space, and they want roads, and they want to drive their ATV everywhere, and they want to log the trees and get that coal out of the ground and develop and build up.

Grant regretted many of the changes he had seen in the time he had lived in the region. Looking back on his environmental activism, he realized that it was motivated partly by trying to prevent change. But now he accepted that change is inevitable:

> One thing I always try to keep in perspective: when I came to Boulder, I was a newcomer with all these great ideas and my vision of what Boulder was. . . . And these newcomers, they move in and they think that's the way Boulder's always been, and they see it change and they think, "Oh god, it can't change." And that's the way I probably was, too, when I first moved here. It had always been in a changing process, and I stepped in in the middle of that and wanted to freeze

it, wanted to fight the roads being built. . . . I think it was naive in a way. But the developments that have happened, they've happened, and they're fine. But I can't help but think, what if Boulder would've not had Boulder Mountain Road built? What if the Burr Trail would've not gotten improved? What if there was still a one-lane little oil road into Boulder? What would it be like? People would be scrambling to get here. And then they'd have to build a bigger road!

While Grant stayed in Boulder and became a different kind of environmentalist, SUWA continued to work on wilderness issues and to grow. As a member of the Utah Wilderness Coalition, it participated in a second, more sophisticated inventory that expanded the amount of wilderness in the proposed America's Redrock Wilderness Act to 9.3 million acres. The main tool SUWA used to protect these areas from activities that might disqualify them from inclusion in the National Wilderness Preservation System, such as roads (see chapter 4), oil and gas development, and mining, was litigation. The organization had a "no compromise" stance toward the issues it worked on, refusing to work with local communities and to participate in collaborative efforts, which it claimed were interest-driven and ignored broader perspectives.[14] SUWA's program to generate grassroots support nationally swelled membership to over twenty thousand at its high point, enabling the organization to raise large sums of money. In the late 1990s it began building an endowment from grants.[15]

Critics of the American environmental movement's propensity to use litigation to challenge the environmental decision-making of federal land management agencies have argued that it is costly in terms of time, money, and human resources.[16] Conflicts become drawn out as they move through different avenues for intervening in decision-making, and the delay often benefits one side. In addition, decisions that result from oppositional processes are more likely to be applied and enforced symbolically rather than substantively. The conflicts over grazing and roads on GSENM (see chapters 3 and 4) illustrate these points. Besides absorbing huge amounts of agency resources that could have been devoted to work on the ground, these legal battles make agency personnel wary of challenges from environmentalists, and avoiding these challenges becomes an unofficial goal of planning efforts, as I observed during the Rangeland Health EIS process (described in chapter 8).

Political scientists Philip Brick and Edward Weber pointed out two underlying assumptions of oppositional approaches to environmentalism, which rely on litigation to force compliance with federally mandated environmental standards. First, in an American culture lacking a strong conception of citizenship, it assumes government is the only institution capable of defending nature. Second, it assumes that environmental aims are so important it may be necessary "to force compliance on unwilling or recalcitrant subjects."[17] Brick and Weber called this approach to American environmental governance "regulatory democracy." In contrast, they held that collaborative conservation relies on "civic democracy," which emphasizes the development of citizens through participation in civic institutions that lie between government and market, devolution of significant authority to citizens, and balancing national environmental law against local ecological, economic, and social conditions.

Despite these critiques of SUWA's approach to environmentalism, this type of environmental power has been effective in confronting powerful entities such as governments and large corporations. Although he split with SUWA, Grant recognized a need for the work they were doing. He pointed out in a letter to the editor that although SUWA was originally supposed to be a grassroots local group, as it "became an urban environmental group, its membership swelled. When SUWA was grassroots, we would hold a meeting in Torrey and be met by angry loggers, then when SUWA went urban they would have a rally in Salt Lake with a crowd of enthusiastic supporters." As a result, "SUWA evolved to incorporate lawyers and infiltrate Washington and became the most effective environmental group for the Canyon Country. They have uncovered and defeated many threats that would have gone unnoticed."[18] He explained, "I still support SUWA, because I think that we need the opposite extreme. But I'm not real happy with the way they . . . it's really an urban organization now. And they have no concept of what it's like to live here."[19] SUWA was able to use this approach to environmentalism in the Grand Staircase-Escalante region partly because it left the region and wielded its power at a safe distance from the ire of those who felt it was aimed against them.

The next section describes what happened when an environmentalist used this approach against the community in which he lived.

Patrick Diehl and the Escalante Wilderness Project

By the time I began my fieldwork in the Grand Staircase-Escalante region, Grant Johnson was no longer the target of anti-environmentalist ire. He had proven himself through hard work and staying power and had become one of "the locals." But after the creation of GSENM in 1996 and the completion of the BLM's wilderness reinventory in Utah in 1999, anti-environmentalist feelings were again running high in the region. They found a new target in Escalante: Patrick Diehl, whose actions at the public hearing in Escalante were described in the introduction, along with his partner, Tori Woodard, who had moved there from Berkeley in 1998.[20]

The trouble started over water—an endless source of trouble in arid parts of the West. The New Escalante Irrigation Company was trying to build a new reservoir because the existing one had lost nearly half of its capacity as a result of sedimentation. Each year Escalante irrigators were running out of water before the growing season was over, losing part of their potential agricultural production. The proposed reservoir was on land managed by GSENM, although not in the monument. After the required environmental assessment, the monument manager gave the project the go-ahead. On April 11, 1999, a construction crew from the Utah National Guard was poised to begin construction on the keyway for the long-awaited reservoir. But construction was suddenly halted. That same day an article in the *Salt Lake Tribune* announced that the BLM had placed the New Escalante Irrigation Company's New Wide Hollow Reservoir project on hold because the Wilderness Society had called for further study of its impacts. The article quoted Patrick Diehl, who questioned the size of the reservoir and the motives of its proponents and suggested they might be planning to use the water for residential development and not just for irrigation.[21]

When Patrick and Tori had first moved to Escalante, residents were very welcoming. They were invited to be on committees, and Patrick sang with the church choir. "It was kind of nice, being part of the community for a while," he said. But Patrick and Tori had already expressed opinions some residents considered "environmental" in letters to the editor of the local paper and at city council meetings. So when construction on the new reservoir was halted, some residents saw them as responsible and turned their disappointment and anger on Patrick and Tori. The couple received threatening phone calls, and on the night of April 15 someone diverted an irrigation pipe from their well-tended garden into an excavation they had just completed for a new building and opened the valve. They incurred not only water damage but also a hefty fine from the New Escalante Irrigation Company for an open pipe.

The *Salt Lake Tribune*'s report of these events took Patrick and Tori's side and represented the "locals" in a derogatory way. An article with the headline "Environmentalists Not Welcome in Town of Escalante" quoted Escalante mayor Lenza Wilson as saying, "The jury [of local public opinion] has returned a very strong verdict, and they are not welcome here. They need a better grip on Escalante's background, customs, and culture."[22] Another local resident stated, "The thing that got Patrick Diehl in trouble is he took the route that we're a bunch of idiots." Patrick disparaged local concerns and judgment and expressed the opinion that local concerns should be overridden: "I'm sorry to see them support a project that is economically unjustified and environmentally damaging. This involved more than the people of Escalante. This is public land, equally owned by everyone."[23]

Local attitudes toward Patrick continued to deteriorate when he showed up at a rally on July 5 at the GSENM visitors' center in Escalante, part of a statewide protest against the BLM's wilderness reinventory, holding a sign supporting wilderness. The county deputy sheriff stepped in to protect him from angry participants. Patrick's actions reinforced many residents' negative stereotypes of environmentalists. Patrick and Tori's home was vandalized again on July 24. This time the *Salt Lake Tribune* headline quoted an Escalante LDS bishop, who called them "lucky."[24] In September the New Escalante Irrigation Company shut Patrick and Tori's irrigation water off because they refused to pay the fine.

Patrick and Tori experienced the paradox between environmental ends and democratic means as conflict with Escalante residents who perceived that their pursuit of environmental goals disregarded the welfare of the community. An Escalante resident expressed these feeling in a letter to the editor of the local newspaper:

> You were accepted into the community. . . . It was only after you began alienating those who befriended you that you were no longer accepted. . . . Your methods are contentious and counterproductive. Instead of seeking common ground on which to build a foundation for success, you have arrogantly belittled the community you were attracted to. . . . Vandalizing your home was wrong. . . . The methods of the vandal are not representative of the citizenry, but I think the sentiment may be. You have made enemies, there is no question about that. But you have created the community you live in.[25]

Undeterred by these events, Patrick and Tori took on a new project, which they must have been aware would again antagonize local residents. The stated goals of the Escalante Wilderness Project were to make most of southern Utah wilderness and eliminate grazing on the public lands. In May 2000 Patrick and Tori set up a booth outside the GSENM visitors' center in Escalante to hand out pamphlets on the impact of livestock grazing on the monument and recruit members to their new organization. They tangled with the BLM over the placement of their table, and Patrick was arrested on two different occasions. Detailed reports of these events were published in the *Salt Lake Tribune*. In June 2001 Patrick and Tori stepped into the middle of the controversy over the cattle impoundment on Fiftymile Mountain that had taken place the previous fall (described in chapter 3) by visiting the allotments involved and reporting to the *Salt Lake Tribune* that cattle were still there.

When I first met Patrick and Tori in the summer of 2001, they were isolated from the rest of the community. Their environmental activities had antagonized many Escalante residents, and the friends they had made in town were afraid to associate with them for fear of drawing antagonism against themselves. But they both spoke calmly, articulately, and with a lot of humor about their experiences. Patrick was in his fifties, and Tori was maybe ten years younger. Tori wore her long, blonde hair in a braid and was thin, quiet, and soft-spoken. Patrick, who holds a PhD in comparative literature from Berkeley, did more of the talking. Tori was the daughter of a Colorado public lands rancher, and Patrick grew up in Texas and Tennessee and still had a bit of a southern accent. In Berkeley, they had both been activists with the anti-nuclear Livermore Action Group. They had moved to Escalante for Tori's health and because they liked the hiking, and despite the difficulties they had been facing in the community, they planned to stay because her health was improving. In addition to the Escalante Wilderness Project, they had another project, called Escalante House, to build housing for people like Tori with multiple chemical sensitivities. At that time I was unaware of what had turned local opinion against Patrick and Tori, and I felt sympathetic to their plight.

They told me that when the New Wide Hollow Reservoir construction was about to start, they had just been trying to keep environmental groups informed about what was going on. They hadn't realized Escalante was such a focal point for environmental politics, and they didn't understand why people thought Patrick had the power to stop the reservoir. But they learned quickly that "if you're not from around here, you're not allowed to speak," although they recognized that the community was not monolithic and that the actions of a few did not represent the attitudes of the whole. They explained, "Some of the most belligerent and anti-environmentalist aren't those who are fifth-generation residents: the outspoken are relative newcomers. Our neighbors are old family. They don't go to meetings, and they come and apologize." And despite local feelings about Patrick's environmental activism, when he broke an ankle hiking in Phipps Wash, the volunteer Escalante Search and Rescue team acted quickly to come to his assistance and carry him out.

When I talked to them in 2001, Patrick and Tori said that things had calmed down and there was a "progressive mood" in the town, but they didn't participate in the community anymore. They admitted that they "didn't have a clue how to deal with a town like this" and "haven't done very well." They attempted to negotiate the paradox between environmental aims and democratic means, which they experienced as ostracism by the local community, by looking for community elsewhere. They were now doing most of their work on the computer, had made new friends in Moab, and helped form the Glen Canyon Chapter of the Sierra Club with like-minded people there, even though they hadn't been members of the Sierra Club before because they felt it was "too middle-of-the-road." Tori "used to think about the future of this town, and I used to care," Patrick said. "But I don't care anymore. Now I focus on protecting the land from them." He added, "People should appreciate us for being the reason the town changes less rapidly. We're helping them get a reputation for being unfriendly. I was surprised at the way they [the federal government] created the monument—very high-handed—but now I understand why they did it that way." As anti-nuclear activists, they had opposed the federal government, but since they had been "cut out of decision-making in the town," they had been working with it more and had "become much more fond of the federal government."

Tori brought out a scrapbook where she kept all the articles that had been published in the newspapers about them, pointing to the most recent ones with pride. Suddenly, my impression of them shifted. They seemed to derive satisfaction from their difficulties and the media attention they drew. I began to wonder how the *Salt Lake Tribune* had been kept informed of Patrick's activities in Escalante and whether the couple's activism had as much to do with being "environmentalists"—giving them an identity of embattled heroes to replace that of anti-nuclear activists—as with being concerned about local environmental issues. This identity needed an opponent against which to define itself; in their Berkeley days, it had been the federal government, but now they were working with the federal government to oppose local land use plans. Tori reinforced my impression when she explained, "This is an extreme climate and it attracts people who are extreme, including us. We're living in a war zone, but we're used to it." She described how they had lived in tents at the site when they were opposing nuclear waste disposal in the California desert. "There's plenty of work to do, but it takes a certain type. We're the right people for the land." My impression was confirmed when, several days later, I watched Patrick's performance at the city council meeting. That experience helped change my perception not only of the locals but of environmentalists as well. Afterward, I had much less sympathy for Patrick and no longer considered him an environmentalist, and I had a much better understanding of the source of local residents' antipathy toward environmentalists.

Following the events of that summer, Patrick and Tori continued their activism against livestock grazing and other uses of the public lands in the region. Their Escalante Wilderness Project (EWP) adopted the same oppositional approach that SUWA used. In 2001 EWP was among the group of environmental organizations that appealed the Kanab BLM Field Office's decision to renew grazing permits on the allotments it managed. The appeal was denied. In 2002, after the BLM had reevaluated the impacts of the New Wide Hollow Reservoir project and given it the go-ahead again, EWP joined several other environmental groups in appealing that decision, and it joined an appeal of a Forest Service decision on the Griffin Springs Resource Management Project, a proposed timber sale in the Dixie National Forest above Escalante. That year EWP also appealed a GSENM decision to reintroduce pronghorn antelope and desert bighorn sheep into the monument because it objected to the predator control component of the program. That appeal was denied too.

Patrick became active in politics as well. In 2002 and 2004 he ran as a Green Party challenger to Democratic representative Jim Matheson in Utah's Second Congressional District using the slogan "The Most Hated Man in Escalante." He joined a protest march against a U.S. first strike in Iraq in Salt Lake City in 2002. In March 2003 he was arrested in Salt Lake City with a group protesting the U.S. invasion of Iraq. Later that same year he was barred from leadership positions in the Sierra Club because of his outspoken criticism of the organization's position on the war in Iraq. He was featured in an April 15, 2004, article in the *Salt Lake Tribune* as a tax protestor "who filed returns for 10 years but never sent the IRS a penny of what he owed." The article went on to note, "A few years ago, he stopped filing altogether." Patrick explained in the article that his "refusal to pay taxes stems from what he sees as faulty US foreign policy, including financial backing for Israel and investment in the war in Iraq." He also divulged how he had been able to avoid paying taxes: among other strategies, he didn't take a regular job because the IRS would garnish his paycheck, so he depended on his partner for support.[26]

Knowing these details gave me a better idea of his character. With his confrontational approach, propensity to appeal every federal agency decision to use resources on the public lands in the Grand Staircase-Escalante region, and disregard for local concerns, Patrick Diehl brought into sharp relief the paradox between environmental aims and democratic means, and "put flesh and bone to every stereotype about environmentalists held in southern Utah."[27] His oppositional approach to environmentalism might have worked for SUWA and for environmental organizations battling the government and large corporations, but his story illustrates what can happen when someone uses this tactic against their neighbors.

In the fall of 2003 Patrick and Tori's house lay empty and had a For Sale sign. It appeared that because their style of "environmentalism" had isolated them from the community, they had abandoned it for Salt Lake City. Eventually, I heard that they had moved to Corsica. I thought this was just another local rumor, but rumors I heard in Escalante always seemed to have some truth to them, and this was later verified in an article in the *Canyon Country Zephyr*.[28] Perhaps the IRS had been closing in on Patrick. He left Escalante with one last thing to remember him by: on July 12, 2005, EWP's appeal of the New Wide Hollow Reservoir was upheld, meaning Escalante would not get a new reservoir.[29]

Jim Catlin and Wild Utah

Jim Catlin exemplified an approach to environmentalism that uses science to legitimate environmental decision-making. Decisions based on science, or rule of experts, would seem to eliminate the need for a democratic process. Jim was the project director for the Wild Utah Project, a group founded in 1996 to provide scientific analysis and geographic information system (GIS) support to other Utah conservation groups. He was a behind-the-scenes environmentalist whose organization and name were not well known in the Grand Staircase-Escalante region like SUWA, the Sierra Club, Patrick Diehl, and Bill Hedden. Nevertheless, he had been extremely active and influential in the environmental movement in Utah since the 1970s. It was to Jim that Grant

Johnson had turned for information in 1977 when Highway 12 was being built, and it was Jim who donated the first copy machine to SUWA when it first organized in 1983.

A native of Utah who lived in Salt Lake City, Jim had been coming to southern Utah since the 1970s to hike and explore its canyons and to work on environmental issues there. He knew the Grand Staircase-Escalante region well and had an amazing memory for the details of the landscape, as well as the details of environmental battles fought and won in southern Utah going back to that time. For example, in the 1970s environmentalists fought a proposal to build a dam on the Escalante River to produce electricity for a coal-fired power plant in the region that would be supplied by coal transported by rail from the Kaiparowits Plateau. They also fought a proposal for an improbable Trans-Escalante Highway, which would traverse the rugged and beautiful country between the Kaiparowits Plateau, the Escalante Canyons, and Waterpocket Fold. Neither project was really feasible or got beyond the conceptual stage.

Jim got a degree in electrical engineering, but after graduating from college, he decided he wasn't "ready to move into a cubicle and be an engineer." He explained, "So I joined the Peace Corps. And that really reshaped my life. I became an activist, wanting to be engaged in civic kinds of things. . . . I was more interested in systems and simulating and planning and systems design, large systems analysis, systems like urban systems or modeling of complex systems." To develop this interest, Jim got a master's degree in urban and regional planning at the University of Utah. During that time he was "very active" with the Sierra Club and other organizations, "working on wilderness issues and public land issues." He continued on for a PhD in environmental science, policy, and management at Berkeley so he could work professionally in the areas in which he had been a volunteer. He studied public policy, how institutions work, natural resources law, and a broad spectrum of public lands issues.

His education and experience equipped him with a broad background and earned him a job running Wild Utah for Dave Foreman's Wildlands Project in Utah in 1997. He described the work of Wild Utah, an organization consisting of Jim and three others, as providing "the science and the ecosystem management tools" that environmental partner organizations requested and that would help the BLM make better land use decisions. "We're unique in that. I don't know of any of the other partners that do that," he said. Jim believed that solutions to environmental problems could be found by using and improving the available science and developing detailed procedures for decision-making. Unlike most environmental organizations, Wild Utah did not pursue particular environmental goals but rather created the processes for other organizations to use.

Jim's description of Wild Utah's first project, helping revamp the Utah Wilderness Coalition's proposal for a wilderness bill for Utah, illustrated this approach. He collaborated with a math PhD to design a comprehensive process for identifying and evaluating "every human impact in over 10 million acres of BLM in Utah" in only two years. They began by identifying four hundred units that needed to be inventoried, then created a training program and field packets for volunteers who spent eight to ten hours of data gathering on each unit, reviewed the fieldwork when it came back, and revisited problem areas. A "silly story" Jim told demonstrated the attention to detail in the process and illuminated the personalities of the collaborators: "We had about two thousand maps we had to file away from all of the fieldwork. So we had to have a standard way of folding maps. We had a two-hour meeting on how to fold a map, and we drove to tears the rest of the coalition members."

The project also included a media plan designed to win support for the reinventory. The team invited the media along as they did fieldwork, showed the journalists where the counties were claiming R.S. 2477 roads existed, and explained, "Here's a track that you can only walk up that they're calling essential for the economy of the county. And it was clear that it was an excuse to fight wilderness, and the media picked up on it right away." The project culminated in a huge rollout, with public meetings designed to impress and convince, wall-size maps, seventy huge boxes with all the fieldwork reports, and a PowerPoint presentation of the whole process to eight hundred people at the University of Utah. Jim was satisfied with the results of this strategy: "We were at a new place in the issue. The media up to that time had been echoing the opposition, saying these areas are developed; they have roads in them; they don't qualify. But the media agreed with us that these lands, in the case of naturalness, they qualify."

Under Jim's leadership, Wild Utah's approach to environmentalism was reflected in its research in GSENM on the effects of livestock grazing. Jim saw the creation of the monument as an opportunity to develop a science-based approach to public land grazing:

> In the Clinton administration, there was a lot of support for using the monument as a model for how grazing should be elsewhere. And there was a real sense that we need to look at the ecological approach to grazing. . . . [GSENM had hired people to do that.] And when the administration changed, these people were no longer welcome. We chose to work on this because it was a real opportunity, and in a new setting. And the monument, more so than other BLM lands, had a responsibility to take care of the land. They had a strong land use plan. If you look at that plan, it was designed by the staff at the time to put a whole bunch of checks in it to ensure that decisions don't ignore key ecological needs.

Based on its research, Wild Utah developed and submitted an alternative for the Draft Rangeland Health Environmental Impact Statement (EIS) in 2003, long before the BLM had made any progress on developing alternatives. Wild Utah's alternative highlighted the fact that the presidential proclamation creating GSENM and the Monument Management Plan both stressed the importance of using the best available science on the monument. It pointed out limitations in the monitoring, data collection, and rangeland health assessment methods that the monument staff was using to gather data for the EIS and in how they were analyzing results, and it made suggestions to improve these processes. Wild Utah also developed its own science-based tools for accomplishing some of the tasks the BLM was required to undertake for the EIS and provided them to the agency, including tools for determining whether livestock grazing was the cause of failure to meet rangeland health standards, for assessing available forage and grazing capacity, and for assessing southwestern stream riparian ecosystems.

Jim displayed the same attention to system design, scientific methods and analysis, and robust data when he talked about Wild Utah's then current project in the monument:

> We got from the Natural Resource Conservation Service their grazing survey for the monument. . . . It took two years to get these. And I went to their office with my copy machine and scanner, and I spent three days copying them—there are over one thousand of them—and organized them all. And right now, we're creating a digital data set from them. And this digital dataset will show plant community composition: which species are there and how much of the species was found on the transect they took. It will show the relative quantity of the biomass that's there, the amount of bare ground they expect to have there, the amount of plant cover, and quite a few other useful variables. This is the best actual measured data of current range condition that we have now. . . . So what we're going to do is use this dataset and, through comparative analysis, look at things like trend, utilization data, and BLM's rangeland health assessments and compare all this data and show where there's consistencies and inconsistencies.

Jim experienced the paradox between environmentalism and democracy as frustration because the BLM is required to make decisions not only based on the best available science but also taking into account the agency's multiple-use mandate, which requires it to balance different resource uses among the present and future needs of the American people. In addition, many of the challenges that the monument staff faced in managing grazing were not technical and could not be tackled using "the science and the ecosystem management tools" that Wild Utah provided. As previous chapters have illustrated, these challenges included a lack of political support, personnel, and funding, as well as a concern for the ranchers who were neighbors. Finally, because the nonequilibrium model of rangeland ecology proposes that rangeland ecosystems evolve unpredictably and have multiple stable states, even when the BLM has better tools for evaluating rangeland health, the agency's rangeland management decisions become decisions about values: which state is preferable.

Advocates of post-normal science and public ecology have argued that science can no longer exempt environmental decision-making from democratic processes because there are many situations where scientific knowledge is incomplete or uncertain and where values differ, and in these situations, decision-making should involve a wide variety of stakeholders. This not only makes the process more democratic but also improves the quality, creativity, and effectiveness of decisions.[30] Instead of decisions based solely on expert knowledge, a more participatory process can "construct a body of knowledge that will reflect the pluralistic and pragmatic context of its use" and "build common ground among competing beliefs and values for the environment."[31] Described in this way, public ecology has much in common with democratic politics as Chantal Mouffe envisioned it.[32] This approach to environmental decision-making would help bridge the paradox between environmentalism and democracy.

Jim's understanding of democracy began from the same recognition of the need for sufficient information and an explicit process in government decision-making as in his approach to environmentalism:

> Well, the ideal model, and I hope that we can work towards that, is where government is open. Where almost all the information that they use and they have you can look at. Where decisions are made on the merits of that issue, publicly, for reasons that they can discuss, leaders can discuss. Where people are elected because they are the best people for the job and not because they come with an association or a predetermined power or money. Where each candidate has an equal chance. Democracy is a certainty that you can trust that what will happen tomorrow is what you talked about yesterday. And democracy is where those in minority have fair consideration and their basic needs are also met.

To illustrate how democracy as it actually works falls short of this ideal, he told a story about grazing and democracy that showed that the BLM was using inaccurate information about how livestock grazing was taking place on public land to make decisions, which is a violation of the National Environmental Policy Act (NEPA). He concluded, "So, going back to democracy, NEPA is actually one of the few laws we have around that holds the government responsible for being open.... One of the frustrations for somebody like myself, and a member of the public, is when you go to the agency to say, 'I'd like to participate in grazing decisions,' they throw this information at you that is at best deception." This story also expressed his belief that with accurate information, you would know "what you need to do," as well as his frustration with the disconnect between his approach to environmentalism and the way the BLM managed public land. The next section illustrates an approach to environmentalism that relied on the market to achieve environmental aims.

Bill Hedden and Grand Canyon Trust

Bill Hedden was the executive director of the Grand Canyon Trust (GCT), a regional nonprofit conservation organization based in Flagstaff, Arizona, whose mission was to protect and restore the Colorado Plateau. (Bill's role in the conflict over grazing was described in chapter 3.) GCT's origin story differs from that of the other environmental organizations working in the Grand Staircase-Escalante region considered so far. Instead of starting out as a grassroots organization like SUWA, a personal crusade like the Escalante Wilderness Project, or a consulting group for other environmental organizations like Wild Utah, it was the brainchild of Interior Secretary Stewart Udall and Arizona governor Bruce Babbitt, who thought there should be an organization to protect the Grand Canyon that bridged Utah and Arizona. With that as its purpose, GCT was incorporated in Washington DC in 1985. The organization's earliest projects involved reducing air pollution from coal-burning power plants in the region and restricting overflights of the Grand Canyon, but it soon broadened both the range and geographic focus of its projects to include the entire Colorado Plateau.

Bill first became involved with GCT in 1995. He lived in Castle Valley, a small community about twenty miles east of Moab, since the mid-1970s. Originally from New Jersey, he first came to southern Utah with his wife, a native Utahn, whom he had met while they were both at Harvard. She took him backpacking in the canyon country of southern Utah, and he fell in love with it, just as she had. They bought property in Castle Valley so they could live in the midst of it. They camped on the property while building the house they still live in. Built of wood, low lying, and nestled among large cottonwoods, it looks like part of the landscape and feels welcoming, comfortable, and well lived in. Bill built most of the furniture himself, and their grown daughter's oil paintings hang on the walls. Since there was no demand for his PhD in neurobiology in southern Utah, Bill started out by making his living as a woodworker and furniture maker.

A tall, lean, and quiet man, Bill did not start out with the intention of becoming an environmental activist. But shortly after they moved to Castle Valley, he learned of plans to build a nuclear waste dump outside Canyonlands National Park. Local residents didn't seem too concerned about it, but with his background, Bill felt that he ought to explain the dangers. "In those days, anyone who got involved was put in charge," so he soon found himself appointed to the governor's commission on nuclear waste and drawn into other environmental issues in the area. He had been president of the local irrigation company and a member of the State Parks Board, as well as of the Grand County Council, doing all this volunteer work in addition to working ten hours a day. In the mid-1990s he began to have work-related health problems, so when a position as the conservation director of GCT came up in 1995, he applied for it. He was offered the position but turned it down when he learned he would have to move to Flagstaff. GCT hired him anyway and put him in charge of its Utah projects, a position he could fulfill from home. In 2003, when the executive director resigned, GCT asked Bill to take the position and he accepted, agreeing to commute between Castle Valley and Flagstaff several times a month.

GCT's market-based approach to public land grazing did not develop by plan. Nor was GCT working on the issue of public land grazing in 1996, when the superintendent of Glen Canyon National Recreation Area first contacted Bill about purchasing the grazing permit for an allotment adjacent to Canyonlands National Park. But the trust, in partnership with the Conservation Fund, agreed to buy the permit if an environmental assessment found the allotment should be closed to grazing. The rancher used the money he received for the permit to get out of debt and rearrange his ranching operation so he could manage it better. A light bulb went on in Bill's head, and he saw this approach as another way that GCT could protect and restore the Colorado Plateau and help ranchers at the same time.

In the next few years the trust had further success retiring grazing permits along the Escalante River (as described in chapter 3), on an allotment that had been added to Arches National Park, and on an allotment in Capitol Reef National Park, experiences that led to the development of its Grazing Retirement Program (GRP). GSENM also looked like a good place to pursue this strategy because the current staff was sympathetic to it and the Interior Department was enthusiastic about market-based approaches to resolving natural resource conflicts. Moreover, Bill believed that the GRP would free the BLM from the local politics of grazing and allow the agency to base grazing decisions purely on science:

> If you've got a rancher sitting there in front of you saying, I don't know how I'm going to put food on the table for my family this winter. I've got to put the cows out there because I can't afford to buy hay for them, well, that's a different situation. But we intentionally created a situation where that pressure didn't have to be there, where in some small part of the monument the main impetus could be, well, what's good for the land. We did it in just a few places, where we thought it was especially important, and where there was an opportunity of a willing rancher. And now it's mired in this controversy.

But he learned that retiring a permit still involved local politics because some local residents saw it as a threat to the ranching community and culture, something the market did not take into consideration.

Bill always insisted that he was not anti-grazing: "Someone like that couldn't have done this. I get along with ranchers. I like these guys." He was on good terms with all the ranchers GCT had dealt with. He explained that GCT had always tried to "work with people who wanted to do it" and to "facilitate the desires of the ranchers." The trust had never filed any lawsuits over grazing. And, he said, "the ranchers we bought out are still in business and wouldn't be if we hadn't bought them out." So he was surprised and dismayed when GCT's next round of grazing permit purchases in GSENM met with hostility and opposition from local government officials and wound up in litigation.

For Bill, "democracy means that we have an opportunity for decisions to be made that reflect the will of the people, and especially for the ones that are really the stakeholders in given issues." He experienced the paradox between environmentalism and democracy as rejection of GCT's Grazing Retirement Program by residents of the Grand Staircase-Escalante region because, while he saw it as a nonconfrontational, market-based means to reduce the effects of livestock grazing in the region, they saw it as undemocratic. What they objected to was not so much GCT's purchase of the permits, which they reluctantly agreed it was qualified to do, but its plans to retire them, because they believed grazing retirements threatened not just the local economy but the ranching culture of the region.

In 2003, when the ranchers appealed the denial of their applications for the permits held by GCT's Canyonlands Grazing Corporation, it looked to Bill as though the opposition had won. GCT's donors were nervous about the outcome, and money for grazing retirements had dried up. Ranchers who wanted to sell their permits were still approaching Bill, but he had to turn them down. "I would still maintain it's a fairly small group of people who have created all that controversy," he said, but that small group had been able to "eliminate a whole other market for permits" and "dictate for all the ranchers what they could do." Kane and Garfield Counties had even had him investigated to try to get him kicked off the State Parks Board. But he defied assumed differences of class and residence between environmentalists and rural residents that allowed the latter to dismiss the former as outsiders. He explained, "They hate it because the trouble is, I am who I say I am. They can't say I am an environmentalist from outside. I've lived here over twenty years, and I have been a working person like they are."

In 2004 GCT was still waiting—waiting for the drought to let up so it could invest in cows and waiting to see what happened with the appeal. In the face of local opposition and an about-face by Bush administration officials in the Interior Department, who had initially supported

GCT's market-based GRP, Bill admitted, "The effort to work with the ranching community and use the market to find balanced solutions is over. They've declared that they don't want to have a larger market for their permits, and they've had support from the highest levels of the Bush administration."

Environmental organizations concerned with public land grazing have tried to negotiate the paradox between environmental ends and democratic means in a variety of ways. Bill explained how GCT's approach to public land grazing differed from that of two other conservation organizations, The Nature Conservancy (TNC) and the Quivira Coalition. Both adopted what they considered a nonoppositional approach that tried to "keep the rancher on the land." Bill's discussion provides insight into more varieties of American environmentalism, as well as his defense of the GRP when it first ran into opposition.

According to Bill, there are no one-size-fits-all approaches to managing grazing on the public lands, and these organizations' different approaches are a result of different conditions where they are being used. GCT's approach is a result of specific conditions in southern Utah. "The answers in different places are very different. It's just differences of geography—a different place, different biology, different land ownership patterns, different everything. What we've developed is a home-grown approach that grew out of this place—out of the tremendously high percentage of federal ownership of the land, the tiny base properties, and the really marginal economic operations that most of the ranchers have got. I don't pretend our answer is relevant to everybody else, but what I see as their main concerns don't apply very well here."

TNC, perhaps the best-known international conservation organization in the United States, uses land acquisition as a principal tool to carry out its mission of protecting biodiversity. It has pursued a policy of purchasing working ranches or conservation easements on working ranches in the American West because much of the biodiversity it wants to protect is on private rangelands and federal grazing allotments. Bill sits on the board of TNC. He explained:

> They made a major high-level policy decision they had to work with ranchers because the ranchers were controlling the land where the

species were. Not because the conservancy thought one way or the other about whether ranchers were good stewards or whether grazing could coexist with their mission of biodiversity or anything else; they just knew inescapably that they had to deal with ranchers. The conservancy's goals are similar to ours, but if buying private land is your principal tool for doing your work and you've set up your whole organization around that, then the big chunks of land you're going to buy are going to be these big, sexy ranches, and so they tend to be dealing in places where there's a very large amount of private land. And then, just by serendipity, they love places where there's trout streams because then their really rich donors can fly in and go fly-fishing and get all excited about the project. So because their main tool is buying land, they're working with places where there's great big private holdings.

Although GCT's and TNC's goals are similar, TNC is an international organization with a large enough budget to use land purchase as a primary tool. In addition, "a lot of those places are further north, where grass actually grows and where there were grazing animals," so ranching is more viable.

The Quivira Coalition is a regional conservation organization based in Santa Fe, New Mexico, that works with interested ranchers, environmentalists, federal and state agency personnel, academics, and members of the public. Its mission was originally to promote "progressive ranch management, scientifically-guided riparian and upland restoration, land health assessment and monitoring, and bridge-building," an approach it called the New Ranch.[33] At the time I talked to Bill, it was providing support for ranchers in the form of outreach and education, demonstration projects, and a network of consultants, specialists, and mentors. Bill explained that conditions in the region where the Quivira Coalition worked were different from conditions both farther north and in the Grand Staircase-Escalante region. Rapid development in that region was seen as the greatest threat to the landscape.

They have made the assumption that because they work in places where you tend to have a very large private landholding, and some of those private landholdings are in places that are desirable for people to live, they made the decision that the best thing to do was to keep those ranches intact and prevent there from being subdivision of that land. And so once you say the best situation is for these ranchers to have these ranches, we want to have favorable economic conditions for the ranchers, we want them to be able to run big enough numbers that their whole operation pencils out, we want to have estate transfer taxes and laws that allows these things to pass down to the families, that's a whole different set of considerations.

In the place where we work, people tend to have a lease on a state section of land, or a 10-acre parcel on the outskirts of Escalante, and the whole concern about the private base lands not being sold off is not such a big concern in this part of the world.... And so we don't start from the position that the most important thing we have to do is keep the rancher on the land.

Quivira starts with the presupposition that environmentalists and ranchers really have the same basic goal, which is to keep ranchers on the land. And that's not true over here. And it's not because we are just more hateful than other people; it's because there's nothing in it for us to keep the rancher on the land like there is in a place where the rancher owns the whole river valley. Quivira has bought the idea that the essential question is cows or condos.[34] ... But in most of the West, the cows versus condos argument is nonsense. Even if the rancher wanted to, there isn't anybody who'd be willing to pay them top dollar and subdivide it. There's no market for homes there.

Recalling stories that local residents had been telling me about developers from Las Vegas buying up ranch property in western Kane and Garfield Counties, I responded, "Yet."

We can view this discussion as one way that Bill was trying to negotiate his experience of paradox between the trust's environmental goals and its means of achieving them. At that time he believed that the particular approach GCT was using to reduce the effects of livestock grazing were determined by conditions in the region. Another way he negotiated the paradox was by developing a new approach. When GCT, in partnership with the Conservation Fund, was given the opportunity to purchase the Kane and Two-Mile Ranches—1,000 acres of private land

and grazing permits for 830,000 acres of public land managed by the BLM and Forest Service in the Arizona strip north of Grand Canyon—the trust decided to use TNC's tool and bought the ranches. However, instead of keeping the rancher on the land, the trust would run the ranches itself. Bill described the new project as "a big experiment: making our primary objective the health of the land rather than the bottom line of the grazing operation." The new approach would be to "change the way grazing is done in order to put the needs of that natural system first." But in this arid region, the trust faced different challenges than TNC, as Bill pointed out: "I don't know whether sustainable ranching is feasible on the Colorado Plateau.... Somewhere there is a number that could go out there and still help the grasslands and help the populations of native species. But is that number high enough that somebody could actually make a living doing that? That's an unanswered question."

With a $1 million contribution from Walmart to the $4.5 million price tag for the Kane and Two-Mile Ranches, the purchase was completed in September 2005, the same month Bill testified at the hearing for the ranchers' appeal. Anticipation of the new project awaiting GCT, one that he hoped would avoid the difficulties the GRP had run up against, may have helped Bill keep his cool during the aggressive questioning by the attorney for the appellants.

GCT's website in 2007 reflected lessons learned from the failure of the GRP to gain support in the Grand Staircase-Escalante region. It described GCT's approach as "advocat[ing] collaborative, common sense solutions to the significant problems affecting the region's natural resources" and expressed concern for local communities whose "quality of life" was at stake in the "economic and demographic transformation as the 'old economy' based in resource extraction competes with a 'new economy' based in tourism and recreation." It affirmed, "In an area facing so many challenges, we believe enduring conservation can only take place when ecology, economy and community come together to support balanced conservation goals."[35] It also described the progress that had been made toward "implementing scientifically rigorous and ecologically appropriate livestock management and restoration activities" on the Kane and Two-Mile Ranches, now collectively called the North Rim Ranches. The trust had hired a ranch manager from Wyoming, assembled a science advisory council consisting of experts from a variety of scientific disciplines and universities, conducted a baseline ecological assessment, begun restoration work with the help of volunteers, and purchased livestock. However, while some of the ranch hands hired were from the local area, it was not clear what role local communities would play in the project or whether it would address local concerns about ranching, community, and culture that had aroused opposition to the GRP.

The trust's new approach to public land ranching, based on purchasing a ranch, was still market-based. It still suffered from the shortcomings pointed out in chapter 3: markets aren't really free, they are unable to take noneconomic values into account, and they interpellate a self-centered individual subject instead of a democratic citizen. In addition, since they must rely on large contributions from donors to buy land, organizations that use this approach may have to attend to donors' wishes and not just to ecological considerations. This strategy may also provoke opposition from local people, for whom these organizations represent big money from outside. As a result, GCT continued to negotiate the paradox between market-based environmentalism and democratic process. Quivira's approach offered a promising alternative, even for the Grand Staircase-Escalante region. It didn't use the coercive power of government or the economic power of the dollar to overcome opposition and accomplish its goals because it worked with ranchers, scientists, and federal land management agency personnel who already shared their goals. The next section explores an individual approach to environmentalism that avoided many of the problems the first four environmentalists encountered.

Bill Wolverton and Russian Olive

Bill Wolverton's approach to environmentalism did not rely on the courts, science, the market, membership dues, or donor funding. He had lived in Escalante since 1986, and while he belonged to several environmental organizations and had participated in many of their activities, he launched his own environmental crusade without attracting the attention or the ire of other local residents. A National Park Service botanist recognized his work as "extraordinary, especially when you consider how incredibly difficult it is" and "unheard of for anything in the Park Service," and a Sierra Club public lands specialist described him as "the most resourceful guy I've ever met," adding, "He has identified a problem and decided to single-handedly go out and solve it."[36]

The battle that Bill was fighting was in the Escalante Canyons, but it was not for wilderness or against grazing or roads, the BLM, the ranchers, or the counties. He was fighting an invasive species, Russian olive (*Elaeagnus angustifolia*), a fast-growing tree introduced into the United States in the late nineteenth century as an ornamental and a windbreak. It was taking over river and stream banks and washes in the Colorado Plateau, crowding out native cottonwoods and willows, threatening wildlife that depended on them, using much more water than native species, and with its long, wicked thorns, making life miserable for hikers and boaters in the Escalante Canyons.

I first met Bill Wolverton in the spring of 1999, when I was on my way to Escalante for the first time. I had heard that the public meeting in Escalante on the results of the BLM's wilderness reinventory had been disrupted by a confrontation between the locals and environmentalists, and I was feeling nervous about my reception. Along the way, I stopped to see the spectacular rock art in Horseshoe Canyon, a detached unit of Canyonlands National Park. It was a cold, rainy, windy day, and I had the canyon to myself. The utter quiet and solitude added to the awe-inspiring experience of seeing the brooding, life-size figures in the Great Gallery. The rain stopped as I was hiking out, and the sun illuminated the swirling clouds. In Horseshoe Shelter, I saw a lone figure, a park ranger, a type of official I had learned to avoid from my experience climbing in Yosemite National Park. However, being an aspiring anthropologist, I decided I should approach him.

Bill turned out not to be the officious park ranger I expected. He worked as a backcountry ranger for the National Park Service (NPS) so he could live in Escalante in the midst of the canyon country he loved. He had also been a backcountry ranger in Zion National Park, so he knew a wide swath of southern Utah's canyon country intimately. He was often called on by search and rescue to locate missing hikers in its complex topography. In 2000 he transferred to Glen Canyon National Recreation Area, which borders GSENM and encompasses the lower Escalante River canyons, so he could work closer to the canyons he called home. Tall, slender, agile, and fit, Bill looked much younger than his fifty years. I attribute it to living a life doing what he loves. We hiked out together, in animated conversation all the way, and he invited me to visit him in Escalante. I was delighted to have already found a friend there. That was only the first of many amazing hikes together and many conversations we would share about hiking routes, his work for the NPS and environmental organizations, local politics, and anything related to the Escalante canyon country, about which he had an incredible memory and propensity to talk in detail.

Bill was originally from Sacramento, California, where, as a member of the Sierra Club, he had enjoyed hiking and scrambling in the Sierra Nevada and floating down the mountain rivers. He worked as a mechanical engineer for the Southern Pacific Railroad. It was his dream job since his father had worked for the railroad, and Bill had been a train fanatic all his life. In the late 1970s he had taken several backpacking trips to southern Utah, and he was powerfully drawn to the canyon country. When he got laid off from his job in 1982, he decided to move to Escalante. With the proceeds from selling his house in California, he bought a fixer-upper and figured he could survive on the remainder by living frugally and working seasonally.

Bill used his engineering skills to create a lifestyle that would allow him the freedom to spend as much time as he wanted in the canyons. He collected scrap wood and metal and worked it into the lumber and hardware he needed to remodel his house, designed and built a solar hot water heating system and an efficient wood-burning system for heat, and rebuilt appliances he found at the dump. He drove a 1983 Toyota pickup with over three hundred thousand miles on it that he worked on himself. "He doesn't need all the stuff the rest of us have," a friend said of him. "I don't know that I'd call him a loner, but he's very comfortable being by himself."[37]

Bill was a longtime member of the Sierra Club and SUWA, he participated in the Citizens' Wilderness Survey in the 1990s, and he had traveled to Washington DC to help lobby for America's Redrock

Wilderness Act. He was a proponent of wilderness and protection of the public lands, but he was practical and not fanatical. For example, when the monument closed long-established car-camping sites next to roads in wilderness study areas, he pointed it out as an example of adhering too strictly to the letter of the law. When Escalante's new irrigation reservoir was put on hold, he used his engineering know-how to come up with an alternative plan that would address the concerns of environmental organizations and still allow the reservoir to be built. He tried to interest both SUWA and the New Escalante Irrigation Company in his plan but without success.

Bill also belonged to the Glen Canyon Institute, which advocated draining Lake Powell, the reservoir behind the Glen Canyon Dam. He kept a photographic record of the effects the rise and fall of the reservoir level had on the Escalante River canyons. That was what got him started on his crusade against Russian olive. He noticed that there was no Russian olive in the photos he had taken on his first trip to the canyons, but later photos showed it creeping in, until the canyons had become choked with it. He couldn't stand to see it taking over the canyons he loved. "From an ecological standpoint, this is a huge disaster," he said. "Tamarisk and Russian olive have basically turned our riparian areas into weed farms. . . . Nothing else can compete with it."[38]

In 1993 he began to do something about it, starting first with tamarisk (*Tamarix* spp., also known as salt cedar) in Coyote Gulch, the most popular hike in the Escalante Canyons. In 2000 he switched his focus to Russian olive, which he saw as a worse scourge. Without waiting years for the results of scientific studies or environmental assessments, funding, or an official assignment from the NPS, he began chopping down the trees, treating the stumps with herbicide, and leaving the debris to be washed away in the next big rainstorm or burned later. "Nobody told me to do this," he explained in an interview for the *Christian Science Monitor*. "It's fair to say I don't work for the Park Service. I work for these canyons."[39]

Bill made it his life's mission to eliminate Russian olive from the Escalante River canyons. Sometimes he worked with groups put together by the Sierra Club or other environmental organizations, but more often he worked by himself. He worked on his own time, as well as the federal government's. Starting at the mouth of the Escalante River, and working his way slowly upstream, by 2007 Bill had cleared Russian olive from thirty-five miles of the river and the tributary canyons feeding into it. He had no interest in recognition, but he began to be acknowledged for his work by his employers, other environmentalists, and the national media. Consequently, Glen Canyon National Recreation Area officially assigned him to his personal project. His boss described Bill as "an environmentalist and an outdoorsman, one of those lone wolves who spends all his time exploring. He's a true desert rat and with that passion has been able to go out and do something truly remarkable."[40] Nevertheless, each year he still faced the possibility that he would lose his position as a result of funding cuts. Bill's work inspired GSENM to start a similar project in the part of Escalante canyon country it manages upstream. In 2007 Bill figured he had about five more years of work to do to finish the Escalante Canyons up to the Glen Canyon boundary, but he planned to continue the work even after he stopped working for the NPS. "It doesn't feel like a losing battle yet," he said. "It's still too early in the game."[41]

Like Grant Johnson, Bill's choice of lifestyle made him a "radical environmentalist" in Guha's sense. But he was also a radical environmentalist in the sense that his individual approach to environmentalism was radically different from the approaches of the environmentalists and the organizations considered so far. Bill avoided the negative experience of other environmentalists described in this chapter because he worked locally, was aware of the perceptions of environmentalists in the community where he lived, and recognized that he needed to be sensitive to its needs and respectful of its values to live there. He chose a project suited to his personality and lifestyle, with a very specific focus, that did not appear to threaten other groups' uses of the public lands. In that way he was able to avoid experiencing the paradox between environmentalism and democracy. Because his efforts were remarkably effective, required little funding, did not create any controversy, and reflected positively on the NPS, he was able to continue and even had his personal project made an official one. The drawback to his individual approach was that without an organization that shared his vision, the project might never be completed.

However, in June 2009 the Escalante River Watershed Partnership, composed of federal and state agencies, local governments, environmental organizations, businesses, nonprofits, and individuals who lived and worked near or on the Escalante River, formed to carry on Bill's work and to expand and coordinate Russian olive removal and riparian restoration efforts in the entire Escalante River watershed. By 2020, thanks to funding from the Walton Family Foundation, federal and state agencies, and other donors and the labor of groups of Conservation Corps volunteers, the initial removal of Russian olive had been completed along the main stem of the Escalante River. But with the larger and more visible organization, the efforts attracted more attention and stirred up some controversy locally.

"We Are the Environmentalists"

To complete the range of approaches to environmentalism in the Grand Staircase-Escalante region, this section considers the perspective of longtime residents who told me, "We are the environmentalists." They pointed out that if they had not taken good care of the land, why would environmentalists want to make it wilderness, why would so many hikers come, and why would the government have made it a national monument?

A pioneer descendant Escalante resident explained why "environmentalist" is a label with negative connotations for many residents of the Grand Staircase-Escalante region. While "Garfield County has faced the gamut of public land use issues," she didn't give the environmentalists credit for being real environmentalists anymore because they had corrupted the idea of wilderness that Congress had in mind in their pursuit of "job security." She felt that some of their policies were destroying the land they claimed to care for. For example, she claimed their opposition to timber sales on the Dixie National Forest had allowed the spruce beetle to spread, resulting in the loss of "spruce trees in all of Dixie." Because of the tactics of environmental groups, "BLM and the Forest Service are too busy to manage." In her view, the efforts of these groups had become "a harmful thing instead of a good conservation effort."

Another example she gave of how environmentalists had gone wrong was in their opposition to the new irrigation reservoir for Escalante. In her view, the reservoir would have allowed Escalante to remain agricultural and not become "another Moab." But she felt that environmentalists opposed it because they didn't want to see it interfere with "their playground." "We are the environmentalists," she insisted. "We who live on the land know how to take care of it to maintain a living." Their love for the land was a "deep, abiding love year-round," rather than the "weekend love affair" of environmentalists. Part of the problem, as she saw it, was that many of the environmentalists and federal land management agency employees were not from the West, and "westerners and easterners see the land differently. They don't understand the West."

It wasn't just longtime residents who felt this way about environmentalists. Some newer residents explained that their attitude toward environmentalists had changed since moving to the region and acquiring a better understanding of the perspective of longtime residents. One Escalante man said that the environmentalists "think they know what is right, but people here have a different idea. They [the environmentalists] are not willing to take the middle ground and include local people." A woman who worked in environmental justice before moving to Escalante and saw herself as an environmentalist explained, "These principles they are applying to us are not environmentally minded. They are not to preserve the environment. They are to shut us down, to control it." A Boulder woman described environmentalists as "shrill, insensitive," and having "no empathy."

Thus to many residents of the Grand Staircase-Escalante region, an environmentalist usually meant someone from outside who did not understand them or their way of life and was not interested in learning about them, whose approach was most often confrontational, who professed to care about the environment but whose actions indicated other motives, and who was part of a group that had undue influence over the federal land management agencies, kept them from doing their jobs, and had contributed to the decline of rural resource-based economies. Another Escalante pioneer descendant explained, "The people in this community are not anti-environment. What we are is anti-exclusionist, anti-environmentalist. We live here because we enjoy it. But at the same time, we realize that you have to make a living here. There is a difference between development and exploitation of natural resources, and we believe that you can have development and that we have done so."

Local residents experienced the paradox between environmentalism and democracy as being excluded by environmentalists from the process of deciding how to manage the public lands. Their objections to environmentalists were based on this experience. They valued community and often conceived of democracy in terms of community, so this experience generated strong feelings, just as their experience of exclusion when the monument was created had. At the same time, some, like one woman from Escalante, were able to imagine a more democratic process: "What hurts is that people are no longer part of the equation. It's hard for me to fathom. There's enough land for every use, for everyone. Why can't we sit down and work it out? The public lands belong to everyone, but that doesn't include us, the ones using the land, the ones caring for the land for decades."

These accounts illustrate different ways that environmentalists in the Grand Staircase-Escalante region have experienced and struggled with a paradox between their understanding of democracy and their goal of protecting the environment. Viewed with an agonistic understanding of democracy, they are practicing democracy as they try to work through the tensions they experience. The accounts also reveal limitations in the underlying assumptions of the environmental political theorists who proposed an opposition between democracy and environmentalism and suggested how the opposition could be diminished at the local level.

To begin with, these theorists assumed limited conceptions of both democracy and environmentalism. Their conception of environmentalism is limited to being founded on either the perception that environmental problems are so dire that they threaten survival or the principle of the intrinsic value of nature. The latter could be said to have characterized SUWA's exclusive focus on wilderness, Patrick Diehl's protectionist approach, and GCT's initial approach to grazing retirements. Significantly, these were the approaches that generated the most opposition from local residents. But this chapter illustrates other approaches to environmentalism. Bill Wolverton saw Russian olive as a problem so dire that it threatened the survival of riparian areas in the Escalante Canyons, but since his solution did not threaten other human groups, it did not appear to pose a threat to democracy. However, an individual environmental crusade runs the risk of exceeding the individual's capacities and failing to continue beyond the individual. Grant Johnson's approach was based more on personal experience of the environmental damage of mining than on a perception of crisis or an underlying principle.

Local residents proposed a more expansive understanding of environmentalism that included them. The approaches to environmentalism of local residents, Johnson, and Bill Hedden after he began to work with local ranchers broadened its scope to encompass the welfare of rural residents who worked for a living on the public lands. Humans were seen as part of nature instead of separate from it, and the health of ecosystems and human communities were seen as intertwined. This brings environmentalism closer to democracy because decisions about how to protect the environment take into account the welfare of those who depend on it for their livelihood and cannot be based on science alone.

These environmental political theorists' conceptions of democracy are also limited. They conceive of democracy as a set of procedures (Goodin), principles that must be upheld (e.g., autonomy; Dobson), or communicative rationality, achieving mutual understanding and agreement through successful communication.[42] While democratic imaginaries include ideas about procedures, principles, and communication, they include personal experiences as well, such as "living in Escalante" and, as Dell LeFevre said, the ability to "get on my horse . . . [and] ride on the Boulder Mountain, without being told where and how and what to do." They can even include feelings, such as Brent Robinson's "feeling in my heart."[43] Grant Johnson initially gave democracy a procedural meaning—"one vote, one person"—but then admitted that it got "tricky" when it came to the question of public lands because "outsiders from elsewhere," "[t]he majority, not just the locals here," could determine how they should be managed. Jim Catlin initially focused on communication and transparency in his understanding of democracy: "[It is] where government is open. Where almost all the information that they use and they have you can look at.... [Where] you can trust that what will happen tomorrow is what you talked about yesterday." But he realized that democratic decision-making requires more than just accurate information because the BLM bases its decision-making on more than just information. Bill Hedden's experience with the Grazing Retirement Program led him to recognize the difficulty in reconciling decisions "that reflect the will of the people," meaning the American people, with the will of "the ones that are really the stakeholders in given issues." Their dilemmas suggest that in order to protect the environment, they were beginning to integrate contradictory experiences into new understandings of democracy and environmentalism that recognized the need to engage adversaries who perceived the environment differently.

By using expanded understandings of democracy and environmentalism, environmental philosophers Ben Minteer and Robert Manning did not find democracy and environmentalism in opposition. Drawing on American pragmatist John Dewey's "faith in the capacity of the intelligence of the common man to respond with common sense to the free play of facts and ideas which are secured by effective guarantees of free inquiry, free assembly, and free communication," they conceived of democracy as a "way of life" in which people have genuine conversations about meanings and values that challenge them to clearly articulate their own positions and to understand those of others. They conceived of environmentalism as pluralistic—not based solely on the principle of respecting the intrinsic value of nonhuman nature—and practical, emerging from the experience of environmental problems and from public deliberation about them supported by "democratic toleration of public ethical pluralism." Combining these understandings of democracy and environmentalism, Minteer and Manning found that environmentalism dovetails with democratic culture because both thrive on diversity in moral thinking and experience. They pointed out that it is "the conversation about moral claims regarding nature within democratic communities—that ultimately legitimates environmental ethics and allows us to creatively address our myriad concerns surrounding the natural world."[44] Minteer and Manning's "conversation" resonates with Mouffe's agonistic model of democratic politics as a constant process of engaging with agonists with whom we have some common ground—in this case, the earth itself—to find temporary, pragmatic, unstable, and precarious negotiation of our differences. The diversity of environmental ethics means that in a democratic society, the search for solutions to environmental problems will always involve these conversations.

For the most part, the environmentalists in this chapter were working through the tension between democracy and environmentalism as individuals. To effectively address large-scale issues, from rangeland health on GSENM to climate change, such conversations need to occur at larger and larger scales. To institutionalize these conversations, environmental political theorists have continued to develop models of democracy, ranging from reformist to radical, that promote collectively working through the paradox of democracy and environmentalism.[45] Environmental democracy models propose to reform existing institutions of liberal democracy and capitalism to incorporate environmental values and expand participatory governance. Ecological models of democracy are more radical. They are critical of existing institutions and aim to be more transformative, participatory, and ecocentric. They are more inclusive in terms of environmentalism, which must promote both human and nonhuman well-being, and in terms of democracy, which must ensure that the interests of both nonhumans and future generations are represented, as well as those of present-day humans.

8   The BLM Employees

DEMOCRACY AND BUREAUCRACY

GSENM botanist: I care passionately about the idea of public lands being available and belonging to the people. I feel that we have an obligation and responsibility to make sure the best thing happens for the land, regardless of any kind of political regimes that come and go. There should be dedication to the principles of good land management by the people on the ground, regardless of what the philosophy is—it changes all the time.

I feel like this is a fight, this is something that you really have to fight for. It's not an ethic that a lot of administrators in the federal government have. I'm a new employee. People have said that "you're new and you're young, you're enthusiastic, you've got this idealism thing going. You need to get into the groove of just doing what the managers want." The day I do that is the day I quit.

GSENM planning supervisor: Anything that's done that involves this monument is controversial, and it's not going forward without approval by the Washington office.

GSENM botanist: We're the monument, and if we had the political guts, we could manage for perfection.

GSENM planning supervisor: We're the BLM; we're not going to manage for perfection.

The quotes above, from Bureau of Land Management (BLM) employees who were members of the interdisciplinary team preparing the

Monument Management Plan Amendment and Rangeland Health Environmental Impact Statement (EIS) for Grand Staircase-Escalante National Monument (GSENM), illustrate different ways that members of the EIS Team conceived of their work and illuminate a paradox between democracy and bureaucracy that they experienced.[1] This chapter follows the development of the Rangeland Health EIS and considers how the team negotiated this paradox, what democracy means to BLM employees who worked at GSENM, and how the process of developing the EIS shaped the development of the BLM's new role as manager of national landscapes.

German political economist and sociologist Max Weber (1864–1920) considered the relationship between democracy and bureaucracy as part of a broader discussion of the development of the modern state. He saw bureaucracy as emerging when the grounds for legitimate authority began to shift from tradition or charisma to rationality. Modern democracy began to emerge in the same shift, so for Weber, the developments of democracy, bureaucracy, and rationality were deeply intertwined. Bureaucracy offered the most efficient and objective means of exercising authority over human beings, where "objective" meant "according to *calculable rules* and 'without regard for persons.'" And it seemed supportive of democracy because its objectivity provided the "equality before the law" and "legal guarantees against arbitrariness" that legitimated mass democracy.[2]

But Weber also saw bureaucracy as a threat to democracy. He feared that bureaucrats would become "a privileged 'caste'" because of their extensive training, specialized knowledge, tenure, and tendency to secrecy, and that their goal would become maintaining their position and power instead of providing efficient administration. He also questioned bureaucracy's "spirit of formalistic impersonality," which allowed bureaucrats to carry out their duties "without hatred or passion" but also "without affection or enthusiasm" and without the "personal responsibility" that a politician or entrepreneur felt. He predicted that a rational but "dehumanized" bureaucracy would "unavoidably collide" with the democratic ethos of the masses. In the face of bureaucracy's "irresistible advance," "growing indispensability," and "corresponding increase in power," Weber asked, "How can one possibly save *any remnants* of any 'individualist' freedom in any sense?" And therefore, "How will democracy even in this limited sense be *at all possible*?"[3] Thus for Weber, the relationship between bureaucracy and democracy was paradoxical and a constant source of tension and conflict.

To show how this tension and conflict played out in the process of writing the Rangeland Health EIS, I first describe the context in which monument staff began working on it. The rest of the chapter considers how team members experienced the paradox and the tension between democracy and bureaucracy and how this affected the process.

"Opportunity and Challenge"

When President Clinton proclaimed Grand Staircase-Escalante National Monument in 1996, he explicitly directed that the new monument would remain under the management of the BLM, making it the first national monument the BLM would manage.[4] Thus the proclamation not only created the largest national monument in the United States outside Alaska but also initiated a new role for the BLM. The BLM had received its authority to manage public land from the Federal Land Policy and Management Act (FLPMA) in 1976, which also gave the agency its multiple-use mandate. FLPMA defined multiple use as "the management of the public lands and their various resource values so that they are utilized in the combination that will best meet the present and future needs of the American people."[5] In its attempts to determine this combination, the agency had been unable to shake a reputation for catering to extractive resource interests. When GSENM was created, the opportunity to manage the monument challenged the BLM to reevaluate the combination of resource values that would best meet the needs of the American people as public land was coming to be seen as national landscape and, in doing so, to reinvent itself.

To start the BLM off on the right foot, Congress gave the new monument a big budget: $6.4 million for the first and several subsequent years. With this generous budget, monument management began to hire a staff of specialists that would be the envy of any field office, including ecologists, botanists, a hydrologist, a soils scientist, an additional archaeologist, a paleontologist, more wildlife biologists, National Environmental Policy Act (NEPA) specialists, a geographic information system (GIS) specialist, more recreation staff, and more planners. Many of the new employees came from the U.S. Forest Service or the National Park Service (NPS). Many told me they had come because of the landscape and because they had been informed that the monument would "have a different management philosophy and style than a typical field office": it would "be run like a park." One said he "liked the idea of BLM trying something new." Another confessed, "I didn't think of it as working for the BLM. I thought it was working for the monument." A new employee described at length the feeling when he arrived:

> The week I got here, the plan was approved, and we just got our marching orders really—had an administration that supported the monument, had a manager that had been here pretty much from the beginning, and he was really motivated to do some innovative things. And it just seemed like a dream. It was really great. And so much new stuff to learn. And it just being a new monument, being the first monument, the first one with a plan, and figuring out things as we went.
>
> I had worked for BLM as a volunteer back in '87 at [another site], and my impression of it then as an organization was not quite as favorable as it was when I came here in 2000. Because people were just tired of their job and weren't really doing anything—that was my impression. And that was one of the other things about the new monument was that everybody was hired new. . . . It was for the most part people who came to the monument and wanted to work, . . . were getting an opportunity to work in a place that they really liked.

With all the new hiring, monument staff increased more than five times in size. In Kanab, there were now two BLM entities—the Kanab Field Office and GSENM—resulting in some uncertainty about their respective responsibilities and strained relationships between them. Some of the local ranchers and outfitters also noticed strained relationships between the old BLM staff who remained with the monument and the new staff who came when it was created. According to one rancher, "It seemed like the office people got more uptight. When we talked to them about it, they said that there was a lot of people that came in thinking they knew more than the people that had been working with this particular area for several years. And it's basically the same thing that some of the ranchers thought about them in the past."

By the time the Monument Management Plan (MMP) was signed in November 1999, Kate Cannon was the monument manager. She had come from the NPS and contrasted its preservationist mandate with the multiple-use mandate of the BLM in this way: the BLM "facilitates the use of public land," while the NPS "sees its role as protecting public land from abuse." According to Cannon, "The BLM complains the Park Service doesn't have ties to communities and considers it a weakness," while the NPS "considers this a strength because they are not swayed by local feelings and would say BLM is carrying out local wishes." She believed there was "room for improvement" in how the BLM managed public lands and said, "How we manage the monument will help make that improvement." In her view, the "challenge" for the BLM was "to take on a role as a conservation organization." Because grazing was "a symbolic issue," she felt it was a good place to start. As described in chapter 3, she immediately set about making that "improvement."

Not all GSENM employees were excited about the changes the new designation brought about. The old staff soon became aware that working on the monument was going to be different from working for the old BLM. For example, when Cannon ordered the impoundment and removal of cattle from Fiftymile Mountain in 2000, an old BLM employee contrasted her approach with the way the BLM formerly did things. "If they had tried to impound in 1990, it never would have happened. BLM people wouldn't have let it. I didn't believe [the managers] would go as far as they did. . . . Helicopters! That kind of shocked me." Another old employee got in trouble with Cannon for driving on a road that was closed to the public but open for administrative access in the Transportation Plan in the MMP. Cannon interpreted administrative access to mean that only permittees who needed access to their allotments could drive on these roads; monument employees had to walk. "Things went downhill from there," the employee noted. Yet another old employee chafed under Cannon's enforcement of a new policy that required special management units like GSENM to wear the BLM uniform. He said he had never had to wear a uniform before she came, and "it's because she comes from the Park Service."

With a big budget and staff, as well as a presidential administration, a monument manager, and a large part of the monument staff who wanted to see the BLM change, change seemed likely on GSENM. One of the biggest initial issues to deal with was grazing permits that had expired or were about to expire. Recognizing that livestock grazing in the monument was one of the most controversial issues and that trying to renew them would hold up the MMP, the EIS planning team that had drawn up the Monument Management Plan had deferred decision-making on this to a later process and set a deadline for its completion: July 1, 2003.[6]

This was the situation when the process that eventually became known as the Monument Management Plan Amendment and Rangeland Health EIS began officially as the Grazing Permit Renewal EIS in August 2000. It became a principal arena for initiating change. A close examination of the dynamics of the EIS process offers insight into how team members experienced the paradox between democracy and bureaucracy and how it affected the process as the BLM addressed the challenge of managing livestock grazing on GSENM and fashioning a new role as manager of national landscapes.

"Trying Something New"

The Rangeland Health EIS process on GSENM had many innovative aspects. First, monument staff would be among the first in the BLM to implement the 1995 changes to federal grazing regulations that required the agency to comply with the Fundamentals of Rangeland Health and Standards and Guidelines for Grazing Administration (43 CFR 4180), using a new technical reference released in 2000, *Interpreting Indicators of Rangeland Health*.[7] Second, the EIS would cover the whole monument, making it the first time the BLM would attempt this at such a large scale. Grazing permit renewals were usually done as individual environmental assessments (EAs) for each allotment.

The expanded monument staff eagerly got to work doing the rangeland health assessments that were the first step in the process (see fig. 24). The assessments were carried out by interdisciplinary teams

24. Riparian assessment, October 2003. The body language of the old BLM employee on the right, a rangeland specialist, speaks volumes. Courtesy of the author.

composed of monument staff from a variety of scientific disciplines, as well as nonscientists, who had received training in the new assessment process. In early 2000 a PhD ecologist joined the monument staff and assumed leadership of the project. He upgraded the assessment process the teams had been following by systematizing the sampling process for collection of rangeland health data; adding optional assessment criteria, including evaluation of biological soil crust; and revising the data collection worksheets. GSENM was now poised on the leading edge of landscape-scale rangeland management.

In 2001 Cannon made the EIS top priority on the monument and had everyone on the staff working on the Livestock Management EIS, as it was known by then. It was an exciting time for many of the new staff members. One member, who was not a scientist, recalled:

It was really a good thing, I think, for the monument staff as a whole, doing the assessments as interdisciplinary teams, because we came to understand each other's jobs a little more, we knew each other better—it created a more cohesive feel at work, I think. I learned a tremendous amount out on the assessments just from the different people—a lot from the range people. I spent maybe half my assessment time with a range person. So I probably spent less time with them than I wanted to. But still it was good to be out with the hydrologists, the wildlife biologists, the geologists, just to get their interpretation of what's going on in the landscape, even just kind of informally as we were waiting to get to the next place we were going to assess. It was really a neat experience—probably the most fun I've ever had on the job.

And then the George W. Bush administration took office. Cannon left, and soon many of the eager young scientists she had brought on board also left, including the ecologist who was the project's leader. Dave Hunsaker, a career BLM employee, became monument manager in November 2002. By this time most of the rangeland health assessments had been completed, and the EIS Team was ready to move into the next phase of the EIS process: writing the Draft EIS. The monument hired a planning specialist to be the new team leader. In early 2003 high-level Interior Department officials directed that representatives from the NPS from Glen Canyon National Recreation Area, Garfield and Kane Counties, and the state of Utah be included on the EIS Team as "cooperating agencies" to make the process more collaborative.[8] The new interior secretary, Gale Norton, had instructed the BLM to use "consultation, cooperation, and coordination" with a wide variety of stakeholders in its decision-making processes to air concerns before decisions were made and thereby produce better outcomes.[9] The full team began meeting in June 2003. The name of the EIS was changed again, to Rangeland Health Plan Amendment and Environmental Impact Statement.

Like his predecessor, the new monument manager told his staff that the Rangeland Health EIS was top priority for the monument. But some reported that they began to receive mixed messages about their superiors' commitment to the process. Mixed messages were conveyed to one team member through repeated schedule changes: team members were initially given what this person felt was an unrealistic schedule that stressed people out, then the schedule changed and scheduled meetings were canceled several times. Another team member noted that when a new staff position became available, a wildlife biologist was hired instead of a desperately needed range staff person. Yet another pointed to the fact that the monument manager rarely attended meetings. In addition, the monument's budget was shrinking: from the initial $6.4 million in 1996 to $5.9 million in 2003, then $4.9 million in 2004. So when positions on the team were vacated, they were not always refilled.

When I began attending meetings in October 2003, the EIS Team was meeting every other week for two or three days, sometimes even more frequently, and the Draft EIS was scheduled to be released in October 2004, only a little over a year late. Between meetings, team members worked full-time on their individual EIS assignments. Despite this effort, by May 2004 the deadline had been extended to February 2005. It continued to be pushed back. As time wore on, the team lost members, who were not replaced, and met less frequently. Team members were assigned other projects. I decided to extend the length of my fieldwork to see the process through to the end.

What was happening? Why was it taking so long to write the EIS? This may seem like the normal state of affairs to those who think of government bureaucracies as slow, inefficient, and staffed by people who care more about job security than about doing their job and serving their clients well. But given the initial passion and enthusiasm of the EIS Team, answering these questions calls for deeper insight into the EIS process and the experience of team members. To begin to address them, I draw on a theoretical framework provided by public administration theorist Gary M. Woller, who built on Weber's insights about the paradox between democracy and bureaucracy.

"The Bureaucratic and Democratic Ethos"

Woller characterized this paradox as a tension between the bureaucratic and the democratic ethos, which present the ethical responsibility of public bureaucrats in divergent ways. He argued that the tension arises because "many of the values we associate with democracy—equality, participation, and individuality—stand sharply opposed to the hierarchy, specialization, and impersonality we ascribe to bureaucracy."[10] This tension is not just theoretical; it is actually experienced by public bureaucrats.

According to Woller, the bureaucratic ethos emerged from the writings of Max Weber and Woodrow Wilson, the twenty-eighth president of the United States, whose 1887 essay "The Study of Administration" is considered to have inaugurated public administration as a field of study. It begins from the assumption that since ends and values cannot be determined by rational analysis, they must be determined by the political process. The public administrator's ethical duty, then, is to enforce the laws and implement the policies enacted by the people's democratically elected representatives. The bureaucratic ethos further assumes a direct line of communication from the people, through their elected representatives, to bureau heads and on down the bureaucracy to those responsible for administering and implementing laws and public policies. Administrators use scientific knowledge and techniques to determine the most efficient and effective means for achieving the given ends. Their actions should be judged solely by the value-free criteria of efficiency and effectiveness, because it is only through the efficient and effective implementation of policies decided by the people that the greater good they have decided on can be achieved.

The democratic ethos grew out of a concern, like Weber's, that while bureaucracies might be efficient, they are not legitimate, because they are "inhumane, unresponsive, and democratically unaccountable."[11] In addition, by operating solely according to specific objectives and scientific principles, they miss opportunities to further broader social goals, such as reducing inequality or improving people's lives in other ways. They are also too easily used as a tool of oppression. Nazi Germany serves as a reminder of the dangers inherent in a public bureaucracy where efficiency and effectiveness are the chief standards of administrative conduct. The democratic ethos rejects the top-down model of democratic governance, which the bureaucratic ethos assumes, and argues that administrators can never be value-free implementers of the public will. Some indeterminacy, or ethical space, in interpreting what the public has willed always exists. Therefore, administrators must be guided by an alternative set of higher-order values, specifically those embedded in the concept of democratic government.

Woller pointed out that the bureaucratic and the democratic ethos are not entirely opposed; they overlap in many ways. For example, proponents of the democratic ethos agree that public administrators have an ethical duty to carry out the public will efficiently and effectively but argue that bureaucratic values, such as hierarchical accountability, technical expertise, and scientific rationality, should not take precedence over democratic values. Supporters of the bureaucratic ethos share a commitment to democracy and the public interest but are concerned that administrators, in following their own understanding of core democratic values, may fail to give sufficient consideration to the public will.

Woller located the source of the tension between the bureaucratic and the democratic ethos in their very different ethical foundations, utilitarianism and deontology, respectively, which he defined thus: "Utilitarianism holds that moral behavior consists in doing that which will bring about the greatest good for the greatest number of people. Deontology, on the other hand, holds that ethical behavior is determined by certain higher order, or a priori, moral principles from which lower order rules—and hence one's moral duty—can be deduced."[12] Utilitarianism is teleological and employs instrumental rationality, while deontology is based on an attachment to substantive principles that are morally binding regardless of their implied consequences. The philosophical debate between them has a long history in Western ethical theory, and studies of human behavior suggest that human nature exhibits a tendency toward both ways of thinking about morality. This led Woller to conclude that the tension between utilitarian and deontological reasoning is unavoidable: "Although we may philosophically tend to adhere more to one way of thinking than the other, *in practice*, we are constantly required to weigh the trade-off between outcomes and principle."[13] Woller's thinking resonates with the beliefs of the environmental political theorists who wrestled with the paradox between environmental aims and democratic means and of the environmental philosophers who suggested the paradox could be resolved through practical environmental ethics (discussed in the previous chapter).

This discussion informs my consideration in the next section of how the EIS Team experienced the tension between the bureaucratic and the democratic ethos as they wrote the Draft EIS and confronted inexperience with the EIS process, lack of guidelines for implementing it, the inadequacy of the science and decision-making tools they were using, the changing composition of the team and divisions within it, and decisions handed down from higher up.

The Rangeland Health EIS Process

THE EIS TEAM: INEXPERIENCE

The National Environmental Policy Act of 1969 established protection of the environment as a national policy. It requires federal agencies whose actions might have a significant impact on the environment to study and report on the impacts of the proposed actions and alternatives to them. NEPA mandates that the study should use a systematic, interdisciplinary approach that integrates the natural and social sciences and environmental planning. The BLM further requires that EISs be prepared for the land use planning process required by FLPMA. The EIS Team was created to fulfill these requirements.

Since the passage of NEPA, an accepted process for developing EISs and a format for writing them have come into use. As evidence of its complexity, federal agencies employ NEPA specialists, and specialized courses exist to train federal employees in the NEPA process. The Rangeland Health EIS Team was, for the most part, inexperienced in this process. Many of the new employees had never worked on an EIS before, and now, in the words of one team member, they were being "thrown into the middle of a huge EIS where there's no precedent for it anyway." No EISs had been written for public lands in the region since the 1980s, so most of the old staff did not have experience with the process either. Those who had participated in the process with the Forest Service found this one "not very well organized" and "frustrating," with one person saying the team was "different from any NEPA teams I have been on."

In the team meetings I attended early on, the unprecedented nature of the Rangeland Health EIS process and the inexperience of the EIS Team members resulted in a lot of discussion about what exactly they were supposed to be doing and what the difference was between a

Livestock Management EIS and a Rangeland Health EIS, the new name for the process. There were questions and debate about the meanings of general terms, such as "issue" and "alternative," and more specific terms, like "current grazing management." Progress would be made on defining a process or a term, but then a question about a specific example would lead to a rehashing of the discussion. There was also much confusion about how to interpret the rangeland health assessment data.

Further complicating the EIS process was the fact that the BLM was in the process of revising the federal grazing regulations for public land. Between December 2003, when the Proposed Revisions to Grazing Regulations for the Public Lands Draft EIS was released, and June 2005, when the Final EIS appeared, the EIS Team was unsure what the final changes would be and what effects they would have on its own EIS.[14] Even after the Final EIS for the proposed revisions came out, one of the team leaders admitted, "No one can interpret what it means." The BLM received so many comments on the Final EIS that it published an addendum. The new grazing regulations were not finalized until July 2006.

These initial difficulties illustrate several problems with the assumption of the bureaucratic ethos that there is a direct line of communication from the people, through their elected representatives, to bureau heads and on down the bureaucracy. They reinforce Woller's assertion that there is an ethical space in public administration where other than purely bureaucratic values come into play. First, the public will is never expressed so clearly in laws and policies that they do not need some interpretation. In addition, the way they are interpreted depends on many factors, including the prior experience of the person or group doing the interpreting, as well as whether any precedents exist.

SCIENCE

The EIS Team also ran into difficulties with the scientific tools they were required to use to evaluate the impacts of livestock grazing and make recommendations for management actions. First, the *Interpreting Indicators of Rangeland Health* technical reference they were using for the rangeland health assessment process stated that it was not intended to be used for decision-making.[15] One of the team members explained that it was a more qualitative process, designed to indicate whether rangelands are meeting standards, not to determine why they aren't or what to do to improve them. When assessment results indicated there was a problem, monitoring, a more quantitative process, should be used to gather more specific information necessary for decision-making. Yet the EIS Team was required to make determinations for allotments that did not meet rangeland health standards. A determination meant answering two questions: "1. Is it more likely than not that existing grazing management practices or levels of grazing use are significant factors in failing to achieve the Standards or conform with the guidelines? 2. Is it more likely than not that existing grazing management needs to be modified to ensure that the Fundamentals of rangeland health are met, or making significant progress toward being met?"[16] While *Interpreting Indicators of Rangeland Health* stated that the procedure should not be used for making decisions, according to one of the team leaders, the *BLM Manual* said it had to be, "so we're in a bind." This situation illustrates that the supposedly rational bureaucratic apparatus can contain contradictions.

Historical monitoring data would help make these determinations, but it was sparse for allotments on the monument. At one of the early meetings, one of the team scientists pointed out that because there is rarely just one cause for conditions that fail to meet rangeland health standards—they could be caused by drought, climate change, or invasive species, as well as livestock grazing—the team needed to depend heavily on the experience of the range staff to make determinations. When another team member asked the range staff how they could tell whether a site was not meeting standards due to grazing or drought, one of the rangeland specialists responded, "Memory. Three of us have been here since '93. But sometimes there are too many factors to say for sure, and at some point, an expert just has to make a call." One of the team leaders recognized that this solution was in tension with the democratic ethos, as it could be seen to infringe on the democratic principle of accountability: "Pushing it into the realm of specialists puts us in the role of making calls on scientific experience that can't be verified by the public. That's not a good place for us to be."

The growing acceptance of the state and transition models of rangeland ecology has eliminated the more certain basis for range management decision-making that the range succession model had provided. This meant that not only was it difficult to determine causes of failure to meet rangeland health standards, but there was also no longer one climax plant community to manage for. The EIS Team engaged in lengthy, acronym-filled discussions of whether it should manage for the "PNC" (potential natural vegetative community) for a particular ecological site, "DFC" (desired future condition), "DPC" (desired plant community), or "precontact condition."[17] In addition to vegetation, there were questions about wildlife. For example, should the team manage for deer? There were few in the region historically, but they had now become abundant and important to sport hunters. These were decisions that could not be answered by science alone; they depended on values and on what the agency could realistically accomplish given available resources. Team members were in a quandary because even using the available scientific knowledge and techniques, they were not able to determine the most efficient and effective means for achieving the politically determined end of rangeland health, as the bureaucratic ethos assumed, nor even what rangeland health was. The uncertainty of science created ethical space where other than purely bureaucratic values could come into play.

The county representatives on the team recognized that in such a situation, one expert's opinion could be contested by that of another. So the counties hired their own expert: a range consultant with a distinguished reputation who had previously worked many years for the BLM. The county representatives introduced him at one of the early meetings and informed the team that if it made a decision to reduce or eliminate grazing on a particular allotment, the counties would have their own expert evaluate the allotment and suggest alternative management strategies.

The bureaucratic ethos's reliance on science as a decision-making tool often boiled down to what the EIS Team called a focus on numbers. The team leaders reminded the members of this continually: "BLM and environmentalists—they're trained to look at numbers. They're really going to look at the numbers." "I guarantee you, all next year we're going to be arguing about numbers." "Everybody is going to focus on the numbers, but there's a lot of really good stuff in the text." One wished one of the county representatives were there "because [he's] got a lot of interest in these numbers." But at the same time, they recognized, "We don't have science good enough to give numbers." Therefore, they said, they would have to write the EIS using language that was "predictive," "generic," "on a large scale," "not specific," and "qualitative."

The determination process was also made more difficult because the range staff was reluctant to identify livestock grazing as a factor contributing to failure to meet rangeland health standards. For them, the ethical space created by the uncertainty of science was filled by a concern for how the EIS Team's decisions would affect the permittees, which can be seen as a democratic concern with how policy affects real people's lives. From experience, they knew what the outcome of such a determination was likely to be. As one rangeland specialist said, "I've been in the government fifteen years. The result will be a cut in season or numbers, not money to fix the problem." In light of the new understanding of rangeland ecology, they realized that this decision would adversely affect the permittee without addressing the real problem, but it was politically expedient because it made it look as if the BLM were doing something. As a result, the range staff's perceptions of a permittee's capacity, how well the permittee managed the allotment, and how easy the person was to work with affected the types of solutions they proposed for allotments not meeting standards.

For example, when discussing options for one of Steve Sorensen's allotments (the millionaire from California mentioned in chapter 6), a rangeland specialist suggested a rapid rotation through five or six pastures. Sorensen had a lot of hired help, which most of the local ranchers lacked, so he was "able to have someone out there" to move the herd frequently. In addition, if his season or numbers were reduced, "this permittee has leased land, so he can feed hay or do spring grazing elsewhere." On another allotment where erosion was a major problem, the rangeland specialist strongly advocated not reducing grazing, but monitoring conditions closely, because the permittees "are good to work with" and "say they'll do whatever it takes."

On an allotment where a seeding was proposed, which would require closing the area to grazing until the seeding was well established, the rangeland specialist was in a quandary. On the one hand, "If we close the whole seeding, [the permittee] will be looking at going out of business." On the other hand, he wasn't sure whether, if they did go ahead with the seeding, the permittee would "uphold his end of the agreement" because "he doesn't have a good history of working with the BLM." But the rangeland specialist didn't want to be too "heavy-handed." As he struggled with a democratic ethos that prompted him to take the welfare of the permittee into account, another rangeland specialist reminded him that he also needed to consider the hierarchical accountability of the bureaucratic ethos: "Is what we're doing consistent with what we're doing on the other allotments? These are the types of questions the public is going to ask and we have to have answers for." The range staff also supported using non-native plants in the seedings, although the MMP specified that native plants were a priority for all projects in the monument. Non-native plants had been used in the seedings that were being replaced, and the range staff argued that they were more likely to grow and were more productive and less expensive than native plants, whereas the new team members felt that it was important to stick to the philosophy and guidelines of the MMP.

Critics of the BLM might interpret these discussions as evidence that the BLM has been "captured" by private interests.[18] But advocates of the democratic ethos would say that the effects of laws and policies on people's lives should be taken into consideration. Range staff members were especially reluctant to take a heavy-handed approach after their recent experience participating in the livestock impoundment orchestrated by former monument manager Cannon. From the statemaking perspective, being too heavy-handed could threaten "the delicate balance between autonomy and control in the relationship between state and society," in this case between the BLM and local residents.[19] Whatever management actions were decided on, the rangeland specialists recognized, "We can't force the permittees to do anything."

Another factor that affected the decision-making of the EIS Team was a desire to avoid "being sued," a term they used to include a variety of different legal avenues that organizations could employ to intervene in agency decision-making. Since the 1965 recognition of an organization's standing to sue the federal government and the 1969 passage of NEPA, avoiding being sued occupied a great amount of federal land management agencies' time and budgets.[20] The BLM, because of its multiple-use mandate, was especially vulnerable to being sued as it attempted to find the combination of resource uses that would "best meet the present and future needs of the American people."[21] The EIS Team was aware that the Rangeland Health EIS would be scrutinized by many interested parties, including the counties, environmentalists, recreationists, and the general public. For example, one of the team leaders reminded the team that for environmental groups, it had become "almost routine to appeal every EA." So to avoid being sued, the team needed to have alternatives that were "negative to us: that you don't like. If we don't, we'll lose in court."

In a particularly contentious discussion of one allotment, one of the county representatives used humor to draw attention to the very real possibility that even though the counties were part of the EIS Team, they were likely to sue if they didn't like the outcome. The team had arrived at an impasse in the discussion, and one of the team leaders admitted, "I don't know what to do when we get to this point. We need to come up with a way to settle impasses." One team member suggested, "The boss needs to make a decision. We'll live with them." The county representative retorted, "We'll appeal 'em." Everyone laughed, but aware of the counties' ongoing appeal of grazing permits purchased by Grand Canyon Trust, they recognized the wisecrack as not just a joke.

The EIS Team also took public scrutiny and negative public perceptions of public land grazing into consideration. The recreation specialist reminded them of negative comments about livestock grazing left by hikers in registers at the trailheads of popular hikes on certain allotments. In considering an allotment close to the road, a team member pointed out that it "gets the most attention because it's right by the road." On another allotment, "to enhance the monument image," the team decided on a burn to treat a sagebrush die-off by the road. When discussing how much acreage to burn, one member recommended, "Anything we can add to give the public a little better picture." These examples suggest that team members experienced the tension between the democratic and bureaucratic ethos when they made decisions intended to appease or out of a concern for being sued, rather than using the value-free criteria of efficiency and effectiveness to achieve the greater good of rangeland health. They also illustrate that in contrast to the assumption of the bureaucratic ethos, in a pluralistic democracy, different groups of people will have different ideas about the greater good, which laws and policies enacted by elected representatives cannot adequately reflect.

Despite these difficulties and complications, the EIS Team began its work with enthusiasm. The team had a sense of purpose and anticipation because, as one member put it, "In this whole EIS we are really out on the edge of a new direction for BLM." By March 2004 the team had completed the determinations for all eighty-nine allotments managed by the monument using a method they had decided on together.[22]

What happened at this point reflects another paradox within bureaucracies in the executive branch of the federal government, whose high-level officials are political appointees: these appointees often interject politically motivated interpretations into the direct line of communication from the people, represented by laws and regulations, on down the bureaucracy. In this case, the Utah State Office of the BLM informed the team it had to use a different method for determinations, so the team would have to go through the whole process again. The demoralized team did the determinations a second time, putting the EIS behind schedule again. The next step was to decide what management actions could be taken for allotments not meeting rangeland health standards, a preliminary step to developing the alternative management actions for the Draft EIS.

THE EIS TEAM: COMPOSITION

When the EIS Team began meeting in 2003, twenty to twenty-five people attended the meetings, including representatives from Garfield and Kane Counties, Glen Canyon National Recreation Area, the Kanab Field Office, and the state of Utah. There were about seventeen GSENM employees on the team, including three members of the management team who acted as leaders, an ecologist, two botanists, a wildlife biologist, a hydrologist, a soils scientist, four rangeland specialists, an archaeologist, a GIS specialist, an outdoor recreation planner, and a backcountry ranger.

Most of them had also participated in the rangeland health assessments. Because the team was interdisciplinary and included groups from outside the BLM, team members were exposed to different types of knowledge and different viewpoints. BLM team members saw the participation of groups outside the agency as valuable, not only for the input they provided but also because "they see all the things BLM deals with," which the team members hoped would make the EIS process more transparent, understandable, and legitimate, and its outcome more acceptable, to outsiders.

However, for some, the team's composition wasn't inclusive enough. "One of the flaws in the composition of the group," according to one member, "was that we had [county] commissioners, which essentially represent the ranchers, and then we had the government, but we consciously excluded any environmental groups. Simply, you've got to either include everybody or keep it small." This member recognized that the democratic ethos requires inclusion, while the bureaucratic ethos dictates efficiency, and the composition of the group bought them into tension. At the same time, he felt, "We don't have really good representation from the country as a whole. It seemed like the local interests had everything. And what the rest of the country would want, what the people who are paying us and the people who own this land would want, as a whole, has kind of been ignored. Partially I guess that's what our jobs as land managers are: to operate in the best interests of the people by the rules enacted by their elected representatives." His words neatly echoed the bureaucratic ethos. He followed this up with a query that suggested he experienced its tension with the democratic ethos: "But if that were the entire case, then why would we need any local input?"

THE EIS TEAM: DIVISIONS

Even with limited representation of groups outside the BLM on the EIS Team, the practical problems with trying to make the EIS process more democratic by using more "consultation, cooperation, and coordination" with cooperating agencies became apparent in a variety of divisions that developed within the team. One BLM member felt that the group had become polarized, which had an adverse effect on discussion and defeated the purpose of inclusive deliberation. "Right at the very beginning the lines got drawn really quick. The [county] commissioners were in the meetings. My feeling from it, and they said it explicitly, 'We trust these range guys, but we don't trust the rest of you.' So there was kind of a line drawn that said, 'These are our allies, these are our enemies, and this is how we're going to approach it.' Most of us were pretty quiet in the meetings with the whole group. So I think there was a lot of stuff held back at that time." One of the team leaders described the problem with having the county commissioners at the meetings this way: "With us, it's just a show. We're all actors when they're here."

These comments indicate that team members were aware that just including more people does not necessarily make deliberation more inclusive. Democratic theorist Iris Marion Young expressed this theoretically by identifying two forms of exclusion that violate democratic norms of inclusion as a criterion of political legitimacy of outcomes.[23] The first is external exclusion, the form referenced by the EIS Team member who said, "You've got to either include everybody or keep it small." The second, internal exclusion occurs when individuals and groups are nominally included in deliberative processes but lack effective opportunity to influence the thinking of others because their communication style does not conform to that assumed by deliberative norms. When the structure of EIS meetings made some members uncomfortable speaking up, it was a form of internal exclusion. Young considered various ways internal exclusion could be overcome. The team member who said that "most of us were pretty quiet in the meetings with the whole group" found that "when we had the meetings where either the commissioners didn't show up or it was something where it was a smaller group meeting, a lot more transpired. There was a lot more communication going on in those meetings, I thought. When we split into small groups, we actually had pretty good submeetings with that group. But I was surprised in that situation at how easy it was to come to some sort of understanding and agree with it."

In the long run, this team member decided that the disadvantages of including the counties as cooperating agencies outweighed the advantages:

As time went on, it became clearer and clearer to me that it was not a good idea [to include the counties]—at least with these dynamics. It reduced input, it reduced communication, increased defensiveness, and just really slowed everything down, and not in a thoughtful way, but more in a defensive way. From my perspective, I think there was some increased trust and willingness to listen to each other, especially with [certain county representatives]. But other people were more antagonistic. And personal attacks on people. It's like because we're the agency, we have to follow some sort of code of conduct, while these guys can just beat on us.

He concluded not only that it was more efficient timewise not to include the counties but also that it was difficult for BLM personnel to follow the bureaucratic "code of conduct"—Weber's "spirit of formalistic impersonality"—in the face of antagonistic sentiments. He also felt that the way the BLM was conducting a similar process on two other new national monuments in the region was much more effective: a small core group met weekly, wrote up documents, and sent them out for review to the rest of the much larger EIS Team. The whole team met once a month, where members had an opportunity to give input on the decisions made by the core group and presented by the team managers. For him, as the EIS process dragged on, this approach came to seem more efficient and rational, and the utilitarian ethic of the bureaucratic ethos was gaining more appeal. It eliminated antagonism, defensiveness, and arguments among the BLM staff in front of other members of the group, and, he noted, it "seems so much more legitimate when the [county] commissioners come in." But it erected different barriers to inclusive deliberation.

Divisions also developed within the BLM staff on the EIS Team. One obvious one was between the range staff and the ecologists, biologists, geologists, and so on, whom the range staff sometimes referred to as the "ologists." This division existed in part for historical reasons: it was between an old profession that had always been part of the BLM and new professions that had more recently been represented in the agency, and they had different ways of looking at the landscape.[24] In addition, the range staff consisted mainly of BLM employees who had worked in the region before GSENM was created, whereas the "ologists" had mostly been hired since its creation. This division was also part of the monument's organizational structure: the range staff and the scientists, although they managed the same physical landscape, did not usually work together. Moreover, the range staff worked directly with permittees and came to know the people who would be affected by the decisions they made, while the scientists did not.

One of the "ologists" described the difference between the two groups as "a culture clash: all of the range guys are from Utah." Being from Utah encapsulated several differences in background between the groups. Members of the range staff were mostly from rural areas and working-class families, belonged to the LDS Church, had grown up around ranching, and were accustomed to the arid landscape. The "ologists" mostly came from urban areas and middle-class families, many were originally from the East or Midwest, and they were accustomed to seeing cows grazing in fields of green grass and were predisposed to see grazing as a problem. As a result, the range staff, who were a minority on the team, felt as though they were on the defensive. Differences in background between the range staff and the "ologists" were also evident in the way they spoke, dressed (cowboy hats and boots versus fleece jackets and hiking boots), what they drank at the meetings (Mountain Dew versus coffee), and where they went for lunch (Subway versus cafés that served quiche and wraps).

At the EIS Team meetings, the range staff would usually sit together in chairs lining the wall of the meeting room and not at the main table. They seldom spoke unless questioned directly. Then they could provide a wealth of information about specific allotments and the activities and character of the permittees that was essential to the discussion. In political scientist Jane Mansbridge's study of a participatory workplace in the United States, she also observed that members with a working-class background seldom spoke at meetings.[25] Some of these differences, and the way they affected relationships among team members, are evident in figure 24, where the rangeland specialist on the rangeland health assessment team can be seen standing apart from the rest of the group.

Several of the BLM nonrange staff said they had learned a lot from working with the range staff on the EIS Team, especially out in the field doing the rangeland health assessments, and wished they were able to work with them more. One explained how his ideas about grazing had changed as a result:

> I started to understand more things about the whole grazing management thing, the whole process, the whole history, and how it's done and things like that. And I probably backed off of the "cows [are] bad" viewpoint considerably, I think, and saw that under proper conditions and proper management, there could be probably pretty good grazing done and pretty good rangeland health. And it became a less black-and-white issue for me. And I can also see how a lot of the people that are doing the ranching operations, the permit holders, I can see how they really love it. And how that's important to them in a way that has some personal history, something that goes back.

For him, working with the range staff was the kind of transformative experience that Bill Hedden experienced working with ranchers and for which Chantal Mouffe argued that democratic politics should provide more opportunities. Another EIS Team member described a division within the team between "the people who want to change the grazing program considerably or to a greater degree to benefit either the vegetation or the aesthetics or the soil health or the riparian or the recreation conflicts" and "those who would prefer to maintain the status quo." Rumor had it that the county commissioners were trying to get people in the former group removed from the EIS Team. As a result of these different kinds of divisions, one of the team leaders felt that "the whole process has been skewed by who's [at meetings] and who's not."

The divisions among the BLM staff illustrate that bureaucratic decision-making processes can never be based purely on criteria of efficiency and effectiveness because human relationships always come into play. In addition, different people interpret the ethical space in the bureaucratic ethos in different ways. These divisions generated tensions within the team, which affected their interactions. There was much joking during EIS Team meetings, which I came to understand as an attempt to defuse these tensions. For example, in a meeting when one of the county representatives found the team leader expressing an opinion he agreed with, he pronounced, "It's scary. [The team leader] is getting to know me too well." The team leader responded, "You probably won't have to worry about that the whole time."

THE EIS TEAM: ATTRITION

The EIS Team also suffered from attrition. As time went on, the team gradually shrank in size, and the meetings got smaller and smaller. Of the twenty-six GSENM staff who participated in the rangeland health assessments, only eight were still there when I left in September 2005. The first GSENM staff person to leave was the ecologist, followed by one of the botanists, the hydrologist, the lead rangeland specialist, one of the team leaders, the other botanist, another rangeland specialist, and the soils scientist. Few of their positions on the EIS Team were refilled.

Most of those who left were among the new people hired after the monument was created. They left for a variety of reasons, but most expressed disappointment with the way the monument was being managed. Among those remaining, one person said he had come "because of the monument," because "they were going to do it differently here," and that he would "leave if they don't." He felt that many people would leave if that happened. The person who had come because it was going to be "run like a park" said, "The most powerful managers we have are old; they've been here a long time. They're used to doing it a certain way. They frankly really don't know what to do with the monument, and so they're just trying to manage it like they've always managed at every place they've been." A third person didn't like the "management style," explaining, "We're paid to be experts, but they don't listen to their experts. They make decisions and we're not allowed to disagree. They won't let the staff do anything. This is the only place I've been like that." A fourth person lamented, "There's too much politics. We're not doing what's good for the land anymore." Another agreed: "There have been a lot of people on the monument who realized that and left." Many of the staff observed that the job turnover rate at the monument was unusually high—higher than at any other federal land management agency office where they had worked.

These kinds of feelings were seldom evident at EIS meetings, where BLM employees maintained the "spirit of formalistic impersonality" proper to a public bureaucrat. But outside of the meetings, EIS Team members—both those who left and those who stayed—often communicated their dissatisfaction with the process to me, sometimes with a just brief comment, sometimes with an elaborate tirade. In this way, I gained valuable insight into how team members actually experienced the process. I also developed friendships with several of the women scientists on the team. I had great admiration for their knowledge, enthusiasm, and dedication to the landscape, and I felt a camaraderie with them because, like me, they didn't have children and preferred to spend their free time outdoors. We sometimes went hiking, horseback riding, or skiing together outside of work. When they left, I was sad, and I lost my best sources of inside information on the monument.

Attrition made the job of the remaining members of the EIS Team more difficult. For example, during discussions of specific allotments, it was often necessary to consult people who had participated in the rangeland health assessments for those allotments for information. When those people left the team, this valuable information was lost. In one discussion of a particular allotment, when the names of several former team members who had been on the assessment team came up, humor served to defuse the uncomfortable feeling that arose. When one team member suggested dryly, "As long as we're naming people who aren't here anymore . . . ," another rejoined, "Well, that could take half an hour."

As a result of the attrition, one of the last remaining "ologists" found herself in a minority. "It used to be that we had representatives, several people from recreation, several people from veg[etation], several people from range," she said. "But you know, people in the veg program quit, so now it's just me. But it's still three or four people from range. So there's times when it becomes a voice vote, and since there's more of them, it goes their direction." This team member eventually left, too, explaining, "I'm an outlier anyway. I want to work where there's camaraderie."

GSENM employees were not the only casualties on the EIS Team. At first the county representatives attended EIS meetings regularly. One believed, "We do make a difference." Another said he thought the monument was changing because of their participation. He explained that when he first went to EIS meetings, he was wary of other attendees and felt he had to "head 'em off at the pass." But he came to feel the counties were "being listened to." "You have to participate," he added, but he still didn't know "how it's all going to turn out." However, as the meetings went on and on, and the county representatives became involved in more adversarial relationships with the monument over roads and grazing retirements, they stopped coming to the meetings. One EIS Team member suggested triumphantly, "We wore 'em down." But he also realized, "As a side effect, we've worn ourselves down too."

Attrition also occurred among the monument management. Manager Dave Hunsaker left in March 2006 to take a position in Washington DC as deputy director of the National Landscape Conservation System. The planning supervisor who was one of the EIS Team leaders assumed the position of acting monument manager, then left shortly afterward. The person who assumed the EIS Team leadership in his place was soon promoted to another position on the monument. A new hire took charge of the EIS Team, but then he left, after which an old BLM employee who hadn't even been on the original team was put in charge.

THE EIS TEAM: HIERARCHY

The EIS Team gradually overcame the initial difficulties posed by their inexperience and the inadequacy of the science and decision-making tools they had to use but continued to struggle with the changing composition of the team and the divisions within it. However, the greatest challenge for many members was an increasing tension between their ethical duty as monument employees to determine the most efficient and effective means to achieve rangeland health and their obligation to follow directives handed down by their superiors. Their dilemma illustrates a tension within the bureaucratic ethos: Which of these duties should take precedence?

This is especially problematic in the federal land management agencies where the highest-ranking officials are political appointees. When a presidential administration of a different party than the previous one takes office, it usually appoints new people to these positions. Thus agency employees may find themselves with a superior who interprets the laws and policies governing the agency differently than the previous supervisor did and directs them to change projects they are working on midcourse, requiring them to abandon or redo work they have already done. The change in presidential administrations from Clinton to Bush, which occurred during the Rangeland Health EIS process, had a huge impact on the work of the EIS Team.

It began with mixed messages the team began to receive after the George W. Bush administration appointed a new monument manager, Dave Hunsaker, and higher-level BLM officials started taking more interest in the EIS process. The monument manager, who had not been attending EIS meetings, reappeared at one in March 2004 as the EIS Team was beginning to develop alternatives and informed the team that "the Washington office has been approached for additional guidance" on formulating the alternatives. This exchange followed:

> County representative: Why do we have to do what the state office and Washington wants? I have much more faith in the expertise in this room.
> Monument manager: We have to make sure we follow procedures.
> GSENM planning supervisor: Use the best science, come up with the best plan, then throw it to the wolves.

The team's interpretation was that instead of being guided by science, it would now be guided by politics. Many team members felt torn between doing what they thought was right and doing what they were told by their superiors. Later in the meeting, the planning supervisor elaborated on his attempt at humor: "Anything that's done that involves this monument is controversial, and it's not going forward without approval by the Washington office. Our job is to get to the draft, then we're subject to the whims of other people."

Shortly after this meeting, BLM officials from the Utah State Office also began attending meetings, reinforcing the impression that the process was being closely scrutinized from above. Instead of being allowed to continue to work on developing alternatives, the team was presented with an already formulated outline of the alternatives and informed that their job would be to fill in the details. The monument manager announced, "Expectations passed down from on high, that is the way of the world."

In the fall of 2004 more "expectations" were "passed down from on high." The previous summer, the range staff had been meeting individually with permittees to get their input on allotment-specific actions to include in the alternatives (see fig. 25), while the EIS Team as a whole worked on management issues common to all allotments for each alternative. The team had come up with management guidelines based on specific numbers for forage utilization and stubble height.[26] Both methods of setting management targets were supported by the current literature on grazing management. The team members felt they were making progress and were encouraged. As one put it, "Now we've started to actually get some stuff together. . . . We've gotten to the point where we think we have a pretty good range of alternatives."

However, in the fall, the GSENM management team received direction from Washington that they could not use specific figures for utilization or stubble height. One of the team leaders explained this development to the rest of the team: "Forest Service plans used specific figures, and they were sued and lost. Washington doesn't want to build in absolutes. Direction as specific as this was a big surprise to the state office—especially since it is common to have a utilization figure in EAs. . . . It's thrown everybody for a loop. Our alternatives were built on a utilization target; they're gutted. This is going to make a big difference in our schedule." Since they could not use utilization and stubble height figures as common guidelines in the EIS, the team would have to come up with specific management goals for each individual allotment. This would be a time-consuming process. The deadline was pushed back to October 2005.

To help develop ideas for managing each allotment, the team went back through the records to get more information about what had been done in the past. From the 1978 Management Framework Plan, which was the most recent planning document for some parts of the monument, they learned that the allotments they had identified as not meeting rangeland health standards were the same ones that has been identified as having problems in that document. In addition, many of the changes in grazing management and the range improvements they were proposing had been proposed at that time but never implemented. This confirmed what permittees on these allotments had been saying all along about planned projects never materializing. One team member realized, "We're suggesting things they suggested then. It just didn't get done." A major reason that range improvements had not been implemented was lack of funding. This example reveals another weakness in the bureaucratic ethos's assumption of a direct line of communication from elected representatives down through the bureaucracy: representatives may enact laws and policies but fail to provide adequate means of implementing or enforcing them.

The management preferred alternative for the EIS was also handed down to the team in the fall of 2004. Many were disappointed with both of these higher-level decisions. One member explained his feeling this way:

> We got the management preferred alternative. When it came out, [the botanist] and myself and wildlife were really disappointed. It's essentially alternative B: make progress in twenty years. The decision essentially comes from Washington to the state office. [The team leaders] went up there and they said Washington was freaked out about their "radical" proposal of 40 percent utilization. They want to keep things as they are.
>
> It just seemed so lame, *so* weak, and such a joke. Because here we've spent an enormous amount of money on this project, put a lot of resources into it with our people, and if it's just to maintain the status quo, it's a pretty rotten thing to do to us. They should have said, "We're going to maintain the status quo. You guys go ahead and do the jobs you'd normally be doing."

In his history of the BLM, James Skillen provided insight from a high-level view into what the EIS Team members experienced. From its inception, attempts to change the BLM failed or only incrementally succeeded in the face of efforts to maintain the status quo and current power structure among public land users and between the Interior Department and Congress. In particular, to privilege economic development on public

25. Ranchers and EIS Team members conferring over a grazing allotment in GSENM, June 2004. Courtesy of the author.

lands in the face of the strength of the environmental movement, the Bush administration developed an extremely centralized administration of public lands. It exercised tight control over information flow, limiting administrative transparency, and routed "both high-profile and routine decisions through Washington, . . . making centralized decision making its default mode of operation."[27] These means of executive control were an attempt by the Bush administration to roll back the reterritorialization of public land as national landscape and maintain it as resource. As this chapter has illustrated, the administration and its appointees reached far down the BLM's chain of command and affected the work of the EIS Team.

As the EIS meetings went on and on, and the team's decisions, which represented years of hard work, were overruled by Washington, the remaining members lost their enthusiasm. Eventually, it felt as if they were just going through the motions at meetings. One team member admitted, "I gotta say, at this point I'm thinking that the people in power really don't want anything to change, and that what we do won't really matter that much." Many began to complain that the EIS was taking too much of their time and they couldn't get their other work done. One member gave up on the process, but not on her passion for the public lands and her belief in "dedication to the principles of good land management by the people on the ground," expressed in the quote that begins this chapter. She decided, "Okay, screw the EIS. What matters is what we're doing on the ground. Because we're not going to get any support or governance from the EIS doesn't mean we can't do things that are technically good on the ground. We have good permittees; we have good range staff. I think there's a possibility." She sighed. "It's a long shot, but it's not completely impossible."

The way some team members explained what democracy meant to them helps bring to light the tension they experienced between their democratic values and the obligation to follow directives handed down by their superiors, expressed in their disappointment and frustration with the EIS process. For one member, democracy meant "rule by the people of themselves according to a generally agreed-upon set of rules. . . . If it worked in practice the way it's designed, it would be really very effective." He felt the EIS Team was doing a pretty good job of following the agreed-upon rules in writing the EIS, and he experienced decisions handed down from above that were based on political goals, instead of on interdisciplinary knowledge and negotiation, as contrary to the way the federal government was designed and as "taking apart some of those mechanisms that were made to prevent concentration of power." For another team member, democracy meant "rule by the majority but with protection of the viewpoints of the minority." For her, the "Founding Fathers . . . were trying to make a place so it was not like a monarchy—that was fair for everybody." She experienced dictates from above as being "like a monarchy" and therefore not "fair for everybody." For these team members, the rules of a bureaucracy were meant to promote equality and fairness, not the power of those at the top of the hierarchy.

The last EIS meeting I attended, in August 2005, was officially the final meeting of the EIS Team. Afterward, the team leaders sent the Draft EIS to BLM headquarters in Washington for final approval, with a planned release date in December of that year. They returned to their regular duties, and I returned to Seattle. In November I received an email announcing that Washington had not given approval to print the Draft EIS: "A surprise but not a setback.... This is just sensitive enough that the agency leadership wants to make sure they clearly understand what is being proposed before they get called about it." The Draft EIS was now scheduled to be released in March 2006. In the spring of 2006, as a member of the interested public, I received a notice in the mail that the Draft EIS would be coming out that summer. But it never appeared. In August 2007 I emailed the BLM employee who was the team leader when I left to ask about the current status of the EIS. He had been promoted to another position and was no longer the EIS Team leader, but he informed me the EIS had been placed on hold for a year while the Washington office developed an official policy on relinquishment. That had been released in February 2007, work had started on the EIS again the previous spring, and the Draft EIS was now expected in September 2007. However, it was another year before it was finally released in October 2008, over five years later than its original July 2003 deadline.

Chapters 3 and 4 showed the role that delay on the part of the federal government played in defusing conflicts over livestock grazing and roads on GSENM and how it served to maintain "the delicate balance between autonomy and control in the relationship between state and society."[28] In the case of the Rangeland Health EIS, delay on the part of the BLM in Washington served to extinguish the enthusiasm of BLM employees at GSENM who wanted the BLM to become an agency that would, in the words of one of the EIS Team members quoted at the beginning of this chapter, "make sure the best thing happens for the land, regardless of any kind of political regimes that come and go." This vision represented a threat from within the agency to high-level politically appointed officials who wanted to make sure that the status quo would be maintained on GSENM and that the Rangeland Health EIS would only propose actions that were nonthreatening to their political goals. The delay also served to deflect the counties', the ranchers', the environmentalists', and the general public's interest in the outcome of the process, as their reactions might challenge the status quo.

"Exit, Voice, and Loyalty"

To better understand why some team members left and others stayed, and what effect team attrition had on the EIS process and on the BLM's attempt to redefine itself as manager of national landscapes, I use a theoretical framework developed by economist Albert O. Hirschman. In *Exit, Voice, and Loyalty*, he considered the relationship between the options of exit and voice that members of an organization or any human group have when the benefit they derive from belonging to the organization decreases. In his formulation, "exit" means leaving the organization, and "voice" means expressing dissatisfaction in some way to attempt to recover the lost benefit. A series of positive and negative correlations influence the choice of exit or voice. First, the greater the ease of exit, the less likely it is that the voice option will be chosen. Second, the greater the costs of exit, the more likely the voice option will be attempted first. Third, the more likely it is that voice will lead to improvement, the more likely that option will be chosen. Finally, the amount of loyalty members have toward the organization will affect their choice between the two options, further complicating the relationship between them. In addition, in a democratic society, group members would expect to have a voice, which would also increase the likelihood that they would attempt that option. Hirschman argued that both exit and voice are signs of decline in an organization, and if voice is not an option and those who are dissatisfied leave, the organization loses the opportunity for feedback that could help it recover.

Using Hirschman's terminology, the exit option is easy for permanent BLM employees at GSENM because they can find jobs elsewhere in the BLM or other federal land management agencies. In fact, federal land management agency employees often seek new positions to advance their careers. However, attachment to the community in which they live is a form of loyalty that makes the cost of taking a job elsewhere higher. If the work they are doing is meaningful to them personally, such as "working for the monument," that also makes the cost of exit higher.

Members of the EIS Team who chose the exit option were those who experienced the greatest decrease in job satisfaction when the presidential administration changed and the tension between their bureaucratic and democratic values increased. Most of them were new employees and scientific specialists hired under the Clinton administration after GSENM was created, with the expectation they would use science to manage the monument and fashion a new direction for the BLM as manager of national landscapes. In the words of one of the team members quoted at the beginning of the chapter, they were dedicated to "the idea of public lands being available and belonging to the people" and to the landscape of GSENM, and they felt "an obligation and responsibility to make sure the best thing happens for the land." Their loyalty was to the land, not to the BLM. When they first joined the EIS Team, their personal feelings and motivations, as well as their interpretation of the ends handed down to them by the American public and those of their superiors, were in alignment. In EIS meetings, they could use the voice option to express dissatisfaction and disagreement with team members "who would prefer to maintain the status quo," and their opinions would be taken into consideration. They experienced a low level of tension between the bureaucratic and the democratic ethos and a high level of job satisfaction.

But when the administration changed and team members began receiving mixed messages from their superiors, saw their work being discarded, and had their decisions overruled by "expectations passed down from on high," the tension between their democratic and bureaucratic values increased, and their job satisfaction decreased. Since they were relatively new employees, they were less likely to have developed loyalty to the community, but they felt a loyalty to the landscape, which made exit more difficult for them. So they stayed and continued to try to use the voice option in EIS meetings. When it ceased to have an effect or they found themselves in a permanent minority and were always outvoted, their dissatisfaction increased further.

Voice can also mean attempting to recover job satisfaction in other ways. For example, several EIS Team members, armed with the knowledge they gained in the EIS process, conceived and wrote EAs for restoration projects in some of the areas identified and prioritized by the team and secured funding from outside the BLM to do the work. Some of those projects were underway long before the Draft EIS was released. Other team members concluded they could be more successful in realizing the goal of "mak[ing] sure the best thing happens" for the public lands by working for a federal land management agency elsewhere. The point at which individuals finally chose the exit option depended on the level of tension and dissatisfaction each one felt, as well as personal factors such as employment opportunities for their spouses. According to Hirschman's framework, the high level of attrition on the EIS Team was a sign of a problem in the BLM. With the loss of so many new employees, the agency lost the opportunity for feedback that could help it address the challenge and reinvent itself as manager of national landscapes.

Members of the EIS Team who stayed either experienced less dissatisfaction with their jobs or perceived the cost of exit to be higher. They may have experienced less dissatisfaction because they were old BLM employees who were accustomed to the way the BLM operated and had no desire to change it. As old employees, they would have lived in the region longer and developed more loyalty to the communities they lived in, increasing the cost of exit. Those who experienced a high level of dissatisfaction but stayed would have had to find a way to reduce the tension between their bureaucratic and democratic values. One way to do this might be to keep hoping that things would get better, as this member of the team did: "I really don't know if I had much in expectations going in because it was all so new. And it was kind of at the beginning of my time with the BLM, when the monument was new, during the administration that created the monument. We had good funding. We were hiring talented scientists. People were coming and not leaving, like they are now.... I haven't given up on it. I hope. No, I haven't given up on it."

Another way to reduce the tension might be to increase adherence to bureaucratic values in relation to democratic values, so that just doing what their superiors told them to do would be less problematic. This also reflected a loss for the BLM; to find efficient and effective ways to implement land management policies, the agency needed the voice of employees working in the field. The evidence in this chapter suggests that the EIS Team leaders and the managers at GSENM were more willing to adhere strictly to the bureaucratic ethos than ordinary team members. Because they had seniority and were closer to retirement, they may have felt they had more to lose by exercising voice. In addition, they did not express their attachment to the landscape in the way many of the new team members did. They may have started out in their careers with attitudes similar to those of the new employees, but over time, their attitudes had shifted. The exit of those whose loyalty was to the land, along with a gradual shift to the bureaucratic ethos among those who stayed, helps explain the resistance of the BLM to change.

This account of the Rangeland Health EIS process suggests that one reason the BLM was slow to rise to the challenge represented by GSENM and to take on a new role as manager of national landscapes is that monument employees who were hired to envision and actualize that role were not actually given the latitude to perform their duties according to how they imagined democracy should work. Using Hirschman's framework to analyze the experience of the Rangeland Health EIS Team suggests that to redefine itself as manager of national landscapes, the BLM should have better supported dedicated, enthusiastic public administrators with loyalty to the public lands, like those who initially staffed the EIS Team; encouraged rather than discouraged their voices; and reflected on the feedback they provided.

President Woodrow Wilson recognized that the key to overcoming the paradox between bureaucracy and democracy was to make sure that public bureaucracies served not just the state or the public but also the people who worked in them. In "The Study of Administration," he suggested that bureaucracies should be administered so that "it shall always be to the interest of the public officer to serve, not his superior alone but the community also, with the best efforts of his talents and the soberest service of his conscience." Then he asked how bureaucracies could serve the public officer's "commonest interest by contributing abundantly to his sustenance, . . . dearest interest by furthering his ambition, and . . . highest interest by advancing his honor and establishing his character."[29]

This account of the Rangeland Health EIS process also illustrates the hard work and dedication to public land of many BLM employees, how their work can be undone by executive branch politics, and why many leave in frustration and disappointment. Throughout its history, the BLM has been subject to interference from special interests, western representatives, and the executive branch, rendering it unable to develop a vision for public land and steer its own course.[30] When we are tempted to vilify agency employees for their apparent inability to manage and maintain healthy public rangelands, we should keep their dedication and the paradox between bureaucracy and democracy they must negotiate in mind, consider the effect high-level interference has on their morale, and ask instead how we could better support BLM employees' "highest interest" so they can focus on what is best for public land and the American public as a whole.

Events after 2009

Bringing the story of the Rangeland Health EIS up to date does little to change the conclusions of this chapter. In October 2008 the Draft Monument Management Plan Amendment and Draft Rangeland Health EIS for GSENM was finally released by the BLM. The BLM held the required public meetings, designed to give the public an opportunity to ask questions and offer comments, on November 18, 19, and 20 in Salt Lake City, Escalante, and Kanab, respectively. The public comment period for the Draft EIS ended on January 8, 2009. Shortly afterward, President Barack Obama took office, and a Democratic administration came to power. The final EIS was never released.

Instead, in November 2013 the BLM initiated a new planning process: the Livestock Grazing Monument Management Plan Amendment and Associated Environmental Impact Statement. Scoping meetings were held in December 2013 and January 2014. In January 2015 further scoping meetings were held to seek public comment on preliminary alternatives. In June 2016 a newsletter from monument manager Cynthia Staszak presented the draft alternatives and announced the planned release of the Draft EIS at the end of the year. I could find no further references to the Draft EIS. The Obama administration's apparent lack of interest in public lands issues has been noted by others.[31] In 2017 President Donald Trump took office, and the party of the presidential administration changed again.

President Trump reduced the size of GSENM in December 2017, and the BLM proceeded with alacrity to develop a new management plan for the monument and lands formerly within it. The Grand Staircase-Escalante National Monument and Kanab-Escalante Planning Area Draft Resource Management Plans and Environmental Impact Statement included the management of livestock grazing and was released in August 2018.[32] The final document was released in August 2019, and the decision was recorded in 2020. In two years the BLM under the Trump administration accomplished what it had not been able to do since the creation of GSENM in 1996: release a management plan for livestock grazing on the monument. The effort was part of the Interior Department's effort to streamline all EIS processes and give them a one-year time limit and a 150- or 300-page limit.[33] Among other actions that facilitated livestock grazing, the EIS reopened allotments along the Escalante River that had been retired from grazing in 1996 and in which the Escalante River Watershed partnership had invested years of funding and effort to remove invasive Russian olive.

In October 2021 Democratic president Joe Biden restored GSENM to its former size. The interim management guidance directed the BLM to prepare a new management plan for GSENM, to be approved by March 2024.[34] The 2020 Monument Management Plan would remain in effect until that plan was finalized. Undoubtedly, the new plan would change grazing management again.

The erratic trajectory of the Rangeland EIS vividly illustrates effects of the paradox between democracy and bureaucracy. When the science- and data-driven decision-making and multiparty negotiation written into the EIS do not align with the political agendas of high-ranking politically appointed Interior Department officials in Washington DC, they either hand down guidelines or directives designed to produce outcomes more to their liking or let EISs languish. As the presidential administrations alternate between Democratic and Republican, the EIS changes course, and thousands of hours of the EIS Team's work and millions of taxpayer dollars are thrown away to further the political goals of the new administration. As EIS Team members who care passionately about the public lands get frustrated and leave, those who are willing to follow orders remain. Little changes, and BLM employees and the public land beloved by so many Americans suffer.

While each of the groups considered in the four chapters of part 3 imagined democracy differently, their democratic imaginaries had several things in common. First, what are considered basic principles and institutions of a democratic political system, such as voting, respect for individual rights, rule of law, and inclusive decision-making (and which were prominent in part 2 of this book), were seldom mentioned when people were asked, "What does democracy mean to you?" Instead, they identified democracy with how they wanted to be able to live their lives and do their chosen work: residents of the communities adjacent to GSENM wanted to live with those who shared their pioneer values; ranchers wanted to be able to run their ranching operations in the way they saw fit; environmentalists wanted to protect the environment from damage by human activities; BLM employees wanted to use interdisciplinary knowledge to create the best plan possible to promote rangeland health on GSENM. Democracy had a very personal and specific meaning to them that gave the idea of democracy emotional force. And just as it is not possible to find a balance between the democratic and liberal logics of modern liberal democracy, and there can only be "temporary, pragmatic, unstable, and precarious negotiations of the tensions between them," each group found that trying to realize its democratic ideal was a struggle in the face of outside circumstances that made this impossible to attain.[35] But in pursuing the struggle, they were practicing democracy.

Conclusion

GSENM's Tenth Anniversary

In commemoration of the tenth anniversary of the creation of Grand Staircase-Escalante National Monument (GSENM), in 2006 the *Salt Lake Tribune* interviewed some of the people who had played prominent roles in conflict over its creation and management, seeking to learn whether their feelings about it had changed. Environmentalists reiterated feelings about the uniqueness of the landscape and approval of the greater protection the monument provided. Bill Hedden of the Grand Canyon Trust told reporters that GSENM should be appreciated and celebrated as "one of the greatest treasures of wilderness in the lower 48 states." Scott Groene, the executive director of the Southern Utah Wilderness Alliance, stated, "Every time there has been a bold conservation decision, there has been a lot of controversy. Then with the passage of time, it becomes appreciated. That's certainly true in Utah. And there's a lesson here. It proves it's a wise decision to protect the beauty of the state."[1] His words echoed the accepted wisdom about controversy over the creation of national monuments expressed by monument manager Kate Cannon in 2001: "Although the controversy is heated initially, over time these places prove their values and become popular. The Grand Canyon and Grand Teton initially were monuments and with a great deal of controversy around them, and now they are some of the best-loved pieces of protected land."[2] This accepted wisdom dismisses the concerns of those involved in the controversy and justifies what Utah representative Enid Green referred to as the "autocratic process" used to create protected areas.[3]

The responses of Utah's elected officials demonstrated, however, that ten years later their feelings about the undemocratic way GSENM was created continued to dominate their perceptions of it. Garfield County commissioner Maloy Dodds replied, "I feel about the same way as the day they created it. It was a bad idea. It's been bad for the counties, bad for the country. It's tied up all our natural resources. It took away a big part of our economic future. A lot has been lost with this. We're still fighting the battle, but it's gone from doing away with the monument to gaining access for things like grazing and even tourism."[4]

Bill Orton, the lone Democrat in Utah's congressional delegation when GSENM was created, recalled, "They lied to my face, which shows you the kind of backstabbing that goes on, even within one's own political party. There was no public debate. No policy discussion. No scientific research. This all happened because somebody had an epiphany." State senator Tom Hatch of Panguitch responded, "I don't think there's any question the monument has created economic activity. But the economic loss we sustained in terms of the future, I don't think we'll ever make up what was lost. I don't know a soul that wouldn't agree that there are areas [of GSENM] that deserve world-class protection. But it was the size of the monument and the way it was done that left a bad taste."[5]

What was also lost was the feeling that the welfare of local residents mattered to the federal government. After ten years they were "still fighting the battle" to try to make up for perceived economic losses, maintain their custom and culture, be recognized and respected, and have a say in the reterritorialization of public land as national landscape.

The monument staff celebrated the tenth anniversary of GSENM by organizing the Learning from the Land science symposium, which would highlight the value of GSENM for scientific research. Held September 12–14 in Cedar City, it followed up on an earlier Learning from the Land symposium that had been held when GSENM was created and showcased research that had been carried out on the monument in the ten years since. Symposium attendees who were interviewed by the *Salt Lake Tribune* extolled the opportunity that GSENM provided for scientific research.[6] Except for those who were government employees, few residents of the region were able to attend the symposium because of its timing, location, and cost. The monument also held local celebrations at each of the new visitors' centers in Big Water, Cannonville, Escalante, and Kanab on September 18, the actual anniversary date.

By 2009 on-the-ground conflict over the management of GSENM had died down. Garfield and Kane Counties were running out of avenues and money to fight the monument, many local residents had given up on attending public meetings where their opinions were ignored, and ranchers, who had to work long hours, didn't have time to write letters, attend meetings, or organize to speak up for themselves. As one Escalante resident put it, "They say after ten years, people think it's a good thing, but it's a different bunch of people. All of the people in the front lines have been shot down." So local residents were learning to live with the monument.

In 2009 the issues that had created the most controversy—livestock grazing and roads—were not yet resolved. There was still no livestock grazing management plan for GSENM. Ranchers remained uncertain about the future of their allotments and were not able to construct range improvements agreed on years in the past. Although the Draft Monument Management Plan Amendment and Rangeland Health Environmental Impact Statement was finally released in October 2008, the administration changed again in 2009, and no final version was ever released. It had not been decided who owned rights-of-way for roads on GSENM, but the latest court decisions had seemed to go against Kane and Garfield Counties. Change in how the public land that became GSENM was managed since its designation as a national monument was incremental. But its status as a national monument changed irrevocably the way it was viewed by many Utah elected officials and the American public.

What Democracy Means

The conclusions I draw in this book about what democracy means to ordinary Americans fall into three categories corresponding to the three parts of the book: landscape, conflict, and democracy.

LANDSCAPE

In part 1 I proposed that the western landscape has shaped what democracy means to ordinary Americans in ways they may not be aware of.

From the founding of the new nation until the end of the nineteenth century, the vast public domain lands provided space for it to expand and for Euro-American settlers to seek landownership and a better life. Western historian Frederick Jackson Turner argued that the existence of "free lands" on the frontier encouraged a distinctly American version of democracy characterized by "individualism, economic equality, freedom to rise."[7]

At the same time, Americans' ideas about democracy shaped the western landscape. The Anti-Federalist vision of a nation of small farmers and small-scale, decentralized government that promoted citizen participation and the development of civic virtue foundered when it encountered the arid landscape west of the 100th meridian. Homesteading laws that embodied this vision of democracy resulted in much public domain land remaining under federal control. Where small farmers could not succeed, livestock entrepreneurs assembled vast herds and ran them freely on the unregulated public domain lands. The image of the cowboy—wild and free—displaced that of the respectable, public-spirited farmer in American democratic imaginaries. As a result of this history, individual freedom and "freedom to rise," or the American dream, have become prominent features in American democratic imaginaries. The idea that resources are free for the taking and developers have a right to them is also informed by this history.

However, an outpouring of new scholarship by Native American authors and on settler colonialism has laid bare the extent to which the existence of so much "free" land depended on the ruthless extirpation and removal of the Indigenous population.[8] Nor has mainstream history acknowledged that the land was not free for everyone: African Americans faced unique difficulties in homesteading the land, and laws in some states barred Asian immigrants from owning land. Concepts such as manifest destiny and American exceptionalism dismissed this history. Failure to acknowledge it still haunts American democracy.

The existence of "free" land also led to careless and wasteful resource extraction and devastation wrought by unregulated logging, mining, and livestock grazing. This served to legitimate the development of a strong federal government to retain and manage some of the public domain lands. The laws and regulations passed to manage these lands have been informed by the Federalists' and Anti-Federalists' contrasting visions for a strong federal government and local control, making conflict over its management endemic. As perceptions of public land change and new forms of governing it emerge, it continues to be a site where the forms and legitimations of federal power and the meaning of democracy in specific local contexts are negotiated. Those living adjacent to these lands, whose livelihoods are most affected by changing management, continue to call attention to their situation and make their voices heard in these negotiations.

Western writers have explored the ways that feelings evoked by the physical characteristics of the western landscape still inform Americans' democratic imaginaries and compel attachment to both. While "free" land is no longer available, the experience of distance and space, the result of aridity, can evoke strong feelings of unrestricted freedom, unlimited opportunity, and the need for self-reliance. These feelings engender attachment to the landscape, motivate people to participate in conflicts over the management of public land, and help explain the passion and endurance of conflicts over GSENM. The existence of so much public land in the United States and laws that mandate public participation in its management provide Americans with a unique opportunity to practice democracy by participating in agonistic confrontations with others who are attached to the landscape for different reasons and have different ideas about how it should be managed.

CONFLICT

My analyses in part 2 of conflicts over the management of grazing and roads on GSENM shed light on what democracy means to ordinary Americans in relation to government. As participants in these conflicts engaged with the federal government and each other, they evinced democratic imaginaries that encompassed understanding democracy as the ability to participate in decision-making; other principles of democratic government, such as equality, freedom of expression, and rule of law; and how the democratic system of government in the United States is supposed to work. They also demonstrated acceptance of the procedures and institutions for participation and of the results because they perceived them to be based on democratic principles. The detailed analyses of these conflicts showed that these understandings are fluid and flexible. They shift as participants adapt to changing circumstances by developing new strategies, tactics, alliances, and oppositions, in the process reworking democratic imaginaries. The analyses also illuminated the micropolitics of statemaking: the ways that the federal government seeks to maintain the balance between local autonomy and state control in these conflicts. Viewed through the lens of agonistic democracy, enduring conflict over the management of public land does not indicate that democracy is not working but rather that those with differing views about how the land should be managed are engaging in agonistic confrontations with each other, finding temporary solutions to the current problem but never a final resolution.

DEMOCRACY

Part 3 presented descriptions of the daily lives of members of different groups of participants in the conflict over GSENM, their concerns regarding the monument, and their own words on what democracy means to them. Interviewees' responses demonstrate that ordinary Americans conceive of democracy in a wide variety of ways and not primarily in terms of a democratic political system. Their diverse democratic imaginaries reflect ideas about democracy and ways of practicing it that are derived not just from political science, education, popular culture, the media, and political rhetoric, but also from their group identity and unique individual experiences. In general, they identified democracy with how they wanted to be able to live their lives and do their chosen work. Democracy had a very personal and specific meaning to them that gave it emotional force. Yascha Mounk attributed confusion over the meaning of democracy to the fact that "we have fallen into the bad habit of expanding its definition to all kinds of things we like."[9] I suggest that this is not a "bad habit," but an indication of what we value about democracy and why we are so attached to it.

Part 3 also showed that even at the individual level, democracy entails paradox. Each group experienced the democratic paradox in their daily lives as they struggled to realize their democratic ideal in the face of outside circumstances that made it impossible to attain. Democratic paradoxes can be a source of creative tension from which new understandings of democracy and new ways of practicing it emerge. Together with the diversity of American democratic imaginaries, attempts to negotiate the democratic paradoxes in individuals' lives represent a fund of creativity from which new individual and collective ways of imagining and practicing democracy can emerge.

The approach to democracy I take in this book fosters optimism about democracy in America. It avoids the limitations of mainstream realist approaches to democracy and shows that democracy means much more to ordinary Americans than the limited conceptions of it proposed by these theorists. This approach provides a broader conception of political life than simply participation in political institutions and reveals the ways ordinary people value democracy and practice it in their daily lives. It allows us to see ongoing and seemingly endless disputes over the management of GSENM not as failures of democracy, but as the way that democratic politics works. And it highlights the value of public land as a site that helps create democratic citizens as people are motivated by their attachment to the landscape and empowered by collective ownership to engage with diverse others in agonistic struggles over its management.

Since 2009 momentous events that seem to threaten both GSENM and democracy in America have occurred. In light of these events, is it still possible to view democracy in America so optimistically? In the following sections, I describe these events and recent scholarship on democracy, revisit my earlier conclusions, and consider whether what democracy means to ordinary Americans may be changing. The chapter ends by examining, in the words of Tocqueville, "what we have to fear or hope" for democracy in America in the twenty-first century.[10]

Public Land and the Trump Administration

Not much changed in how GSENM was managed during the Obama administration. Little progress was made on resolving the grazing and roads conflicts, nor had the need for more funding and personnel for GSENM and for federal land management agencies more generally been addressed. Although his administration had devoted little attention to public lands issues, before leaving office President Obama used the Antiquities Act to create more national monuments than any president before him, including the 1.35-million-acre Bears Ears National Monument in southeast Utah. Significant for American democracy, the proposal for Bears Ears was led by Native American tribes for whom the land was culturally important and who would, for the first time in U.S. history, have a substantial say in its management. However, its creation also revived Utah elected officials' simmering anger over GSENM.

By the time I moved back to Escalante in 2017, many new businesses had been established in the region to serve both local and visitor needs. Escalante had a locally owned Home Store, new medical clinic and volunteer Fire Department buildings, and the old theater had been renovated and turned into the Showhouse for local gatherings. The local telecommunications company was beginning to install fiber-optic cable throughout the region, aided by stimulus funding from the American Recovery and Reinvestment Act of 2009. There were many new "move-ins," and one was building Escalante's first trophy home. Many property owners had converted their properties to short-term rentals, driving up home prices and rents and creating a severe housing shortage for lower-income families and seasonal workers. There were also many houses flying Trump flags and other flags that announced their political affinity. I had not seen such displays of enthusiasm for politics during the 2004 presidential election and was surprised to see so much support in a predominantly Mormon community for a person who flaunted his immorality. And it seemed to me that the division between pioneer descendant residents and move-ins, which was perceptible when I was doing fieldwork, even though both sides treated each other respectfully for the most part, had become more overt and antagonistic.

Rural anger had helped elect President Donald Trump in 2016, a fact that helped stimulate research seeking to understand how the situation of rural residents had contributed to a "politics of resentment."[11] This research identified long-term effects of neoliberal economic policies that have created a widening income gap between educated elites and working-class and rural Americans; hollowed out the American dream, which promised that hard work would be rewarded with success; and contributed to the latter groups' feeling of being left behind and having their concerns ignored by both political parties. A meritocratic ideology that rationalizes inequality as the outcome of differential effort or talent creates hubris in the winners and shame and anger in the losers. Additionally, as an increasing percentage of nonwhite citizens are predicted to become a majority in 2042, some white Americans perceive a threat to their historic dominance. Conservative mass and social media have successfully worked to turn discontent into fear and anger and channel it toward liberals, progressives, and the urban elite. At the same time, contempt expressed by those groups for conservatives and rural residents has served to deepen their anger and resentment. Some of these dynamics were already evident in my fieldwork: a stagnating or declining standard of living among longtime residents of the communities adjacent to GSENM, the feeling of being left out of consideration in public land decision-making and American prosperity, and contempt for rural residents expressed by environmental organizations and the mainstream media.

As soon as President Trump took office in January 2021, assumptions that Utahns had come to accept and appreciate GSENM over time were shown to be ill advised. The outrage that many local residents and Utah elected officials had felt when GSENM was created had kept simmering, and the "bad taste" that local officials had expressed at the tenth anniversary of the creation of GSENM had not gone away. An opportunity to transform these negative feelings into action had arisen, and opponents of GSENM wasted no time taking advantage of it. In February the Utah State Legislature passed resolution HCR 12, introduced by Republican state representative Mike Noel, representing the Grand Staircase-Escalante region, asking Trump to reduce the size of GSENM. Kane and Garfield Counties passed similar resolutions.

These resolutions repeated the same arguments that county leaders have long maintained: GSENM has reduced livestock grazing, strangled economic development, and shrunk school enrollment in Garfield County. Each of these claims is countered by facts, which Utah elected officials continue to ignore. Data from the Bureau of Land Management (BLM) show that no reductions in livestock grazing have occurred because of monument designation.[12] There are many contributing factors to reduction in school enrollment, including smaller family size. Studies have shown that the economies of Garfield and Kane Counties continued to grow after GSENM was created.[13] While tourism businesses have thrived in towns surrounding GSENM, elected officials say they want to see job growth associated with resource production that offers year-round employment and better pay.

In March Republican Utah senator Orrin Hatch sent a letter to President Trump asking for reduction of Bears Ears and GSENM.[14] On April 26 Trump issued an executive order instructing Interior Secretary Ryan Zinke to evaluate national monuments that were designated from 1996 through 2017 and over one hundred thousand acres. The starting date ensured that GSENM was included in the process. The first step in the evaluation process, according to the summary report issued by Zinke, was to "gather the facts" on the monuments under review from the BLM to aid in making recommendations.[15] The BLM report, mistakenly released in July 2017, pointed to significant benefits of the designation of GSENM for surveying and protecting cultural resources, increasing scientific discoveries, and supporting nonfederal jobs. It also stated that "no reductions in permitted livestock grazing use have been made as a result of the Monument's designation."[16]

The second step was to "ensure that the local voice was heard by holding meetings with local, state, tribal, and other elected officials as well as meetings with non-profit groups and other stakeholders, as well as providing an online format for public comment."[17] On his visit to GSENM, however, Zinke met only with local elected officials who supported the reduction in size of GSENM and refused to meet with local residents who had gathered from adjacent communities to speak with him. The Department of Interior (DOI) received some 2.8 million online comments, which overwhelmingly (98 percent) supported maintaining the national monuments under review as they existed. In his summary report, Zinke dismissed these comments as evidence of a "well-orchestrated national campaign organized by multiple organizations" and instead dwelled at length on the views of the few who opposed the monuments.[18] Both the facts and public input were ignored when, on December 4, 2017, President Trump reduced the size of GSENM by 46 percent and directed that the remaining monument land be divided into three management units to be managed by the Kanab Field Office.[19] He also reduced Bears Ears National Monument by 85 percent. Trump acknowledged the role of Senator Hatch's pressure and persistence in persuading him to make the boundary changes.[20] His actions were immediately challenged by multiple lawsuits that would take years to settle in court.

The process that President Trump used to reduce the size of GSENM was the same "autocratic process" used by President Clinton to create it, except this time the DOI had solicited public input, and the interior secretary had consulted with some Utah residents and elected officials beforehand. However, input from the former source was ignored, and only a select few Utah residents known to be antipathetic to GSENM were consulted. Predictably, environmentalists and supporters of GSENM were outraged. But rather than engaging in protest actions like local residents had when the monument was created, they filed lawsuits and left the battle to the courts, thereby reducing the opportunity for the general public to participate.

The impression of a targeted attack on GSENM was reinforced when, later in December, Republican Utah representative Chris Stewart introduced H.R. 4558, which would establish the Escalante Canyons National Park and Preserve and make the reduced size of GSENM permanent. An article in the *New York Times* described the bill as a "Trojan horse" because it appealed to Americans' love of national parks, while hiding an agenda that promoted resource extraction.[21] Hunting and livestock grazing would be core purposes of the proposed park, and it would be managed by a management council composed of two presidential appointees, four Utah county commissioners, and one Utah state representative.

The development of new management plans for the reduced GSENM and lands formerly within it proceeded with a speed uncharacteristic of the BLM. On January 18, 2018, a sixty-day scoping period was announced. Departing from the accepted BLM practice of holding public scoping meetings in nearby cities as well as local communities to maximize participation, only two meetings were held: in Kanab on March 28 and Escalante on March 29. The Draft Management Plan, which included the management of livestock grazing, was released on August 15, and again only two public meetings to accept comments on the draft were held: in Escalante on October 15 and Kanab on October 16. Nevertheless, when the comment period for the GSENM plan closed on November 30, over five hundred thousand public comments had been received.

The Draft Management Plan opened with a statement of the BLM's mission: "to sustain the health, diversity, and productivity of the public lands for the use and enjoyment of present and future generations." In jarring contradiction, the BLM's preferred alternative stated that it "conserves the least land area for physical, biological and cultural resources," "is the least restrictive of energy and mineral development," and "has the greatest potential for adverse effects on resources among other proposed alternatives."[22] The Final Management Plan, released August 23, 2019, confirmed this alternative with a few minor changes and was approved February 20, 2020. Meanwhile, in the Grand Staircase-Escalante region, life carried on as usual, without the eruption of protest against the reduction of GSENM that had punctuated the years after its creation.

The reduction of GSENM and Bears Ears National Monument was only one action in a concerted attack on the public lands during the Trump administration. Efforts to privatize the public lands or transfer them to the states have a long history that began when the federal government first withdrew land from the public domain and attempted to manage resource use. These actions became most vigorous during Republican administrations and resumed as soon as President Trump took office.[23] In February 2017 Republican Utah representative Jason Chaffetz introduced a bill, the Disposal of Excess Federal Lands Act, which directed the DOI to offer 3.3 million acres of public lands for sale. The bill was withdrawn in the face of strong protest by Utah residents. The same month Republican Alaska representative Don Young introduced H.R. 232, which would allow states to purchase national forest land. Because Americans strongly support the public lands, such bills have little chance of passing in Congress, but members from certain western states continue to submit them. Consequently, proponents of privatizing public lands, transferring them to the states, or opening them to extensive resource development have begun to pursue their objectives by subtler means that slowly transfer management authority away from the public and into the hands of sympathizers.[24] Their methods include curtailing the public process by shortening comment periods, holding fewer public meetings, and withholding information; ignoring or "losing" public input; streamlining the permit process for resource development projects; and defunding land management agencies.

The public process used to review national monuments in 2017, develop management plans for GSENM, and review the draft plan in 2018 employed the first two tactics. Other examples from the 2017–18 Congress include H.J. Res. 44, which rolled back the BLM's Planning 2.0, a long-awaited modernization of the BLM's land planning process that included an improved public process; H.R. 6087, which would require the public to pay fees to comment on oil and gas leases; and H.R. 6106, which expanded the use of categorical exclusions, streamlining the oil and gas leasing process and sidestepping public input.[25] In August 2017 Zinke ordered DOI agencies to limit future environmental impact statements to a one-year time limit and a 150- or 300-page limit.[26] That same month he announced that he was reviewing the status of public lands advisory boards, whose purpose is to give outside advice to public land managers; since then, few scheduled meetings have been held, effectively shutting out public input.[27] In January 2018 the BLM issued a memorandum that instructed field offices to take actions that would effectively avoid National Environmental Policy Act analysis of oil and gas leasing. Its implementation was blocked by a federal judge in September.[28] In March 2018 the BLM blamed a technological breakdown for the disappearance of tens of thousands of comments on proposed revisions to the greater sage-grouse conservation plan.[29]

Defunding the federal agencies that manage the public lands makes it impossible for them to manage effectively and undermines public support for the agencies. Data from the BLM, U.S. Forest Service (USFS), and National Park Service (NPS) show that the number of people using the public lands continues to increase over time, prompting many recent articles about "loving public lands to death."[30] While use is increasing, funding and staffing for the agencies that administer them is not. For example, the 2018 BLM budget of $1.1 billion represented a $162.7 million decrease from 2017.[31] While appropriations for the NPS increased since 2009, staffing remained about the same.[32] In fiscal year 2020 there was $14.37 billion in deferred maintenance for the NPS, $5.87 billion for the USFS, and $4.08 billion for the BLM.[33] In addition, as wildfires increase on public lands, more of the agency budgets are being used to fight them. In 2015 addressing wildfires used 52 percent of the USFS budget, compared with 16 percent in 1995.[34] The same trends have occurred during Democratic administrations.

Surprisingly, a bright spot occurred during the Trump administration. The Great American Outdoors Act, passed in August 2020, provided up to $1.9 billion a year for five years to begin to address the maintenance backlog in national parks, forests, and other public lands.[35] But it did not address the need for additional funding and staffing to manage these lands. To further disempower the BLM, the Trump administration moved its headquarters from Washington DC to Grand Junction, Colorado. The move isolated upper-level BLM employees from lawmakers, other federal officials, and resources in Washington. It also resulted in the loss of many of the BLM's most experienced employees, who declined to make the move.

In light of my argument that public land promotes democracy, this multipronged attack on it was effectively an attack on democracy. During the period of the Trump presidency, the word "democracy" came into circulation again in the United States, voiced by critics in response to other, more overt presidential actions they saw as a threat to democratic norms and institutions. Whereas I began this book with the observation that in 2009 one seldom heard the word "democracy" in the United States, ten years later Astra Taylor began her book *Democracy May Not Exist, but We'll Miss It When It's Gone* by telling us, "The word *democracy* is all around us."[36] The culmination, and most shocking, of Trump's actions was his assertion that the 2020 presidential election had been stolen, followed by attempts to have the results overturned and inciting his followers to attack the U.S. Capitol on January 6, 2021, in an effort to prevent the transfer of power.

Update on GSENM

During his presidential campaign, Joe Biden pledged to restore GSENM and Bears Ears. He honored that commitment immediately after taking office on January 20, 2021, by directing the DOI to review the boundaries and conditions of GSENM, Bears Ears, and two other national monuments. Utah elected officials' response was predictable. In February the Garfield County Commission passed a resolution opposing changes to the boundaries set by President Trump's proclamation. Utah's congressional delegation warned the president not to exacerbate what had already become the "political football of national monuments in Utah" and stressed the need for "a permanent solution approved by Congress."[37] Interior Secretary Deb Haaland visited GSENM and Bears Ears in April and met with a wider variety of affected and interested parties than Zinke had: the BLM and USFS; Utah elected officials at the national, state, county, and city levels; tribal leaders; ranchers; business owners; environmental organizations; outdoor recreation permit holders; mining companies; and scientists. She submitted her recommendations to fully restore the original boundaries on June 4. On October 8 President Biden issued two proclamations, 10286 and 10285, restoring the original boundaries of GSENM and Bears Ears National Monument, respectively.[38]

GSENM's twenty-fifth anniversary occurred in 2021 during the COVID-19 pandemic and before the monument was restored. As it approached, I was not in the mood for celebrating, still dismayed by the concerted attack on public land and democracy during the Trump administration and concerned about the future of both. Although Congress had passed the Great American Outdoors Act in 2020 and it appeared President Biden would restore the boundaries of GSENM and Bears Ears, public lands were still taking a backseat to more pressing national concerns. Reflecting pandemic caution toward public events and perhaps the equivocal status of GSENM, the celebration was also more subdued. In contrast to the science symposiums the BLM had held in the past, this time it organized scientist-led educational tours held outside and open to the public. For example, the monument paleontologist introduced participants to the fossil-bearing geological formations near Escalante and gave them an opportunity to look for fossils themselves; an ecologist took participants to a spring near Henrieville, explained the protocol for a survey of springs underway on the monument, and gave them an opportunity to try it out; and the monument archaeologist took participants on a tour of archaeological sites near Kanab. These tours were less formal and more accessible to local residents than a science symposium and seemed to me the perfect way to experience and celebrate the unique landscape of GSENM and the opportunities for scientific research it affords.

In July 2022 the BLM began the process of writing the Grand Staircase-Escalante Resource Management Plan and Environmental Impact Statement (RMP/EIS) for the restored GSENM, scheduled to be released in March 2024. The agency attempted to reproduce the timeline of the 2000 plan, but not the curtailment of public input. During the thirty-day scoping period, it held meetings in Escalante, Kanab, and Panguitch and online via Zoom. The Draft RMP/EIS was released in August 2023, and during the ninety-day comment period, the BLM held meetings in the same venues plus Salt Lake City. The Garfield County commissioners were alarmed by the proposed management in the BLM's preferred alternative and hosted a public information meeting on October 26 to provide an opportunity for their constituents to discuss the plan and to encourage them to submit comments. Commissioner Leland Pollock took the opportunity to inform attendees that the plan was formulated by "special interest groups like SUWA and Western Watershed and Grand Canyon Trust," whom he called "'Al-Qaeda' because they're like terrorists . . . they're the scum of the planet. . . . These terror organizations like SUWA and all the bad people that this is coming from—they're running the federal government right now."[39]

This language illustrates the more overt antagonism of some longtime residents toward people with different political views that I noticed when I moved back to Escalante. The men who were Garfield County commissioners when I was doing my original research would never have spoken like that in public, no matter their personal views. Pollock's statement elicited alternating letters to the editor in one of the current local newspapers, the *Insider*, from people who objected to language that encouraged violence and respondents who dismissed it as hyperbole. The final plan was released on August 29, 2024. As of this writing, it awaits review by the governor of Utah.

Setting up the next play in the "political football of national monuments," on August 24, 2022, the state of Utah and Garfield and Kane Counties filed two lawsuits challenging Biden's authority to restore

GSENM and Bear Ears, arguing that the size of the two monuments violated the Antiquities Act and challenging the Antiquities Act itself. In November, following the lead of the Hopi Tribe, Navajo Nation, Ute Mountain Ute Tribe, and Pueblo of Zuni, the Southern Utah Wilderness Alliance, Grand Staircase Partners, and other conservation groups filed a motion to intervene in the lawsuits. In March 2023 intervenor status was granted. The lawsuits were dismissed in August, but the state, in characteristic fashion, immediately filed an appeal. The "political football" is now being played in a federal courtroom, rendering the American public unaware and uninvolved. More insidiously, treating the public lands as just another way to score points in partisan politics shifts their significance in American democratic imaginaries away from "our" public lands—lands that we are willing to stand up for and to engage with others to maintain and enhance—to just another partisan issue.

There have been significant changes in the physical and social landscape of the Grand Staircase-Escalante region as well. When the COVID-19 pandemic began in 2020, to escape lockdowns, visitors came in unprecedented numbers to public land managed by the BLM, which was less subject to COVID restrictions than national parks and forests and where people could "social distance" by camping along dirt roads in vast, open landscapes. On most BLM land, camping is free, permits are not required, and you can camp where you want. It was estimated that there were ten million first-time visitors that year who were inexperienced with backcountry travel, low-impact camping, waste disposal, and appropriate treatment of resources and artifacts. Numbers plus inexperience resulted in substantial resource damage. Backcountry rangers reported more garbage, vandalism, and graffiti than they had ever seen before. On GSENM, every trailhead and camping spot was overflowing with vehicles, trailers, and motor homes with license plates from all over the country. Increased visitation serves to increase public awareness of and support for public land, but GSENM is still woefully underfunded and understaffed, and the BLM still lacks the resources to manage it. The region has also been withered by the worst drought on record, possibly wounding the land in a more grievous, visible, and lasting way than humans can. While politicians battle over boundaries instead of addressing the lack of funding for federal land management agencies, the land suffers.

GSENM still attracts people from more crowded places who are captivated by the landscape and want to live here. State and local governments are actively trying to create new job opportunities and affordable housing to attract new residents and make it possible for local youths to remain in the area. With high-speed internet available, the region is attractive to the growing number of people who discovered during the COVID-19 pandemic that they can work anywhere. The Escalante Canyons Art Festival, which was first organized in 2004, is still going strong, but it is mostly attended by more recent residents and out-of-town visitors. Grand Staircase Escalante Partners is also going strong, and in 2020 it purchased and remodeled a building in Escalante for its new headquarters. The region feels energized and growing, and the "political football" over monument boundaries does not seem to have had much effect on people's daily lives.

However, the division between longtime and multigenerational residents, who are primarily conservative and are still Trump supporters, and the move-ins, who are primarily liberal or progressive, has widened since the first time I lived here. Many of the older-generation residents I came to know and interviewed when I was doing fieldwork have passed on. Maloy Dodds, Dell LeFevre, and Clare Ramsay, who were the three members of the Garfield County Council then, died within a couple of months of one another in 2020, two from COVID-19. My neighbor Delane Griffin, the cowboy poet, passed away in March 2021, ninety-seven years young. The older generation seemed more willing to tolerate differences and to believe that with new residents, "it's a state of mind and not an issue of [their] background," as one pioneer descendant Escalante resident was quoted as saying in chapter 5. The younger generation is more attuned to the messages of conservative media. Some alarming incidents have occurred in Escalante. During a small and peaceful Black Lives Matter march organized by a newcomer in 2020, local men in pickup trucks drove alongside and harassed the marchers. One of the participants was confronted by a multigenerational resident she knew who yelled, "Are you going to burn down my town?" When a restaurant that had posted a Masks Required sign during the COVID-19 pandemic denied entry to a local resident not wearing a mask, he returned later, armed and wearing camouflage, and asked whether they would let him in now.

On the other hand, many of the new move-ins express animosity and contempt toward longtime residents, whom they call "stupid" and "ignorant" and whose views they caricature as "right-wing," "redneck," and other epithets, without ever having engaged in a meaningful conversation with them. There are not as many Church-sponsored events where longtime and more recent residents can mingle and get to know each other as there were when I lived in Escalante before. I heard a rumor from a nonpracticing Mormon that the LDS Church had handed down a decision to circle the wagons and not be as welcoming to non-Mormons.

Reflecting on these developments and experiences, I wondered how they might change this book's propositions about what democracy means to ordinary Americans. And at the same time they were happening, something was happening to democracy in America.

Democracy in America in the Twenty-First Century

While I was doing fieldwork, democracy was on the rise in the world and had been since 1973. At that time, about a quarter of countries were considered democracies (meaning leaders were elected by regular, free, and fair elections); by 1992 the proportion had increased to one-half, and by 2000 it had reached three-fifths.[40] Between 1980 and 2000 eighty-one countries moved from authoritarianism to democracy. In 2011 most of the world population lived in democratic political systems. This trend led democratic theorists to conclusions similar to those of David Held, quoted in the introduction: "We live in the age of democracy," which has become "the fundamental standard of political legitimacy in the current era."[41] Political scientist Francis Fukuyama announced "the end of history" following the collapse of the Soviet Union and the end of the Cold War, concluding that liberal democracy had clinched a final victory over other political ideologies.[42] With hindsight, I can see how these global and national contexts informed my research. The first democratic elections in South Africa in 1996 were part of this democratic expansion, and my experience of them primed me to participate in the optimistic assessment of the future of democracy. The election of Barack Obama in 2008, the first person of color to hold the office of president of the United States, reinforced this optimism, signaling hope, change, and an expansion of democratic rights and equality in the United States.

However, according to political scientists, by that time liberal democracy had already begun to falter worldwide and in the United States, and since then the trajectory of democracy has undergone a stunning reversal. Using several different scales that measure democracy in different ways, political scientists have argued that democracy peaked around 2006, when 63 percent of all states had democratic political systems, it has been declining since, and authoritarianism is on the rise.[43] Freedom House, which measures and tracks the quality of democracy around the world in terms of political rights and civil liberties, reported in 2022 that countries with declining yearly aggregate freedom scores outnumbered those with increasing scores every year from 2005 to 2021. Whereas 46 percent of the world population lived in a country Freedom House considered free in 2005, by 2021 only 20.3 percent did.[44]

Democracy index scores for the United States have declined alarmingly since 2010. In 2020 Democracy Matrix ranked the United States as number 36 out of 176 countries, calling it a "deficient democracy," and in 2022 the Economist Intelligence Unit Democracy Index rated it a "flawed democracy."[45] Its freedom score declined from 94 in 2010, ranking it near the top, to 83 in 2020. Its Polity score, which measures the level of autocracy to democracy on a scale of −10 to +10, has also been declining and dropped to +5 in 2021 after the attack on the U.S. Capitol.[46] According to Freedom House in 2023, this declining score is due to "rising political polarization and extremism, partisan pressure on the electoral process, bias and dysfunction in the criminal justice system, harmful policies on immigration and asylum seekers, and growing disparities in wealth, economic opportunity, and political influence."[47] Reasons for declining scores cited by other democracy indices include the influence of money in politics and policymaking, a politicized Supreme Court, threats to freedom of the press, the degradation of civil discourse and norms of compromise with those in opposition, and the weakening of institutional checks on the executive.[48]

In addition to indices that measure political democracy, surveys that measure people's attitudes toward democracy throughout the world also show troubling trends. While support for democracy is still high, it has declined, and willingness to express support for authoritarian alternatives has increased.[49] A majority of those surveyed in advanced economies feel their political system needs major changes.[50] Political scientist Barbara Walter offered these statistics in 2022 from surveys done in the United States: the percentage of those surveyed with a negative view of democracy grew from 9 percent in 1995 to 14 percent; faith in government fell from 77 percent in 1964 to 17 percent in 2019; those who think "army rule" would be a good thing rose from 7 percent in 1995 to 18 percent; those who don't have confidence in the electorate to make good decision rose from 35 percent in 1997 to 59 percent; and 3.5 percent said they would vote for their preferred candidate even if the person did or said something anti-democratic.[51]

The decline of democracy in the United States has generated a spate of books that attempt to identify processes contributing to what many call a "crisis of democracy" or a "crisis of legitimacy." The processes identified by these authors have been underway for many years but attracted increasing attention in the United States as the 2008 recession, the rise of the Tea Party, the hard right turn of the Republican Party, and the election of Donald Trump occurred. Most of these authors see neoliberalism as a major contributor to democracy's decline. It has produced the most extreme income inequality in U.S. history, along with a stagnating or declining standard of living, and made the American dream unreachable for most Americans.[52] Political theorist Wendy Brown argued that in extending the model of the market to all domains and activities and constructing human beings solely as economic actors, neoliberalism has undone the demos—the sense of a "we" as a living political body that governs—and the possibility of democracy understood as rule by the people.[53] In the name of freedom from government, it seeks to activate traditional morality in place of legislated social justice, eroding the political equality of the historically excluded and ultimately equating freedom with unregulated personal license.[54] Four decades of neoliberal markets and moral-based rationality have produced a profoundly anti-democratic political culture and contributed to the rise of the anti-democratic right.

Yascha Mounk cast his net wider than just neoliberalism. He attributed the decline of U.S. democracy to changes in three conditions that its past stability depended on: the dominance of mass media, which created a set of shared facts and values and limited the distribution of extreme ideas; a rising standard of living that held out hope for a better future; and dominance of one ethnic group.[55] He pointed out that the U.S. Constitution was designed not to promote democracy but to limit it. He referred to "the founding myth of liberal democratic ideology" as "the improbable fiction that representative government would facilitate the rule of the people," saying that this myth "proved to be one of the most powerful ideological forces in the history of mankind. And though it had never been exactly correct, it retained sufficient footing in reality to keep a hold over the democratic imagination."[56] That footing is crumbling as the rise of the internet and social media has empowered once marginal movements and politicians; a stagnating or declining standard of living is creating fear of greater hardship in the future; and white dominance is threatened. As a result, democracy is decomposing into its component parts, giving rise to illiberal democracy and undemocratic liberalism.

Chantal Mouffe made a similar assessment. Neoliberal hegemony has led to processes of "oligarchization"—the concentration of wealth and power among fewer and fewer people—and of "pauperization and precarization" of the middle class. At the same time, it has led to a situation she called "post-democracy," in which the two pillars of the democratic ideal—equality and popular sovereignty—have eroded, and democracy has been reduced to its liberal component, the presence of free elections and the defense of human rights. Agonistic spaces where alternatives to neoliberalism could be debated have disappeared. Economic deprivation coupled with erosion of people's ability to exercise their democratic rights has created a "populist moment" in which "the people" seek to regain a voice in a political-economic system perceived to be controlled by "privileged elites who are deaf to the demands of the other groups in society."[57]

The indices, surveys, and scholars cited in this section approached democracy as a political regime and suggested that democracy as "the fundamental standard of political legitimacy in the current era" is being challenged.[58] In light of the events affecting both GSENM and democracy in America, what insights can this book's approach to democracy add to understanding the current crisis? I revisit the three interrelated sets of conclusions about what democracy means to ordinary Americans from the first section of this chapter to consider "what we have to fear or hope" for democracy in America in the third decade of the twenty-first century.

LANDSCAPE

What we have to fear for democracy in regard to the landscape is loss of access to our public lands or the ability to participate in managing them. While overt attacks by conservative opponents who want to privatize them or give them to the states subside during Democratic administrations, covert attacks that slowly transfer management authority away from the public and into the hands of sympathizers who will direct their management toward private ends continue. As our ability to participate significantly in managing public lands is reduced, so is the opportunity to become democratic citizens and to practice democracy by participating in agonistic confrontations with others who are attached to the landscape for different reasons and have different ideas about how it should be managed, and this reduces the strength of our democracy as well. If they are no longer "our" public lands, we lose the sense of a "we" as a living political body that owns and manages them. If we lose access to the public lands, we lose the opportunity to experience the western landscape and be inspirited by what writer Terry Tempest Williams called "the open space of democracy."[59] When public lands are used in "political football," we have to fear that they will become just another partisan issue and that Americans' attachment to and willingness to stand up for them will be eroded. Another concern is the proliferation of new national monuments for the BLM to manage under the Biden administration without a corresponding increase in funding for the agency. Without adequate management, overcrowding and overuse can have adverse effects on the ecosystems, resources, and values the designation is supposed to protect.

What we have to hope for democracy is that the public lands will continue to inspire Americans, attract their support, and motivate them to work together to maintain and manage these lands. With greater acknowledgment of American settler colonial history and recognition of Indigenous knowledge and management of these lands in the past, efforts are being made to include Native Americans in public land management. Efforts are also being made to increase the participation of underrepresented groups in recreation and management activities on public lands. We can hope that these efforts to democratize the public lands will improve their management and also contribute to making democracy in America more genuine and inclusive.

CONFLICT

What we have to fear for democracy regarding conflict is that in the face of strong support for the public lands, but with a wide diversity of opinions about how they should be managed, purely scientific or neoliberal rationality could be used to bypass the messy and lengthy process of public participation. We also have to fear that as political divisions in the United States deepen and become more antagonistic, it could become more difficult for participants in conflict over public lands to transform antagonism into agonism and work together to find mutually acceptable resolutions.

What we have to hope for democracy is that Americans' attachment to their public lands will continue to motivate them to participate in agonistic engagements with others who value the land for different reasons and have different ideas about how it should be managed, to recognize common ground, and to find mutually acceptable solutions. This experience can show people how to begin to bridge the political divide that is threatening democracy in America today. As participation in conflicts over the public lands becomes more diverse, we can also hope that new perspectives will help us address complex issues such as species loss and climate change.

Mouffe emphasized the role of emotions, affects, and passions in democratic politics.[60] It is not through rational argument that antagonism can be transformed into agonism, but through recognition of our shared allegiance to democratic values and of other common ground that creates empathy and disposes us to give others a more open-minded and compassionate hearing. For that reason, I find it encouraging that with the rise of the Tea Party and the election of Donald Trump, social scientists have begun to use ethnographic methods to investigate the experience of rural residents and members of conservative groups in the United States, the basis for their political views, and the sources of the rage and resentment that infuse right-wing rhetoric.[61] I am hopeful that their writing will increase understanding of and empathy for others currently seen as the "enemy" by some liberal and progressive readers so they may come to see them as legitimate adversaries.[62] As sociologist Parker Palmer stated, "The more you know about another person's story, the less possible it is to see that person as your enemy."[63] I am disappointed that few of these books have been written by anthropologists who for the most part have failed to take up anthropologist Julia Paley's challenge to undertake research specifically focused on democracy in the United States. The need is even more urgent now than when she posed it.[64]

Other social scientists are beginning to emphasize that recognition of common experiences and affects are essential for creating the mutual understanding and respect that the functioning of diverse democracies like the United States depends on. As long as the United States is a democracy, we will share it with people whose democratic imaginaries are different from our own. As sociologist Ruth Braunstein argued, "If one accepts the view that widespread citizen participation is necessary for a functioning democracy, then one must welcome even the participation of those citizens with whom one disagrees."[65] Journalist and community activist Erica Etelson explained, "Our choice is whether to communicate with them [those with whom we disagree] in a manner that fosters understanding and goodwill, or that stirs up hatred."[66] Understanding others' points of view makes it more likely we can communicate without being defensive and will welcome debate. Recognizing common ground creates empathy and helps us find something we can agree on. Both Braunstein and sociologist Parker Palmer suggested that working- and middle-class Americans throughout the political spectrum are "heartbroken" about threats to democracy, the condition of our society, and the loss of the American dream, however these things are perceived, and that shared grief could be a source of common ground for working- and middle-class Americans.[67] I have suggested that attachment to public land and to democracy could be a source of common ground.

Channeling Mouffe, these scholars have also recognized the paradoxical nature of democracy and the inevitability of conflict. Braunstein concluded, "As long as multiple groups cultivate and enact different stories of America, and no single story becomes dominant, then citizens can productively interrogate their respective benefits and drawbacks."[68] Palmer asserted that political life in a democracy is a "nonstop flow of contradictions and conflicts." But "our sharpest disagreements need not be the seeds of democracy's destruction. If we know how to hold their tensions in ways that open our hearts, they can become proof of democracy's genius and drivers of its renewal." He praised the Constitution for enshrining ongoing political negotiation in which "all resolutions are tentative" and "no such thing as a last word would ever be uttered."[69] Astra Taylor structured her book around "seeming oppositions that are foundational to democracy": the "paradoxes, contradictory elements that, while liable to clash, must coexist." Those she pointed out are freedom and equality, conflict and consensus, inclusion and exclusion, coercion and choice, spontaneity and structure, expertise and mass opinion, the local and the global, and the present and the future. She emphasized that "there can be no unambiguous resolution on one or the other side" of any of these binaries.[70]

DEMOCRACY

If democracy means to ordinary Americans being able to live their lives the way they want, we have to fear that as the effects of neoliberal globalization make this increasingly difficult for many Americans, they will lose faith in democracy and turn to other forms of government. Or that in the face of divisive partisan politics and modern forms of power, they will lose hope. We have to fear the appeal of those who catalyze their discontent and disillusionment with democracy into blame and anger against specific enemies—the government, liberals, immigrants, ethnic minorities—in ways that deflect these feelings away from economic elites who conceive of, benefit from, and support neoliberal policies and restrict democracy. These right-wing populists claim they will bring back popular sovereignty, democracy as rule of "we the people," but the "people" they have in mind excludes numerous categories. Because freedom also figures prominently in American democratic imaginaries, we also have to fear the neoliberal promotion of individual freedom over democracy.[71] Neoliberal freedom is reduced to freedom to compete in the market without government intervention, to be a winner or loser, ultimately to be unequal.[72] It is freedom *from* any kind of coercion without being restricted by collective freedom, social consciousness, or political equality. At its extreme, it is "unregulated personal license" and casts principles of equality and inclusion as "tyrannical political correctness."[73]

What we have to hope for democracy is that it will continue to retain its personal meaning and value for ordinary Americans and that their attachment to it will see the United States through the current crisis. Despite the documented decline of democracy throughout the world, Mouffe's agonistic understanding of democracy allowed her to see a way to reverse that trend, which she outlined in her two most recent books as of this writing. She began by observing that many of the current struggles against oppression are expressed as democratic demands, demonstrating that the affective force of the democratic imaginary is still potent and motivates people to act. She observed that many of these demands come from groups who are the main losers of neoliberal globalization and cannot be satisfied within the neoliberal project. She suggested that to counter right-wing populism, what is needed is a left populism that links together these heterogeneous struggles and creates a "people" by activating passions that are central to the democratic imaginary and drawing a political frontier that presents the adversary of the people as being constituted by the forces of neoliberalism. Mouffe also recognized that the democratic project needs to be reformulated in view of the current ecological and climate crises and that the democratic principles of liberty and equality need to be redefined and extended to new domains, including humans and nonhumans. Additionally, the antineoliberal struggle needs to be articulated with the ecological one, and these struggles need to mobilize affects of both a democratic and an ecological nature. However, Mouffe was operating on the theoretical plane and did not provide any practical suggestions for how to do this.[74]

Applying some of Mouffe's ideas to conflicts over the management of public lands, a populist public lands politics would mean that instead of local residents, environmentalists, and the federal government in various "us-versus-them" combinations, a "we" would be constructed by mobilizing democratic affects and attachment to the landscape, and a political frontier would be established that presents the adversary as the opponents of the public lands: those who want to privatize them, give them to the states, or transfer management authority away from the public. They are also opponents of democracy.

My hope for democracy is that the stories in this book will open up understanding of the points of view of participants in conflicts over GSENM—and over the public lands more generally—as well as the role of conflict in democracy, so that Americans will be able to engage in productive debate about how best to manage our public lands. Whether we choose to be active participants in these debates or just open our minds and actively listen to those with whom we disagree, each of us has the power to contribute to the revitalization of democracy in America.

Notes

Preface

1. Although some sources spell the name with an en dash, I prefer to use a hyphen, per the U.S. Department of the Interior's Bureau of Land Management and other government references.
2. This phrase was suggested by an anonymous reader, to whom I am deeply grateful for suggesting how I could make the research more relevant to the current political context.
3. Turner, *Dramas, Fields, and Metaphors*, 35.
4. The title of this book is inspired by the first ethnographer of democracy, Alexis de Tocqueville, author of *Democracy in America*.
5. Paley, "Toward an Anthropology," 471.
6. For example, MacLean, *Democracy in Chains*; Mounk, *People vs. Democracy*; Levitsky and Ziblatt, *How Democracies Die*.
7. Edwards, Haugerud, and Parikh, "Introduction"; Brugger, "'Other' and the 'Enemy.'" Some exceptions are Bessire, *Running Out*; Bjork-James, *Divine Institution*; Westermeyer, *Back to America*.
8. Ginsburg, *Contested Lives*.
9. Marcus, "Ethnography."
10. Unless otherwise noted, unattributed quotes in this book are from my interviews or observation. When they are attributed, I use the real names of people who have given me their permission to do so, are public servants in their official capacity, or were quoted in media accounts.
11. Eaton, "Consultation."
12. Nafisi, *Reading Lolita in Tehran*, 268.

Introduction

1. In 1998 the Utah Schools and Land Exchange Act and Public Law 105-335 carried out the president's intent to acquire state trust lands within GSENM, increasing its size to 1,865,420 acres. BLM, Grand Staircase-Escalante National Monument Management Plan (hereafter Management Plan).

2. Proclamation No. 6920, 61 Fed. Reg. 186 (September 18, 1996).
3. "Kane County Holds a Bitter Wake after Monument Decision," *Salt Lake Tribune*, September 19, 1996, A7.
4. Jim Woolf, "A Pretty, Great Monument?" *Salt Lake Tribune*, September 19, 1996, A1.
5. Paul Larmer, "A Bold Stroke: Clinton Takes a 1.7 Million-Acre Stand in Utah," *High Country News*, September 30, 1996.
6. Woolf, "Pretty, Great Monument?"
7. Larmer, "Bold Stroke."
8. Laurie Sullivan Maddox, "Taking Swipes at Clinton, Utahns Vow to Fight Back," *Salt Lake Tribune*, September 19, 1996, A5.
9. Laurie Sullivan Maddox, "It's a Monumental Day for Utah," *Salt Lake Tribune*, September 19, 1996, A1.
10. Maddox, "Taking Swipes."
11. I use the Grand Staircase-Escalante region to refer to the area of Garfield and Kane Counties that includes GSENM and the communities adjacent to it.
12. Goodman and McCool, *Contested Landscape*, table 14.1. A large proportion of federal land within a county also poses a hardship for the county, because federal lands are not subject to property taxes. Utah counties use property taxes to fund schools and other services for county residents. To help offset the loss of revenue, the federal government makes payments in lieu of taxes to local governments. However, the counties do not have the control over this revenue stream that they would have with local taxes.
13. Andalex Resources was a Dutch-owned company that held leases for coal on the Kaiparowits Plateau at the time GSENM was created.
14. Kaibab Forest Products Company, a lumbermill in Fredonia, a few miles south of the Arizona border from Kanab, was one of Kanab's major employers from the 1940s until it shut down in 1995. Trainor, "Conflicting Values."
15. The School and Institutional Trust Lands Administration administers Utah's state trust lands: the sections (640 acres each) of a township granted, by the act of Congress that established a state, to the state to be held in trust for the benefit of the state's public school system and other public institutions. The federal government granted all western states two sections (16 and 36) from each township for the support of their public schools. In the case of Arizona, New Mexico, and Utah, the federal government granted four sections (2 and 32, in addition to 16 and 36). Revenue is generated by selling the land or putting it to use in some income-generating way, such as leasing the land for grazing.

16. A complete transcript of the meeting was published in the *Garfield County News*, July 26, August 2, 9, 2021. Quotes in this account are from the transcript.
17. Held, *Models of Democracy*, xi.
18. Whitehead, "Vexed Issue," 124.
19. Sen, "Democracy."
20. Norris, *Democratic Deficit*.
21. Dahl, "Democratic Paradox?," 38.
22. Mounk, *People vs. Democracy*.
23. C. Taylor, "Modern Social Imaginaries."
24. Braunstein, *Prophets and Patriots*, 73.
25. Mouffe, *Democratic Paradox*.
26. Mouffe, *Democratic Paradox*.
27. Mouffe, *Democratic Paradox*, 45, 15.
28. Mouffe, *Democratic Paradox*, 102.
29. This discussion of the nature of the state draws on Abrams, "Notes"; Brown, "Finding the Man"; Gupta, "Blurred Boundaries"; Mitchell, "Limits of the State."
30. Gerth and Mills, *From Max Weber*, 78.
31. Abrams, "Notes," 76.
32. Sivaramakrishnan, "Crafting the Public Sphere," 433.
33. Sivaramakrishnan, "Crafting the Public Sphere," 433.
34. Held, *Models of Democracy*, xi.
35. Vandergeest and Peluso, "Territorialization and State Power."
36. Foucault, "Governmentality"; Foucault, *Birth of Biopolitics*. Foucault uses "government" to describe the mode of rule (i.e., managing the relationship between "men and things") and "governmentality" to describe its rationale (i.e., to ensure "the welfare of the population"). To avoid confusion with my own references to the U.S. federal government, when I use the term in his sense, I put it in quotes.
37. Foucault, "Governmentality," 93; Braun, "Producing Vertical Territory," 12.
38. Braun, "Producing Vertical Territory," 28.
39. In 2018 Russell M. Nelson, the president of the Church of Jesus Christ of Latter-day Saints, requested that "Mormon" and "LDS" no longer be used to refer to the Church or its members. Instead, he said, the religion should be referred to by its full name, as the Church of Jesus Christ, or the Church, and members should be called Latter-day Saints. For the most part, I try to use these terms. But where their use is awkward, as in "Latter-day Saints pioneers," I continue to use the nicknames. Sarah Jane Weaver, "'Mormon' Is Out: Church Releases Statement on How to

Refer to the Organization," Church of Jesus Christ of Latter-day Saints, August 16, 2018, https://www.churchofjesuschrist.org/church/news/mormon-is-out-church-releases-statement-on-how-to-refer-to-the-organization?lang=eng.
40. Tocqueville, *Democracy in America*, 19.

1. National Landscape

1. Only Canada has more, and much of this land is in the Far North and inaccessible to most of the country's population.
2. Vincent, Hanson, and Bermejo, *Federal Land Ownership*.
3. Vincent, Hanson, and Bermejo, *Federal Land Ownership*.
4. For the history of the relationship between public land and ideas about democracy in the United States, I draw on Bailyn et al., *Great Republic*; Baldwin, *Highway Rights of Way*; Kemmis, *Community*; Rose, *Property and Persuasion*; Vincent et al., *Federal Land Management Agencies*; White, *"It's Your Misfortune"*; Worster, *Under Western Skies*.
5. Rose, *Property and Persuasion*, 84.
6. Rose, *Property and Persuasion*, 84.
7. Tocqueville, *Democracy in America*, 279.
8. Faragher, *Rereading Frederick Jackson Turner*, 1.
9. Faragher, *Rereading Frederick Jackson Turner*, 91–92.
10. Faragher, *Rereading Frederick Jackson Turner*, 47, 67.
11. Faragher, *Rereading Frederick Jackson Turner*, 55.
12. For example, Limerick, *Legacy of Conquest*.
13. Scott, *Seeing like a State*.
14. The history of ranching draws on Jordan, *North American Cattle-Ranching*; and Sayre, "Cattle Boom."
15. Foucault, "Governmentality."
16. Mitchell, *Rule of Experts*.
17. Hays, *Conservation*.
18. Foucault, "Governmentality," 100.
19. White, *"It's Your Misfortune,"* 58.
20. Spence, *Dispossessing the Wilderness*.
21. Jacoby, *Crimes against Nature*.
22. Merrill, *Public Lands*.
23. For the section on national monuments, I draw on National Park Service, "Antiquities Act of 1906," accessed May 2006, https://www.nps.gov/subjects/archeology/antiquities-act.htm; Righter, "National Monuments"; Rothman,

America's National Monuments; Thompson, "Antiquities Act of 1906"; Vincent and Baldwin, *National Monuments*.
24. American Antiquities Act of 1906, 16 USC 431–433.
25. Righter, "National Monuments," 291, 285.
26. This section draws on C. Davis, "Politics and Public Rangeland"; Donohue, *Western Range Revisited*; Klyza, *Who Controls the Public Lands?*; Makley, *Open Spaces*; Merrill, *Public Lands*; Rowley, "From Open Range"; Skillen, *Nation's Largest Landlord*; Skillen, *This Land*.
27. Taylor Grazing Act of 1934, Public Law 73-482, "Grazing Lands," 43 USC Ch. 8A.
28. McConnell, *Private Power*.
29. Wilderness Act of 1964, 16 USC 1131–1136.
30. Federal Land Policy and Management, 43 USC 1702(c).
31. Examples include the American Legislative Exchange Council (1973), the National Legal Center for Public Interest (1975, merging with the American Enterprise Institute in 2007), the Mountain States Legal Defense Fund (1977, now called Mountain States Legal Foundation), the Public Lands Council (1968), and the League for the Advancement of States' Equal Rights (1977).
32. Skillen, *This Land*, 54.
33. Pinchot, "Conservation Means the Wise Use." This paragraph draws on S. K. Davis, "Fighting over Public Lands"; Jacobs, "'Wisdom' but Uncertain Future"; Klyza, *Who Controls the Public Lands?*; McCarthy, "First World Political Ecology"; Skillen, *This Land*.
34. "Grazing Administration—Exclusive of Alaska," 43 CFR Part 4100.
35. S. K. Davis, "Fighting over Public Lands."
36. Rasband, "Questioning the Rule."
37. The BLM had found that 2.5 million of the 23 million acres it managed in Utah possessed wilderness characteristics and were eligible to be designated wilderness study areas.
38. A detailed history of the citizen's wilderness inventory and the continuing struggle for wilderness in Utah can be found in the newsletters of the Southern Utah Wilderness Alliance (SUWA) and on its website at https://suwa.org.
39. Foucault, *Birth of Biopolitics*.
40. Proclamation No. 6920, 61 Fed. Reg. 186 (September 18, 1996).
41. According to the monument manager, Dave Hunsaker, in 2003, the GSENM's annual budget was $6.4 million for the first few years after it was created; it was reduced to $5.9 million in 2003 and was projected at $4.9 million for 2004. This was far more than the typical budgets of BLM field offices. In 1999 a BLM employee at the Monticello Field Office, where the budget was

$500,000 to manage nearly 1.8 million acres, suggested that the administration was trying to "buy off the conflict."
42. Newell and Barnes, *Untold History*.
43. Newell and Talbot, *History of Garfield County*.
44. Frye, *From Barrier to Crossroads*.
45. Southern Utah Oral History Project, Grand Staircase-Escalante National Monument and Utah Division of State History, accessed 2008, https://spcoll.li.suu.edu/collections/HO1ncH8BnM5_0W5sFc6P/items.
46. BLM, accessed October 17, 2008, http://www.blm.gov/wo/st/en/prog/blm_special_areas/NLCS.html (site discontinued).
47. Interview with Charles Wilkinson and Patricia Limerick, Center of the American West, Boulder, Colorado, April 20, 2004, http://www.centerwest.org/projects/secretaries/interviewpdf/babbitt.pdf. Babbitt tells essentially the same story in Babbitt, *Cities in the Wilderness*, 163–65. Critics of the president's action have pointed out that the decision to create a monument in Utah was mostly likely influenced by the fact that Utah is solidly Republican and was already lost to the Clinton campaign.

2. Regional Landscape

1. Bailyn et al., *Great Republic*, 1:425.
2. Areas where the average annual precipitation is less than 250 mm (10 inches) are usually considered arid lands or desert; those where it falls between 250 and 500 mm (10 and 20 inches) are considered semiarid. "What Is a Desert?" USGS, last modified December 18, 2001, http://pubs.usgs.gov/gip/deserts/what/.
3. John Tierney, "The Sagebrush Solution," *New York Times*, July 26, 2008, A17.
4. Roundy, *"Advised Them."*
5. BLM, Management Plan.
6. Goodman and McCool, *Contested Landscape*, table 14.1; BLM, Management Plan.
7. The former name for this group, Anasazi, is still in widespread use. Local residents also use the term Moqui to refer to traces the former inhabitants left on the landscape, such as Moqui steps carved into steep walls for access.
8. For the geological history of the Colorado Plateau, I draw on Barnes, *Canyon Country Geology*; Doelling et al., "Geology"; Fillmore, *Geology of the Parks*; John D. Grahame and Thomas D. Sisk, "Canyons, Cultures and Environmental Change: An Introduction to the Land-Use History of the Colorado Plateau," 2002, accessed December 17, 2007, site archived at https://web.archive.org/web/20060208054415/http://www.cpluhna.nau.edu/index.htm.

9. Since the late nineteenth century, humans have also had a significant impact on the physical landscape, so much so that their activities could be compared to another geological force. Recognizing this, geologists are debating whether the current geological age should be called the Anthropocene.
10. Waters et al., *Landscape-Scale Assessment*.
11. BLM, Grand Staircase-Escalante National Monument Draft Monument Management Plan Amendment and Draft Rangeland Health Environmental Impact Statement (hereafter Draft Amendment and Draft EIS).
12. Waters et al., *Landscape-Scale Assessment*.
13. For the geological history of the Colorado Plateau, I draw on Doelling et al., "Geology"; Grahame and Sisk, "Canyons, Cultures"; Kelly and Fowler, "Southern Paiute"; Newell and Talbot, *History of Garfield County*; Spangler and Zweifel, *Deep Roots*.
14. Janetski et al., "Paleoarchaic to Early Archaic."
15. Louderback and Pavlik, "Starch Granule Evidence."
16. For reasons explained in the preface, this chapter does not consider the regional landscape from the perspective of Native Americans.
17. Proclamation No. 6920, 61 Fed. Reg. 186 (September 18, 1996).
18. Milton, *Loving Nature*.
19. Francaviglia, *Believing in Place*.
20. Worster, *Under Western Skies*, 82–83.
21. Worster, *Under Western Skies*, 234–36.
22. Stegner, *American West*, 80.
23. Williams, *Red*, 201.
24. Williams, *Open Space of Democracy*, 76.
25. For the Mormon experience, I draw on Alexander, *Utah*; Arrington, *Great Basin Kingdom*; Arrington and Bitton, *Mormon Experience*; Bailyn et al., *Great Republic*, vol. 1; Francaviglia, *Mormon Landscape*; Krakauer, *Under the Banner*; Nelson, *Mormon Village*.
26. Arrington and Bitton, *Mormon Experience*.
27. Stegner, "On the Mormons," 109.
28. Latter-day Saints sometimes refer to people who are not members of their Church as Gentiles.
29. Bailyn et al., *Great Republic*, 1:434.
30. Francaviglia, *Mormon Landscape*.
31. Larson, *"Americanization" of Utah*.
32. "The Mormons," *American Experience*, PBS, April 30, 2007, http://www.pbs.org/mormons/.
33. Arrington, *Great Basin Kingdom*.
34. Francaviglia, *Mormon Landscape*.

35. Nelson, *Mormon Village*, 128.
36. Riebsame and Robb, *Atlas of the New West*. Less celebrated is the "Nuclear West," the landscape defined by radiation exposure from nuclear testing in Nevada in the 1950s and 1960s and uranium mining. Residents of the Grand Staircase-Escalante region are among the "downwinders" whose concerns were dismissed by the federal government, contributing to mistrust of the government in the region. Fox, *Downwind*. In 1990 Congress passed the Radiation Exposure Compensation Act to provide some compensation to those affected. The program was extended until June 2024.
37. Taylor Grazing Act of 1934, Public Law 73-482, "Grazing Lands," 43 USC Ch. 8A.
38. Sayre, *Working Wilderness*.
39. *Billings Gazette*, October 7, 2004.
40. BLM, Draft Amendment and Draft EIS; Walker, "Reconsidering 'Regional' Political Ecologies."
41. McCarthy, "First World Political Ecology"; "Rural Poverty and Well-Being," Economic Research Service, U.S. Department of Agriculture, last updated November 15, 2023, https://www.ers.usda.gov/topics/rural-economy-population/rural-poverty-well-being/#historic. In 2021 per capita income was $49,895 in rural areas and $66,440 in urban areas, and the poverty rate was 15.4 percent and 12.3 percent, respectively. "State Fact Sheets: United States," Economic Research Service, U.S. Department of Agriculture, last updated February 7, 2024, https://data.ers.usda.gov/reports.aspx?ID=17854.
42. Walker, "Reconsidering 'Regional' Political Ecologies."
43. Sayre, *Working Wilderness*.
44. "Estimates Show Slowest Growth on Record for the Nation's Population," U.S. Census Bureau, December 21, 2021, https://www.census.gov/newsroom/press-releases/2021/2021-population-estimates.html.
45. Walker, "Reconsidering 'Regional' Political Ecologies," 17–18.
46. Matt Canham, "Mormon Portion of Utah Population Steadily Shrinking," *Salt Lake Tribune*, July 24, 2005; "Mormons Now a Minority in Utah's Biggest County, New Figures Show," *Los Angeles Times*, December 15, 2008.
47. Rasker et al., *Public Lands Conservation*.
48. Sonoran Institute, *Population, Employment: Garfield County*; Sonoran Institute, *Population, Employment: Kane County*.
49. Power, "Fiscal Impacts."
50. Preceding statistics in this paragraph are from BLM, Draft Amendment and Draft EIS.
51. Rasker et al., *Public Lands Conservation*.

52. BLM, Draft Amendment and Draft EIS.
53. Hamilton, Martin, and Sutton, Births.
54. Rasker et al., *Prosperity*.
55. Headwaters Economics, *Grand Staircase-Escalante*.
56. Muhn and Stuart, *Opportunity and Challenge*.

3. Conflict over Grazing

1. Gupta, "Blurred Boundaries"; McConnell, *Private Power*.
2. Brunson and Wallace, "Perceptions of Ranching."
3. Hardin, "Tragedy of the Commons." Anthropologists Nathan Sayre and Maria Fernández-Giménez pointed out that it should more accurately be referred to as a tragedy of open access. Sayre and Fernández-Giménez, "Genesis of Range Science."
4. Knight, "Ecology of Ranching."
5. This paragraph draws on many texts on "new ecology" and rangeland ecology: Sayre, *Ranching*; Sayre, *Politics of Scale*; Scoones, *Living with Uncertainty*; Vavra, Laycock, and Pieper, *Ecological Implications*; Westoby, Walker, and Noy-Meir, "Opportunistic Management."
6. In this section, quotes that are not cited are from interviews; information is drawn from these interviews and the following newspaper articles: Nancy Bostick-Ebbert, "The Lady Ain't No Cowboy, She Just Broke All Those Rules," *Salt Lake Tribune*, December 3, 2000, AA4; Judy Fahys, "Maverick Cows on Off-Limits on the Monument," *Salt Lake Tribune*, July 6, 2001, D1; Mark Havnes, "Copter That Crashed Was Killing Cows," *Salt Lake Tribune*, December 16, 2005; Brent Israelsen, "Cows Remain on Overgrazed Area of Monument," *Salt Lake Tribune*, September 25, 2000, B2; Israelsen, "Feds to Pluck Cattle from Public Land," *Salt Lake Tribune*, October 17, 2000, A1; Israelsen, "Airborne Wranglers Round Up Wayward Cattle in Monument," *Salt Lake Tribune*, January 9, 2001, B1; Israelsen, "Bovine Casualties: Problem Cows Gunned Down from the Air," *Salt Lake Tribune*, November 27, 2001, A1; Israelsen, "Range Rebels Agree to Fines," *Salt Lake Tribune*, June 18, 2003; Brent Israelsen and Thomas Burr, "Ranchers and Sheriff Defy Feds, Take Back Seized Herd of Cattle," *Salt Lake Tribune*, November 9, 2000, C1; Israelsen and Burr, "Irked Ranchers Retake Cattle Seized in Grazing Dispute," *Seattle Post-Intelligencer*, November 10, 2000, A22; Shia Kapos, "Feds, State Agency Agree on Livestock Seizure Rules," *Salt Lake Tribune*, January 20, 2001, B2; Kapos, "The Last Roundup?" *Salt Lake Tribune*, March 3, 2001, A10; Kapos, "Fiftymile Faux Pas," *Salt Lake Tribune*, July 11, 2001; and *Garfield County News*, September 7, 28, October 5, 12, 19, 26, November 2, 9, 16, 23, 30, December 21, 2000.

7. For example, Loring et al., "Science, Data."
8. Israelsen, "Cows Remain."
9. Israelsen, "Feds to Pluck Cattle."
10. Israelsen and Burr, "Irked Ranchers Retake Cattle."
11. Israelsen, "Feds to Pluck Cattle"; *Garfield County News*, November 16, 2000.
12. Israelsen, "Airborne Wranglers."
13. The act costs the BLM a significant amount of money to administer. For example, in November 2008, the Government Accountability Office reported that the cost of keeping horses for future adoption had jumped from $7 million in 2000 to $21 million in 2007. Patty Henetz, "GAO Analysis: Wild Horses in Captivity Giving Feds Fits," *Salt Lake Tribune*, November 11, 2008. By 2022 it had ballooned to $137 million. Vincent, *Wild Horse*.
14. Tom Kenworthy, "Land Agency Accused of Personnel 'Purge,'" *USA Today*, March 11, 2002.
15. Michelle Nijhuis, "Change Comes Slowly to Escalante Country," *High Country News*, April 14, 2003.
16. In this section, quotes that are not cited are from interviews and notes taken during the May 9–11 and September 8–9, 2005, Department of the Interior Office of Hearing and Appeals hearing in Kanab; quotes that are cited are from DOI, Decision in Docket Numbers UT-030-04-01, UT-030-04-02, UT-030-04-03, or newspaper accounts of events. Information is drawn from personal knowledge of events and from the following newspaper articles: Joe Baird, "Activists Win Fight on Rights to Grazing," *Salt Lake Tribune*, January 31, 2006, D1; Baird, "New Suit Challenges Ruling on Grazing Permits," *Salt Lake Tribune*, March 29, 2006, B6; Felicity Barringer, "A Strategy to Restore Western Grasslands Meets with Local Resistance," *New York Times*, December 1, 2005; Joe Bauman, "Grazing Permit a Threat?" *Deseret Morning News*, January 31, 2006; Lisa Church, "Utah Ranchers Agree to Sell or Trade Grazing Rights inside Grand Staircase-Escalante National Monument," *Salt Lake Tribune*, January 5, 1999, B2; Church, "Fun-Hogs to Replace Cows in Utah Monument," *High Country News*, February 1, 1999; "Common Enemy," editorial, *Salt Lake Tribune*, February 2, 2006, A10; "Counties Appeal Ruling That Left Grazing Rights Intact for Arizona Trust," *Salt Lake Tribune*, March 20, 2006, B2; Mark Havnes, "Restoration: Projects Meant to Upgrade S. Utah," *Salt Lake Tribune*, February 5, 2007; Havnes, "Judge Bars Counties from Using Public Funds for Ranchers' Grazing Suits," *Salt Lake Tribune*, April 17, 2007; Brent Israelsen, "Grazing May End on Chunk of Land in Grand Staircase," *Salt Lake Tribune*, February 28, 2001, A1; Israelsen, "Plan Would Reduce Grazing in Grand Staircase," *Salt Lake Tribune*, May 4, 2002, D4; Israelsen, "Plan to Cut Grazing in Monument Hits Snag," *Salt Lake Tribune*,

November 10, 2002, B1; Israelsen, "Grazing Permits to Retire," *Salt Lake Tribune*, January 14, 2003, A1; Israelsen, "State Funds Granted for Grazing Suit," *Salt Lake Tribune*, November 23, 2003, B1; Israelsen, "Rancher Tries to Keep Another's Cows off Acreage," *Salt Lake Tribune*, January, 27, 2004; Michelle Nijhuis, "Change Comes Slowly to Escalante Country," *High Country News*, April 14, 2003; "Poisoning the Well," editorial, *Salt Lake Tribune*, November 25, 2003, A18; Nicole Warburton, "2 Counties Sue over Grazing," *Deseret Morning News*, January 28, 2005; and Glen Warchol, "Ranchers Vow Fight over Grazing Rights," *Salt Lake Tribune*, March 7, 2002, D1.

17. Grand Canyon Trust, accessed July 28, 2004, https://www.grandcanyontrust.org/ (the mission and website have since been updated).
18. Grand Canyon Trust, accessed July 28, 2004.
19. Church, "Utah Ranchers Agree."
20. Church, "Fun-Hogs."
21. Church, "Fun-Hogs."
22. Tierney, "Sagebrush Solution."
23. Grand Canyon Trust, accessed July 28, 2004 (the website no longer mentions this approach or a grazing retirement program).
24. DOI, Decision in Docket Number UT-030-04-01.
25. Israelsen, "Grazing May End."
26. Harvey, *Brief History of Neoliberalism*, 2.
27. Harvey, *Brief History of Neoliberalism*, 3.
28. Israelsen, "Grazing May End."
29. Warchol, "Ranchers Vow Fight."
30. DOI, Decision in Docket Number UT-030-04-01.
31. Abrams, "Notes," 79.
32. Warchol, "Ranchers Vow Fight."
33. Israelsen, "Plan Would Reduce Grazing."
34. Israelsen, "State Funds Granted."
35. *Salt Lake Tribune*, April 22, 2006; "Poisoning the Well."
36. Grand Canyon Trust, accessed July 28, 2004.
37. Nijhuis, "Change Comes Slowly."
38. Israelsen, "State Funds Granted."
39. Groesbeck, "Preliminary Analysis"; Groesbeck, "Tax Revenue Impacts."
40. Power, "Fiscal Impacts," 21, 24, 20.
41. DOI, Decision in Docket Number UT-030-04-01.
42. Mouffe, *Democratic Paradox*.
43. DOI, Decision in Docket Number UT-030-04-01.
44. DOI, Decision in Docket Number UT-030-04-01.

45. Walmart contributed $1 million to the $4.5 million purchase price. Ironically echoing an earlier editorial that described the state of Utah Community Impact Board's grant to the counties for the appeal as "poisoning the well," an editorial in the *Salt Lake Tribune* answered charges that the grant from Walmart was "tainted money" with the justification, "We beggars cannot be too choosy." "Poisoning the Well"; Randy Parker, "Tainted Money," *Salt Lake Tribune*, April 15, 2005, A16.
46. Brent Israelsen, "Greens Snapping Up Huge Swath of Land," *Salt Lake Tribune*, July 13, 2004.
47. Joe Baird, "Environmentalism and the New West," *Salt Lake Tribune*, October 30, 2005, A1.
48. DOI, Decision in Docket Number UT-030-04-01.
49. Mark Habbeshaw, "Kane County's Perspective on Its Grazing Appeal," *Salt Lake Tribune*, April 22, 2006.
50. Clare Ramsay, "County Officials Will Defend the Right to Graze on Public Lands," *Salt Lake Tribune*, October 28, 2006.
51. Tom Wharton, "Kane County Can't Cope with Free Enterprise," *Salt Lake Tribune*, April 13, 2006; Randy Parker, "Grazing Rights Essential to Protect Livestock Industry," *Salt Lake Tribune*, April 22, 2006.
52. Habbeshaw, "Kane County's Perspective."
53. Baird, "Environmentalism."
54. BLM, Relinquishment of Grazing Preference on BLM Administered Lands, Instruction Memorandum No. 2007-067, February 20, 2007, https://www.blm.gov/policy/im-2007-067.
55. State representative Mike Noel, quoted in Barringer, "Strategy to Restore."
56. Freyfogle, *Land We Share*, 198.
57. Sivaramakrishnan, "Crafting the Public Sphere," 433.
58. This approach has been promoted by the Quivira Coalition and found much success in New Mexico.

4. Conflict over Roads

1. This background draws on Rasband, "Questioning the Rule."
2. Baldwin, *Highway Rights of Way*; Vincent, Hanson, and Argueta, *Federal Land Ownership*.
3. These arguments are taken from two SUWA fact sheets: "RS 2477 and Disclaimer Rule: Environmental, Economic, and Policy Impacts," last updated March 31, 2003, https://secure.suwa.org/site/DocServer/Impacts_Env_Econ_Policy.pdf?docID=622; and "RS 2477: Impacts on Private Property,"

accessed December 6, 2008, https://secure.suwa.org/site/DocServer/PrivateProperty_FactSheet.pdf?docID=601.
4. Jana Smith and Ron Smith, "Beware the Consequences of RS 2477 Right-of-Way Claims," *Salt Lake Tribune*, June 21, 2003, A11.
5. Rasband, "Questioning the Rule," 1029, 1031.
6. In this section, quotes are from interviews where not cited and from newspaper accounts of events where cited. Information is drawn from personal knowledge of events, Rasband, "Questioning the Rule," and the following newspaper articles: Joe Baird, "Counties, BLM Ease Tension over Signs," *Salt Lake Tribune*, June 6, 2005, B1; Baird, "Utah Sues Feds over Emery County Road Closures," *Salt Lake Tribune*, June 30, 2005, B3; Baird, "Warning: Bumps Ahead in Dispute over Rural Roads," *Salt Lake Tribune*, September 10, 2005, B1; Baird, "Kane Near Deal with BLM on Road Signs," *Salt Lake Tribune*, December 21, 2005, A1; Baird, "Utah Case Now Model for New BLM Road Policy," *Salt Lake Tribune*, March 22, 2006, A4; Baird, "Rural Utah Counties Submit Road Ownership Claims to BLM," *Salt Lake Tribune*, November 30, 2006; Baird, "Kane Backs Off OHV Stand," *Salt Lake Tribune*, December 13, 2006; Joe Baird and Mark Havnes, "Kane County Up Ante in Road Feud with Feds," *Salt Lake Tribune*, March 19, 2005, B1; Baird and Havnes, "Grand Staircase to Nature," *Salt Lake Tribune*, September 16, 2006; Joe Baird, Mark Havnes, and Robert Gehrke, "Rebellion in Kane County," *Salt Lake Tribune*, November 21, 2005, A1; Felicity Barringer, "In Utah, Trying to Undo a Federal Claim Bit by Bit," *New York Times*, November 24, 2005, A22; Joe Bauman, "Utah Drops Lawsuit against Feds over 6 BLM Roads," *Deseret Morning News*, December 19, 2007; Thomas Burr, "Lawmaker Seeks to Curb BLM Power," *Salt Lake Tribune*, June 16, 2007; "End Run," *Salt Lake Tribune*, February 16, 2008; "Environmentalists: Court Rules Issue Is Settled, Suit Is Moot," *Salt Lake Tribune*, August 17, 2006; Judy Fahys and Joe Baird, "Road War Ruling Favors the Feds," *Salt Lake Tribune*, May 17, 2008; "Feud over Monument Signs Just Keeps Heating Up," *Salt Lake Tribune*, November 15, 2006, D1; "GAO Says Roads Deal Illegal," *Salt Lake Tribune*, February 11, 2003, B1; Robert Gehrke, "Senate Democrat Weighs In on Fight over Kane Signs," *Salt Lake Tribune*, June 8, 2005, C1; Gehrke, "Monument Road Dispute May Lead to Action against Kane County," *Salt Lake Tribune*, June 30, 2005, B3; Gehrke, "Activists Suing Kane County over Roads," *Salt Lake Tribune*, October 14, 2005, C2; Gehrke, "Bill Would Boost Power of Counties, States to Claim Roads," *Salt Lake Tribune*, October 4, 2006; Gehrke, "Lawmaker Assails Judge's Ruling on Road in National Monument," *Salt Lake Tribune*, May 21, 2008; Robert Gehrke

and Joe Baird, "Kane County, BLM Land Dispute Heats Up," *Salt Lake Tribune*, April 27, 2005, A1; Mike Gorrell, "Feds Sue to Halt Road Work in Wild Utah Areas," *Salt Lake Tribune*, October 19, 1996, A1; Hillary Gubler, "County, Officials Fight for Road Access," *Spectrum*, September 10, 2003; Mark Havnes, "County Is Again Raising Kane over Roads," *Salt Lake Tribune*, February 16, 2005, B4; Havnes, "Kane Readies Monument Suit," *Salt Lake Tribune*, November 8, 2005, B5; Havnes, "Road Battle Roused Commissioner out of His Retirement," *Salt Lake Tribune*, November 21, 2005, A6; Havnes, "Some Kane County Residents Don't Like Officials' Road Stance," *Salt Lake Tribune*, December 14 2005, D4; Havnes, "New Escalante Monument Manager Named," *Salt Lake Tribune*, August 15, 2006; Havnes, "A Decade Cools the Controversy," *Salt Lake Tribune*, September 14, 2006; Havnes, "Kane County, BLM Can't Agree on Road-Maintenance Solution," *Salt Lake Tribune*, January 26, 2009; Patty Henetz, "Judge Rebuffs Kane, Garfield Claims on Grand Staircase-Escalante Roads," *Salt Lake Tribune*, July 3, 2007; Henetz, "Kane, Garfield to Appeal Ruling on Road Ownership," *Salt Lake Tribune*, July 11, 2007; Henetz, "BLM Allows Claim, Hands Road to Kane County," *Salt Lake Tribune*, September 14, 2007; Henetz, "Activists Assail Kane Road Signs," *Salt Lake Tribune*, September 25, 2007; Henetz, "Utah Guv Stakes a Claim on Roads," *Salt Lake Tribune*, January 28, 2008; Henetz, "Bill to Help Fund Road Fight with Feds Advances," *Salt Lake Tribune*, February 3, 2009; Henetz, "Kane, Garfield Lose Again in Monument Fight," *Salt Lake Tribune*, April 13, 2009; Henetz, "Road Warriors to Roar vs. BLM Ban," *Salt Lake Tribune*, May 6, 2009; Henetz, "Peaceful Picnickers to Take Stand against Off-Roaders," *Salt Lake Tribune*, May 7, 2009; Henetz, "U.S. Attorney Reviewing Evidence from Protest Ride," *Salt Lake Tribune*, May 11, 2009; Christine Hoekenga, "The Road More Traveled," *High Country News*, September 25, 2007; Dawn House and Joe Baird, "Rural Road-Sign Rage Erupting Again," *Salt Lake Tribune*, July 16, 2005, B1; "Incendiary Inanities," *Salt Lake Tribune*, July 19, 2005, A12; Brent Israelsen, "Removal of Signs Reignites Road War," *Salt Lake Tribune*, August 20, 2003, A1; Israelsen, "Monument Fray Heats Up," *Salt Lake Tribune*, September 9, 2003, A1; Israelsen, "Kane Residents Split on BLM," *Salt Lake Tribune*, September 29, 2003, D1; Israelsen, "BLM, Greens Win Round in Route Dispute," *Salt Lake Tribune*, February 25, 2004; Israelsen, "Monument Probe Ends," *Salt Lake Tribune*, March 5, 2004; Israelsen, "Monument Wins in Court," *Salt Lake Tribune*, April 20, 2004; "Kane County Loses Sign Request," *Salt Lake Tribune*, June 19, 2008; "Kane County Rescinds OHV Ordinance," *Southern Utah News*, December 20, 2006; "Latest Lawsuit Is Un-American," *Southern*

Utah News, November 23, 2005; "Merging on Monument Roads?" *Salt Lake Tribune*, September 26, 1999, AA1; "Monument Neighbors Aren't Adding Opinions to Planning," *Salt Lake Tribune*, January 8, 1999, B3; Michelle Nijhuis, "Road Warriors Back on the Offensive," *High Country News*, February 3, 2003; Nancy Perkins, "BLM Bald Knob Decision a Precedent?" *Deseret Morning News*, November 1, 2007; "Road Deal Is Stalled by Court," *Salt Lake Tribune*, August 27, 2000, B2; "Road Warriors," *Salt Lake Tribune*, August 21, 2003, A1; Christopher Smith, "Deal Struck on Control of Roads on Public Land," *Salt Lake Tribune*, April 10, 2003, A1; Donna Kemp Spangler, "Removal of Signs Adding Fuel to Kane-BLM Feud," *Deseret Morning News*, August 23, 2003, B1; "Unfair to Kane," *Salt Lake Tribune*, August 27, 2003, A12; Glen Warchol, "Conservationists Smell Victory in Road Ruling," *Salt Lake Tribune*, June 28, 2001, D3; Jim Woolf, "Monument Roads Issue Resolved," *Salt Lake Tribune*, December 11, 1998, D3; Woolf, "Leavitt Takes On Dirt-Road Ownership," *Salt Lake Tribune*, March 17, 2000; and "A Wrong Road: Norton Policy Would Open Up Lands to Overuse," *Salt Lake Tribune*, April 27, 2006.

7. San Juan County also participated in this action and the subsequent litigation.
8. Gorrell, "Feds Sue."
9. Gorrell, "Feds Sue."
10. Gorrell, "Feds Sue."
11. "Monument Neighbors."
12. The BLM was aware that the transportation plan in the MMP might conflict with existing rights-of-way. A footnote in the "Transportation and Access" section of the final MMP states, "It is unknown whether any R.S. 2477 claims would be asserted in the Monument which are inconsistent with the transportation decisions made in the Approved Plan or whether any of those R.S. 2477 claims would be determined to be valid. To the extent inconsistent claims are made, the validity of those claims would have to be determined. If claims are determined to be valid R.S. 2477 highways, the Approved Plan will respect those as valid existing rights. Otherwise, the transportation system described in the Approved Plan will be the one administered in the Monument." BLM, Management Plan, 46.
13. Woolf, "Monument Roads Issue Resolved."
14. BLM, Management Plan.
15. Woolf, "Leavitt Takes On."
16. Gubler, "County, Officials Fight."
17. Warchol, "Conservationists Smell Victory."
18. Nijhuis, "Road Warriors Back."

19. Smith, "Deal Struck."
20. "2003 Memorandum of Understanding on RS 2477," SUWA, accessed February 3, 2024, https://suwa.org/mou/; Smith, "Deal Struck."
21. Spangler, "Removal of Signs Adding Fuel."
22. Israelsen, "Removal of Signs Reignites."
23. Gubler, "County, Officials Fight."
24. Spangler, "Removal of Signs Adding Fuel."
25. Spangler, "Removal of Signs Adding Fuel."
26. Young, *Inclusion and Democracy*, 50.
27. Spangler, "Removal of Signs Adding Fuel."
28. "Unfair to Kane."
29. Israelsen, "Removal of Signs Reignites."
30. Israelsen, "Removal of Signs Reignites."
31. SUWA to Kane County residents, October 2, 2003.
32. Letter to the editor, *Southern Utah News*, October 8, 2003.
33. Grand Staircase-Escalante Partners, accessed January 3, 2007, http://www.gsenm.org (the mission and website have since been updated).
34. Kane County and Garfield County commissioners, Kanab mayor, state representative, and state senator to BLM state director Sally Wisely, August 25, 2003.
35. Israelsen, "Monument Probe Ends."
36. "Road Warriors," August 21, 2003.
37. Israelsen, "Monument Fray Heats Up."
38. SUWA, "Kane Kounty Kapers."
39. Touraine, *What Is Democracy?*, 46.
40. McCarthy, "First World Political Ecology."
41. Jarosz and Lawson, "Sophisticated People versus Rednecks."
42. For example, Cramer, *Politics of Resentment*; Hochschild, *Strangers*; Pilgeram, *Pushed Out*; Sherman, *Dividing Paradise*; Sherman, *Those Who Work*; Wuthnow, *Left Behind*.
43. According to Utah Code 72-3-105(1), a class D road is "any road, way, or other land surface route that has been or is established by use or constructed and has been maintained to provide for usage by the public for vehicles with four or more wheels that is not a class A, class B, or class C road." Class A roads are state highways, class B roads are county roads, and class C roads are city streets.
44. Havnes, "County Is Again Raising Kane."
45. Baird and Havnes, "Kane County Up Ante."
46. Rose, *Property and Persuasion*.
47. Havnes, "County Is Again Raising Kane."

48. Mark Habbeshaw, "Rural Roads—a County Perspective," *Salt Lake Tribune*, April 17, 2005, AA5.
49. Baird, "Utah Sues Feds."
50. BLM state director Sally Wisely to Kane County, received April 26, 2005.
51. Baird, "Counties, BLM Ease Tension."
52. Sivaramakrishnan, "Crafting the Public Sphere," 433; Gehrke, "Monument Road Dispute."
53. Gehrke, "Senate Democrat Weighs In."
54. House and Baird, "Rural Road-Sign Rage."
55. "Incendiary Inanities," *Salt Lake Tribune*, July 19, 2005, A12.
56. Baird, "Warning."
57. Baird, "Warning."
58. Baird, Havnes, and Gehrke, "Rebellion in Kane County"
59. Gehrke, "Monument Road Dispute."
60. Advertisement, "Latest Lawsuit Is Un-American."
61. Havnes, "Some Kane County Residents."
62. Baird, "Kane Near Deal."
63. Baird, "Utah Case Now Model."
64. Baird, "Rural Utah Counties."
65. Gehrke, "Bill Would Boost Power."
66. Baird, "Kane Backs Off."
67. "Kane County Rescinds."
68. The Quiet Title Act (1972) allows a party to make a real property claim against the federal government, which otherwise has immunity from any legal claim made against it.
69. Henetz, "Judge Rebuffs Kane."
70. Bauman, "Utah Drops Lawsuit."
71. Henetz, "Utah County Stakes a Claim."
72. Henetz, "Utah County Stakes a Claim."
73. Fahys and Baird, "Road War Ruling."
74. Gehrke, "Lawmaker Assails Judge's Ruling."
75. Havnes, "Kane County, BLM."
76. Havnes, "Kane County, BLM."
77. Henetz, "Peaceful Picnickers."
78. Sivaramakrishnan, "Crafting the Public Sphere," 433.
79. "Kane County Wins Its First R.S. 2477 Road—the Skutumpah Road," *Southern Utah News*, August 31, 2010.
80. Brooke Adams, "Judge Rules Largely in Favor of Utah on Rural Roads Dispute," *Salt Lake Tribune*, March 22, 2013.

81. Brian Maffly, "Environmentalists, Federal Government Partially Prevail in 10th Circuit Road Ruling; Setback for State of Utah," *Salt Lake Tribune*, December 2, 2014.
82. John Swallow and Anthony Rampton, "Utah Deserves Title to Thousands of Road," *Salt Lake Tribune*, May 12, 2012.
83. "R.S. 2477: Bellwether Initiative and Trial," Utah Public Lands Policy Coordinating Office, accessed February 2, 2024, https://publiclands.utah.gov/rs-2477/.
84. Brian Maffly, "Bellwether Trial Starts on Utah's Claims to 12,000 Roads on Federal Land," *Salt Lake Tribune*, February 4, 2020.
85. Tocqueville, *Democracy in America*.
86. Brown, *Undoing the Demos*; Sandel, *What Money Can't Buy*.
87. Skillen, *Nation's Largest Landlord*.
88. For example, in an interview with the *Salt Lake Tribune*, a Kame County rancher described how he lost his grazing lease without recourse when the state of Utah traded its sections within GSENM to the federal government. Tom Wharton, "Small Ranchers Keep Battling a Grim Future," *Salt Lake Tribune*, February 3, 2001.
89. Peter Staler, "Land Sale of the Century," *Time*, August 23, 1982.

5. The Locals

1. C. Taylor, "No Community, No Democracy," 34.
2. For readers who would like to enjoy these stories too, the Southern Utah Oral History Project recorded interviews with many of these residents. See "Register of the Southern Utah Oral History Project (UUA Ms.130A)," 1998–2018, Special Collections, Gerald R. Sherratt Library, Southern Utah University, https://spcoll.li.suu.edu/collections/HO1ncH8BnM5_0W5sFc6P/items.
3. Professor Tim Heaton of Brigham Young University, who studies LDS demographics, estimated in 2005 that between one-half and two-thirds of Church members were active in the faith. Canham, "Mormon Portion."
4. Although its birth rate declined in recent years, Utah still has one of the highest birth rates in the United States. "Birth Rate by State," World Population Review, accessed February 16, 2023, https://worldpopulationreview.com/state-rankings/birth-rate-by-state.
5. Stephanie Simon, "Utah Town Divided over Values," *Seattle Times*, July 4, 2006, A6.
6. Burr et al., *Front Country Visitor Survey*.
7. The sawmill reopened, but employees were mostly from the Navajo reservation or immigrants from Mexico. Longtime residents were no longer

interested in sawmill jobs because the wages were too low. The sawmill closed again permanently after a fire.
8. For example, Doukas, *Worked Over*.
9. John Heilprin, "New Federal Parks a Monument to the Changing West," *Los Angeles Times*, August 11, 2002, B6.
10. Walker, "Reconsidering 'Regional' Political Ecologies," 17–18.
11. Bellah et al., *Habits of the Heart*, 91.
12. Bellah et al., *Habits of the Heart*, 134.
13. Bellah et al., *Habits of the Heart*, 200.
14. Bellah et al., *Habits of the Heart*, 335, 72.
15. Bellah et al., *Habits of the Heart*, 333, 191–92.
16. Dell LeFevre, Southern Utah Oral History Project (hereafter SUOHP), 1998.
17. C. Taylor, "No Community, No Democracy," 31.
18. C. Taylor, "No Community, No Democracy," 37.
19. C. Taylor, "No Community, No Democracy," 34.
20. C. Taylor, "No Community, No Democracy," 38.
21. C. Taylor, "No Community, No Democracy," 41.
22. U.S. Census Bureau, "U.S. Rural Population 1960–2024," Macrotrends, accessed March 6, 2024, https://www.macrotrends.net/global-metrics/countries/USA/united-states/rural-population.
23. C. Taylor, "No Community, No Democracy," 39.
24. C. Taylor, "No Community, No Democracy," 39.
25. Mouffe, *Democratic Paradox*, 102.
26. C. Taylor, "No Community, No Democracy," 39.

6. The Ranchers

1. Taylor Grazing Act of 1934, Public Law 73-482, "Grazing Lands," 43 USC Ch. 8A.
2. Tierney, "Sagebrush Solution."
3. LeFevre, SUOHP, 1998.
4. LeFevre, SUOHP.
5. LeFevre, SUOHP.
6. LeFevre, SUOHP.
7. Church, "Utah Ranchers Agree."
8. LeFevre, SUOHP.
9. LeFevre, SUOHP.
10. LeFevre, SUOHP.
11. Tierney, "Sagebrush Solution."
12. LeFevre, SUOHP.
13. LeFevre, SUOHP.

14. Heilprin, "New Federal Parks."
15. For example, Dietrich, *Final Forest*.
16. Berlin, "Two Concepts of Liberty," 131.
17. DOI, Decision in Docket Number UT-030-04-01.
18. Sayre, *Working Wilderness*.
19. Permittees work with a BLM rangeland specialist (formerly called a range conservationist, hence they are referred to as "range cons") to formulate an allotment management plan, which specifies dates when grazing can begin and must end, as well as a schedule for rotating livestock among different pastures on the allotment.
20. Tamarisk or saltcedar (*Tamarix ramosissima* Deneb) and Russian olive (*Elaeagnus angustifolia*) are both invasive species on the Colorado Plateau.
21. Sayre, "Viewpoint."
22. Nash, *Grand Canyon for Sale*.
23. Carr Childers, *Size of the Risk*.
24. Carr Childers, *Size of the Risk*, 219.

7. The Environmentalists

1. Dryzek, *Politics of the Earth*.
2. Dobson, "Democratising Green Theory."
3. Dobson, "Democratising Green Theory," 146.
4. Ball, "Democracy."
5. H. Wilson, "Environmental Democracy."
6. Information and quotes in this section that are not cited are drawn from personal interviews and personal knowledge; "The Hiker and the Cowman Should Be Friends," PBS interview, September 17, 2003; SUWA, "Landscape Finds It Voice"; and "Suit Targets Tar-Sand Oil Development," *Salt Lake Tribune*, March 18, 2007.
7. Trainor, "Conflicting Values," 302.
8. Trainor, "Conflicting Values."
9. Cronon, "Trouble with Wilderness," 80.
10. White, "Are You an Environmentalist?," 171.
11. White, "Are You an Environmentalist?," 185, 173.
12. Cronon, "Trouble with Wilderness," 85.
13. Guha, "Radical American Environmentalism," 82–83.
14. SUWA, "Why One Advocacy Group Steers Clear of Consensus Efforts," *High Country News*, May 30, 1994.
15. Jim Styles, "Take It or Leave It: SUWA Can You Spare a Dime?" *Canyon Country Zephyr*, April–May 2006.
16. For example, Brick et al., *Across the Great Divide*.

17. Brick and Weber, "Will Rain Follow?," 18.
18. Grant Johnson, letter to the editor, *Canyon Country Zephyr*, August–September 2005.
19. Trainor, "Conflicting Values," 302.
20. Information about the events described in the following paragraphs is drawn from personal interviews and from the following newspaper articles: "Activist Defies Monument Permit Rule, Distributes Leaflets," *Salt Lake Tribune*, September 3, 2000; Joe Baird, "Sierra Club Removes Member from Leadership," *Salt Lake Tribune*, June 15, 2003, B5; Kevin Cantera, "Wilderness Group Clash over Protest Booth Site," *Salt Lake Tribune*, May 30, 2000, B4; "Diehl, District 2 Candidate Is Used to Being on the Outside," *Salt Lake Tribune*, October 24, 2002, A12; Judy Fahys, "BLM, Activists Bring Dispute to the Table," *Salt Lake Tribune*, June 2, 2000, B2; Fahys, "Maverick Cows on Off-Limits Monument," *Salt Lake Tribune*, July 6, 2001, D1; Mark Havnes and Joanne Rideout, "Activist Who Threatened Hunger Strike Is Released from Jail," *Salt Lake Tribune*, May 31, 2000, D2; Brent Israelsen, "Environmentalists Not Welcome in Town of Escalante," *Salt Lake Tribune*, May 7, 1999, D1; Israelsen, "Greens Not Welcome in Escalante," *High Country News*, May 24, 1999; Israelsen, "Couple in Feud Loses Water," *Salt Lake Tribune*, September 17, 1999, B2; Israelsen, "In Wake of Arrests, Protestors Regain Voice at Monument Entry," *Salt Lake Tribune*, June 3, 2000, B1; Israelsen, "New Rules Irk Monument Protestors," *Salt Lake Tribune*, September 2, 2000, D2; Mary Brown Malouf, "A Sense of Duty Compels Utahns to Act," *Salt Lake Tribune*, March 18, 2003, B1; Kurt Repanshek, "Reservoir Project on Escalante Is Delayed for Further Studies," *Salt Lake Tribune*, April 11, 1999, C5; Michael Vigh and Hilary Groutage, "Activists Cited for Failing to Move Booth Near Staircase-Escalante," *Salt Lake Tribune*, May 28, 2000, B4; Rebecca Walsh, "Tired of Only Two Political Parties? There Are Others," *Salt Lake Tribune*, March 29, 2004, B1; and Glen Warchol, "Protestors March," *Salt Lake Tribune*, October 7, 2002, D1; as well as from Rangenet, accessed February 7, 2007, http://www.rangenet.org/directory/diehlp (site discontinued).
21. Repanshek, "Reservoir Project."
22. Israelsen, "Environmentalists Not Welcome."
23. Judy Fahys, "Canyon Quarrel," *Salt Lake Tribune*, July 10, 2000, B1.
24. Kelly Kennedy, "Home of Escalante Environmentalists Is Vandalized," *Salt Lake Tribune*, July 27, 1999, B2.
25. Karen Munson, letter to the editor, *Garfield County News*, August 5, 1999.
26. Pamela Manson and Lesley Mitchell, "Tax Protestors' Mantra—'No Way, We Won't Pay,'" *Salt Lake Tribune*, April 15, 2004, A1.

27. Bill Boyle, publisher of the *San Juan Record*, quoted in "Feedback: More on Greening," *Canyon Country Zephyr*, August–September 2005.
28. "Feedback: More on Greening."
29. DOI, Decision in Docket Numbers UT-030-04-01, UT-030-04-02, UT-030-04-03.
30. Ravetz, "What Is Post-Normal Science."
31. Robertson and Hull, "Public Ecology," 399.
32. Mouffe, *Democratic Paradox*.
33. Quivira Coalition, accessed February 13, 2008, http://www.quiviracoalition.org (the mission and website have since been updated).
34. This is the argument made by anthropologist Thomas Sheridan in "Cows, Condos."
35. Grand Canyon Trust, accessed December 8, 2007, http://www.grandcanyontrust.org (the mission and website have since been updated).
36. Ethan Gilsdorf, "The Man Who Saves the National Park Vistas," *Christian Science Monitor*, June 28, 2007, 20; Joe Baird, "Invasive Weeds Threaten Native Species, Cause Havoc," *Salt Lake Tribune*, July 6, 2006.
37. Gilsdorf, "Man Who Saves," 20.
38. Baird, "Invasive Weeds."
39. Gilsdorf, "Man Who Saves," 20.
40. Baird, "Invasive Weeds."
41. Gilsdorf, "Man Who Saves," 20.
42. Dobson, "Democratising Green Theory."
43. These quotes are all from chapter 6.
44. Minteer and Manning, "Pragmatism in Environmental Ethics," 202, 193, 202.
45. Pickering, Bäckstrand, and Schlosberg, "Between Environmental and Ecological Democracy."

8. The BLM Employees

1. I refer to the interdisciplinary team writing the EIS as the EIS Team, as team members did. These quotes and others throughout the chapter are from observation during EIS Team meetings and interviews with some of its member between 2003 and 2005.
2. Gerth and Mills, *From Max Weber*, 215, 220.
3. Weber, *Economy and Society*, 999, 225, 1403, 975, 979, 1403.
4. The heading of this section is the title of the Department of the Interior's history of the BLM, Muhn and Stuart, *Opportunity and Challenge*.
5. Federal Land Policy and Management, 43 USC 1702(c).
6. BLM, Management Plan.
7. BLM, *Interpreting Indicators of Rangeland Health*.

8. Glen Canyon National Recreation Area adjoins GSENM and is administered by the National Park Service, but the BLM is responsible for administering livestock grazing there.
9. BLM, accessed October 7, 2007, http://www.blm.gov/nhp/efoia/wy/2004im/wy2004-021.htm (site discontinued).
10. Woller, "Toward a Reconciliation," 87.
11. Woller, "Toward a Reconciliation," 89.
12. Woller, "Toward a Reconciliation," 90.
13. Woller, "Toward a Reconciliation," 91 (my emphasis).
14. BLM, Proposed Revisions to Grazing Regulations for the Public Lands, Draft Environmental Impact Statement DES 03-62; BLM, Proposed Revisions to Grazing Regulations for the Public Lands, Final Environmental Impact Statement FES 04-39.
15. BLM, *Interpreting Indicators of Rangeland Health*.
16. "Process for Evaluating Status of Land Health and Making Determinations of Causal Factors When Land Health Standards Are Not Achieved," *BLM Manual*, Rel. 4-107, January 19, 2001, III-16.
17. The *potential natural vegetative community* refers to the climax plant community for a particular ecological site as it was previously understood. The National Resource Conservation Service developed the concept of ecological site to provide information on native plant communities for ecological restoration and for predicting change in plant communities due to disturbance. It defines an ecological site as "a distinctive kind of land with specific physical characteristics that differs from other kinds of land in its ability to produce a distinctive kind and amount of vegetation." It is a product of soils, climate, topography, and natural disturbances, such as herbivory, fire, or drought. "Ecological Site Description," National Resource Conservation Service, U.S. Department of Agriculture, accessed March 10, 2024, https://www.nrcs.usda.gov/getting-assistance/technical-assistance/ecological-sciences/ecological-site-descriptions.

The BLM defines *desired future conditions* as "the condition of rangeland resources on a landscape scale that meet management objectives. It is based on ecological, social, and economic considerations during the land planning process." BLM, "Glossary of Common BLM Terms," accessed March 10, 2024, https://eplanning.blm.gov/public_projects/lup/22652/34861/36285/1.2_Glossary_of_Common_BLM_Terms.pdf. By definition, this is a decision based on considerations other than science. *Desired plant community* is the species composition most compatible with these management objectives. *Precontact condition* refers to the plant community that existed at the time

of European settlement. This is what environmentalists and laypersons often refer to as "natural."
18. For example, McConnell, *Private Power*; Klyza, *Who Controls the Public Lands?*; Donohue, *Western Range Revisited*.
19. Sivaramakrishnan, "Crafting the Public Sphere," 433.
20. Muhn and Stuart, *Opportunity and Challenge*; Wondolleck and Yaffee, *Making Collaboration Work*.
21. Federal Land Policy and Management, 43 USC 1702(c).
22. The number of allotments included in the EIS process changed as the understanding of the process, as well as allotment identities and boundaries, changed.
23. Young, "Communication and the Other."
24. Muhn and Stuart, *Opportunity and Challenge*.
25. Mansbridge, *Beyond Adversary Democracy*.
26. *Forage utilization* is the proportion of the current year's forage production that is consumed or destroyed by grazing animals. Forage is all herbaceous and woody biomass that is available and acceptable to grazing animals. The Rangelands Partnership, "Utilization," Rangelands Gateway, accessed March 10, 2024, https://rangelandsgateway.org/inventorymonitoring/utilization. *Stubble height* is the height of a plant left after it has been grazed. It is one way of estimating utilization. Huss, "Rangeland Ecosystem."
27. Skillen, *Nation's Largest Landlord*, 167.
28. Sivaramakrishnan, "Crafting the Public Sphere," 433.
29. W. Wilson, "Study of Administration."
30. Skillen, *Nation's Largest Landlord*.
31. For example, Skillen, *Federal Ecosystem Management*.
32. BLM, Grand Staircase-Escalante National Monument and Kanab-Escalante Planning Area Draft Resource Management Plans and Environmental Impact Statement, Executive Summary.
33. Molly Marcello, "Interior Sets New Limits on Deadlines, Length for EIS Submissions," *Times Independent*, September 14, 2017.
34. BLM director to Utah state BLM director, memorandum on "Interim Management of the Grand Staircase-Escalante National Monument," December 16, 2021, https://www.blm.gov/sites/blm.gov/files/docs/2021-12/GSENM_Interim_Guidance_12-16-21_Final508_0.pdf.
35. Mouffe, *Democratic Paradox*, 45.

Conclusion

1. Joe Baird and Mark Havnes, "Grand Staircase to Nature," *Salt Lake Tribune*, September 16, 2006.

2. Eric Pianin, "Long Arm of the Government Rankles Western Landowners," *Washington Post*, April 29, 2001, A5.
3. Laurie Sullivan Maddox, "It's a Monumental Day for Utah," *Salt Lake Tribune*, September 19, 1996, A1.
4. Baird and Havnes, "Grand Staircase to Nature."
5. Baird and Havnes, "Grand Staircase to Nature."
6. Mark Havnes, "A Decade Cools the Controversy," *Salt Lake Tribune*, September 14, 2006.
7. Faragher, *Rereading Frederick Jackson Turner*, 91–92.
8. Some examples include Blackhawk, *Rediscovery of America*; Cattelino, "Thoughts on the U.S."; Dunbar-Ortiz, *Indigenous People's History*; Hixon, *American Settler Colonialism*; Rana, *Two Faces*.
9. Mounk, *People vs. Democracy*, 26.
10. Tocqueville, *Democracy in America*, 19.
11. Ashwood, *For-Profit Democracy*; Braunstein, *Prophets and Patriots*; Brown, *Undoing the Demos*; Brown, *In the Ruins*; Cramer, *Politics of Resentment*; Hochschild, *Strangers*; Maskovshy and Bjork-James, *Beyond Populism*; Mounk, *People vs. Democracy*; Mutz, "Status Threat"; Piketty, *Capital and Ideology*; Pilgeram, *Pushed Out*; Sandel, *Tyranny of Merit*; Sherman, *Those Who Work*; Sherman, *Dividing Paradise*; Silva, *We're Still Here*; Smarsh, *Heartland*; Westermeyer, *Back to America*; Wuthnow, *Left Behind*.
12. Brian Maffly, "A Report on Monuments Showed the Benefits of Utah's Grand Staircase—but Then the Feds Blacked Out Those Portions," *Salt Lake Tribune*, July 24, 2018.
13. Rasker et al., *Prosperity*; Rasker et al., *Public Lands Conservation*; Headwaters Economics, *Grand Staircase-Escalante*; Jakus and Akhundjanov, "Neither Boom nor Bane."
14. Chris D'Angelo, "Trump's Monument Review Was a Big Old Sham," *Huffington Post*, March 14, 2019, https://www.huffpost.com/entry/trump-national-monuments-review_n_5c8835c8e4b038892f486792.
15. Zinke, "Report Summary."
16. Maffly, "Report on Monuments."
17. Zinke, "Report Summary."
18. Zinke, "Report Summary."
19. Proclamation No. 9682, 82 Fed. Reg. 235 (December 4, 2017).
20. Amy Joi O'Donoghue, "'Political Football'? Biden Wants Review of Bears Ears, Grand Staircase Boundaries," *Deseret News*, January 20, 2021.
21. Christopher A. Ketcham, "Trojan Horse Threatens the Nation's Parks," *New York Times*, January 18, 2018.

22. BLM, Grand Staircase-Escalante National Monument and Kanab-Escalante Planning Area Draft Resource Management Plans and Environmental Impact Statement, Executive Summary.
23. Makley, *Open Spaces*; Leshy, *Our Common Ground*.
24. Tania Lown-Hecht, "Look Closer: The New Public Land Heist Is a Wolf in Sheep's Clothing," Outdoor Alliance (blog), October 22, 2018, https://www.outdooralliance.org/blog/2018/10/22/look-closer-the-new-public-land-heist-is-a-wolf-in-sheeps-clothing; Ben Goldfarb, "How the Public Is Losing Its Voice on Public Lands," *Audubon*, September 20, 2018, https://www.audubon.org/news/how-public-losing-its-voice-public-lands.
25. Disapproving the Rule Submitted by the Department of the Interior Relating to Bureau of Land Management Regulations That Establish the Procedures Used to Prepare, Revise, or Amend Land Use Plans Pursuant to the Federal Land Policy and Management Act of 1976, H.J. Res. 44, 115th Cong. (2017–18); Removing Barriers to Energy Independence Act, H.R. 6087, 115th Cong. (2017–18); Bus Operator and Pedestrian Protection Act, H.R. 6106, 115th Cong. (2017–18); Bobby McEnaney, "Congress and Trump Curtail Public Input on Public Lands," Natural Resources Defense Council (expert blog), June 19, 2018, https://www.nrdc.org/experts/bobby-mcenaney/congress-and-trump-curtail-public-input-public-lands.
26. Marcello, "Interior Sets New Limits."
27. Alastair Gee, "Dozens of Public Lands Advocates Say Trump Administration 'Shut Them Out,'" *Guardian*, February 26, 2108, https://www.theguardian.com/environment/2018/feb/26/public-lands-advisory-groups-ryan-zinke-trump-shut-out.
28. Western Watersheds Project, "Judge Blocks Trump Policy Cutting Public Out of Oil and Gas Leasing Decisions on Public Lands," September 24, 2018, https://www.westernwatersheds.org/2018/09/judge-blocks-trump-policy-cutting-public-out-of-oil-and-gas-leasing-decisions-on-public-lands/.
29. Goldfarb, "How the Public Is Losing."
30. BLM, Grand Staircase-Escalante National Monument and Kanab-Escalante Planning Area Proposed Resource Management Plans and Environmental Impact Statement; U.S. Forest Service, *U.S. Forest Service National Visitor Use Monitoring Survey*; National Park Service, "Annual Visitation Summary Report for 2022," accessed May 8, 2023, https://irma.nps.gov/Stats/SSRS Reports/National%20Reports/Annual%20Visitation%20Summary%20Report%20(1979%20-%20Last%20Calendar%20Year).
31. Department of the Interior, "Bureau of Land Management: Bureau Highlights, 2018."
32. Comay, *National Park Service Appropriations*.

33. Vincent, *Deferred Maintenance*.
34. Tom Vilsack, "The Cost of Fighting Wildfires Is Sapping Forest Service Budget," U.S. Forest Service, August 6, 2015, https://www.fs.usda.gov/features/cost-fighting-wildfires-sapping-forest-service-budget.
35. Outdoor Alliance, "Great American Outdoors Act," accessed August 8, 2021, https://www.outdooralliance.org/great-american-outdoors-act.
36. A. Taylor, *Democracy May Not Exist*, 1.
37. Mitt Romney, "Utah Delegation, State Officials Oppose Executive Order on Bears Ears, Grand Staircase-Escalante National Monuments," newsletter, January 20, 2021, https://www.romney.senate.gov/utah-delegation-state-officials-oppose-executive-order-bears-ears-grand-staircase-escalante; O'Donoghue, "'Political Football'?"; K. Sophie Will, "Who Can Save Grand Staircase-Escalante and Bears Ears from Political Chaos, Vacillation?" *St. George Spectrum & Daily News*, March 5, 2021.
38. Proclamation No. 10286, 86 Fed. Reg. 197 (October 8, 2021); Proclamation No. 10285, 86 Fed. Reg. 57321 (October 8, 2021).
39. Kadi Franson, "Garfield Co. Reps Hold Community Meeting to Discuss the GSENM Draft RMP," *Insider*, November 2, 2023, A1.
40. Diamond, "Democracy's Third Wave Today."
41. Held, *Models of Democracy*, xi.
42. Fukuyama, *End of History*.
43. Diamond, "Democracy's Third Wave Today." For example, in Turkey, India, Hungary, Poland, the Philippines, Sri Lanka, Thailand, and Venezuela, democratically elected leaders have gradually weakened democratic institutions to increase their own power.
44. Freedom House, *Freedom in the World 2022*.
45. Democracy Matrix, "Ranking of Countries by Quality of Democracy: Complete Ranking: Total Value Index 2020 (Context Measurement)," Deutsche Forschungsgemeinschaft, accessed May 3, 2023, https://www.democracymatrix.com/ranking; Economist Intelligence Unit, "Democracy Index 2022," accessed May 3, 2023, https://www.eiu.com/n/campaigns/democracy-index-2022/.
46. Walter, *How Civil Wars Start*. The decline in democracy in the United States has also been documented by International IDEA, "The Global State of Democracy 2023," https://www.idea.int/; Varieties of Democracy (V-Dem), "Democracy Report 2023," March 2023, https://www.v-dem.net/; UNESCO, "The Global Democracy Index," last updated 2020, https://www.unesco.org/en/world-media-trends/global-democracy-index; and Brookings Institution, "The Brookings Democracy Dashboard," June 2, 2016, https://www.brookings.edu/interactives/the-brookings-democracy-dashboard/.

47. Freedom House, "Freedom in the World 2023," accessed May 3, 2023, https://freedomhouse.org/country/united-states/freedom-world/2023.
48. Galston and Kamarck, "Is Democracy Failing?"
49. For example, Foa and Mounk, "Danger of Deconsolidation"; Pew Charitable Trust, "In 2017, Ideological Right More Supportive of Strong Leader Ruling without Constraints," December 2, 2021, https://www.pewresearch.org/global/2021/12/07/global-public-opinion-in-an-era-of-democratic-anxiety/pg_2021-12-07_democracy_0-05/; Norris, *Democratic Deficit*; Elizabeth J. Zechmeister and Noam Lupu, "Support for Democracy Is Waning across the Americas," *Conversation*, March 8, 2022, https://theconversation.com/support-for-democracy-is-waning-across-the-americas-174992.
50. Pew Research Center, "Many See Need for Significant Political, Economic and Health Care Reform," October 20, 2021, https://www.pewresearch.org/global/2021/10/21/citizens-in-advanced-economies-want-significant-changes-to-their-political-systems/pg_2021-10-21_democracy_0-01/.
51. Walter, *How Civil Wars Start*.
52. Piketty, *Capital and Ideology*. In addition to Brown, Mounk, and Mouffe, the three scholars mentioned in the text, political theorist Nancy Fraser made an important contribution on what she called a "crisis of hegemony." Fraser, *Old Is Dying*.
53. Brown, *Undoing the Demos*.
54. Brown, *In the Ruins*.
55. Mounk, *People vs. Democracy*.
56. Mounk, *People vs. Democracy*, 56–57.
57. Mouffe, *For a Left Populism*, 10. Mouffe defined "populism" as a discursive strategy in which a political frontier is constructed that divides society into two camps and calls for the mobilization of the "underdog" against those in power.
58. Held, *Models of Democracy*, xi.
59. Williams, *Open Space of Democracy*.
60. Mouffe, *Democratic Paradox*; Mouffe, *For a Left Populism*; Mouffe, *Towards a Green*. Mouffe explained that emotions are usually associated with individuals, while affects and passions are more appropriate for attachments to collective identities.
61. These include Ashwood, *For-Profit Democracy*; Braunstein, *Prophets and Patriots*; Cramer, *Politics of Resentment*; Etelson, *Beyond Contempt*; Hochschild, *Strangers*; Pilgeram, *Pushed Out*; Sherman, *Those Who Work*; Sherman, *Dividing Paradise*; Silva, *We're Still Here*; Walker, *Sagebrush Collaboration*; Westermeyer, *Back to America*; Wuthnow, *Left Behind*. I am not aware of similar literature, based on ethnographic research with members of liberal

and progressive groups, that aims to make their views understandable to conservatives.

62. Brugger, "'Other' and the 'Enemy.'"
63. Palmer, *Healing the Heart*.
64. Paley, "Toward an Anthropology."
65. Braunstein, *Prophets and Patriots*, 188.
66. Etelson, *Beyond Contempt*, 11.
67. Braunstein, *Prophets and Patriots*; Palmer, *Healing the Heart*.
68. Braunstein, *Prophets and Patriots*, 188.
69. Palmer, *Healing the Heart*, 74, 59, 76.
70. A. Taylor, *Democracy May Not Exist*, 10–11.
71. Mouffe, *For a Left Populism*.
72. A. Taylor, *Democracy May Not Exist*.
73. Brown, *In the Ruins*, 45, 41.
74. Mouffe, *For a Left Populism*; Mouffe, *Towards a Green*.

Bibliography

Abrams, Philip. "Notes on the Difficulty of Studying the State (1977)." *Journal of Historical Sociology* 1, no. 1 (1998): 58–89.

Alexander, Thomas G. *Utah: The Right Place*. Salt Lake City: Gibbs Smith, 1996.

Arrington, Leonard J. *Great Basin Kingdom: An Economic History of the Latter-day Saints, 1980–1900*. Cambridge MA: Harvard University Press, 1958.

Arrington, Leonard J., and Davis Bitton. *The Mormon Experience: A History of the Latter-day Saints*. 2nd ed. Urbana: University of Illinois Press, 1992.

Ashwood, Loka. *For-Profit Democracy: Why the Government Is Losing the Trust of Rural America*. New Haven CT: Yale University Press, 2018.

Babbitt, Bruce. *Cities in the Wilderness: A New Vision of Land Use in America*. Washington DC: Island, 2005.

Bailyn, Bernard, Robert Dallek, David Brion Davis, David Herbert Donald, John L. Thomas, and Gordon S. Woods. *The Great Republic: A History of the American People*. 2 vols. 4th ed. Lexington MA: D. C. Heath, 1992.

Baldwin, Pamela. *Highway Rights of Way: The Controversy over Claims under R.S. 2477*. Washington DC: Congressional Research Service, Library of Congress, 1993.

Ball, Terence. "Democracy." In *Political Theory and the Ecological Challenge*, edited by Andrew Dobson and Robyn Eckersley, 131–47. Cambridge: Cambridge University Press, 2006.

Barnes, F. A. *Canyon Country Geology*. Salt Lake City: Wasatch, 1978.

Bellah, Robert N., Richard Madsen, William M. Sullivan, Ann Swidler, and Steven M. Tipton. *Habits of the Heart: Individualism and Commitment in American Life*. Updated ed. Berkeley: University of California Press, 1996.

Berlin, Isaiah. "Two Concepts of Liberty." In *Four Essays on Liberty*, 118–72. London: Oxford University Press, 1969.

Bessire, Lucas. *Running Out: In Search of Water on the High Plains*. Princeton NJ: Princeton University Press, 2021.

Bjork-James, Sophie. *The Divine Institution: While Evangelicalism's Politics of the Family*. New Brunswick NJ: Rutgers University Press, 2021.

Blackhawk, Ned. *The Rediscovery of America: Native Peoples and the Unmaking of U.S. History*. New Haven CT: Yale University Press, 2023.

Bradley, Martha Sonntag. *A History of Kane County*. Salt Lake City: Utah State Historical Society, 1999.

Braun, Bruce. "Producing Vertical Territory: Geology and Governmentality in Late Victorian Canada." *Ecumene* 7, no. 1 (2000): 7–50.

Braunstein, Ruth. *Prophets and Patriots: Faith in Democracy across the Political Divide*. Berkeley: University of California Press, 2017.

Brick, Philip, and Edward P. Weber. "Will Rain Follow the Plow? Unearthing a New Environmental Movement." In *Across the Great Divide: Explorations in Collaborative Conservation and the American West*, edited by Philip Brick, Donald Snow, and Sarah Van De Wettering, 13–24. Washington DC: Island, 2001.

Brick, Philip, Donald Snow, and Sarah Van De Wettering, eds. *Across the Great Divide: Explorations in Collaborative Conservation and the American West*. Washington DC: Island, 2001.

Brown, Wendy. "Finding the Man in the State." In *States of Injury: Power and Freedom in Late Modernity*, 166–96. Princeton NJ: Princeton University Press, 1995.

———. *In the Ruins of Neoliberalism: The Rise of Antidemocratic Politics in the West*. New York: Columbia University Press, 2019.

———. *Undoing the Demos: Neoliberalism's Stealth Revolution*. Brooklyn: Zone, 2015.

Brugger, Julie. "The 'Other' and the 'Enemy': Reflections on Fieldwork in Utah." *North American Dialogue* 10, no. 1 (2007): 6–10.

———. "Public Land and American Democratic Imaginaries: A Case Study of Conflict over the Management of Grand Staircase-Escalante National Monument." PhD diss., University of Washington, Seattle, 2009.

Brunson, Mark, and George Wallace. "Perceptions of Ranching: Public Views and Personal Reflections." In *Ranching West of the 100th Meridian: Culture, Ecology, and Economics*, edited by Richard L. Knight, Wendell C. Gilgert, and Ed Marston, 91–105. Washington DC: Island, 2002.

Bureau of Land Management (BLM). Grand Staircase-Escalante National Monument and Kanab-Escalante Planning Area Draft Resource Management Plans and Environmental Impact Statement, Executive Summary. Accessed August 31, 2018. https://eplanning.blm.gov/epl-front-office/projects/lup/94706/155930/190910/GSENM-KEPA_Executive_Summary-508.pdf (site discontinued).

———. Grand Staircase-Escalante National Monument and Kanab-Escalante Planning Area Proposed Resource Management Plans and Environmental

Impact Statement. Vol. 2, appendixes A–E. Accessed August 31, 2018. https://eplanning.blm.gov/epl-front-office/projects/lup/94706/155936/190916/GSENM-KEPA_RMPs-EIS_Vol_2-508.pdf (site discontinued).

———. Grand Staircase-Escalante National Monument and Kanab-Escalante Planning Area Proposed Resource Management Plans and Final Environmental Impact Statement, Executive Summary. Salt Lake City: Bureau of Land Management, October 2019. https://eplanning.blm.gov/public_projects/lup/94706/20005728/250006731/01_GSENM-KEPA_modified_Proposed_RMPs-Final_EIS_Executive_Summary.pdf.

———. Grand Staircase-Escalante National Monument Draft Monument Management Plan Amendment and Draft Rangeland Health Environmental Impact Statement BLM-UT-PL-08-007-1610, UT-030-00-028-EIS, DES-08-36. Salt Lake City: Bureau of Land Management, 2008.

———. Grand Staircase-Escalante National Monument Management Plan. Kanab UT: Bureau of Land Management, 1999.

———. *Interpreting Indicators of Rangeland Health*. Technical Reference 1734-6, Version 3. Denver: Bureau of Land Management, 2000.

———. Proposed Revisions to Grazing Regulations for the Public Lands, Draft Environmental Impact Statement DES 03-62. 2003.

———. Proposed Revisions to Grazing Regulations for the Public Lands, Final Environmental Impact Statement FES 04-39. 2004.

Burr, Steven W., Dale J. Blahna, Doug Reiter, Erin C. Leary, and Nathan M. Wagoner. *A Front Country Visitor Survey for Grand Staircase-Escalante National Monument*. IORT Professional Report PR2006-01. Logan UT: Institute for Outdoor Recreation and Tourism, Utah State University, 2006.

Carr Childers, Leisl. *The Size of the Risk: Histories of Multiple Use in the Great Basin*. Norman: University of Oklahoma Press, 2015.

Cattelino, Jessica R. "Thoughts on the U.S. as a Settler Society." *North American Dialogue* 14, no. 1 (2011): 1–6.

Comay, Laura B. *National Park Service Appropriations: Ten-Year Trends*. Congressional Research Service. Last updated July 10, 2018. https://crsreports.congress.gov/product/pdf/R/R42757/32.

Cramer, Katherine J. *The Politics of Resentment: Rural Consciousness in Wisconsin and the Rise of Scott Walker*. Chicago: University of Chicago Press, 2016.

Cronon, William. "The Trouble with Wilderness; or, Getting Back to the Wrong Nature." In *Uncommon Ground: Rethinking the Human Place in Nature*, edited by William Cronon, 69–90. New York: W. W. Norton, 1996.

Dahl, Robert A. "A Democratic Paradox?" *Political Science Quarterly* 115, no. 1 (2000): 35–40.

Davis, Charles. "Politics and Public Rangeland Policy." In *Western Public Lands and Environmental Politics*, 2nd ed., edited by Charles Davis, 87–109. Boulder CO: Westview, 2001.

Davis, Sandra K. "Fighting over Public Lands: Interest Groups, States, and the Federal Government." In *Western Public Lands and Environmental Politics*, 2nd ed., edited by Charles Davis, 11–34. Boulder CO: Westview, 2001.

Department of the Interior (DOI). "Bureau of Land Management: Bureau Highlights, 2018." Accessed February 13, 2019. https://www.doi.gov/sites/doi.gov/files/uploads/fy2018_bib_bh007.pdf (site discontinued).

———. Decision in Docket Numbers UT-030-04-01, UT-030-04-02, UT-030-04-03. Office of Hearings and Appeals. January 26, 2006.

———. Interior Board of Land Appeals Decisions: Southern Utah Wilderness Alliance, et al. 166 IBLA 140. July 12, 2005.

———. "Secretary Haaland Wraps Three-Day Visit to Utah." DOI News, April 9, 2021. https://www.doi.gov/news/secretary-haaland-wraps-three-day-visit-utah.

Diamond, Larry. "Democracy's Third Wave Today." *Current History* 110, no. 739 (2011): 299–307.

Dietrich, William. *The Final Forest: The Battle for the Last Great Trees of the Northwest*. New York: Penguin, 1992.

Dobson, Andrew. "Democratising Green Theory: Preconditions and Principles." In *Democracy and Green Political Thought: Sustainability, Rights, and Citizenship*, edited by Brian Doherty and Marius de Geus, 132–48. London: Routledge, 1996.

Doelling, Hellmut H., Robert E. Blackett, Alden H. Hamblin, J. Douglas Powell, and Gayle L. Pollock. "Geology of Grand Staircase-Escalante National Monument, Utah." In *Geology of Utah's Parks and Monuments*, 2nd ed., edited by D. A. Sprinkel, T. C. Chidsey Jr., and P. B. Anderson, 189–231. Salt Lake City: Utah Geological Association, 2003.

Donohue, Debra. *The Western Range Revisited: Removing Livestock from Public Lands to Conserve Native Biodiversity*. Norman: University of Oklahoma Press, 1999.

Doukas, Dimitra. *Worked Over: The Corporate Sabotage of an American Community*. Ithaca NY: Cornell University Press, 2003.

Dryzek, John S. *The Politics of the Earth: Environmental Discourses*. Oxford: Oxford University Press, 1997.

Dunbar-Ortiz, Roxanne. *An Indigenous People's History of the United States*. Boston: Beacon, 2015.

Eaton, Marietta W. "Consultation on Grand Staircase-Escalante National Monument from Planning to Implementation." *American Indian Quarterly* 25, no. 1 (2001): 28–34.

Edwards, Jeanette, Angelique Haugerud, and Shanti Parikh. "Introduction: The 2016 Brexit Referendum and Trump Election." *American Ethnologist* 44, no. 2 (2017): 195–200.

Etelson, Erica. *Beyond Contempt: How Liberals Can Communicate across the Great Divide*. Gabriola Island BC: New Society, 2019.

Faragher, John Mack. *Rereading Frederick Jackson Turner: "The Significance of the Frontier in American History" and Other Essays*. New York: Henry Holt, 1994.

Fillmore, Robert. *The Geology of the Parks, Monuments, and Wildlands of Southern Utah*. Salt Lake City: University of Utah Press, 2000.

Foa, Roberto Stefan, and Yascha Mounk. "The Danger of Deconsolidation: The Democratic Disconnect." *Journal of Democracy* 27, no. 3 (2016): 5–17.

Foucault, Michel. *The Birth of Biopolitics: Lectures at the Collège de France, 1978–79*. Edited by Michel Senellart. Translated by Graham Burchell. Basingstoke: Palgrave Macmillan, 2008.

———. "Governmentality." In *The Foucault Effect: Studies in Governmentality*, edited by Graham Burchell, Colin Gordon, and Peter Miller, 87–104. Chicago: University of Chicago Press, 1991.

Fox, Sarah Alisabeth. *Downwind: A People's History of the Nuclear West*. Lincoln: University of Nebraska Press, 2018.

Francaviglia, Richard A. *Believing in Place: A Spiritual Geography of the Great Basin*. Reno: University of Nevada Press, 2003.

———. *The Mormon Landscape: Existence, Creation, and Perception of a Unique Image in the American West*. New York: AMS, 1978.

Fraser, Nancy. *The Old Is Dying and the New Cannot Be Born: From Progressive Neoliberalism to Trump and Beyond*. New York: Verso, 2019.

Freedom House. *Freedom in the World 2022: The Global Expansion of Authoritarian Rule*. February 2022. https://freedomhouse.org/sites/default/files/2022-02/FIW_2022_PDF_Booklet_Digital_Final_Web.pdf.

Freyfogle, Eric T. *The Land We Share: Private Property and the Common Good*. Washington DC: Island, 2003.

Frye, Bradford J. *From Barrier to Crossroads: An Administrative History of Capitol Reef National Park, Utah*. 2 vols. Denver: National Park Service, 1998.

Fukuyama, Francis. *The End of History and the Last Man*. New York: Free Press, 1992.

Galston, William A., and Elaine Kamarck. "Is Democracy Failing and Putting Our Economic System at Risk?" Brookings Institution, January 4, 2022.

https://www.brookings.edu/research/is-democracy-failing-and-putting-our-economic-system-at-risk/.

Gerth, H. H., and C. Wright Mills, trans. and ed. *From Max Weber: Essays in Sociology*. New York: Oxford University Press, 1958.

Ginsburg, Faye D. *Contested Lives: The Abortion Debate in an American Community*. Updated ed. Berkeley: University of California Press, 1998.

Goodman, Doug, and Daniel McCool. *Contested Landscape: The Politics of Wilderness in Utah and the West*. Salt Lake City: University of Utah Press, 1999.

Graeber, David. *The Democracy Project: A History, a Crisis, a Movement*. London: Penguin, 2014.

Groesbeck, John. "Preliminary Analysis of the Economic Impact of aum Loss in Kane and Garfield Counties, Utah." Unpublished report prepared for the Kane County Commission, 2002.

——. "The Tax Revenue Impacts on Kane and Garfield Counties Due to Reductions in Productive aum on the Grand Staircase-Escalante National Monument." Unpublished report prepared for the Kane County Commission, 2004.

Guha, Ramachandra. "Radical American Environmentalism and Wilderness Preservation: A Third World Critique." *Environmental Ethics* 11, no. 1 (1989): 71–83.

Gupta, Akhil. "Blurred Boundaries: The Discourse of Corruption, the Culture of Politics, and the Imagined State." *American Ethnologist* 22, no. 2 (1995): 375–402.

Hamilton, Brady E., Joyce A. Martin, and Paul D. Sutton. *Births: Preliminary Data for 2003*. National Center for Health Statistics. National Vital Statistics Reports 53, no. 9 (November 23, 2004). https://www.cdc.gov/nchs/data/nvsr/nvsr53/nvsr53_09.pdf.

Hardin, Garrett. "The Tragedy of the Commons." *Science* 162, no. 3859 (1968): 1243–48.

Harvey, David. *A Brief History of Neoliberalism*. Oxford: Oxford University Press, 2005.

Hays, Samuel P. *Conservation and the Gospel of Efficiency: The Progressive Conservation Movement, 1820–1920*. Pittsburgh: University of Pittsburgh Press, 1999.

Headwaters Economics. *Grand Staircase-Escalante National Monument: A Summary of Economic Performance in the Surrounding Communities*. Spring 2017. https://headwaterseconomics.org/wp-content/uploads/Escalante.pdf.

Held, David. *Models of Democracy*. 2nd ed. Stanford CA: Stanford University Press, 1996.

Hirschman, Albert O. *Exit, Voice, and Loyalty: Responses to Decline in Firms, Organizations, and States*. Cambridge MA: Harvard University Press, 1970.

Hixon, Walter L. *American Settler Colonialism: A History*. New York: Palgrave McMillan, 2013.

Hochschild, Arlie Russell. *Strangers in Their Own Land: Anger and Mourning on the American Right*. New York: New Press, 2016.

Huss, Donald L. "The Rangeland Ecosystem." In *The Desertification Process on Rangelands and Its Reversal*. Rome: Food and Agriculture Organization of the United Nations, 2006. http://www.fao.org/docrep/X5321E/x5321e05.htm.

Jacobs, Harvey M. "The 'Wisdom' but Uncertain Future of the Wise Use Movement." In *Who Owns America? Social Conflict over Property Rights*, edited by Harvey M Jacobs, 29–34. Madison: University of Wisconsin Press, 1998.

Jacoby, Karl. *Crimes against Nature: Squatters, Poachers, Thieves, and the Hidden History of American Conservation*. Berkeley: University of California Press, 2001.

Jakus, Paul M., and Sherzod B. Akhundjanov. "Neither Boom nor Bane: The Economic Effects of a Landscape-Scale National Monument." *Land Economics* 94, no. 3 (2018): 323–39.

Janetski, Joel C., Mark L. Bodily, Bradley A. Newbold, and David T. Yoder. "The Paleoarchaic to Early Archaic Transition on the Colorado Plateau: The Archaeology of North Creek Shelter." *American Antiquity* 77, no. 1 (2012): 125–59.

Jarosz, Lucy, and Victoria Lawson. "Sophisticated People versus Rednecks: Economic Restructuring and Class Difference in America's West." *Antipode* 34, no. 1 (2002): 8–27.

Jordan, Terry G. *North American Cattle-Ranching Frontiers: Origins, Diffusion, and Differentiation*. Albuquerque: University of New Mexico Press, 1993.

Kelly, Isabell T., and Catherine S. Fowler. "Southern Paiute." In *Handbook of North American Indians*, vol. 11, *Great Basin*, edited by Warren L. D'Azevedo, 368–97. Washington DC: Smithsonian Institution, 1986.

Kemmis, Daniel. *Community and the Politics of Place*. Norman: University of Oklahoma Press, 1990.

Klyza, Christopher McGrory. *Who Controls the Public Lands? Mining, Forestry, and Grazing Policies, 1870–1990*. Chapel Hill: University of North Carolina Press, 1996.

Knight, Richard L. "The Ecology of Ranching." In *Ranching West of the 100th Meridian: Culture, Ecology, and Economics*, edited by Richard L. Knight, Wendell C. Gilgert, and Ed Marston, 123–44. Washington DC: Island, 2002.

Krakauer, Jon. *Under the Banner of Heaven: A Story of Violent Faith*. New York: Doubleday, 2003.

Larson, Gustive O. *The "Americanization" of Utah for Statehood*. San Marino CA: Huntington Library, 1971.

Leshy, John D. *Our Common Ground: A History of America's Public Lands*. New Haven CT: Yale University Press, 2021.

Levitsky, Steven, and Daniel Ziblatt. *How Democracies Die: What History Reveals about Our Future*. London: Viking, 2018.

Limerick, Patricia Nelson. *The Legacy of Conquest: The Unbroken Past of the American West*. New York: Norton, 1987.

Loring, Phillip A., Hannah L. Harrison, Valencia Gaspard, Sarah Minnes, and Helen M. Baulch. "Science, Data, and the Struggle for Standing in Environmental Governance." *Society & Natural Resources* 34, no. 12 (2021): 1584–601. https://doi.org/10.1080/08941920.2021.1979150.

Louderback, Lisbeth, and Bruce M. Pavlik. "Starch Granule Evidence for the Earliest Potato Use in North America." *Proceedings of the National Academy of Sciences* 114, no. 29 (2017): 7606–10.

MacLean, Nancy. *Democracy in Chains: The Deep History of the Radical Right's Stealth Plan for America*. New York: Viking, 2017.

Makley, Michael J. *Open Spaces, Open Rebellions: The War over America's Public Lands*. Amherst: University of Massachusetts Press, 2017.

Mansbridge, Jane J. *Beyond Adversary Democracy*. New York: Basic, 1980.

Marcus, George E. "Ethnography in/of the World System: The Emergence of Multi-Sited Ethnography." *Annual Review of Anthropology* 24 (1995): 95–117.

Maskovsky, Jeff, and Sophie Bjork-James, eds. *Beyond Populism: Angry Politics and the Twilight of Neoliberalism*. Morgantown: West Virginia University Press, 2020.

McCarthy, James. "First World Political Ecology: Lessons from the Wise Use Movement." *Environment and Planning A* 34 (2002): 1231–302.

McConnell, Grant. *Private Power and American Democracy*. New York: Vintage, 1966.

Merrill, Karen R. *Public Lands and Political Meaning: Ranchers, the Government, and the Property between Them*. Berkeley: University of California Press, 2002.

Milton, Kay. *Loving Nature: Towards an Ecology of Emotion*. London: Routledge, 2002.

Minteer, Ben A., and Robert E. Manning. "Pragmatism in Environmental Ethics: Democracy, Pluralism, and the Management of Nature." *Environmental Ethics* 21, no. 2 (1999): 191–207.

Mitchell, Timothy. "The Limits of the State: Beyond Statist Approaches and Their Critics." *American Political Science Review* 85, no. 1 (1991): 77–96.

———. *Rule of Experts: Egypt, Techno-Politics, Modernity*. Berkeley: University of California Press, 2002.

Mouffe, Chantal. *The Democratic Paradox*. New York: Verso, 2000.

———. *For a Left Populism*. New York: Verso, 2018.

———. *Towards a Green Democratic Revolution: Left Populism and the Power of Affects*. New York: Verso, 2022.

Mounk, Yascha. *The People vs. Democracy: Why Our Freedom Is in Danger and How to Save It*. Cambridge MA: Harvard University Press, 2018.

Muhn, James, and Hanson R. Stuart. *Opportunity and Challenge: The Story of BLM*. Washington DC: U.S. Department of the Interior, Bureau of Land Management, 1988.

Mutz, Diana. "Status Threat, Not Economic Hardship, Explains the 2016 Presidential Vote." *PNAS* 115, no. 19 (2018): 4330–39.

Nafisi, Azar. *Reading Lolita in Tehran: A Memoir in Books*. New York: Random House, 2004.

Nash, Stephen. *Grand Canyon for Sale: Public Lands versus Private Interests in the Era of Climate Change*. Oakland: University of California Press, 2017.

Nelson, Lowry. *The Mormon Village: A Pattern and Technique of Land Settlement*. Salt Lake City: University of Utah Press, 1952.

Newell, Linda King, and Vivian Linford Talbot. *A History of Garfield County*. Salt Lake City: Utah State Historical Society, 1998.

Newell, Maxine, and Terby Barnes. *The Untold History of Utah's Grand Staircase-Escalante National Monument*. Moab UT: Canyon Country, 1998.

Norris, Pippa. *Democratic Deficit: Critical Citizens Revisited*. New York: Cambridge University Press, 2011.

Paley, Julia. "Toward an Anthropology of Democracy." *Annual Review of Anthropology* 31 (2002): 469–96.

Palmer, Parker J. *Healing the Heart of Democracy: The Courage to Create a Politics Worthy of the Human Spirit*. San Francisco: Jossey-Bass, 2011.

Pickering, Jonathan, Karin Bäckstrand, and David Schlosberg. "Between Environmental and Ecological Democracy: Theory and Practice at the Democracy-Environment Nexus." *Journal of Environmental Policy and Planning* 22, no. 1 (2020): 1–15.

Piketty, Thomas. *Capital and Ideology*. Translated by Arthur Goldman. Cambridge MA: Harvard University Press, 2020.

Pilgeram, Ryanne. *Pushed Out: Contested Development and Rural Gentrification in the US West*. Seattle: University of Washington Press, 2021.

Pinchot, Gifford. "Conservation Means the Wise Use of the Earth and Its Resources." Washington DC: American Forest Institute, n.d.

Power, Thomas Michael. "The Fiscal Impacts of Closing Certain Federal Grazing Allotments in the Grand Staircase-Escalante National Monument." Unpublished report prepared for the Grand Canyon Trust, 2004.

Rana, Aziz. *The Two Faces of American Freedom*. Cambridge MA: Harvard University Press, 2010.

Rasband, James R. "Questioning the Rule of Capture Metaphor for Nineteenth Century Land Law: A Look at R.S. 2477." *Environmental Law* 35, no. 4 (2005): 1005–47.

Rasker, Ray, Ben Alexander, Jeff van den Noort, and Rebecca Carter. *Prosperity in the 21st Century West: The Role of Protected Public Lands*. Tucson AZ: Sonoran Institute, 2004.

———. *Public Lands Conservation and Economic Well-Being*. Tucson AZ: Sonoran Institute, 2004.

Ravetz, Jerome R. "What Is Post-Normal Science." *Futures* 31, no. 7 (1999): 647–53.

Riebsame, William, and James J. Robb, eds. *Atlas of the New West*. New York: W. W. Norton, 1997.

Righter, Robert W. "National Monuments to National Parks: The Use of the Antiquities Act of 1906." *Western Historical Quarterly* 20, no. 3 (1989): 281–301.

Robertson, David P., and R. Bruce Hull. "Public Ecology: An Environmental Science and Policy for Global Society." *Environmental Science and Policy* 6 (2003): 399–410.

Rose, Carol M. *Property and Persuasion: Essays on the History, Theory, and Rhetoric of Ownership*. Boulder CO: Westview, 1994.

Rothman, Hal. *America's National Monuments: The Politics of Preservation*. Lawrence: University of Kansas Press, 1994.

Roundy, Jerry C. *"Advised Them to Call the Place Escalante."* Springville UT: ArtCity, 2000.

Rowley, William D. "From Open Range to Closed Range on the Public Lands." In *Land in the American West: Private Claims and the Common Good*, edited by William G. Robbins and James C. Foster, 96–118. Seattle: University of Washington Press, 2000.

Sandel. Michael J. *The Tyranny of Merit: What's Become of the Common Good*. New York: Farrar, Straus and Giroux, 2020.

———. *What Money Can't Buy: The Moral Limits of Markets*. New York: Farrar, Strauss and Giroux, 2012.

San Juan County. "Politically Motivated, Technically Flawed: A Review of the BLM Wilderness Re-inventory in the State of Utah." 1999. Papers of Congressman James V. Hansen, 1970–2013, Series VI: Committee on Resources, box 34, folder 3. Special Collections and Archives, Merrill-Cazier Library, Utah State University, Logan.

Sayre, Nathan F. "The Cattle Boom in Southern Arizona: Towards a Critical Political Ecology." *Journal of the Southwest* 41, no. 2 (1999): 239–71.

———. *The Politics of Scale: A History of Rangeland Science*. Chicago: University of Chicago Press, 2017.

———. *Ranching, Endangered Species, and Urbanization in the Southwest: Species of Capital.* Tucson: University of Arizona Press, 2002.

———. "Viewpoint: The Need for Qualitative Research to Understand Ranch Management." *Journal of Range Management* 57, no. 6 (2004): 668–74.

———. *Working Wilderness: The Malpai Borderlands Group and the Future of the Western Range.* Tucson AZ: Rio Nuevo, 2005.

Sayre, N. F., and M. Fernández-Giménez. "The Genesis of Range Science with Implications for Current Development Policies." *Proceedings of the VIIth International Rangeland Congress* (2003): 1976–1985. https://archive.jornada.nmsu.edu/biblio/genesis-range-science-implications-current-development-policies.

Scokpol, Theda, and Vanessa Williamson. *The Tea Party and the Remaking of Republican Conservatism.* Oxford: Oxford University Press, 2012.

Scoones, Ian, ed. *Living with Uncertainty: New Directions in Pastoral Development in Africa.* London: Intermediate Technology, 1994.

Scott, James C. *Seeing like a State: How Certain Schemes to Improve the Human Condition Have Failed.* New Haven CT: Yale University Press, 1998.

Sen, Amartya. "Democracy as a Universal Value." *Journal of Democracy* 10, no. 3 (1999): 3–17.

Sheridan, Thomas. "Cows, Condos, and the Contested Commons: The Political Ecology of Ranching on the Arizona-Sonora Borderlands." *Human Organization* 60, no. 2 (2001): 141–52.

Sherman, Jennifer. *Dividing Paradise: Rural Inequality and the Diminishing American Dream.* Oakland: University of California Press, 2021.

———. *Those Who Work, Those Who Don't: Poverty, Morality, and Family in Rural America.* Minneapolis: University of Minnesota Press, 2009.

Silva, Jennifer M. *We're Still Here: Pain and Politics in the Heart of America.* Oxford: Oxford University Press, 2019.

Sivaramakrishnan, K. "Crafting the Public Sphere in West Bengal: Democracy, Development, and Political Action." *American Ethnologist* 27, no. 2 (2000): 431–61.

Skillen, James R. *Federal Ecosystem Management: Its Rise, Fall, and Afterlife.* Lawrence: University Press of Kansas, 2015.

———. *The Nation's Largest Landlord: The Bureau of Land Management in the American West.* Lawrence: University Press of Kansas, 2009.

———. *This Land Is My Land: Rebellion in the West.* New York: Oxford University Press, 2020.

Smarsh, Sarah White. *Heartland: A Memoir of Working Hard and Being Broke in the Richest Country on Earth.* New York: Scribner, 2018.

Sonoran Institute. *Population, Employment, Earnings and Personal Income Trends: Garfield County, UT*. Bozeman MT: Sonoran Institute, 2003.

———. *Population, Employment, Earnings and Personal Income Trends: Kane County, UT*. Bozeman MT: Sonoran Institute, 2003.

Southern Utah Wilderness Alliance (SUWA). "Kane Kounty Kapers." *Redrock Wilderness* 20, no. 3 (2003): 18.

———. "A Landscape Finds Its Voice: Inception of the Southern Utah Wilderness Alliance." *Redrock Wilderness* (Spring 1998).

Spangler, Jerry D., and Matthew K. Zweifel. *Deep Roots: A 10,000 Year Indigenous History of the Grand Staircase-Escalante National Monument*. Utah Bureau of Land Management Cultural Resources Series No. 30. Grand Staircase-Escalante National Monument Special Publication No. 5. September 29, 2021. https://www.blm.gov/utah/blm-library/cultural-resource-series/deep-roots-10000-year-indigenous-history-grand-staircase.

Spence, Mark David. *Dispossessing the Wilderness: Indian Removal and the Making of the National Parks*. New York: Oxford University Press, 1999.

Stegner, Wallace. *The American West as Living Space*. Ann Arbor: University of Michigan Press, 2001.

———. "On the Mormons." In *Stegner: Conversations on History and Literature*, rev. ed., edited by Wallace Stegner and Richard W. Etulain, 101–22. Reno: University of Las Vegas Press, 1996.

Taylor, Astra. *Democracy May Not Exist, but We'll Miss It When It's Gone*. New York: Metropolitan, 2019.

Taylor, Charles. "Modern Social Imaginaries." *Public Culture* 14, no. 1 (2002): 91–124.

———. "No Community, No Democracy." In *The Communitarian Reader: Beyond the Essentials*, edited by Amitai Etzioni, Andrew Volmert, and Elant Rothschild, 27–43. Lanham MD: Rowman & Littlefield, 2004.

Thompson, Raymond Harris. "The Antiquities Act of 1906 by Ronald Freeman Lee." *Journal of the Southwest* 42, no. 2 (2000): 197–269.

Tocqueville, Alexis de. *Democracy in America* [1835, 1840]. Translated by George Lawrence. Edited by J. P. Mayer. New York: HarperCollins, 2000.

Touraine, Alain. *What Is Democracy?* Translated by David Macey. Boulder CO: Westview, 1997.

Trainor, Sarah Fleisher. "Conflicting Values, Contested Terrain: Mormon, Paiute, and Wilderness Advocate Values of the Grand Staircase-Escalante National Monument." PhD diss., University of California, Berkeley, 2002.

Turner, Victor. *Dramas, Fields, and Metaphors*. Ithaca NY: Cornell University Press, 1974.

U.S. Forest Service (USFS). *U.S. Forest Service National Visitor Use Monitoring Survey Results National Summary Report: Data Collected FY 2014 through FY 2018*. U.S. Department of Agriculture, September 2019. https://www.fs.usda.gov/sites/default/files/2019-09/5082018_national_summary_report_070219.pdf.

Vandergeest, Peter, and Nancy Lee Peluso. "Territorialization and State Power in Thailand." *Theory and Society* 24 (1995): 385–426.

Vavra, Martin, William A. Laycock, and Rex D. Pieper, eds. *Ecological Implications of Livestock Herbivory in the West*. Denver: Society for Range Management, 1994.

Vincent, Carol Hardy. *Deferred Maintenance of Federal Land Management Agencies: FY2011–FY2020 Estimates and Issues*. Congressional Research Service. Updated November 30, 2021. https://www.everycrsreport.com/files/2021-11-30_R43997_e9e0adda228777651a9f2e18821dff68ca3677ca.pdf.

———. *Wild Horse and Burro Management: Overview of Costs*. Congressional Research Service. Updated July 13, 2022. https://crsreports.cpongress.gov/product/pdf/IF/IF11060.

Vincent, Carol Hardy, and Pamela Baldwin. *National Monuments and the Antiquities Act*. RL30528. Washington DC: Congressional Research Service, 2000.

Vincent, Carol Hardy, Laura A. Hanson, and Lucas F. Bermejo. *Federal Land Ownership: Overview and Data*. Congressional Research Service. Updated February 21, 2020. https://sgp.fas.org/crs/misc/R42346.pdf.

Vincent, Carol Hardy, M. Lynne Corn, Ross W. Gort, Sandra L Johnson, and David Whiteman. *Federal Land Management Agencies: Background on Land and Resource Management*. Washington DC: Congressional Research Service, 2004.

Walker, Peter. "Reconsidering 'Regional' Political Ecologies: Toward a Political Ecology of the Rural American West." *Progress in Human Geography* 27, no. 1 (2003): 7–24.

———. *Sagebrush Collaboration: How Harney County Defeated the Takeover of the Malheur Wildlife Refuge*. Corvallis: Oregon State University Press, 2018.

Walter, Barbara F. *How Civil Wars Start: And How to Stop Them*. New York: Crown, 2022.

Waters, M. Alycia, Thomas J. Stohlgren, Paul H. Evangelista, Debra A. Guenther, Nathaniel W. Alley, and Greg J. Newman, eds. *Landscape-Scale Assessment of Grand Staircase-Escalante National Monument*. Technical report. Fort Collins: Natural Resource Ecology Laboratory, Colorado State University, 2004.

Weber, Max. *Economy and Society*. 2 vols. Edited by Guenther Roth and Claus Wittich. Berkeley: University of California Press, 1978.

Westermeyer, William. *Back to America: Identity, Political Culture, and the Tea Party Movement.* Lincoln: University of Nebraska Press, 2019.

Westoby, Mark, Brian Walker, and Imanuel Noy-Meir. "Opportunistic Management for Rangelands Not at Equilibrium." *Journal of Range Management* 42, no. 4 (1989): 266–74.

White, Richard. "'Are You an Environmentalist or Do You Work for a Living?': Work and Nature." In *Uncommon Ground: Rethinking the Human Place in Nature,* edited by William Cronon, 171–85. New York: W. W. Norton, 1996.

———. *"It's Your Misfortune and None of My Own": A New History of the American West.* Norman: University of Oklahoma Press, 1991.

Whitehead, Laurence. "The Vexed Issue of the Meaning of 'Democracy.'" *Journal of Political Ideologies* 2, no. 2 (1997): 121–35.

Williams, Terry Tempest. *The Open Space of Democracy.* Barrington MA: Orion Society, 2004.

———. *Red: Passion and Patience in the Desert.* New York: Pantheon, 2001.

Wilson, Harlan. "Environmental Democracy and the Green State." *Polity* 38, no. 2 (2006): 276–94.

Wilson, Woodrow. "The Study of Administration." In *Classics of Public Administration,* edited by J. M. Schafritz and A. C. Hyde, 11–24. Pacific Grove CA: Brooks/Cole, 1992.

Woller, Gary M. "Toward a Reconciliation of the Bureaucratic and Democratic Ethos." *Administration and Society* 30, no. 1 (1998): 85–109.

Wondolleck, Julia M., and Steven L. Yaffee. *Making Collaboration Work: Lessons from Innovation in Natural Resource Management.* Washington DC: Island, 2000.

Woolsey, Nethella Griffin. *The Escalante Story: A History of the Town of Escalante and Description of the Surrounding Territory, Garfield County, Utah, 1875–1964.* Springville UT: Art City, 1964.

Worster, Donald. *Under Western Skies: Nature and History in the American West.* New York: Oxford University Press, 1992.

Wuthnow, Robert. *The Left Behind: Decline and Rage in Rural America.* Princeton NJ: Princeton University Press, 2018.

Young, Iris Marion. "Communication and the Other: Beyond Deliberative Democracy." In *Democracy and Difference: Contesting the Boundaries of the Political,* edited by Seyla Benhabib, 120–35. Princeton NJ: Princeton University Press, 1996.

———. *Inclusion and Democracy.* New York: Oxford University Press, 2000.

Zinke, Ryan. "Report Summary by U.S. Secretary of the Interior Ryan Zinke." U.S. Department of the Interior, August 24, 2017. https://www.doi.gov/sites/doi.gov/files/uploads/monument-report-summary.pdf.

Index

Page numbers in italics refer to illustrations.

agonistic democracy, 15–17, 114–15, 126–28, 167–68, 171, 291–92, 356–57
American West. *See* the West
America's Redrock Wilderness Act (1989), 45, 225, 260
Ancestral Pueblo, 64–65, 366n7. *See also* Native Americans
Andalex Resources, 7, 54, 255, 362n13
Anthropocene as term, 367n9
Anti-Federalists, 30–31, 34, 36–37, 202–3, 336
Antiquities Act (1906), xi, xv, 1, 36, 37, 38–39, 50, 339–40, 348–49
apartheid, xii, xiii–xiv
ATVs (all-terrain vehicles), 131, 137t, 145, 153, 155, 158, 161, 259

Babbitt, Bruce, 2, 44, 48, 50–51
Bears Ears National Monument, 339–40, 342, 346–47
Bellah, Robert, 197–200
Berlin, Isaiah, 217
Biden, Joe, xvi, 331, 346–47, 348
Biden administration, 355
Big Bowns Bench allotment, 99t, 104–5, 107, 115–16, 124
birth rates, 79, 378n4
Boulder UT, 5, 183, 201, 213, 246

Braunstein, Ruth, 14, 357–58
Brick, Philip, 261
Bryce Canyon National Park, 6, 46–47, 181
Bulloch, Mary, 89, 93–94, 95–96
bureaucracy: and bureaucratic ethos, 301–3, 305, 307–8, 309, 315–16, 322, 328–29; democracy and, 294–95, 310–11, 312, 327
Bureau of Land Management (BLM): about, 40, 344, 346; budget of, 295–96, 365n41; employees of, 18–19, 93, 229, 293, 295–97, 300, 314–16, 326–27; grazing allotments and, 90, 109–10, 115–21; local perceptions of, 122, 228–29, 238–39; and management of GSENM, xi, 2, 295–96, 329; and management of public land, 28, 45–46, 49, 97, 329, 349, 365n37; multiple-use mandate of, 119, 272, 295, 297, 310; ranchers and, 220–21, 228–30, 238–39; range improvements under, 228–29; road conflicts and, 130, 146, 153, *154*, 155–56, 160. *See also* EIS Team
Burr Trail, 134, 252–54
Bush, George W., 168

405

Bush administration (G. W.), 95, 106, 110–11, 119, 142, 143, 167, 173, 300, 320–23

Cannon, Kate, 86, 92, 94–96, 97–98, 105, 118–19, 142, 297–98, 333

Canyon Country Ranchers Association, 107–8

Canyonlands Grazing Corporation (CGC), 102–3, 114, 121–22, 220, 277. *See also* Grand Canyon Trust (GCT)

Capitol Reef National Park, 6, 47–48, 134, 211

Carr Childers, Leisl, 248

Carter administration, 39, 133

Catlin, Jim, 268–74

cattle: feral, 92, 95, 96, 235–37; impoundment of, 89, 92–94, 97–98, 125, 239–40, 264, 297; removal of, 89–96. *See also* grazing

Church of Jesus Christ of Latter-day Saints, 67–74, 183–87, 363n39. *See also* Mormons

Clark Bench allotment, 99t, 104–5, 107, 114, 115–16, 124, 219

climax plant community, 88, 307, 383n17

Clinton, Bill, xi, 1, 2, 39, 45, 47, 48, 50, 295, 343

Clinton administration, 44, 50–51, 133, 143, 271

Cochran, Bob, 241–47

Cochran, Sioux, 241–47

collaborative conservation, xiii, 15–16, 41, 89–90, 261

Colorado Plateau region, 53–54, 58–59, 63–64, 281

community: of association, 198–99; of belonging, 197–98, 204; democracy and, 201–6; demographic changes in, 191–94, 246; dynamics in, 177–79, 194–201; of Escalante UT, 8, 179–81, *184*, *185*, 188, 193, 196, 200–203, 262–63, 340; exclusionists in, 200–201; identity of, 187–94, 203–4, 205–6; as lifestyle enclave, 199; in a strong sense, 199–200, 206; types of, 197–200. *See also* local residents; longtime residents; newcomer residents

conflict, 15–17, 337–38, 356–58. *See also* agonistic democracy

conservation, 15–16, 36, 41, 89–90, 106, 261

Conservation Fund, 120–21, 275, 280–81

conservation movement, 36

COVID-19 pandemic, 349, 350

cowboys, 35, 208, 211, 243, 336

crisis of hegemony, 388n52

Cronon, William, 257–58

Dahl, Robert, 12–13

decision-making, 139–40, 144–45, 167–68, 273, 306–9, 337–38

democracy: aggregative model of, 198–99; agonistic, 15–17, 114–15, 126–28, 167–68, 171, 291–92, 356–57; bureaucracy and, 294–95, 310–11, 312, 327, 328–29; civic, 261; community and, 201–6; conflict and, 337–38, 356–58; decision-making and, 139–40, 144–45, 167–68, 273, 337–38; decline of, 352–55; definitions of, 12–13; and democratic ethos, 301–3, 309–12; freedom and, 216–18, 223–25, 247–48; inclusion and, 10–11, 204–5, 313; landscape and, 335–37;

minimalist conception of, 12–13; participation in, 10–13, 139–41, 170, 171–72; public lands and, 169–73, 259–60, 346; on the range, 40, 87, 93, 97, 117–18, 126, 170; regulatory, 261; in the United States, 30–33, 35–36, 351–55, 358–60; violations of, 2–3, 6, 8, 13, 20, 122, 138, 143, 164, 313
democracy, understandings of: author's interest in, xi–xix; by BLM employees, 294, 324; by environmentalists, 259, 273–74, 277; by environmental political theorists, 290–91; by ranchers, 171, 216–18, 231, 237; by residents, 3–6, 14–15, 201–3
Democracy in America (Tocqueville), 31, 68, 170, 339
democratic imaginaries: about, 13–15, 290; American West and, 31–32, 35, 67, 80, 336–37; Constitution and, 31; of decentralized government, 144; of decision-making, 139–40, 144–45, 167–68; of equality, 68; of federal government supremacy, 138–39; of freedom, 336; of free speech, 159; of Mormons, 70, 72; of participatory democracy, 139–41; and public land, 27; of rule of law, 93, 105–6, 139, 167–68, 171
democratic paradoxes: about, 203–6, 338–39; bureaucracy and, 293–94, 301–3; community and, 201–6; environmentalism and, 255–58, 263–68, 272–74, 277–78, 280–81, 282, 289–92; freedom and, 247–48; liberal democracy and, 16, 159–60; liberty and, 217–18; market-based solutions and, 282

demographic changes, 77–80, 150–51, 191–94, 213, 246
deontology, 303
Department of the Interior, U.S. (DOI), 27, 106–7, 109, 111–12, 144, 159
Department of the Interior, Utah, 144–45, 151, 153
Deseret, state of, 70
desired future conditions (DFCs), 307, 383n17
desired plant community (DPC), 307, 383n17
Diehl, Patrick, 10–11, 261–68
Dobson, Andrew, 250
Dodds, Maloy, 112, 139–40, 144, 334
downwinders as term, 368n36
droughts, 89, 104, 110, 114, 226, 349–50

Eaton, Marietta, xvii–xviii
economy: and economic shifts, 75–80, 150–51, 213; in Garfield and Kane Counties, 78–80, 156–57, 189, 341–42; and market-based solutions, 106–7, 112–13, 123, 126, 156–57, 277–78; and neoliberal economic policies, 340–41
Edmunds Act (1882), 71
EISs. *See* environmental impact statements (EISs)
EIS Team: attrition within, 317–18, 326–28; composition of, 298–301, 311–12; county representatives and, 307, 313–14, 318–19; divisions within, 312–17; hierarchy in, 319–24; job satisfaction of, 327–28; ranchers and, 323; and understanding of democracy, 324. *See also* Bureau of Land Management

INDEX 407

EIS Team (cont.)
(BLM); Monument Management Plan Amendment and Rangeland Health EIS
employment, 77–79, 189–91
environmental assessments (EAs), 105, 107, 110–11, 116, 118–19
environmental groups: EIS Team and, 312; Escalante Wilderness Project, 264, 267; local residents and, 131–32, 262, 287; ranching and, 230–31; road conflicts and, 131–32, 133, 139, 144, 158; Sierra Club, 252, 266, 267, 284; Utah Wilderness Coalition, 45, 133, 260, 270; Wilderness Society, 158, 161, 162, 262; Wild Utah Project, 268–72. *See also* Grand Canyon Trust (GCT); Southern Utah Wilderness Alliance (SUWA)
environmental impact statements (EISs), 41, 304–5. *See also* EIS Team; Monument Management Plan Amendment and Rangeland Health EIS
environmentalism: democracy and, 249–50, 255–58, 263–68, 272–74, 277–78, 280–81, 282, 289–92; and environmental movement, 41, 260–61; and environmental political theory, 250, 289–91; in Grand Staircase-Escalante region, 269; individualist approach to, 282–86; resource production and, 258. *See also* environmental groups; Grand Canyon Trust (GCT); Southern Utah Wilderness Alliance (SUWA)
environmentalists: backgrounds of, 256–57, 288; class and, 257–58; harassment of, 253–54, 263–64; landscape knowledge of, 256–57; locals and, 263–64, 265, 266–67, 277, 287–89; perceptions of, 263, 266–67, 287–88; radical, 244, 259, 286; and understanding of democracy, 259, 273–74, 277; use of term, 249. *See also individual environmentalists*

Escalante Center, xiii, 89–90, 188, 239–40
Escalante UT: about, 5, 56; community of, 8, 179–81, *184*, *185*, 188, 193, 196, 200–203, 262–63, 340; demographics of, 75–76; houses in, 57, 58; Planning and Zoning Committee, 200; response of, to GSENM, 2
Escalante Wilderness Project (EWP), 264, 267
exclusion, 200–201, 204–5, 313
Exit, Voice, and Loyalty (Hirschman), 326

federal government: Church of Jesus Christ of Latter-day Saints and, 71–72; conflicts within branches of, 18–19, 110–11, 311; delays within, 115, 124, 158, 324–25; and Department of the Interior, 27, 106–7, 109, 111–12, 144, 159; individual freedom and, 224, 247; and land laws, 33–34, 336–37; and land management agencies, 27–28, 172–73, 345–46; land owned by, 27–28, 29, 56, 172; lawsuits including, 50, 111–12, 134, 138–39, 310; local governments and, 202–3, 319–20, 338; perceptions of, 7, 105–6, 139–40, 150, 266; power of, 30–31, 35–37, 39–40; road conflicts and, 132–34,

138–39, 142–44, 158–59, 161–63, 166, 169. *See also* presidential administrations
Federalists, 30–31. *See also* Anti-Federalists
Federal Land Policy and Management Act (FLPMA), 41–46, 130–31, 134, 143, 165, 166, 295
federally owned land, 27–28, 56, 80, 172. *See also* public domain lands; public lands
feral cattle, 92, 95, 96, 235–37
Fiftymile Mountain, 90–98, 233–35, 237–38, 240–41
forage utilization, 321, 384n26
Foucault, Michel, 20–21, 363n36
freedom, 216–18, 247–48, 259
free-market. *See* market-based solutions
Fremont people, 64
Friends of the Monument, 147, 188, 192
Fundamentalist Church of Jesus Christ of Latter-day Saints (FLDS), 72. *See also* Church of Jesus Christ of Latter-day Saints

Garfield County: about, 4, 5, 56, 79; federally owned land in, 6, 362n12; lawsuits including, 115–22, 134, 143, 159, 162, 310, 348–49; livestock grazing and, 108; on RMP/EIS, 348; roads in, 131, 138–39. *See also* Kane County
General Revision Act (1891), 36, 37
Ginsburg, Faye, xvi–xvii
Glen Canyon National Recreation Area, 101, 284, 285–86, 383n8
Grand Canyon Trust (GCT): about, 274, 281–82; approach of, to grazing, 47–48, 120–21, 275–76, 278, 281–82; and Canyonlands Grazing Corporation, 102–3, 114, 121–22, 220, 277; and grazing permit purchases, 101–2, 104–5; and Grazing Retirement Program, 102–4, 106–9, 111–12, 117, 124–25, 276, 277; and purchase of Kane and Two-Mile Ranches, 120–21, 280–81; ranchers and, 276–77; ranching by, 122, 281
Grand Staircase-Escalante National Monument (GSENM): about, 4, 5, 53–56, 58–65, 60, 61, 62, 91, 350, 383n17; budget of, 125, 295, 301, 345–46, 365n41; community identity and, 187–90; creation of, xi, 1–3, 8, 50–51, 295, 333–34, 366n47; management of, 2, 295–96, 329; and Monument Management Plan, xiii, 7–8, 55, 110, 134, 139–42, 159, 343–44, 375n12; and Monument Management Plan Amendment and Rangeland Health EIS, 86, 110, 123–24, 294, 298, 324–25, 330, 335; name of, 36n1 (pref.); plants and wildlife in, 59, 63, 88, 95, 215, 245, 283, 285–86, 287; proclamation of, 1–3, 295; size of, xv, 341–44, 346–47, 36n1 (intro.); tenth anniversary of, 333–35; as third reterritorialization, 45; twenty-fifth anniversary of, 347–48. *See also* monument managers
Grand Staircase-Escalante National Monument and Kanab-Escalante Planning Area Draft Resource Management Plans and EIS, 331
Grand Staircase Escalante Partners, 147, 350

INDEX 409

grazing: about, 85–86; agonistic democracy and, 126–28; allotments, 90, 109–10, 115–21, 306–7, 308, 321–22, 323; in Capital Reef National Monument, 47–48; hikers and, 210, 244–45; impacts of, 125; and intent to graze, 116–17, 124–25; permits, 87, 121–22, 275–76; public lands and, 39–42, 87–89, 125, 220–21, 230–31, 243–45, 271, 278, 310–11, 380n19; public perceptions of, 87–89, 208, 231, 244, 247; regulations on, 43–44, 121–22, 305; as a right, 89. *See also* cattle; grazing retirements; Taylor Grazing Act (1934) (TGA)

Grazing Permit Renewal EIS, 86, 298

Grazing Retirement Program (GRP), 102–4, 106–9, 111–12, 117, 124–25, 276, 277. *See also* Grand Canyon Trust (GCT)

grazing retirements: (1996–99), 101–4; (2000–2001), 104–7; (2002), 107–10; (2003–4), 110–15; (2005), 115–21; (2006), 121–24; about, 98; lawsuits against, 98, 99t, 115–22; local opposition to, 124–26; reterritorialization and, 124–28, 378n88; timeline of, 99t

Great American Outdoors Act (2020), 346, 347

green political theory, 250, 289–91. *See also* environmentalism

Griffin, Delane, 233–35, 236, 237, 240–41

Griffin, Gene, 89, 234, 237

Griffin, Quinn, 88–89, 94–98, 237–41

Groesbeck, John, 113

GSENM. *See* Grand Staircase-Escalante National Monument (GSENM)

Guha, Ramachandra, 258

Habbeshaw, Mark: about, 105–6; as county commissioner, 107–8, 159; on Grazing Retirement Program, 111, 117, 122–23; on Monument Management Plan, 140–41; road conflicts and, 145–46, 151, 153, 155–56, 161–62

Habits of the Heart (Bellah), 197–200

Hatch, Orrin, 3, 148, 342

Hedden, Bill, 2, 101–2, 110, 112, 114, 120–21, 274–81, 333

hikers, 6, 210, 244–45

Hirschman, Albert O., 326, 328

Homestead Act (1862), 34

horses, 92, 95–96, 239, 243, 247, 251, 370n13

Hunsaker, Dave, 20, 96, 110, 145–46, 239–40, 300, 319, 320, 365n41

Indigenous people, 28, 29, 37, 63–65. *See also* Native Americans

individualism, 33, 66, 68, 182

inner exclusion, 204–5

Interior Department. *See* Department of the Interior, U.S. (DOI)

Interpreting Indicators of Rangeland Health (technical reference), 298, 305–6

irrigation, 262–63, 285, 288

Jarosz, Lucy, 150–51

Johnson, Calvin, 226–32

Johnson, Grant, 251–61

Johnson, Karla, 226–32

Johnson, Que, 226–32

Kaibab Forest Products Company, 362n14
Kanab UT, 2, 5, 56, 147–48
Kane County: about, 4, 5, 56, 78–80, 157; federal land within, 6, 362n12; lawsuits including, 115–22, 143, 159–60, 161–62, 310, 348–49; livestock grazing in, 108; road conflicts and, 131, 138–39, 141–43, 161–62, 168, 169; road signs in, 153, *154*, 155–56, 163–64. *See also* Garfield County
Kane Ranch, 120, 280–81
Kincaid, Clive, 253

Land Ordinance (1785), 33
landscape, 72–74, 181–82, 216–17, 355–57
landscape knowledge, 221–22, 269
Last Chance allotment, 104–5, 114, 115–16, 124, 212
Latter-day Saints. *See* Church of Jesus Christ of Latter-day Saints; Mormons
Lawson, Victoria, 150–51
lawsuit participants: federal government, 50, 111–12, 134, 138–39, 310; Garfield County, 115–22, 134, 143, 159, 162, 310, 348–49; Kane County, 115–22, 143, 159–60, 161–62, 310, 348–49; Mountain States Legal Foundation, 50; Southern Utah Wilderness Alliance, 138, 143, 160, 163; Utah Association of Counties, 50; Utah School and Institutional Trust Lands Administration, 50; Utah state government, 111–12, 142, 144, 162–63, 164, 168–69
lawsuits: BLM and, 310; environmental movement and, 260–61; grazing retirements and, 98, 99t, 115–22; public land grazing and, 109–10; road conflicts and, 111–12, 134, 136t, 157–59, 160, 162–63, 168–69
LDS as term, 363n39. *See also* Church of Jesus Christ of Latter-day Saints; Mormons
Learning from the Land science symposium, 334
Leavitt, Mike, 3, 142, 144, 147
LeFevre, Dell, 48, 102, 104, 108–9, 118, 208–18
liberal democracy, 16, 159–60
liberalism, 13, 16, 159–60, 205. *See also* neoliberalism
liberty, 32, 217–18
litigation. *See* lawsuits
Livestock Grazing Monument Management Plan Amendment and Associated EIS, 330
livestock industry, 34–35, 40, 117, 126. *See also* cattle; ranchers; ranching; Taylor Grazing Act (1934) (TGA)
Livestock Management EIS, 299, 304–5
local governments, 202–3, 319–20, 338. *See also* Garfield County; Kane County; Utah
local residents, 131–32, 165, 177–79, 187–88, 262, 287, 289–90, 350–51. *See also* community; longtime residents; newcomer residents; rural Americans
longtime residents, 178–79, 196–99, 200–201, 205–6, 213, 350–51
Lyman, Arthur, 101–2
Lyman, Ivan, 209, 256
Lyman family, 209–10

Mandela, Nelson, xii

INDEX 411

Manning, Robert, 291
Marcus, George, xvii
market-based solutions, 106–7, 112–13, 123, 126, 156–57, 277–78, 282
Meredith, Jerry, 8, 141
Mining Act (1866), 33, 130, 143, 150
Mining Act (1872), 33
mining industry, 7, 192, 251–52, 253, 368n36
Minteer, Ben, 291
Missouri, 68–69
Mollie's Nipple allotment, 226
Monument Management Plan (MMP), xiii, 7–8, 55, 110, 134, 139–42, 159, 343–44, 375n12
Monument Management Plan Amendment and Rangeland Health EIS, 86, 123–24, 294, 298, 324–25, 330, 335. *See also* EIS Team
monument managers: Cynthia Staszak, 330; Dave Hunsaker, 20, 96, 110, 145–46, 239–40, 300–301, 319, 320; Jerry Meredith, 8, 141; Kate Cannon, 86, 92, 94–96, 97–98, 105, 118–19, 142, 297–98, 333
Moqui, 366n7
Mormon landscape, 72–74
Mormons, 71–72, 74–75, 77–78, 178, 182–83, 186–87, 195, 363n39. *See also* Church of Jesus Christ of Latter-day Saints
The Mormon Village (Nelson), 75–76
Morrill Anti-Bigamy Act (1862), 71
Morris, Dick, 50
Mouffe, Chantal, 15–17, 114, 206, 273, 354, 356, 359–60, 388n60
Mounk, Yascha, 13, 338, 354
multiple-use mandate, 119, 272, 295, 297, 310

Nafisi, Azar, xviii–xix
National Conservation Lands, 48, *49*
National Environmental Policy Act (1969) (NEPA), 41, 93, 139, 273–74, 304, 345
National Landscape Conservation System, 48, *49*
national monuments: evaluation of, 342; generally, 2–3, 27–28, 36–39, 48, *49*, 333, 339–40, 345; in Utah, 6, 47–48, 240, 314, 347, 349–50
national parks, 6, 37–38, 46–48, 55, 134, 181, 211, 346
National Park Service (NPS), 27–28, 47, 255–56, 286, 296, 297, 345
National Wilderness Preservation System, 41, 44–45, 130, 133–34, 260
Native Americans, xvii–xviii, 28, *29*, 37, 63–65, 69, 129, 336, 340, 356
natural as term, 384n17
The Nature Conservancy (TNC), 278–79
Nauvoo IL, 69
Nelson, Lowry, 75–76
Nelson, Russell M., 363n39
neoliberalism, 106, 111–13, 119, 127, 172, 340–41, 353–54
neoliberalization, 106–7
newcomer residents, 191–96, 201, 245, 259–60, 265, 288, 350–51. *See also* local residents
New Deal legislation, 39–41
New Escalante Irrigation Company, 262–63, 285
New West, 76–80, 105, 196–97
New Wide Hollow Reservoir, 262, 265, 267, 268
"No Community, No Democracy" (Taylor), 204–6
Noel, Mike, 112, 163, 164, 341

North Rim Ranches. *See* Kane Ranch; Two-Mile Ranch
Norton, Gale, 106, 110–11, 144, 156–57, 160, 300
Norton policy, 160, 161–62
nuclear testing, 368n36

Obama, Barack, xv, 339, 352
Obama administration, 173, 330, 339
"October surprise," 50–51
Orton, Bill, 3, 334

Paleo-Indians, 63–64
Paley, Julia, xiv, 357
Palmer, Parker, 357–58
pioneer values, 182–83, 192
Plat of the City of Zion, 73
politics of resentment, 340–41
polygamy, 69, 70, 71, 72
popular sovereignty, 16, 30–31, 146, 273, 354, 359
populism, definition of, 388n57
post-normal science, 273
potential natural vegetative community (PNC), 307, 383n17
Power, Thomas Michael, 113
precontact condition, 307, 383n17
presidential administrations: Biden, 355; Carter, 39, 133; changes depending on, 157–58, 166, 319–20, 326–27; Clinton, 44, 50–51, 133, 143, 271; G. W. Bush, 95, 106, 110–11, 119, 142, 143, 167, 173, 300, 320–23; Obama, 173, 330, 339; Reagan, 42, 133, 172; Trump, xv–xvi, 330–31, 340–43, 344–46, 357. *See also* federal government
Proclamation 9682 (2017), xv–xvi
Progressive movement, 35–36
property ownership, 153

public administration, 302–3. *See also* bureaucracy
public domain lands: definition of, 27; democracy and, 28; management of land in, 35–37; reterritorialization of, 32–35, 36, 41–43, 45, 48
public ecology, 273
public input processes, 41, 139–40, 342, 343–44, 346, 348
public lands: conservative movement against, 173; definition of, 27–28, 42; democracy and, 114–15, 246–48; grazing on, 39–42, 87–89, 125, 220–21, 230–31, 243–45, 271, 278, 310–11; local control and privatization of, 172–73, 344–45; management of, 41–42, 171–72; public perceptions of, 35, 41, 87–88, 109–10, 127, 187, 189, 208, 244, 337; reterritorialization of, 165–68, 170; value of, 172. *See also* Taylor Grazing Act (1934) (TGA)
Pueblo peoples, 64–65, 366n7. *See also* Native Americans

Quiet Title Act (1972), 377n68
quiet titles, 162, 168–69, 377n68
Quivira Coalition, 278, 279–80, 282, 372n58

radiation exposure, 368n36
ranchers: about, 207–8; Bureau of Land Management and, 220–21, 228–30, 238–39, 323; Canyon Country Ranchers Association and, 107–8; families of, 227, 243; Grand Canyon Trust and, 118, 276–77; knowledge of, 221–22, 229, 231–32; The Nature Conservatory and, 278–79; priorities of, 247; and understanding of democracy, 171,

ranchers (cont.)
216–18, 223–25, 231, 237. See also individual ranchers
ranching, 113, 214–16, 221–25, 227–31, 243, 245, 279–80. See also grazing
rangeland ecology, 88, 272, 308
rangeland health, 125, 272, 298–99, 299, 304–7, 310, 321
Rangeland Health EIS. See Monument Management Plan Amendment and Rangeland Health EIS
Rangeland Health Plan Amendment and EIS, xvii, 300–301
Rangeland Reform '94, 44, 101
Reading Lolita in Tehran (Nafisi), xviii–xix
Reagan administration, 42, 133, 172
recreational fees, 172–73
Red (Williams), 67
"redneck" discourse, 150–51. See also rural Americans
Relinquishment of Grazing Preference on BLM Administered Lands, 123–24
research methodology, xvi–xix
residents. See community; local residents; longtime residents; newcomer residents; rural Americans
Resource Management Plan and Environmental Impact Statement (RMP/EIS), 348
resource production, 7, 44, 188–89, 230–31, 258
reterritorialization: about, 20–21; grazing retirements and, 124–28, 378n88; of GSENM, 119; of public land, 32–35, 36, 41–43, 45, 48, 165–68, 170; of Utah, 69–72. See also territorialization, overview of

Revised Statutes (R.S. 2477), 33–34, 44, 130, 132–33, 136t. See also rights-of-way; road conflicts; roads
rights-of-way, 375n12; guidelines for, 160; lawsuits regarding, 134, 157, 158, 169; and property rights, 153; and recognition of road claims, 164; R.S. 2477 and, 33–34, 130
road conflicts: (1996), 138–39; (1998–99), 139–41; (2000), 141–43; (2001–3), 143–45; (2003, August), 145–51; (2004), 151, 153; (2005), 153–60; (2006–7), 160–63; (2008–9), 163–65; (2009–present), 168–69; agonistic democracy and, 167–68; BLM and, 130, 146, 153, *154*, 155–56, 160; environmental groups and, 131–32, 133, 139, 144, 158; federal government and, 132–34, 138–39, 142–44, 158–59, 161–62, 166, 169; guidelines for resolving, 160; Kane County and, 131, 138–39, 141–43, 161–62, 168, 169; lawsuits regarding, 111–12, 134, 156–59, 160, 162–63, 168–69; and mapping of roads, 133–34; Mark Habbeshaw and, 145–46, 151, 153, 155–56, 161–62; media coverage of, 147, 148, 149t; nonbinding determinations and, 162; Norton policy and, 160, 161–62; quiet titles and, 162, 168–69, 377n68; Southern Utah Wilderness Alliance and, 158, 169; state government and, 111–12, 142, 144, 162–63, 164, 168–69; timeline of, 136t. See also Revised Statutes (R.S. 2477); rights-of-way
roads: definitions of, 129–30, 143, 376n43; legislation on, 155; maintenance of, 164, 167; management

of, 44–45, 141, 142–43; mapping of, 133–34; negative impacts of, 131; regulations of, 132–33; and roadless lands, 44–45. *See also* Revised Statutes (R.S. 2477)

road signs: and ATV use, 145, 153, 155–56, 158, 161; in Kane County, 153, *154*, 155–56, 162, 163–64; lawsuits over, 163–64; removal of, 145–48, 151, *152*, 156; types of, 142–43

Robinson, Brent, 104, 114, 218–25, *225*

Robinson, Lynette, 218, 225

Roosevelt, Franklin, 38–39, 47

Roosevelt, Theodore, 36, 38

R.S. 2477. *See* Revised Statutes (R.S. 2477)

rugged individualism, 33

rule of experts, 36, 90, 93, 97, 268

rural Americans, 8–9, 76–77, 150, 202–3, 205–6, 231, 248, 340–41, 357

Russian olive, 283, 285–86, 287, 380n20

Sagebrush Rebellion, 42

saltcedar. *See* tamarisk

Salt Lake Tribune, 123, 148–50, 149t, 152, 157, 263

sawmill, 190, 378n7

School and Institutional Trust Lands Administration, 8, 50, 362n15

science-based decision-making. *See* decision-making

Sierra Club, 252, 266, 267, 284

"The Significance of the Frontier in American History" (Turner), 32, 35

Skillen, James, 42, 322

Skutumpah Ranch, 218–21

Skutumpah Road, 164, 168

Smith, Joseph, 67–69

Smith, Lamont, 145–46

social drama, xi

Sorensen, Steve, 209, 240, 308

South Africa, xii, xiii–xiv

Southern Paiute, 65

Southern Utah News, 147, 148, 159

Southern Utah Wilderness Alliance (SUWA): Grant Johnson and, 251, 256; on GSENM, 333; lawsuits including, 138, 143, 160, 163; local residents and, 147, 159; origins of, 134, 251, 253; road conflicts and, 158, 169; work of, 254–55, 260, 261

Staszak, Cynthia, 330

State Land Use Management Plans Amendments (H.B. 264), 115, 155

statemaking, 19–20, 116, 309, 338

Stegner, Wallace, 66, 67

"The Study of Administration" (Wilson), 302, 329

Sullivan, Carol, 6–7, 187, 188, 194–95, 201

tamarisk, 245, 285, 380n20

taxes, 362n12

Taylor, Charles, 13, 179, 204–6

Taylor Grazing Act (1934) (TGA), 39–41, 43–44, 87, 89, 97, 117–18, 123

Tenth Circuit Court of Appeals, 151, 157, 164, 165, 168

territorialization, overview of, 17–22. *See also* reterritorialization

TGA. *See* Taylor Grazing Act (1934) (TGA)

Tocqueville, Alexis de, 24, 31–33, 65, 68, 170, 339

tourism industry, 77, 153, 155, 189–90, 193, 213, 259, 341–42

"Toward an Anthropology of Democracy" (Paley), xiv

Transportation Plan, 141–43, 159, 297, 375n12. *See also* Monument Management Plan (MMP)
tribal groups. *See* Native Americans
Trump, Donald, xv, 151, 173, 330, 340, 353, 357
Trump administration, xv–xvi, 330–31, 340–43, 344–46, 357
Turner, Frederick Jackson, 32, 35, 336
Turner, Victor, xi
Two-Mile Ranch, 120–21, 124, 280–82

unemployment, 79
uranium mining, 7, 192, 251–52, 368n36. *See also* mining industry
U.S. Capitol riot (2021), xvi
U.S. Fish and Wildlife Service (FWS), 27–28
U.S. Forest Service (USFS), 27–28, 41, 345–46
Utah: birth rate in, 79, 378n4; Mormons and the reterritorialization of, 69–72; state government and road conflicts in, 111–12, 142, 144–45, 162–63, 164, 168–69; and State Land Use Management Plans Amendments, 115; and state of Utah–Interior Department MOU, 144–45, 151, 153
Utah Association of Counties, 50
Utah Permanent Community Impact Board Fund, 111–12, 372n45
Utah School and Institutional Trust Lands Administration, 50
Utah Schools and Land Exchange Act and Public Law (105-335), 361n1 (intro.)
"Utah War," 70–71
Utah Wilderness Coalition, 45, 133, 260, 270

utilitarianism, 303

"The Vexed Issue of the Meaning of 'Democracy'" (Whitehead), 12

Walker, Peter, 196–97
Walmart, 281, 372n45
Weber, Edward, 261
Weber, Max, 19, 294–95, 302
Weed, Robert, 253, 255
the West: conceptions of, 53–54, 65–67; democratic imaginaries and, 31–32, 336–37; economic and demographic shifts in, 77–80, 150–51, 213; and New West, 76–80, 105, 196–97; settlement of, 28–29
West Clark Bench allotment, 99t, 104–5, 107, 114, 115–16, 124, 219
western writers, 337
White, Richard, 37, 257–58
Whitehead, Laurence, 12
wilderness: dualism of, 257; experience of, 257–58; reinventory of, 45, 133–34; and wilderness areas, 41, 49; and wilderness study areas, 44–45, 49
Wilderness Act (1964), 41
Wilderness Society, 158, 161, 162, 262
Wild Utah Project, 268–72
Williams, Terry Tempest, 2, 67, 255
Wilson, Woodrow, 302, 329
Wisely, Sally, 110, 148, 155–56, 239
Wise Use movement, 43, 140, 172
Woller, Gary M., 301–3
Wolverton, Bill, 282–86
Woodard, Tori, 262–68
Worster, Donald, 65–66

Young, Brigham, 67–68, 69
Young, Iris Marion, 146, 313

Zinke, Ryan, 342, 345

In the Anthropology of Contemporary North America series:

America's Digital Army: Games at Work and War
Robertson Allen

Governing Affect: Neoliberalism and Disaster Reconstruction
Roberto E. Barrios

Public Land and Democracy in America: Understanding Conflict over Grand Staircase-Escalante National Monument
Julie Brugger

Come Now, Let Us Argue It Out: Counter-Conduct and LGBTQ Evangelical Activism
Jon Burrow-Branine

White Gold: Stories of Breast Milk Sharing
Susan Falls

Mexicans in Alaska: An Ethnography of Mobility, Place, and Transnational Life
Sara V. Komarnisky

Holding On: African American Women Surviving HIV/AIDS
Alyson O'Daniel

Rebuilding Shattered Worlds: Creating Community by Voicing the Past
Andrea L. Smith and Anna Eisenstein

Songs of Profit, Songs of Loss: Private Equity, Wealth, and Inequality
Daniel Scott Souleles

Back to America: Identity, Political Culture, and the Tea Party Movement
William H. Westermeyer

Religious, Feminist, Activist: Cosmologies of Interconnection
Laurel Zwissler

To order or obtain more information on these or other University of Nebraska Press titles, visit nebraskapress.unl.edu.

www.ingramcontent.com/pod-product-compliance
Lightning Source LLC
Chambersburg PA
CBHW030601230426
43661CB00053B/1794